THE
DISAPPEARANCE
OF THE UNIVERSE

the disappearance of the universe

STRAIGHT TALK ABOUT ILLUSIONS, PAST LIVES, RELIGION, SEX, POLITICS, AND THE MIRACLES OF FORGIVENESS

gary r. renard

FEARLESS BOOKS
Berkeley CA

First Edition, Spring 2003 • Second printing, July 2003

FEARLESS BOOKS
1678 Shattuck Avenue #319 • Berkeley, CA 94709
www.fearlessbooks.com

Portions from *A Course in Miracles*, copyright 1975, 1985, 1992, 1996,
Psychotherapy: Purpose, Process, and Practice, copyright 1976, 1992, and
The Song of Prayer, copyright 1978, 1992, reprinted by permission of the
Foundation for *A Course in Miracles*, 41397 Buecking Drive, Temecula,
California, 92590-5668.

A Course in Miracles® and ACIM® are registered service marks and
trademarks of the Foundation for *A Course in Miracles*.

Publisher's Cataloging-in-Publication
(provided by Quality Books, Inc.)

Renard, Gary R.
   The disappearance of the universe : straight talk
about illusions, past lives, religion, sex, politics,
and the miracles of forgiveness / Gary R. Renard.
      p. cm.
   LCCN 2002116849
   ISBN 0-9656809-5-9

   1. Spirituality. 2. Reincarnation. 3. Forgiveness.
4. Bible—Criticism, interpretation, etc. 5. Course in
miracles. 6. Metaphysics. I. Title.

BV4501.3.R46 2003   248
                            QBI33-1053

Design and typography by D. Patrick Miller
Printed on recycled stock in the USA by
Data Reproductions Corp., Auburn Hills, Michigan USA

CONTENTS

Publisher's Foreword

I SHOULD have my head examined. When Gary Renard contacted me about getting a professional assessment of the manuscript that would become this book, my initial responses were perfectly sensible. First, when Gary told me that his manuscript was 150,000 words long, I told him that no publisher in his right mind would produce such a book in one volume. He'd either have to split it into two books, or better yet, have it edited down into one manageable project under 100,000 words. That much I could tell him without even seeing the manuscript.

Gary said he didn't think that either approach was possible with what he had written, but he'd think about it. In the meantime, would I take a look at this project, largely comprising a series of extended conversations with two "ascended masters"?

That's when I had my second perfectly sensible response, which I didn't share with Gary: *Oh no*, I thought, *another long-winded manifesto of spiritual claptrap written by some poor sap who thinks the voices in his head are manifestations of something divine.* In almost two decades of working as a journalist, reviewer, editor, and publisher in the field of alternative spirituality, I had seen more piles of such dreck than I cared to remember. I couldn't help but recall a quote from St. John of the Cross, complaining of deluded scribes in his own day: "This happens very commonly, and many persons are greatly deceived by it, thinking they have attained to a high degree of prayer and are receiving communications from God. Wherefore, they either write this down or cause it to be written, and it turns out to be nothing, and to have the substance of no virtue, and it serves only to encourage them in vanity."

But this Renard fellow was willing to pay for a full critique of his work; that got him on my good side. I'd learned from writing scores of literary assessments that one can always find *something* helpful to say about a writer's work, some kind of "constructive criticism" that will do more than encourage an aspiring author's vanity. So I said sure, he could send me his wannabe-book and I'd do a courteous and thorough examination.

I was not far into this manuscript before I was glad I hadn't shared my second, private response with Gary, because that meant I wouldn't have to eat my words. As bizarre as his story appeared on the surface, it was nonetheless surprisingly readable, even captivating. The conversations that Gary had recorded with his un-expected and most unusual spiritual instructors, Arten and Pursah, were smart, funny, and free of the unctuous pseudo-profundity that I'd come to expect from so-called "channeled" material. Moreover, the work did not seem to do much in the way of encouraging Gary's vanity. In fact, his otherworldly companions ribbed him mercilessly about being a slacker and a smart ass, although they also gave him a lot of caring encouragement about the spiritual discipline in which they were urging him along.

Readers will soon discover that this discipline is the one known to millions worldwide through the modern spiritual guidebook called *A Course in Miracles®* (ACIM®). No doubt Gary contacted me because of my published work regarding the Course, including the book which launched my publishing company, *The Complete Story of the Course,* a journalistic overview of this teaching's history, chief teachers and popularizers, as well as its critics and a few contro-versies it has spawned. It was also possible that Gary contacted me because he had an unconscious recognition of our psychological similarities. While I am by no means a slacker like Mr. Renard, I've certainly got my share of smart-ass tendencies.

As a supplemental teaching guide of Course principles, Gary's manuscript had another remarkable characteristic: It was absolutely uncompromising in its commitment to ACIM's spiritual philosophy of "pure non-dualism" and its inwardly activist creed of forgiving, forgiving, and then more forgiving until forgiveness becomes a 24-7 habit of mind. While there has been a handful of very successful books relying on Course principles for their primary appeal, the most popular ones have also been the most diluted, and often blended with more palatable notions of the New Age and self-help variety. I was impressed to see that Gary's manuscript stayed true to both the hardcore metaphysics and the exacting mind-training discipline of the Course, usually in no uncertain terms. Whatever they were and wherever they came from, Arten and Pursah were clearly not shills for the latest vapid Enlightenment-in-a-Weekend workshop.

Thus, as I read through the manuscript for the first time, I was beginning to feel that it deserved publication after all — but it had even greater odds stacked against it than I had first estimated. It was indeed too long; it was written in a three-way conversational format that would be a no-no in the eyes of most mainstream publishers; and finally, it claimed metaphysical sources that would relegate it to the New Age realm while the text was too tough-minded for much of that audience. There were just too many potential points of controversy — historical, religious, metaphysical, psychological, and political — and too much self-confrontation required for the kind of readers accustomed to step-by-step, feel-better prescriptions that could be quickly digested and then forgotten by the time the next best-selling spiritual nostrum hit the bookstands.

As my professional concern shifted from providing Gary with an assessment of his manuscript to helping him find a publisher, I realized that I could not think of a single house, large or small, that would take on this project and resist the very practical urge to slice it, dice it, and "mainstream" it. Gary's communications made it clear that he sought a publisher who would preserve this work in its entirety, maintaining both its format and its thematic consistency — and rack my brains as I might, I couldn't think of any publishers who would take all the risks required to uphold its integrity.

Except one, that is.

That's why I should have my head examined. Hell, I don't even believe in ascended masters, largely because none has ever popped up in my admittedly narrow field of vision. Despite the great good that *A Course in Miracles* has brought into my life, I've always felt ambivalent about its own alleged spiritual authorship. As shocking as it may sound to other ACIM students, I've never much cared whether Jesus Christ had anything to do with it. The authenticity of the Course has been verified for me because it *works*, creating positive and dramatic change in my life and the lives of many others whom I've met and interviewed — but *not* because it purports to have a divine source. In this sentiment, I'm actually in harmony with Arten and Pursah, who repeatedly remind Gary in this book that it's always the innate truth of the message that counts, not the specialness of the messengers.

Oddly enough, the message of this book came to me at precisely the right time to reinvigorate my own study of the Course, which had entered a phase of fatigue largely because I'd become too fascinated with the story of ACIM as a social phenomenon in the so-called "real world." Several years of reporting on controversies about cults and copyrights had distracted me from the practice of the discipline itself. As I read through Gary's manuscript, I kept thinking, "Oh, *that's* what it was all about" and "I'd forgotten that" and "Forgiveness — I wonder if that really works?"

By the time I came to the close of the manuscript, I realized that it was functioning for me just as Gary's teachers intended it for him and future readers: as a rousing refresher course in the spirituality of the future. I put it that way because, despite the rapid growth of its audience since its publication in 1976, *A Course in Miracles* still has a comparatively small following and I think it's likely to stay that way for generations. Its metaphysics are just too different from what most of the world believes, and its transformative discipline is far too demanding, for it to become the basis of a mass spiritual movement for a long time. Yet as Gary's teachers predict, I sense that such a time will eventually arrive.

While the Course can sound absolutist and unyielding, one of its saving graces is that it claims to be only one version of a "universal curriculum," generally endorsing the world's other spiritual and psychological paths for their innate wisdom. It does assert, however, that the serious student will progress along this path *faster* than by any other method. As a spiritual pragmatist, I appreciate that selling point.

In fact the Course periodically drops the heavy-handed hint that recognizing and fulfilling one's forgiveness tasks will save "thousands of years" in the process of spiritual development. Since I've never put a lot of stock in reincarnation, I don't quite know what to make of *that*. I have had the uncanny sensation of being saved much future suffering by decisions that I've made under the influence of ACIM — decisions that involved the release of habitual resentment, debilitating anger, and self-limiting fear.

Before I encountered the Course, I was decidedly not on a path toward such a sublime and activist wisdom. I ran into that peculiar blue book when I needed it the most, and I'm happy to report that I am not the only one who has benefited from my seemingly chance meeting with a miraculous teaching. I'm certain that I would not have reached thousands of readers in a useful way with my own books had I not undertaken the Course discipline.

When I get my head examined, I guess I'll tell the shrink that I ended up publishing *The Disappearance of the Universe* because I wanted to help instrument other chance encounters with such a profound and pragmatic wisdom. This book is not a substitute for *A Course in Miracles*, but I'm confident that it will serve many as a bracing preview or a radical review of that teaching's fundamental principles. Readers who don't care about the Course may still find much herein to laugh at, argue with, or marvel over. If you're anything like me, you'll discover that this book is not at all what you expect — but it sure is one helluva ride. As Arten and Pursah might say: Have fun!

D. Patrick Miller
Founder, Fearless Books
January 2003

Author's Note
and Acknowledgments

WHILE living in a rural area of Maine I was witness to a series of in-the-flesh appearances by two ascended masters named Pursah and Arten, who eventually identified their previous incarnations as including those of Saint Thomas and Saint Thaddaeus. (Despite popular myth, those lifetimes as two of the original disciples were not their final ones.)

My visitors did *not* come forth in order to repeat some of the spiritual platitudes that many people may already believe. Rather, they revealed no less than the secrets of the universe, discussed the true purpose of life, spoke in detail about *The Gospel of Thomas,* and bluntly clarified the principles of an astounding spiritual document that is spreading throughout the world to usher in a new way of thinking that will become more prevalent in the new millennium.

It is not essential for you to believe these appearances took place in order to derive benefits from the information in this book. However, I can vouch for the extreme unlikeliness of this book being written by an uneducated layman such as myself without inspiration by these masters. At any rate, I leave it up to readers to think whatever they choose about the book's origins.

I personally believe that *The Disappearance of the Universe* can be helpful, time-saving reading for any open-minded person who is on a spiritual path. After you experience this message, it may be impossible for you — as it was for me — ever to look at your life or think of the universe the same way again.

The following text relates events that occurred from December of 1992 through December of 2001. They are presented within the framework of a dialogue that has three participants: *Gary,* (that's me) and *Arten* and *Pursah,* the two ascended masters who appeared to me in person. My narration is not labeled unless it interrupts the dialogue, in which case it is simply labeled "NOTE." The many italicized words you will see indicate an emphasis on the part of the speakers. Please be advised that I did not substantially change this dialogue even though it was difficult for me to review this material and tolerate some of the immature and judgmental things I said over the span of time covered by this book. Looking back, I realized that it was only during the later chapters that I was truly practicing forgiveness.

Even though there are statements made by the masters in these pages that may appear to be harsh or critical in their printed form, I can witness that their *attitude* should always be taken to include gentleness, humor, humility and love. As an analogy, a good parent sometimes knows it is necessary for children to be firmly corrected in a manner they can understand, but the motivation behind the correction is positive in nature. So if these discussions appear to get a little rough it should be remembered that for *my* benefit, Arten and Pursah are deliberately speaking to me in a way I can grasp, with the purpose of gradually bringing me along toward the goal of their teaching. I was told by Pursah that their style was designed to get me to pay attention. Perhaps that says it all.

I've made every effort to do this book right, but I am not perfect and so this book isn't perfect either. But if there are any errors of fact in these chapters you can be certain they are my mistakes and were not made by my visitors. Also, in the interest of full disclosure I feel I should say in advance that I have expanded some of these discussions with dialogue that I recalled after the fact. This was done with the blessing and encouragement of Arten and Pursah, and some of their instructions to me are included in these conversations. Thus this book should be considered a personal project that was both initiated and consistently guided by them, even in the occasional instances where it is not a literal transcript of our meetings.

References to *A Course in Miracles,* including each chapter's introductory quotation, are noted and listed in an Index in the back.

Limitless gratitude goes to the Voice of the Course, whose true Identity is discussed herein.

Deep appreciation also goes to the following people for their many years of helpful conversations and support: Chaitanya York, Eileen Coyne, Dan Stepenuck, Paul D. Renard, Ph.D, Karen Renard, Glendon Curtis, Louise Flynt, Ed Jordan, Betty Jordan, Charles Hudson and Sharon Salmon.

Finally, although I am not affiliated with them, I would like to take this opportunity to extend my sincere thanks to Gloria and Kenneth Wapnick, Ph.D, founders of the Foundation for *A Course in Miracles* in Temecula, California, upon whose work much of this book is based. The reader will see that my visitors suggested I should also become a student of the Wapnicks' teachings, and this book cannot help but reflect all of my learning experiences.

The ideas represented herein are the personal interpretation and understanding of the author and are not necessarily endorsed by the copyright holder of *A Course in Miracles.*

Gary R. Renard

For mom and dad

We are not apart

There are those who have reached God directly, retaining no trace of worldly limits and remembering their own Identity perfectly. These might be called the Teachers of teachers because, although they are no longer visible, their image can yet be called upon. And they will appear when and where it is helpful for them to do so. To those to whom such appearances would be frightening, they give their ideas. No one can call on them in vain. Nor is there anyone of whom they are unaware.[1]

— A COURSE IN MIRACLES

PART I

A Whisper in
Your Dream

1

Arten and Pursah Appear

Communication is not limited to the
small range of channels the world recognizes.[2]

DURING Christmas week of 1992, I realized that the circum-stances of my life and my state of mind had been slowly improving for about a year. At the previous Christmas, things had not been going well at all. Then I had been deeply troubled by the apparent scarcity in my life. Although I had been successful as a pro-fessional musician, I had not managed to save much money. I was struggling in my new career as a stock market trader, and I was in the process of suing a friend and former business partner whom I felt had treated me unfairly. Meanwhile, I was still in the process of recovering from a bankruptcy four years earlier — the result of impatience, reckless spending and seemingly good investments gone bad. I didn't know it, but I was at war with myself and I was losing. I also didn't know back then that practically all people are at war and losing, even when they may appear to be winning.

Suddenly, something shifted deep within me. For thirteen years I had been on a spiritual search during which I had learned a great deal without really taking the time to apply my lessons, but now a new certainty swept over me. *Things have got to change*, I thought. *There's got to be a better way than this.*

I wrote to the friend I was suing and informed him that I was dropping my legal action in order to start removing conflict from my life. He called and thanked me, and we began to rebuild our friendship. Eventually I would learn that this same kind of scenario, in different forms, had played itself out thousands of times in the previous few decades as some people in conflict had begun a process of laying down their weapons and surrendering to a greater wisdom within themselves.

Then I began trying to activate forgiveness and love, as I understood them at the time, in the situations that confronted me on any given day. I had some good results and some very tough difficulties, especially when someone pushed my buttons in just the right (or wrong) way. But at least I felt like I was beginning to change direction. During this period I began noticing little flashes of light out of the corner of my eye, or occurring around certain objects. These crystal clear light flashes did not take up my entire field of vision, but were concentrated on particular areas. I wouldn't understand what they meant until it was explained to me later.

Through this year of change I regularly prayed to Jesus, the prophet of wisdom whom I admired more than anyone else, to help me. I felt a mysterious connection to Jesus, and in my prayers I often told him how I wished that I could go back two thousand years and be a follower of his, so I could know what it was really like to learn from him in person.

Then, during that Christmas week of 1992, something most unusual happened while I was meditating in my living room in a rural area of Maine. I was all alone because I worked at home and my wife, Karen, commuted to Lewiston. We had no children and thus I enjoyed a very quiet environment, except for the occasional barking of our dog, Nupey. As my mind drifted back from my meditation, I opened my eyes and was stunned to see that I was not alone. With my mouth open but no sound coming out, I stared across the room at a man and a woman sitting on my couch, looking directly at me with gentle smiles and lucid, penetrating eyes. There was nothing threatening about them; in fact, they looked extraordinarily peaceful, which I found reassuring. Looking back on the event I would wonder why I had not been more fearful, given that these very solid-looking people had apparently materialized out of nowhere. Still, this first appearance by my soon-to-be friends was so surreal that fear somehow didn't seem appropriate.

The two people looked to be in their thirties and very healthy. Their clothing was stylish and contemporary. They didn't look anything like I might have imagined that angels, or ascended masters, or any other kind of divine beings might look. There was no illumination or glowing aura around them. One could have spotted them in a restaurant eating dinner and not given them a second thought. But I couldn't help but notice them sitting there on my couch, and I found myself looking at the attractive woman more than the man. Noticing this, the woman spoke first.

> 🔥
> **We are appearing to you as symbols whose words will help facilitate the disappearance of the universe.**

PURSAH: Hello, my dear brother. I can see you are astonished, but not really afraid. I am Pursah and this is our brother, Arten. We are appearing to you as symbols whose words will help facilitate the disappearance of the universe. I say we are symbols because *anything* that appears to take on a form is symbolic. The only true reality is God or pure spirit, which in Heaven are synonymous, and God and pure spirit have no form. Thus there is no concept of male or female in Heaven. Any form, including your own body, that is experienced in the false universe of perception must, by definition, be symbolic of something else. That is the real meaning of the second commandment, "Thou shalt not make unto thee any graven image." Most Biblical scholars have always considered that particular commandment to be a mystery. Why would God not want you to make any images of Him? Moses thought the idea was to get rid of pagan idolatry. The real meaning is that you shouldn't make up any images of God because God *has* no image. That idea is central to what we'll be telling you later.

GARY: Do you want to run that by me again?

ARTEN: We'll be repeating things enough for you to pick them up, Gary, and one of the things you'll notice is that we'll speak to you more and more in your own style of language. In fact, we're going to put things to you very bluntly. We think you're big enough to handle it, and we didn't come here to waste time. You asked Jesus for help. He would have been happy to come to you himself, but that's not what's called for right now. We're his representatives. By the way, most of the time we're just going to refer to Jesus as J. We have permission from him to do that, and we'll tell you why when the time is right. You wanted to know what it was like to be there with him two thousand years ago. We were there and we'll be happy to tell you, although you may be surprised to find out there are more advantages to being a student of his today than there were back then. One thing we're going to do is challenge you the way J repeatedly challenged us, whether in the past or in what you think of as the future. We're not going to be easy on you or tell you what you want to hear. If you want to be handled with kid gloves then go to a theme park. If you're ready to be treated like an adult who has a right to know why nothing in your universe can possibly work in the long run, then we'll get down to business. You will also learn both the cause of this situation and the way out of it. So, what do you say?

GARY: I don't know what to say.

ARTEN: Excellent. A fine qualification for a student, another one being the desire to learn. I know you have that. I also know you don't like to talk very much. You're the kind of guy who could go into a monastery for years and not say a word. You also have an exceptional memory — something that will come in handy for you later. In fact, we know everything about you.

GARY: Everything?

PURSAH: Yes, everything. But we're not here to judge you so there's no sense in hiding things or being embarrassed. We're here simply because it's helpful for us to appear right now. Take advantage of us while you can. Ask any questions that come into your mind. You were wondering why we look this way. The answer is that we like to fit in wherever we go. Also, we dress in a secular fashion because we don't represent any particular religion or denomination.

GARY: So you're not Jehovah's Witnesses then, 'cause I already told them I'm not into organized churches.

PURSAH: We are certainly witnesses for God, but Jehovah's Witnesses subscribe to the old belief that except for a select number who will be with Him, God's Kingdom will be on earth with them in glorified bodies, and that is not what we teach. We may disagree with the teachings of others, but we don't judge them and respect the right of all people to believe what they want.

GARY: That's cool, but I don't know if I like this idea of no male and female in Heaven.

PURSAH: There are no differences in Heaven and no changes. Everything is constant. That's the only way it can be completely dependable instead of chaotic.

GARY: Isn't that kind of boring?

PURSAH: Let me ask you something, Gary. Is sex boring?

GARY: Not in my book.

PURSAH: Well, imagine the very peak of a perfect sexual orgasm, except this orgasm never stops. It keeps going on forever with no decrease in its powerful and flawless intensity.

GARY: You have my attention.

PURSAH: The physical act of sex doesn't even come close to the incredible bliss of Heaven. It's just a poor, made-up imitation of union with God. It's a false idol made to fix your attention on the body and the world with just enough of a payoff to keep you coming back for more. It's very similar to a narcotic. Heaven, on the other hand, is a perfect, indescribable ecstasy that never ceases.

GARY: That sounds beautiful, but it doesn't account for all these experiences people have of the other side — out-of-body trips, near-death experiences, communicating with people who have passed on and things of that nature.

ARTEN: What you call this side and the other side are really just two sides of the same illusory coin. It's all the universe of perception. When your body appears to stop and die your mind keeps right on going. You like to go to the movies, right?

GARY: Everyone should have a hobby.

ARTEN: When you make a transition from one side to the other, whether from this life to the afterlife or back to a body again, it's like walking out of one movie and into a different one. Except these films are more like the virtual reality movies people will have in the future where everything will seem completely real, right down to the touch.

GARY: That reminds me of this article I read about a machine in a lab at MIT that you can put your finger in and feel things that aren't there. Is that the kind of technology you're talking about?

ARTEN: Yes, most inventions mimic some aspect of what the mind does. Getting back to the birth and death cycle, when you are seemingly born once again into a physical body you forget everything, or at least most of it. It's all a trick of the mind.

GARY: Are you trying to tell me that my life is all in my head?

ARTEN: It's all in your mind.

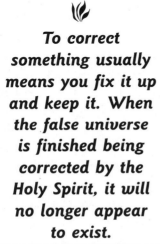

To correct something usually means you fix it up and keep it. When the false universe is finished being corrected by the Holy Spirit, it will no longer appear to exist.

GARY: My head is in my mind?

ARTEN: Your head, your brain, your body, your world, your entire universe, any parallel universes and anything else that can be perceived are projections of the mind. They are all symbolic of just one thought. We will tell you what that thought is later. An even better way of thinking about this is to consider your universe to be a dream.

GARY: It feels pretty solid for a dream, pal.

ARTEN: We'll tell you later why it feels solid, but you need more background first. Let's not get too far ahead of ourselves. What Pursah was trying to impress on you is that nobody is asking you to give up a lot in exchange for nothing. It's really the opposite. You will eventually come to realize that you are giving up nothing in exchange for everything — a state so awesome and joyous that to describe it in words is impossible. To attain this state of Being, however, you must be willing to undergo a difficult process of correction by the Holy Spirit.

GARY: This correction you speak of, does it have anything to do with political correctness?

PURSAH: No. Political correctness, no matter how well intentioned, is still an attack on freedom of speech. You will find we are very free with our speech indeed. The word *correction* is not used by us in the usual way, because to correct something usually means you fix it up and keep it. When the false universe is finished being corrected by the Holy Spirit, it will no longer appear to exist.

I say it will no longer *appear* to exist because it does not exist in reality. The true Universe is God's Universe, or Heaven — and Heaven has absolutely nothing whatsoever to do with the false universe. However, there is a way of *looking* at your universe that will help you return to your true home with God.

GARY: You're talking about the universe like it's some kind of a mistake. But the Bible says that God created the world, and most everybody believes He did, not to mention all the world's religions. My friends and I think that God produced the world so He could know Himself experientially, which I guess is a pretty common New Age belief. Didn't God create polarity, duality and all of the opposites in this world of subject and object?

PURSAH: In a word, no. God did not create duality and He did *not* create the world. If He did He would be the author of "a tale told by an idiot," to borrow Shakespeare's description of life. But God is not an idiot. We'll prove it to you. He can only be one of two things. He is either perfect Love, as the Bible says when it momentarily stumbles upon the truth, or He's an idiot. You can't have it both ways. J was no idiot either, because he wasn't taken in by the false universe. We'll be telling you more about him, but don't expect the official version. Do you remember the story about the prodigal Son?

GARY: Sure. Well, I could probably use a refresher.

PURSAH: Grab your New Testament there and read it to us; then we'll explain something to you. But leave off the last paragraph.

GARY: Why should I leave off the last paragraph?

ARTEN: It was added on later as the story got passed around during the oral tradition. Then it was changed some more by the doctor who wrote both the Book of Luke and the Book of Acts.

GARY: All right. I'll give you the benefit of the doubt for now. Is the Revised Standard Version good enough?

ARTEN: Yes, it's practical. Go to Luke, 15:11.

GARY: O.K. Now this is Jesus talking, right?

ARTEN: Yes. J doesn't speak that much in the Bible, and when he does he's often misquoted. He was misquoted and misunderstood by everyone right from the beginning, including us. We understood him better than most, but we still had a lot to learn. We're speaking to you now with the benefit of subsequent learning. But J was misquoted most often for the purposes of the individual novels that became the mainstream Gospels. They were the popular stories of their time. J didn't say a lot of the things he's quoted as saying in these books but did say some of them — just as he didn't do most of the things he's portrayed as doing in these books, but did do a few of them.

GARY: You mean like one of those TV movies where they say it's based on a true story but most of it's made up?

ARTEN: Yes, very good. The other half of the New Testament comes almost entirely from the Apostle Paul, who was a real crowd pleaser but didn't really teach the same things as J. None of the people who wrote the Bible ever even met J, except for the author of Mark, who was just a child at the time that he met him. Look at the Book of Revelation. It reads like a Stephen King story. Imagine portraying J as a warrior leader riding on a white horse and wearing a robe dipped in blood! No, he is *not* a spiritual warrior — a term that's an oxymoron if there ever was one.

GARY: One more question before the story, if you don't mind.

PURSAH: Go right ahead. We're not in a hurry.

GARY: Isn't the idea that God didn't create the world a Gnostic belief?

ARTEN: The principle certainly did not originate with the Gnostics, predating them in other philosophies and religions. As far as the Gnostic sects are concerned, they were right in believing that God did not create this excuse for a world, but they made the same error that almost everybody else does: They made the miscreated world psychologically real for themselves. They saw it as an evil to be despised. J, on the other hand, viewed the world as the Holy Spirit sees it: a perfect opportunity for forgiveness and salvation.

GARY: So rather than resisting the world, I should look for ways I can use it as a chance to get home?

PURSAH: Exactly. Good boy. J used to say, "You have heard that it was said 'an eye for an eye and a tooth for a tooth.' But I say to you, do not resist one who you think is evil." Not only was that a shocking and direct refutation of the old scripture, but it was also the answer to the question you just asked. To further demonstrate J's attitude, why don't you read that story now?

GARY: All right. I'm a little rusty at this, but here goes.

There was a man who had two sons; and the younger of them said to the father, "Father, give me the share of property that falls to me." And he divided his living between them. Not many days later, the younger son gathered all he had and took his journey into a far country, and there he squandered his property in loose living. And when he had spent everything a great famine arose in that country, and he began to be in want. So he went and joined himself to one of the citizens of that country, who sent him into his fields to feed swine. And he would gladly have fed on the pods that the swine ate; and no one gave him anything. But when he came to himself he said, "How many of my father's hired servants have bread enough and to spare, but I perish here with hunger! I will arise and go to my father, and I will say to him, 'Father, I have sinned against heaven and before you; I am no longer worthy to be called your son; treat me as one of your hired servants.'" And he arose and came to his father. But while he was yet at a distance, his father saw him and had compassion, and ran and embraced him and kissed him. And the son said to him, "Father, I have sinned against heaven and before you; I am no longer worthy to be called your son." But the father said to his servants, "Bring quickly the best robe, and put it on him; and put a ring on his hand, and shoes on his feet; and bring the fatted calf and kill it, and let us eat and make merry; for this my son was dead, and is alive again; he was lost, and is found." And they began to make merry.

ARTEN: Thank you, Gary. The story still stands up pretty well, although I assure you it sounded a lot better in Aramaic. Of course J was using the symbols of the audience he was speaking to, but there's still much to learn by looking at that story with a clean slate.

The first thing you have to understand is that the Son was not kicked out of the house; he was innocently foolish enough to think he could leave and do better on his own. That was J's answer to the

Garden of Eden myth. God didn't banish you from paradise, and He is not responsible in any way, shape or form for your experience of being apart from Him.

The next thing you should notice is that the Son used up his limited resources and began to experience lack, a condition that doesn't exist in Heaven. Being seemingly cut off from his Source, he was now experiencing want for the first time. We'll explore that subject with you when we sense it's appropriate. Once again, we say he is seemingly cut off from his Source because we're speaking of something that only *seemed* to happen but did not actually occur in reality. We understand that's a difficult concept and we'll be dealing more with it as we go along.

With the Son now experiencing scarcity, he tries to fill the lack by joining himself to another citizen of that country. This is symbolic of attempting to find solutions to your problems somewhere outside of yourself, invariably involving some form of special relationship. These endless and hopeless attempts at a solution through external searching continue until you become like the prodigal Son *when he came to himself.* Then the Son realizes that the only meaningful answer to his problem is to return to his Father's house, and doing this becomes more important to him than anything in the world.

Here we come to the most important point of the story: the contrast between what the Son has come to believe is true about himself and what the Father knows to be true. The Son *thinks* that he has sinned and is unworthy to be called the Son of his Father. But the loving Father will hear none of this. He is not wrathful or vengeful and is not the slightest bit interested in punishing His Son. This is what God is really like! He doesn't think like humans because He isn't a person. The story is metaphorical. God's Love *rushes* to meet His Son. God knows that His Son is forever innocent, because He *is* His Son. Nothing that seems to happen can ever change that fact. The prodigal Son is now returning to life. He is no longer lost in dreams of scarcity, destruction and death. It's time to party.

GARY: It's not that you don't make sense, but I have a couple of problems. First of all, the thing about the whole universe being the responsibility of the prodigal Son and not God. The world, nature and the human body all seem pretty awesome to me. I'm not exactly what you'd call a cock-eyed optimist, but there's a lot of beauty, order and intricacy that would appear to me to have the touch of God. Secondly, if I told people that God didn't create the world, I have a feeling it would probably go over about as big as a fart in an elevator.

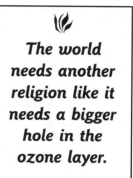

The world needs another religion like it needs a bigger hole in the ozone layer.

ARTEN: Let's handle the fart first. The truth is you don't have to tell anybody anything. It would be entirely possible for you to practice the kind of spirituality we'll be discussing without anyone else ever knowing it. This will all be between you and the Holy Spirit or J, whichever you prefer. The only difference now between the Holy Spirit and J is that one is abstract and the other is specific. They're really the same, and your work will be done in your mind along with Them.

This isn't about trying to save a world that isn't really out there anyway. You save the world by concentrating on your *own* forgiveness lessons. If everybody concentrated on their own lessons instead of somebody else's, the collective, prodigal Son would be home in a New York minute. In time, this won't happen until the end. But we'll also be discussing time and you'll see that nothing in this universe is what it appears to be. In any case, *you* don't have to wait. Your time is at hand, but only if you're willing to follow the Holy Spirit's thought system instead of trying to lead the planet on a wild goose chase.

The world doesn't need another Moses, and it was never J's intention to start a religion. Whether then or now, the world needs another religion like it needs a bigger hole in the ozone layer. J was the ultimate follower in the sense that he eventually listened only to the Holy Spirit. Yes, he shared his experience with us, but he knew we could only understand so much and that we'd learn someday just like he did.

As for the so-called beauty and complexity of the universe, it's as though you painted a picture with a defective canvas and inferior paint, and then as soon as you were finished the painting started to crack and the images in it began to decay and fall apart. The human body appears to be an amazing accomplishment — until something goes wrong with it. I don't have to tell you what your parents looked like just before their earthly lives ended.

GARY: I'd appreciate it if you didn't remind me.

ARTEN: There's nothing in your universe that doesn't follow the pattern of decay and death, and there's nothing here that can seemingly live without something else dying. Your world is quite impressive until you learn to *really* look. But people don't want to really look, not just because it isn't a pretty picture, but because the world is meant to cover over an unconscious thought system that governs their lives but which they are not consciously aware of. So you're going to have to cut us some slack for a while and give us a chance to explain more until you start to get the general idea.

GARY: I guess it wouldn't hurt to give you more of a chance, but don't blame me for being skeptical. I have a cousin who's a minister and he'd say you two are witnesses for Satan, not God.

PURSAH: How predictable. J was repeatedly accused of blasphemy. It's even in the Bible. I guarantee you that if he were here in the flesh he'd be accused of exactly the same thing today — and by Christians. Don't expect us to shy away from heresy or blasphemy any more than he would. What you *can* expect from us is honesty and directness. Some people need to be treated gently and some people can take getting hit over the head, like the old Zen training. We don't have any problem with rattling people's cages. We have no investment in what you think about us. We are free to be teachers and not politicians. We don't have to suck up to you so you can feel all warm and fuzzy about us instead of learning something. Your approval of what we have to say is not required. We have no need to be popular. We have no stake in manipulating the level of form so we can make a tale told by an idiot appear to be going our way. Our condition is one of peace, but our message will be firm.

We'll be offering a clarification of spiritual principles, not a substitute for them. Our words are simply learning aids. Our purpose is to help you understand certain ideas so the Holy Spirit will be more accessible to you in your studies and your everyday experiences.

We have already said we will speak about the past. After that, we'll be discussing J's new teachings, which could not possibly have been understood until now. There is a spiritual document that you, Gary, first heard of back in the early eighties from a fellow participant at the *est* six-day course. You didn't read any of it back then, which is just as well, but you'll begin studying it in the next few weeks. This teaching originated during your lifetime, but you will learn that it is not of this world. It's spreading throughout many countries and is already being generally misunderstood and misinterpreted, just as J's message was distorted two thousand years ago. That's to be expected. But we'll help you get off on the right foot with this metaphysical masterpiece so you can hear it more clearly.

GARY: I'm glad you think you know everything, including my future, but I'll decide what I'm gonna study and when I'm gonna get around to it. I've always thought Jesus was cool though, and you talk about him a lot. Most of my New Age friends don't mention him very much. It's almost as though they're embarrassed by him. What do you make of that?

ARTEN: It's not J who they don't like. It's the behavior-oriented, Biblical version of J who's been shoved down their throats all their lives that they can't stand. There's another issue involved that we'll get into in good time, but can you blame your friends for being confused about J? Christianity is so conflicted it openly promotes teachings that are diametrically opposed to one another. How is one supposed to deal with that? People will eventually have to stop blaming J for some of the ludicrous things Christianity has done and continues to do in his name. He has no more to do with these things than God has to do with this world.

GARY: You're giving me some pretty radical stuff here.

ARTEN: Oh, we're just getting started. There have been several very popular and supposedly unconventional books written in the last few decades that — like all of the world's major religions — have been presented as though they came directly from God or the Holy Spirit while their teachings actually reflect a level of spiritual awareness that could be described as ordinary. For all intents and purposes, dualism — which we'll define during future visits — is the level of thinking of the entire world, even among most people who follow spiritual paths that are non-dualistic. Although it's true that the Holy Spirit works with all people in a way they can understand —

which is why all spiritual paths are necessary — it's one of our challenges to you that teachings of dualism must eventually lead to the
teachings and practices of semi-dualism, non-dualism and ultimately *pure* non-dualism if one is to experience the Love of God. If that
sounds complicated, rest assured that it's really very simple and will
be presented to you in an understand-
able, linear manner.

> ❦
> *Your good
> times in the
> world are good
> only in comparison
> to the bad times.
> You will eventually
> learn that it's
> all a trick.*

There are many in your generation
who imagine they are just about ready
to vibrate off the planet for good. Unfortunately, it's not that easy. If you could
just zap yourself off to never-never land
then everybody would already be experiencing the Kingdom. But your experience is that you are here, or else you
wouldn't be experiencing that you *are*
here. And there's a big problem holding
your friends back that the popular New Age authors didn't tell
them about.

Perhaps the most overlooked error of all religions and philosophies, including the New Age models, is the failure to understand
that although doing things like thinking positively, being "in the
now," saying prayers, affirmations, denying negative thoughts and
listening to famous speakers may have a temporarily helpful impact,
they *cannot* release that which is locked in the deep canyons of your
unconscious mind. Your unconscious mind, which you are completely oblivious to or else it wouldn't *be* unconscious, is under the
domination of a sick thought system that is shared on both a collective and individual level by everyone who comes to the false
universe — or else they wouldn't have come here in the first place.
This will remain the case until your thoughts are examined, correctly forgiven, released to the Holy Spirit and replaced by His thinking instead. Until then your *hidden* beliefs will continue to dominate
and assert themselves in a predetermined way. The world is merely
acting out a symbolic scenario that each one here agreed to participate in before they ever appeared to arrive.

GARY: You don't have to convince me the world sucks sometimes.

But what about the good stuff? We all have our favorite times.

ARTEN: Your good times in this world are good only in comparison to the bad times. The comparison isn't a valid one, because both the seemingly good times and the bad times are *not* Heaven. You will eventually learn that it's all a trick, that your perception — something you value very highly — is simply lying to you. You wouldn't listen to your unconscious thought system if it didn't hide itself and lie to you, because it's so seemingly despicable, and listening to it is so painful, that you'd run away from it if you could really examine it. J can help you examine it. He can show you a way to make your unconscious mind conscious to a degree that Freud could not have imagined. That will be the purpose of some of our later discussions, but we have other things to talk about first.

GARY: Meanwhile, do you have anything more encouraging to tell me?

PURSAH: Certainly, if you want to go home. J is outside the door of the asylum, calling you to come out and join him, and you keep trying to drag him back in. That was the case with the world two thousand years ago and it remains the case today. The person who first said that the more things change the more they stay the same hit the universal nail right on the holographic head. But there *is* a way out, and *that's* what should be encouraging to you.

ARTEN: In helping you we will not be giving you the so-called wisdom of the ages that your contemporary spiritual wizards are so fond of. You will learn instead that most of what the world thinks of as the wisdom of the ages is actually full of it. The "divine intelligence of the universe" is a phrase that's entirely worthy of having the plug pulled on it. You will learn that babies are *not* born with a clean slate or a natural tendency to focus on love and are then corrupted by the world, and you will find that if you are to return to God then you have some work to do — not work in the world, but with your thoughts. During most of this it will appear to you that we are making judgments, a lot of them. There's a good reason for that. The only possible way we can teach you is by contrasting the Holy Spirit's thinking with the thinking of the world. His judgment is sound, and leads to God. Your judgment is poor, and leads you back here, again and again.

PURSAH: During our exchanges you will also find out what you really are, how you got here, exactly why you and all other people behave and feel the way that you do, why the universe keeps repeating the same patterns over and over again, why people get sick, the reason behind all failure, accidents, addictions and natural disasters, the real cause of all of the violence, crime, war and terrorism in the world, the only meaningful solution to all of these things and how to apply it.

GARY: If you can tell me all that, you win a prize.

PURSAH: There is only one prize anybody should be interested in.

GARY: Heaven?

ARTEN: Yes. You have heard that the truth shall set you free. That's true, but nobody tells you what the truth is. You have heard that the Kingdom of Heaven is within you. That is also true, but nobody tells you how to get there. If they did, would you listen? You can lead a human to water but you can't make him drink. We will point you toward the water, but you will only drink it if you are ready for a spirituality that, like the truth, is not of this universe.

One of the fundamental differences between the teachings of J and the teachings of the world is this: The teachings of the world are the product of a split, unconscious mind. Once you have that you have compromise, and once you have compromise you no longer have the truth.

You will not find compromise with us, and you will not always like it. That doesn't matter. If we gave you everything you think you want, you'd be looking for something else a month later. You don't need us to help you feel good about a universe that was never worth the price of admission, and never will be.

There is something much better to feel good about. With God's speed we followed our way home. Our intention now is to help you find yours. We will return to you soon for the second of seventeen appearances. Our next discussion will be the longest, and in the meantime you may want to consider the idea that if the teachings you are hearing are truly of the spirit, then it should be apparent that the principles being expressed did not come from people or from the universe — for they are the correction of both.

2

The J Underground

Be vigilant only for·God and His Kingdom.[1]

ARTEN and Pursah had disappeared in an instant, and my mind
was spinning. Did this really happen? Was it a hallucination?
Would they ever come back? I hadn't even thought to ask them how
they got here or even precisely what they were. Were they angels,
ascended masters, time travelers or what? Most of all, why would
they appear and give advanced metaphysical teachings to me — just
an average guy with an interest in spirituality who had never even
gone to college?

I decided immediately that I wouldn't tell anybody what had happened, not even Karen. She was going through a very stressful and
challenging time at work that required a great deal of concentration.
The last thing she needed right now was to learn that I was pulling
a Joan of Arc with live-action figures.

I did confide in my dog Nupey, who could always be counted on
to be nonjudgmental. Then I attempted to take a step back, try to
relax, and wait to find out if the episode was just a weird delusion
resulting from too much meditation, or if it would happen again.

That night in bed after Karen had fallen asleep, I laid awake for
hours thinking about some of the things my visitors had said. I had a
natural resistance to the idea God hadn't created the world since I'd
been told something else all my life, but as I thought about it I realized that the idea answered a lot of questions. I'd always wondered
how God could allow so much pain, suffering and horror in the
world, and how good people could often be put through unspeakable

hell. If what Arten and Pursah said was true, it would mean that God had nothing to do with any of it. This somehow made God seem less fearful. As I dozed off to sleep, I wondered if believing that God was innocent of making this world would be an insult to God — or merely an insult to an ancient myth that most people had decided to include in their religions. By seriously considering Arten and Pursah's position, how did I know I wouldn't be raising my opinion of God, thus making Him more approachable?

One week later on a Tuesday evening, I was alone in my living room doing some homework for my business when Pursah and Arten surprised me with their second appearance. This time I was on my couch and my two visitors each appeared in a chair. Arten began speaking almost immediately.

ARTEN: We thought we'd visit you tonight because we knew Karen was out with some friends. You made the right decision not to tell her about us yet. She has her own interests right now. Let her learn what she should learn. There are teachers who will try to tell you that life is not a classroom and that you're not here to learn lessons, but simply to experience the truth that is already within you. They are mistaken. Your life is very much a classroom and if you *don't* learn your lessons then you will *not* experience the truth that is within you.

There is nothing wrong with feeling and experiencing the times of your life. Indeed, in your present condition it would be rather difficult for you not to. But there *is* a better way of seeing.

PURSAH: You've been thinking a lot during the past week. Are you ready to proceed?

GARY: First I'd like to know some more about you — like, what are you exactly? How do you materialize here? Why come to me? Why not some guy with a fire in his belly who wants to be a prophet? My main ambitions are to move to Hawaii, commune with nature and drink beer, not necessarily in that order.

ARTEN: We know. First of all, we are both ascended masters. We are not angels. Angels were never born into bodies. Like you, we were each born thousands of times, or at least it appeared that way. Now we have no need to be born. Secondly, our bodies symbolize the last earthly identities we had. We won't tell you when that was, because it's in your future and we don't want to get into a pattern of giving you information about what is seemingly yet to come.

GARY: You don't want to interrupt the space-time continuum, huh?

ARTEN: We couldn't care less about the space-time conundrum. We simply would not want to rob you of your opportunities to learn your lessons first-hand and accelerate your return to God. Most ascended masters use their last earthly identities for teaching purposes, keeping in mind that the term *last* is an illusory, linear concept. Some apparitions claim to be ascended masters when that's really just wishful thinking on the part of the mind that is projecting the apparition. That type of appearance is more like seeing a ghost or lost soul. An even better description would be a seemingly separated soul. But a true ascended master knows that he or she can never really be separate from God or from anyone.

GARY: You said you were there two thousand years ago with J. Were you just putting me on or can you tell me who you were?

ARTEN: At the time we were both people whom you would now refer to as saints. You assume that all saints are ascended masters, but that's not true. Just because a church calls somebody a saint it doesn't make them like J in terms of their attainment. I always thought it was very generous of the church to make me a saint, considering I never belonged to their religion. We were Jews and so was J. If you asked any of us disciples about Christianity we would have said, "What's that?" Yes, some of us did start Jewish sects based on the master, but certainly not a separate religion. It took hundreds of years for most of Christianity to be made up, and it didn't have anything to do with us. It's *still* being made up. How many of your present-day American Christians realize that some of their most sacred ideas, like the Rapture, weren't even named until the 19TH century? Such ideas are cyclical. Some early Christians and many since them have thought J was coming back as a glorified body *very soon*. But as you'll see, J teaches you now like the Holy Spirit does — through your mind.

PURSAH: As far as how we materialize, you wouldn't really be able to grasp that yet, but we'll tell you that the mind projects bodily images. You think bodies make other bodies and then brains do the thinking, but nothing can think except the mind.[2] The brain is just a part of the body. It's the mind that projects every body, including yours. I'm not talking about that tiny little mind you identify with. I'm referring to the entire mind that is outside of time, space and form. This is the mind Buddha got in touch with, although people don't realize that it is still one important step away from joining with God. This mind made the entire universe, each body and every form that appears to be in it. The question is, why?

> ❦
>
> *How would you feel if someone who was as dead as a doornail stopped by to have a chat with you?*

We'll get to the reason, which in your case is unconscious, as to why your body was made, but our state of awareness puts us in a position where we can deliberately make these bodies for the one and only purpose of communicating the Holy Spirit's message to you in a way you can accept and understand. Of ourselves, we know that we have no identity other than the Holy Spirit, so we are manifestations of Him and our words are His. When J appeared to us in the flesh after he was crucified, he had simply made another body to communicate with us. His mind could make his body appear or disappear, like in the tomb. We could not really understand that at the time, so we made the grave error of attaching great significance to J's body, which was really nothing, instead of to the mind, which is the important thing.[3] However, you shouldn't judge some of us for being overzealous. How would you feel if someone who you knew beyond a doubt was as dead as a doornail stopped by to have a chat with you, and even let you touch him so you could know he was legit?

GARY: I wouldn't know whether to take a crap or go blind.

PURSAH: Our reaction was similar, if not our language. Let me ask, do you remember Father Raymond from the Cracille?

GARY: Sure.

PURSAH: Do you remember him telling you about a contemporary of Sigmund Freud's named Groddeck?

NOTE: Although I wasn't a Catholic, I had agreed to go along with the friend I had stopped suing and participate in a three-day spiritual experience called the Cracille, which was held at a Catholic church in Massachusetts. The event emphasized laughter, song, love and forgiveness and came as a big surprise to me, because I didn't know there were Catholic people who were happy. During the weekend I met a priest who was also a psychologist by the name of Father Raymond, who had done some research on someone named Groddeck. The research had made a big impression on him, and he told me a little about it.

GARY: Yeah. He was saying things like what you've been telling me. Father Ray said that Groddeck was respected by Freud and was a real revolutionary. Apparently, Groddeck had come to the conclusion that brains and bodies are actually made by the mind, rather than the other way around, and that the mind — which was described as a force that Groddeck called the It — was doing this for its own purposes.

PURSAH: Close enough, dear student. You have a memory like a steel trap. Dr. Groddeck was correct about his conclusions, even though he certainly didn't have the whole picture like J did. By the way, unlike most of the Apostles and the early founders of Christianity, Dr. Groddeck didn't assume or pretend that he knew everything. He only said what he *did* know, but he was still light years ahead of his brain-worshipping successors. It's almost needless to say that because of Groddeck's views the world kept its distance from him. We mention him now, and will again later, merely to point out that there have always been brilliant people whose level of observation was much more in line with the truth than the thinking of the world is.

GARY: My other question — you're appearing to me rather than someone more appropriate because...?

PURSAH: We already told you the last time, but the explanation was too simple for you. We are here because it is helpful for us to appear right now. That's really all you need to know.

GARY: From what you've said, I'm not sure what my role is in your appearance. Is my mind projecting you, or is it just your mind?

ARTEN: The question is misplaced because there is only one mind. Eventually the question becomes one of purpose. But there are different illusory levels of thinking and resulting experience, and we'll come back to that subject eventually.

GARY: You *know* I have to ask which two saints you were.

PURSAH: Yes. It's only fair that we tell you, but we're not going to dwell on it. We would much rather spend our visits clarifying J's role and teachings for you rather than wasting time attempting to clarify our own rather insignificant roles. We want you to learn, and you're going to have to trust that we know best what to tell you in order to help facilitate that learning. As a matter of record I was Thomas, usually referred to as Saint Thomas and author of part of the now famous *Gospel of Thomas*. You should also know up front that the Coptic language version of that Gospel, discovered near Nag Hammadi in Egypt, was a derivative version and contains some sayings that J didn't say, and that I never had in the original. I will briefly discuss this Gospel with you soon, but as I said, we're not going to dwell on it. I never got to finish it anyway. I would have put the prodigal Son parable last, but I couldn't because I was killed.

GARY: Life's a bitch, isn't it?

PURSAH: That's a matter of interpretation. By the way, I'm going to assume you're sophisticated enough to understand it's not unusual to be male in some lifetimes and female in other lifetimes.

GARY: I can fathom it. How about you, Arten? You're not going to tell me you were the Virgin Mary.

ARTEN: No, but she was a wonderful woman. I probably wasn't famous enough to impress you; that's fine with me. I was Thaddaeus, although my given name was Lebbaeus and J renamed me Thaddaeus. I was humble and quiet, and I was a good learner. The churches call me Saint Thaddaeus as well as Saint Judas of James, not to be confused with Judas Iscariot. I didn't have to do very much to earn the distinction of sainthood. Some people think I wrote the Epistle of Jude. I didn't. I formed a sect with Thomas and visited Persia, but I did *not* play a role in the martyrdom fad, as some people believe. I was just in the right place at the right time to be sainted.

GARY: You lucky bum. Do you have any jobs like that for me, Thaddaeus?

ARTEN: Yes. You're doing it right now. Do you want us to continue teaching you?

GARY: Yes, but mainly because I've found myself thinking differently about God since the last time you were here. I feel like I can trust Him more — like maybe He doesn't have anything against me and He's not responsible for any of my problems and suffering, past or present.

ARTEN: Very good, my brother. Very good.

GARY: But just so I'm clear, you're not saying that God didn't create *some* of the universe. You're saying He doesn't have anything to do with *any* of it, and that the whole Genesis story of creation is bogus?

ARTEN: Very well. We'll take care of old business first. It's not our purpose to put anybody down, although it always offends people when you don't buy into their beliefs. As we've already implied, we simply agree to disagree with the teachings of others. It should be very clear to anyone that one of the most important aspects of the old scripture is the law, and the punishment of anyone who doesn't follow the letter of it. Although the real purpose of this crime and punishment cycle is not what you think, there is still nothing wrong with establishing laws in an attempt to have an orderly society. Two thousand years ago the old scripture was very dear to Thomas and I, but we had already begun to realize that just as with your present day legal system, the law eventually becomes all about the law and nothing about justice.

Aside from the awful, threatening passages, there are *also* some very beautiful and profound passages in the old scripture we could agree with to this very day. If you go back to the creation story of Genesis however, you encounter a very serious problem that good thinking people of many faiths have struggled with ever since the story was first heard — even before it was scripture. As the story goes, God created the world and saw that it was good.

GARY: He writes His own reviews.

ARTEN: So God goes on and creates Adam and then gets him a date, Eve. Life is paradise. *But,* God gives them this one rule. Do anything you want kids, knock yourselves out, but don't you *dare* eat the fruit from that tree of knowledge over there. So the serpent does its thing, Eve takes a bite and tempts Adam just so you can blame women for everything, and then Adam takes a bite. Now there's hell to pay. Big angry Maker kicks Adam and Eve out of paradise. He even tells Eve that she's going to suffer terrible pain during childbirth just for good measure. That'll teach her! But wait just a minute here. If God is God, wouldn't He be perfect? And if He is perfect, then wouldn't He know everything? Even today's parents know that the surest way to get children to do something is to tell them they can't. So if God is God and He knows everything, then what has He done here?

GARY: Well, apparently God has set up His own children to fail just so He can have the pleasure of ruthlessly punishing them for a scenario which He Himself set into motion.

ARTEN: It sure looks that way, doesn't it? But would God do this? If you had a child, would *you* do that? How could you possibly trust a God like that? Nowadays He'd be accused of child abuse. So what's the truth? The answer should be obvious to anyone who is willing to take the blinders off. God would *not* do this. He is *not* an idiot. The story of Genesis is the symbolic story of the making of the world and bodies by the unconscious mind for reasons you are not aware of, but which you *must* become aware of.

GARY: So, from this and what you told me earlier, I gather J didn't subscribe to some of the jurassic thinking of Genesis — as well as much of the old scripture — and he was really teaching something more original that most people couldn't grasp so they substituted their own beliefs?

PURSAH: Yes. J would usually ignore scripture that had little basis in truth but offer the correct interpretation of scripture that did have some basis in truth. He was definitely not into the hellfire and damnation routine. That was John the Baptist, but John had his quieter moments too. It was he who said, "Love your enemies," not J. J wouldn't have any concept of an enemy. People don't realize that John was far more famous than J was in their lifetimes. John had what the crowd *really* wanted. That is the way of success in the world, no matter what your job. Supply and demand. You can be successful if you have something people want.

You have no idea how uninspired it is that people, including your spiritual leaders, are always trying to spiritualize abundance in the world. How much success or money you get has nothing whatsoever to do with how spiritually enlightened you are. They are like apples and oranges. That loaves and fishes story was supposed to be symbolic! It didn't actually happen. It meant there is a way for you to receive *guidance* as to how you should proceed in the world, and we'll cover that. But stop trying to spiritualize money. There's nothing wrong with money or success, but there's nothing spiritual about them either. While we're at it, don't listen to that incredible interpretation the churches put on the saying of J, that you should render unto Caesar that which is Caesar's and render unto God that which is God's.

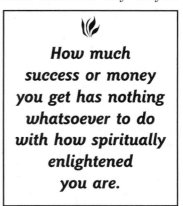

> *How much success or money you get has nothing whatsoever to do with how spiritually enlightened you are.*

The churches use that saying to try to raise money. But J wasn't talking about money. He was saying this: *Let Caesar have the things of this world, for they are nothing. Let God have your spirit, for it is everything.* He was a wisdom teacher of pure love and truth.

A lot of people think that both John and J were members of the Essenes. It's true that they were both visitors to and friends with the Essenes at times, but they were never members of the sect. They were both travelers. J eventually fell out of favor with the Essenes. They had loved John because he respected their laws and beliefs, but they ended up hating J because he saw no need to bow down to their precious rules. Very few tears were shed at Qumran when the news of J's death was heard. Thirty-five years later most of the Essenes went over to Jerusalem to fight against the Romans in the revolt. Like many, they saw it as the Apocalypse. You know, the sons of light against the sons of darkness and all that nonsense. It was a total disaster. In the end, the Essenes lived by the sword and they died by the sword. Today, you try to make them and the Dead Sea Scrolls into something special, just as you try to make so many people from the past into great spiritual masters when they weren't. They were people, like you.

Some in your generation think the Mayans vibrated off the planet in a state of spiritual enlightenment. What makes you think they were enlightened? They practiced human sacrifice. How enlightened do you think that was? They were just people; like the Essenes, like the Europeans, like the American Indians and like you. Accept that and move on.

GARY: So I shouldn't be too impressed by that ancient spiritual book I want to read to help me with my trading — the one about the art of war?

PURSAH: War isn't art, it's psychosis. But why shouldn't you try to spiritualize it? You try to spiritualize everything else. I'm not just talking about *Sun Tsu — The Art of War*. You'll eventually have to realize that you can't spiritualize anything that is not spirit, which means you can't really spiritualize anything in the universe of form. The truly spiritual is only outside of it. That is where you really belong, and will eventually return.

As just one example of spiritualizing objects, you romanticize the South American rainforest by thinking it's one of the holiest spots on earth. If you could observe in accelerated motion what goes on underneath the ground there, you would see that the roots of the trees actually compete with each other for the water, just as all the creatures of the rainforest fight for survival.

GARY: Boy, it's a tree eat tree world out there. Sorry.

PURSAH: All of which brings us back to our brother J and what he was communicating. There are a couple of very important reasons why we couldn't grasp a lot of what he was saying to us. You should take note of them because they will also prevent *you* from being able to understand what he's saying directly to you. First of all, he's not talking to somebody else. There isn't anybody else. There's nobody out there, but it's not enough to just say that. The experience of it will come, and when it does it will be more liberating to you than anything the world can come up with. But the biggest reason we couldn't get J's message was because we took all the things we already believed and superimposed them onto him. People always do that with their spirituality. Here's J, challenging them to come up to his level, and they keep bringing him down to their own.

We were devoted to the old scripture, and I can tell you now there's *no way* we could have seen J except through the filter of what we already believed. He was a savior all right, but not the kind who promoted vicarious salvation. He wanted to teach us how to play our part in saving ourselves. When he said that he was the way, the truth and the life he meant we should follow his *example,* not believe in him personally. You shouldn't glorify his body. *He* didn't believe in his own body, why should you? That was our mistake, but that doesn't mean you have to make it also. Today, many people see him through the eyes of the New Testament or the lens of some of the things they've picked up off of the New Age rack. But his message, when it's understood, *is not really the same as anything else.*

GARY: Yeah, but haven't there always been *some* people who were spiritually enlightened like J, and did understand everything?

PURSAH: Not always, but yes, there have been others in some times. And they don't always come from the same spiritual paths. This brings up another important subject. The religion or spirituality you believe in does not determine how spiritually advanced you are in terms of your awareness. There are Christians who are among the very highest of attainers, and there are Christians who are babbling fools. This is true of *all* religions, philosophies and spiritual forms, without exception.

GARY: And why is that?

PURSAH: Would you like to share the answer to that, Arten?

ARTEN: Certainly. The reason it's true is because there are four major attitudes of learning you will go through during your return to God. Everyone will go through all four of them, and everyone who progresses will occasionally and unexpectedly bounce back and forth from one to the other. Each level brings with it different thoughts and resulting experiences, and you will interpret the exact same scripture differently depending on which attitude of learning you are currently engaged in.

Dualism is the condition of almost all of the universe. The mind believes in the domain of subject and object. Conceptually, it would appear to those who believe in God that there are two worlds which are both true: the world of God and the world of man. In the world of man you believe, very practically and objectively, that there is in fact a subject — you — and an object, namely, anything else. This attitude was well expressed through the model of Newtonian physics. The objects that make up a human's universe, which until the last few hundred years was simply called the world and referred to all of manifestation, are believed to exist apart from you and can be manipulated by you; "you" meaning the body and the brain that seems to run it. In fact, as we have already touched upon, the body and brain that you think are you appear to have been caused *by* the world. As we will see, this idea is exactly backwards.

> *The nonsensical tragedy of duality is considered to be normal by all modern societies, which are themselves as mad as a hatter.*

By necessity the attitude toward God that accompanies this attitude of learning is that He is somewhere outside of you. There are you *and* God, seemingly separated from one another. God, Who is actually real, seems distant and illusory. The world, which is actually illusory, seems immediate and real. For reasons that will be described later, your split mind, which split from the house like the prodigal Son, has unconsciously assigned to God the same qualities that your seemingly separated mind itself possesses. Thus God and the messages that seem to come from Him are conflicted.

Keep in mind that most of this is unconscious — meaning that it *seems* to exist out there in the world rather than in your own split mind. So God is considered to be both forgiving *and* wrathful. He is both loving *and* a killer, apparently depending on what kind of a mood He's in. This may be a good description of the conflict of a dualistic mind, but it is hardly a description of God. Almost needless to say, all of this leads to countless oddities, including the bizarre notion that God would somehow play a role in instructing people to kill other people in order to acquire certain lands and possessions, or bring a certain version of justice or the right religion to everyone. The nonsensical tragedy of duality is considered to be normal by all modern societies, which are themselves as mad as a hatter.

The next attitude of learning you will go through during your return to God is sometimes referred to as *semi-dualism*. This could be described as a kinder, gentler form of dualism because certain true ideas have begun to be accepted by the mind. Once again, it makes no difference what your religion is, which is just one reason why *all* religions have some very nice, gentle and relatively non-judgmental people. One such idea that the mind would be accepting at this time is the simple concept that God is Love. A simple notion like this however, *if it is truly believed,* would bring along with it some very difficult questions. For example, if God is Love, can He also be hate? If God is really perfect Love, then can He also be flawed? If God is a Creator, could He then be vengeful against that which He Himself had created?

Once the answer to such questions is clearly seen to be *of course not,* a long closed door has been nudged open. In the state of semi-dualism your mind has begun to lose some of its hidden but terrible fear of God. Now God is less threatening to you, as you yourself have already expressed to us. A primitive form of forgiveness has taken root within you. You still think of yourself as a body, and both God and the world still seem to be outside of you, but now you sense that God is not the cause of your situation. Perhaps the one person who was always there when things appeared to be going down the toilet was you. Perfect Love can only be responsible for good. So everything else must come *from* somewhere else. But, as we will see in our next attitude of learning, there *is* nowhere else.

PURSAH: So now we come to the subject of *non-dualism.* Keep in mind that whether we are talking about an attitude of learning or spiritual sight, we are always referring to a state of mind — an *inner* attitude and not something that is seen with the body's eyes in the world. We'll begin with a simple idea. Do you remember the old riddle, that if a tree falls in the middle of the forest and there's nobody there to hear it does it still make a sound?

GARY: I sure do. You can't prove it so people always end up arguing about it.

PURSAH: What would you say the answer is? I promise not to argue with you.

GARY: I'd say the tree always makes a sound, whether there's someone there to hear it or not.

PURSAH: And you'd be enormously wrong, even on the level of form. What the tree does is send out sound waves. Sound waves, like radio waves — and for that matter energy waves — require a receiver to pick them up. There are many radio waves going through this room right now, but there is no sound because there's no receiver tuned into them. The human or animal ear is a receiver. If a tree falls in the middle of the forest and there's nobody there to hear it, then it does *not* make a sound. Sound isn't sound *until* you hear it, just as a wave of energy does not appear to be matter *until* you see or touch it.

To make a long story short, it should be evident from this that it takes two to tango. In order for anything to interact you must have duality. Indeed, without duality there is nothing to interact *with*. There can be nothing in a mirror without an image that appears to be opposite it, attached to an observer to see it. Without duality there *is* no tree in the forest. As some of your scientists of quantum physics know, duality is a myth. And if duality is a myth, then not only is there no tree, but there is also no universe. Without you to perceive it the universe is not here, but logic would have to dictate that if the universe is not here then you are also not here. In order to make the illusion of existence you must take oneness and seemingly divide it, which is precisely what you've done. It's all a trick.

The concept of oneness is hardly an original one. However, the question few people ever ask is: What am I really one *with*? Although most of those who do ask this question would say the answer is God, they then make the error of *assuming* they and this universe were created in their present form by the Divine. That is not true, and it leaves the seeker in a position where even if he masters the mind, as Buddha certainly did, he will *still* not reach God in a permanent way. Yes, he *will* achieve oneness with the mind that made the duality waves. This mind, in a non-place that transcends all of your dimensions, is completely outside the system of time, space and form. This is the logical and proper extension of non-duality, yet it is still not God. It is in fact, a dead end. Or better yet, a dead beginning. This explains why Buddhism, which is obviously the world's most psychologically sophisticated religion, does not handle the issue of God. It's because Buddha didn't handle the issue of God while he was still in the body you call Buddha. It's also the reason we'll be making distinctions between non-dualism and pure non-dualism. When Buddha said, "I am awake," he meant he realized that he was not actually a participant in the illusion, but the maker of the entire illusion.

Still, there is another step required, where the mind that is the maker of the illusion chooses *completely against itself* in favor of God. Of course someone of Buddha's tremendous accomplishment had a snap of it, quickly going on to the exact same awareness as J. But this was done by Buddha in a lifetime the world doesn't even know about. It's not unheard of for people to achieve J's level of enlightenment in obscurity, and for the world to think they achieved it in a more famous lifetime when they really didn't. Most people who approach true spiritual mastery are not interested in being leaders. At the same time there are people who are highly visible when, rather than being true masters of spirituality and metaphysics, they are merely exhibiting the symptoms of an extroverted personality.

GARY: So how did J experience his oneness with God?

ARTEN: That's coming. One of the reasons we're telling you these things is so we can put some of his statements into context for you. One of the things he had to realize was not only that the universe doesn't exist, but that he didn't exist on any level other than pure spirit. That's something that practically no one really wants to learn. It's terrifying to all people on an unconscious level because it means the relinquishment of any individuality or personal identity, now and forever.

GARY: I once heard the Ayurvedic physician Deepak Chopra say to his students, "I'm not here." Is that the kind of experience you're referring to?

ARTEN: The doctor you speak of is a brilliant and articulate man, but it doesn't do you much good to know you're not here if you don't have the whole picture. Sure, it's a step in the right direction, but the kind of thing I'm speaking of right now is not just that I'm not here, but that I don't even *exist* in an individual way — not on *any* level. There is no separated or individual soul. There is no Atman, as the Hindus call it, except as a mis-thought in the mind. There is only God.

GARY: So you're not here; you don't even exist, and the mind is projecting these duality waves so they can *seem* to become solid particles by interacting with each other like in a movie. Also, you're saying that few people have ever been aware of the real reason they're appearing here.

ARTEN: Not bad. As we said, *we* are here for the Holy Spirit's purposes, but most people haven't got a clue what they are or how they got here. What you said is too limited. It's not just that I don't exist, *you* don't exist and neither does the false universe. When we talk about returning to reality and God, we're not just blowing hypothetical smoke. You can't have both you *and* God. It's not possible. You can't have both your universe and God. The two are mutually exclusive. You'll have to choose. There's no hurry, for time *is* hypothetical smoke, and we'll relay some of J's teachings to you on how to escape it. It's not easy, but it's doable. The Holy Spirit wouldn't give you a way out that wasn't workable. You'll be afraid of losing your identity at times. That's why we went out of our way earlier to point out that you're really giving up nothing in exchange for everything. But it will take time and more experience for you to have faith in that.

GARY: So, non-dualism is like the old teaching that you live *as if* you are in this world, but your attitude is that of the two seeming worlds, the world of truth and the world of illusion, only the truth is true and nothing else is true.

ARTEN: Yes, a delightful student. Even then, people make the mistake of thinking the illusion was made by truth. So they still make the error of attempting to bring legitimacy to the illusion rather than giving it up. You cannot hope to break the cycle of birth and death as long as you maintain this confusion. The unconscious mind goes to such lengths to avoid God that you will either ignore Him, or even more likely you will attempt to devolve non-dualism into dualism. An extraordinary example of this is what happened to one of the great teachings of Indian philosophy called the Vedanta.

The Vedanta is a non-dualistic spiritual document that teaches that the truth of Brahman is all that there really is and *anything* else is illusion — untrue, nothing, zilch — period. The Vedanta was wisely interpreted by Shankara as Advaita or non-dualistic. Good enough, right? Well, not for about nine hundred and ninety nine out of a thousand people. There are several other major, more popular and untrue interpretations of the Vedanta that represent attempts to destroy its non-dualistic metaphysics and turn it into what it is not, including Madva's effort to take unqualified non-dualism and turn it into unqualified dualism.

This is where we see an astonishing parallel between what happened to Hinduism and what happened to the teachings of J. J taught pure non-dualism, *interpreted by the world as dualism.* The Vedanta was non-dualism, interpreted by the world as dualism. Today, you have two huge religions that are controlled by a reactionary majority, both of which are in competition for the hearts and minds of a world that isn't there — one religion being the symbol of an empire based on money, and the other religion being the symbol of a government that could possibly engage in nuclear war along with its next-door, equally reactionary Muslim neighbor.

Such antics may be good enough for most of the planet, but they don't have to be good enough for you. The attitude of non-dualism tells you that what you are seeing is not the truth. If it's not the truth, then how can you judge it? To judge it is to give it reality. But how can you judge and give reality to that which isn't there? And if it's not there, why would you need to acquire it, or fight a war over it, or make it more holy or valuable than something else? How could one piece of land on earth be more important than another? Why would it matter what happens in an illusion, unless you have given the illusion a power it does not and cannot have? How could it matter what result is produced in a particular situation unless you have made a false idol out of the situation? Why is Tibet more important than anyplace else?

I know you don't want to hear this yet, but it doesn't matter what actions you take or don't take in the world — although your way of seeing and the attitude you maintain while engaging in any action *does* matter. Of course, as long as you appear to exist within the world of multiplicity you will have some temporary earthly concerns, and we do not intend to ignore your worldly needs. The Holy Spirit isn't stupid, and as we said, your experience is that you are here. There is a way to go through life doing many of the same things you'd do anyway, but now you won't do them alone. And thus you will learn that you are never alone.

So we're not suggesting you shouldn't be practical and take care of yourself. It's just that your real boss won't be of this world. You don't even have to tell anybody you're not the boss if you don't want to. If you want to have your own business and *look* like you're the boss then fine. Make it work the best you feel guided to. Be good to yourself. It's your mental attitude we're really concerned with, not *what* you appear to do. Eventually, you will come to see anything you do to make a living as an illusion to support you in the illusion, without really supporting the illusion.

From what we've said, you should get the sense that with the attitude of non-dualism you are acquiring the ability to question all of your judgments and beliefs. Now you realize there isn't really any such thing as a subject and an object, there is only oneness. Still unknown to you is that this is an *imitation* of genuine oneness, for few have learned to make the distinction between being one with the mind that has seemingly separated itself from God, and being one with God. *The mind must be returned to Him.*[4] Yet traditional non-dualism is a necessary step along the way, for you have learned you can't really separate one thing from anything else — nor can you separate anything from you.

As hinted at earlier, this idea is well expressed by the models of quantum physics. Newtonian physics held that objects were real and outside of you with a separate existence. Quantum physics demonstrates that this is not true. The universe is not what you assume it to be; everything that appears to exist is really inseparable thought. You can't even observe something without causing a change in it on the sub-atomic level. Everything is in your mind, including your own body. As aspects of Buddhism correctly teach, the mind that is thinking everything is one mind, and this mind is completely outside the illusion of time and space. What no philosophy except one teaches is a truth that will seldom be well received by anyone: the fact that this mind is itself also an illusion.[5]

It should be self-evident that if there is only oneness, then anything else that appears to exist must have been made up. Furthermore — and this is an issue that no teaching has satisfactorily supplied the motivation for until very recently — it must have been made up for what appeared to be a damn good reason. Thus instead of judging the world and everything in it, perhaps it would be more helpful for you to ask what value you saw in making it up in the first place. It may also be wise to ask yourself what would be a more appropriate response to it *now*.

PURSAH: Which brings us to J's attitude. His is the awareness of *pure non-dualism*, the end of the road, the final stop.

You should keep in mind that each of the four major attitudes of learning are long roads in themselves, and you will sometimes bounce around like a ping pong ball in between them. The Holy Spirit will correct you along the way and set you back in the right direction. Do not feel bad when you temporarily lose your way. There is no one who has ever walked this earth, including J, who did not give in to temptation in some way. The myth of living a perfect life in terms of behavior is self-defeating and unnecessary. All that is necessary is to be willing to receive correction.

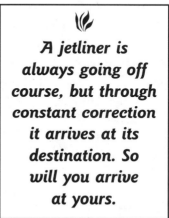

A jetliner is always going off course, but through constant correction it arrives at its destination. So will you arrive at yours.

Just as a navigator or computer constantly corrects the course of a jet airliner along its route, the Holy Spirit is always correcting you, no matter what you may appear to do or on what level of spiritual awareness you may appear to be. It may be possible to ignore Him, but it is never possible to lose Him. The jet airliner is *always* going off course, but through constant correction it arrives at its destination. So will you arrive at your destination. It's a done deal; you couldn't screw it up if you tried. The real question is, how long do you want to prolong your suffering?

It's not too early for you to start thinking along the lines of pure non-dualism. You won't always stick with it, but it doesn't hurt to start. You'll be starting to think like J, listening to the Holy Spirit like he did. But eventually we'll have to break this pure non-dualism down to two levels.

GARY: How come?

PURSAH: Stop dominating the conversation. It's because *you* have seemingly broken yourself into different levels, and the Voice that represents the big Guy must speak to you *as though* you are here in this world. How else would you be able to hear Him?

ARTEN: We'll start off with the more general sort of pure non-dualism and save the specific, practical applications of it for later.

Advanced forgiveness as J practiced it — as opposed to the primitive, backward form of forgiveness the world sometimes practices—requires more understanding than you presently have. So let's continue.

Even a cursory reading of the New Testament by a relatively sane person of rudimentary intelligence should reveal that J was not judgmental or a reactionary.

GARY: That doesn't say much for the Christian Coalition.

PURSAH: You don't care for them, do you?

GARY: I get tired of listening to these unforgiving, right-wing politicians who call themselves Christians but probably wouldn't know Jesus if he came up and bit them on the ass.

PURSAH: Yes, but that's a subtle trap, and you fell headfirst right into it. It may be accurate on the level of form to say that most Christians could easily change the name of their religion to Judgmentalism. But if you judge their judgment then you're doing the same thing as them, which puts you in the same position — chained to a body and a world that you're making psychologically real for yourself by failing to forgive.

It's obvious that most people couldn't completely forgive others if their life depended on it, and your *real* life *does* depend on it. Rather than simply pointing out that J was able to forgive people even when they were killing him — while most of today's Christians can't even forgive people who have done nothing to them — it would be far more beneficial for you to ask how he was able to do that.

Incidentally, you'll find out as we proceed that organizations like the Republicans and the Democrats, the Christian Coalition and the American Civil Liberties Union are there for an entirely different reason than you presently believe.

GARY: I guess you should proceed then, but can I ask you one more question about non-dualism first?

PURSAH: It better be good. You're throwing off my rap.

GARY: I remember once this college physicist student chick, I mean woman, told me that matter appears out of nowhere, and it's almost all empty space. Are you saying that it's thought that makes this matter appear?

PURSAH: It's true that matter appears out of nowhere. What's less obvious, and yet necessary to realize, is that after it appears it is *still* nowhere. All space is empty and non-existent, even the tiny fraction of it that appears to contain something. We'll explain what that something is eventually. As far as thoughts making images appear, a more accurate way of putting it would be that *one thought* made all images appear, because they all represent the same thing in seemingly different forms. Such issues are covered more by J's newer teachings, which are deliberately put in a language that can be comprehended but not easily digested by the people of your time. For now let's concentrate on a little clarification of the past in order to prepare you to meet the present.

GARY: All right, since you're here. I mean, since we once collectively *appeared* to form an image here.

ARTEN: As I said, J was neither judgmental or a reactionary, and our brief outline of non-dualism should have given you the idea that he would not be willing to compromise on this logic: if nothing is outside of your mind, then to judge it is to grant it power over you, and to not judge it is to withdraw its power over you. This certainly contributes to the end of your suffering. But our brother J didn't stop there.

Pure non-dualism recognizes the authority of God so completely that it relinquishes all psychological attachment to anything that is not God. This attitude also recognizes what some people have called the "like from like" principle, which says that anything coming from God must be like Him. Pure non-dualism is not willing to compromise on this principle either. Rather, it says that anything that comes from God must be *exactly* like Him. God could not create anything that is not perfect or else *He* wouldn't be perfect. The logic of that is flawless. If God is perfect and eternal, then by definition anything He creates would also have to be perfect and eternal.

GARY: That certainly narrows it down.

ARTEN: Since there is obviously nothing in this world that is perfect and eternal, J was able to see the world for what it was — nothing. But he also knew that it appeared for a reason, and that it was a trick to keep people away from the truth of God and His Kingdom.

GARY: Why does it have to keep us away from the truth?

ARTEN: That's a couple of discussions away, but you need to

understand that J made a complete and uncompromising distinction between God and everything else — everything else being totally insignificant except for the opportunity it provided to listen to the Holy Spirit's interpretation of it, instead of the world's. Anything involving perception and change would, by its very nature, be imper-

> **Humility is the way — not a false humility that says you are inadequate, but a real humility that simply says God is your only Source.**

fect — an idea Plato expressed but did not fully develop in terms of God. J learned to overlook perception and choose with the perfect Love of spirit on a consistent basis. The vital distinctions between perfect spirit and the world of change allowed him to hear the Voice of the Holy Spirit more and more, which in turn allowed a process to unfold where he could forgive more and more. The Voice for truth got louder and stronger until J got to the point where he could listen to just this one Voice and see right through everything else. Finally, J became, or better, he re-became what this Voice represents — his and your true reality as spirit and oneness with the Kingdom of Heaven.

Remember, if you believe God has anything to do with the universe of perception and change, or if you believe that the mind that made this world has anything to do with God, you will sabotage the process of mastering the ability to listen only to the Holy Spirit's Voice. Why? One reason has to do with your unconscious guilt, which is something we'll eventually have to deal with. Another is that a pre-requisite of gaining the power and peace of the Kingdom is to give up your own pseudo-power and your *own* rather precarious kingdom. How can you give up your miscreations if you believe they are God's Will? And how can you relinquish your weakness if you believe it is strength?

You've got to be willing to surrender the idea of Authorship to God if you want to be able to share in your real power. Humility is the way — not a false humility that says you are inadequate, but a real humility that simply says God is your only Source. You will realize that except for His Love you need nothing, and he who needs nothing can be trusted with everything.

So when J made statements like, "Of myself I can do nothing," and "I and the Father are one," he wasn't claiming any kind of specialness for himself. In fact, he was *giving up* any specialness, individuality or authorship and accepting his true strength — the power of God.

As far as J was concerned there *was* no J, and eventually there wasn't. His reality was now that of pure spirit and outside of the illusion completely. This reality is also completely outside of the mind that made the false universe, a mind that people mistake for the home of their true oneness. J knew that the miscreation of the universe didn't have anything to do with the truth. His Identity was with God and nothing else. The 'Peace of God which passeth under-standing' was no longer something to be strived for. It was his for the asking or better yet, it was his for the remembering. He no longer had to seek after perfect Love, for with his many wise choices he had removed all of the barriers that had divided him from the reality of his perfection.

His Love, like God's, was total, impersonal, non-selective and all embracing. He treated everyone equally, from rabbi to prostitute. He was not a body. He was no longer a human being. He had passed through the eye of the needle. He had reclaimed his place with God as pure spirit. This is pure non-dualism: an attitude that, along with the Holy Spirit, will lead you to what you are. You and J are the same thing. We all are. There *is* nothing else, but you need more training and practice to experience this.

GARY: I've been taught that I'm a co-creator with God. Is that true?

ARTEN: Not on this level. The only place where you are really a co-creator with God is in Heaven, where you would not be aware of being any different than Him or in any way separate from Him. So then how could you *not* be a co-creator with Him? But there is a way here on earth to practice the thought system of the Holy Spirit like J did which *reflects* the laws of Heaven, and *that* is your way home.

We will further discuss the attributes of pure non-dualism and how to practice it as we proceed, but for now just try to remember that if God is perfect Love, then He is not anything *else*, and neither are you. You are in fact, the Love of God, and your real life is with

Him. Like J, you will come to know and experience that God is not outside of you. You will no longer identify yourself with a vulnerable body or anything else that can be limited, and a body *is* anything that has borders or limits. You will learn instead of your true reality as pure spirit that is invulnerable forever.

GARY: You know, I've heard a lot of people lately who ridicule spiritual ideas like these. There's that guy who used to be a magician who now calls himself a professional debunker and skeptic. People like him are always pointing out that spiritual themes are unscientific; he seems to think you should always go with what the body's senses and experience tell you. How can I handle people like that?

ARTEN: Forgive them. We'll tell you how. Besides, such people don't even realize that they're dinosaurs. That man supposedly respects scientists, but wasn't Albert Einstein a scientist?

GARY: I believe he was a rather famous one.

ARTEN: Do you know what he said about your experience of the world?

GARY: What?

ARTEN: He said that a man's experience is an optical delusion of his consciousness.

GARY: Einstein said *that?*

ARTEN: Yes. People like your debunker friend should be a little more humble and a little less arrogant about their assumptions. He's actually a very intelligent man, yet he doesn't use it constructively. But we're not here to talk about him. His turn to become aware of the truth will come when it's supposed to.

Meanwhile, don't expect him or the world to beat a path to your doorstep. Look at J the last day before the part of the illusion where he got crucified. Do you really think most of our people wanted to hear what he had to say? And do you really believe that the Gentiles were any more intelligent? Come on! Those silly bastards wouldn't even catch on to the Arabic number system for another 1200 years. They were too busy slicing and dicing people and keeping the world safe for darkness.

GARY: Are you saying that Christianity is a relic of the dark ages?

ARTEN: I'm saying that the Europeans weren't any more ready for the truth than the rest of the world was. The universe doesn't really want to wake up. The universe wants candy to make it feel better, but the candy is designed to bind you to the universe.

PURSAH: From the brief outline of spiritual progression we just gave you it should now be clear that when J said things like, "Enter by the narrow gate, for the gate is wide and the way is easy that leads to destruction, and those who enter by it are many. For the gate is narrow and the way is hard that leads to life, and those who find it are few," he wasn't trying to scare the hell out of people by threatening them with destruction if they didn't walk the straight and narrow. On the contrary, he was telling them that what they are experiencing here is *not* life, while showing them the way *to* life.

What you are experiencing here *is* destruction, but J knew the way out. That's why he said, "Be of good cheer, for I have overcome the world." If he wasn't a man who had lessons to learn like you, then why would he have to overcome the world in the first place? He understood countless things we didn't, yet all of it was connected to one consistent thought system, the thought system of the Holy Spirit. For instance, he knew the old scripture contained passages that didn't express perfect, non-selective Love, which meant they couldn't be God's Word.

GARY: Like what?

PURSAH: The kind of thing we mean should be obvious. For example, do you really believe, as it says in various verses of Leviticus, Chapter 20, that God told Moses that adulterers, wizards, mediums and homosexuals should be put to death?

GARY: That does seem a little extreme. I've always liked mediums.

PURSAH: Seriously.

GARY: Seriously, no. I don't believe God would say that.

ARTEN: So now you have a fundamental problem.

GARY: Yeah, the fundas are mental.

ARTEN: The world *is* a mental problem, but the problem we're addressing at this time is the attempted reconciliation of two thought systems that cannot be reconciled. And I'm not referring to the Old Testament and the New Testament. The differences between them are about J, not God. Yet the early Christians were desperate to build a bridge between J and the past, and what they really ended up with was simply a new *version* of the past.

What I'm really comparing here is the thought system of the world, which you can find in *either* the Old Testament or the New, and the thought system of J, which is absent from both. Yes, you can get a glimpse of what J was like from a few of his surviving sayings, but that's about it. I'm not telling you that Judaism or Christianity are more or less valid than one another. We've already said that all religions have both exemplary people and jerks. That's an illusion as well because as J knew, the body is an illusion.

And *there* you have the number one reason why the thinking of the world and the thinking of J are mutually exclusive — because J's reality was not the body, and the world's thinking is completely based upon an identification with the body as your reality. Even those of you who glance past the body still maintain the idea of an individual existence, which is actually little different than having a body. In fact, it is with this idea of separation, and all that arises from it, that you sentence yourself to continue in the universe of bodies.

Why do you think the master, unlike the other people of his time, treated all men and women equally?

GARY: You tell me. I assume there's more to it than the fact that he wasn't trying to get the babes into the sack.

PURSAH: It was because he didn't see *either* men or women as bodies. He did not acknowledge differences. He knew each person's reality was spirit, which cannot be limited in any way. So they could not really be male *or* female. Today, your feminists are always trying to build up the greatness of women. They sometimes refer to women as Goddesses and to God as a She instead of a He. That's cute, but all they're really doing is replacing one mistake with another.

When J used the word 'He' to describe God he was speaking metaphorically in the language of scripture. He had to use metaphor to communicate with people, but *you* make everything real. J knew that God cannot be limited by gender, and neither can people — because they're not really people. How can you really be a person if you're not a body? That's far more important for you to comprehend than you presently suspect, and we'll be explaining why. Knowing the truth, J treated each body the same — as though it didn't exist. He was then able to look completely past it to the true light of unchangeable and immortal spirit that is the one reality of us all.

Anyway, like most people today, instead of really listening back then to what J was teaching, most of us saw and heard what we wanted to see and hear so we could use him to validate our own experience — which was the experience of being an individual in a body. Thus we had to make *him* a separate and *very special* individual body, which is how we really saw ourselves, and how you still see yourself.

Although some of us tended to be a little more intellectual, the beliefs of most of the earliest followers were simple enough. We had already seen J after the crucifixion, and since we didn't comprehend his entire message, the inaccurate and majority opinion among the sects was that he was going to return to us again, as he had already done before, and bring in God's Kingdom. It was expected this would happen

> ◟◞
> **For God to create the imperfect must either mean that He was imperfect or that He deliberately made those who were so they could screw up, be punished by Him and suffer here on psycho planet.**

very soon, *not* in the distant future and not anywhere but right on the ground. I didn't agree with that particular scenario because, as J taught in my Gospel, the Kingdom of God is something that is *present* but unseen by people. In any case, there was some diversity even at the beginning, but most of the followers bought into the idea of a return. As the years wore on and the going got tough however, the leaders of a now developing new religion had to improvise if they were going to hold anyone's interest.

Before you knew it you had people relating to J as the body of all bodies. They already believed God had created a flawed world with imperfect people like Adam and Eve who were capable of making mistakes. They completely overlooked the logic that for God to create the imperfect must either mean that He Himself was imperfect or He deliberately made those who were so they could screw up, be punished by Him and suffer here on psycho planet. Then, according to this developing new religion, God takes — incredibly — His big-time special only begotten Son, who would apparently be more Holy than the rest of the scum of the earth, and sends him as a blood sacrifice to suffer and die on a cross as a way of vicariously atoning for people's sins.

Except now there's *another* big problem, because even according to Christianity's own doctrines, this does *not* really atone for anybody else's sins. If it atoned for people's sins, then that would be the end of it. Problem solved. But no! It now becomes necessary for everyone to blindly *believe* in all of the details conveniently set forth exclusively by the Christian religion, or else they will *still* burn in hell, even if they happened to be born — presumably by God's Will — in a place, time or culture that isn't even familiar with this particular religion!

GARY: It does all sound a little bizarre when you put it that way. The whole thought system isn't exactly complimentary to the nature of God.

ARTEN: That's because it's all symbolic of a fearful image of God rather than a loving one. We don't mean to be disrespectful, but we have to make certain controversial statements because there's not exactly an oversupply of people in your society who are willing to point these things out. It *is* true that at the time J was the most advanced spiritual person to ever appear on the earth. But everyone else, including you, will eventually attain the same level of accomplishment as him. There is no exception to this. Thus J is not ultimately different than anyone else, and his attitude was that *no one* will be left out of Heaven, because there is really only *one* of us — not all these separate bodies as you are presently dreaming.

GARY: Are you saying even murderers will end up in Heaven?

ARTEN: Even Saint Paul, or Saul, which was his name before he changed it so he could be a hit with the Gentiles, was a murderer before he turned in his sword. You don't get what we're saying. There *is* no Saint Paul, not really, or anyone else — including J — except in a dream. *There's nobody out there.* There is only *one* Son of God, and you're It. You'll get it, but it takes years of practice to really experience it. You have to want it, but I know you do.

GARY: If we're all dreaming, why do we have our separate experiences, but we also have the same experiences? For example, we all see the same mountain out the window there.

ARTEN: That's because there is only one dream, which explains the common experiences. The mind has seemingly split itself up so that each unit observes the dream from a different *point of view*, which explains your own personal experiences.

We expected these conversations to ramble, which is perfectly all right. But let's try to stick to the subject and we'll get to the other things as they come.

GARY: All right. You're saying that J saw people as being the same as him and God — unlimited and perfect. All other characteristics we put onto other people *or* onto God are really are own *unconscious* beliefs about ourselves?

PURSAH: I knew you weren't as dumb as you look. You know I'm kidding, right?

GARY: Yeah sure, just my luck. I get an ascended master with a chip on her shoulder.

PURSAH: Yes, but the chip is an illusion for teaching purposes, and let me make another point.

GARY: Do I have a choice?

PURSAH: Yes, always. Getting back to business, you have to understand that as Jews we sincerely believed that our religion had made some kind of a giant leap forward with monotheism — the idea of one God — as opposed to polytheism — the belief in many different Gods. Most of us didn't know monotheism actually originated with Akhnaton in ancient Egypt, and all this idea and our continuation of it really did was take all the different personalities and characteristics, good and bad, of all these previously made up Gods and *incorporate* them into one God.

GARY: So now instead of all these different screwed-up Gods you had just one screwed-up God.

ARTEN: Well put! Of course there really *is* only one God and He isn't screwed up at all, and neither was the J guy, who had forgiven the world — his mind had been returned to the Holy Spirit where it belonged. That's where your mind belongs. You took it, and you have to give it back.[6] And I've got a message for you: You'll never really be happy until you do. No matter what you imagine you have accomplished in any lifetime, there will always be a part of you that feels like something is missing—because in your illusions something *is* missing.

GARY: You said you'd tell me what J was like. That reminds me, a lot of people seem to think his first name was Jesus and his last name was Christ.

PURSAH: Yes, and his middle initial was H. Fortunately, a lot of other people realize the word *Christ* is from the Greek psychological term that can be applied to anyone, and not just J exclusively.

> ❦
>
> *J's peace and unalterable love were so total that sometimes people couldn't stand it and they had to look away.*

I'll tell you, we used to feel like fools trying to describe him to people after the crucifixion and his subsequent appearances to us. But wait, I forgot to mention something.

GARY: You made a mistake? Shame on you. One more and you'll be judged severely.

PURSAH: I wanted to point out that I suspected, as a few others believed at the time, that resurrection is something that happens in your mind and has nothing to do with your body. That idea, which was eventually rejected by Paul and the church, was carried forward by some of the Gnostics. I learned eventually that the idea was correct. This brings up something Arten and I can say that Christianity cannot. The newer teachings of J that we'll be talking to you about will eventually be proven to be true, where so many of the things the Bible says have already been debunked, and will continue to be shown false by science. If something really comes from God, wouldn't it make sense that it would eventually be demonstrated to be true rather than false?

Also, because of a story in the Gospels, I have sometimes been referred to as "Doubting Thomas." Just as with J, you shouldn't confuse the Biblical Thomas with the true, historical Thomas. A story in a novel doesn't necessarily represent the absolute truth, even though some people may want it to. The experiences that can be brought about by the genuine teachings of the Holy Spirit speak for themselves.

GARY: And the historical J?

PURSAH: He never cursed a tree and killed it, never got angry and knocked over the tables in the temple, but he *did* heal a few people who were already dead. Also, his body died on the cross but he did not suffer as you would imagine. As for his way of being, mere words cannot do him justice. To be in his presence was an experience so unique it gave you a feeling of wonder. His peace and unalterable love were so total that sometimes people couldn't stand it and they had to look away. His attitude was so calm and sure it made you want to know how he did it. Those of us who spent a lot of time with him and, as in my case, got to speak in private with him were inspired by his complete faith in God.

One of the ironic things — and this is something people don't understand — was that he considered himself to be totally *dependent* on God, yet this dependence was not weakness, as the world usually views dependence. Rather, the result was a state of unbelievable psychological strength. Things that would scare the stuffing out of strong people meant nothing to him, because they *were* nothing to him. Fear was not a part of him. His attitude was the same as if you were having a dream last night asleep in your bed, except you were totally aware of the fact that you were dreaming. And because you knew you were dreaming you also knew that absolutely nothing in the dream could possibly hurt you, because none of it was true; you realized you were merely observing symbolic images, including people, who weren't really there.

J used to tell me when we were alone that the world was just an insignificant dream, but most people weren't ready to accept such an idea because their contrary experience was so strong. He then stressed that *knowing the world is an illusion is not enough.* The Gnostics and some early Christians called the world a dream; the Hindus call it *maya* and the Buddhists call it *anicca*, all meaning pretty much the same thing. But if you don't know the purpose of the dream and how to reinterpret the images you are seeing, which is something we'll get into later, then the general teaching that the world is an illusion is of very limited value. However, he also said the time would come when the Holy Spirit would teach people all things — which is something we hope to contribute to by sharing some of J's newer teachings with you — and that everyone would know only God is real. Sometimes at the end of a conversation with me he would just say "God is," and walk away.[7]

One of the other things about him that's rarely mentioned is that he had an excellent sense of humor. He was quite irreverent. He liked to laugh and bring out the joy in others.

GARY: And he was totally awake?

ARTEN: Yes, but let's be very clear about what we mean by that. We're not saying he was more awake *in* the dream, we're saying he had awakened *from* the dream. That's not just a minor distinction, Gary. Indeed, being more seemingly awake in the dream is what passes for enlightenment among very many, but that's not what we're teaching. You can teach a dog to be more alert and impressive and to live its so-called life to the fullest, and almost any human can be taught to raise his consciousness. You can always be taught to approach the dream with a clever thought pattern in an attempt to bring about something more, different or better. But our brother J was *completely* outside of the dream. He wasn't advocating a way of making your delusion better, or telling you how to strive for self-expression so you won't die with an unmet potential. Such exercises may temporarily make you feel better, but you're still building your house upon the sand.

J wouldn't be *opposed* to making your life better, but he would be more concerned with your Source of guidance than he would be about the guidance itself, because he knew the tremendous long-term benefits that being a true follower of the Holy Spirit could have for your mind. The real goal isn't dressing up your life; it's about awakening from what you *think* is your life! *Then* you're building your house upon the rock. J's message isn't about fixing up the world. When your body appears to die, what are you going to do with what you believe is the world? As far as the world is concerned, you can dress it up, but you can't take it anywhere.

GARY: Aren't some of these ideas touched upon in a few of the Gospels that were rejected by the church?

PURSAH: To say they were rejected is to put it mildly. In many cases Gospels were destroyed by the church, never to be read again. People today overlook the fact that when Constantine made Christianity the official religion of the Roman Empire, it meant that by law any other religious or spiritual ideas were outlawed. So if your beliefs were not a part of the rapidly developing doctrines of

THE DISAPPEARANCE OF THE UNIVERSE 51

the new church, then you were an overnight heretic — which was a crime punishable by death. It was as though your Congress suddenly passed a law saying all religious beliefs that are not exactly in line with the doctrines of the Christian Coalition are banned, and any disagreement by you is a crime equal to murder.

GARY: So Emperor Constantine wasn't into tolerance any more than those before him who had persecuted the Christians.

PURSAH: Constantine was a soldier, a politician and a murderer. He didn't do much of anything that wasn't calculated to increase his own power. He realized that Christianity was *already* becoming the most popular religion in the Roman Empire and he simply made the most of it for himself. You can't possibly think that anyone who just goes right on slaughtering people has had any kind of serious religious experience.

GARY: Don't some people believe holy wars are justified?

ARTEN: Holy war — another oxymoron if there ever was one.

GARY: Even Edgar Cayce said wars are sometimes necessary.

ARTEN: There's a world of difference between Holy and necessary. Edgar was a fine and gifted man, but he would be the first one to tell you that he wasn't J. J laughed at the idea of spiritualizing violence, just as he laughed at the world.

GARY: All right. So getting back to our overrated friend Constantine and some of the early church actions, you're saying a lot of Gospels and alternative ideas about J were wiped out?

PURSAH: Yes, and that begs an observation about what passes for history. You may think we're giving you revised history, but what you don't understand is that it's *all* revised history. Whether it's religious history, natural history or political history, the truth is you don't *know* what your history is. History, or Herstory for your feminist friends, is a story written by whoever wins the war. If the Axis powers had won World War Two you'd be reading today about what great men Hitler, Mussolini and Tojo must have been, and the Holocaust and the rape of Nanking would only be spoken about by a few rebels who didn't mind taking their lives into their hands. Fortunately for you, the Allies won the war and you're free to study spirituality instead of fascism. People weren't always fortunate enough to believe whatever they wanted to.

My ministry after the crucifixion was mostly in Syria — I was there fourteen years before Paul — and I also made extended trips to Egypt, Arabia, Persia and even India. My witnessing for J was pretty straightforward and based completely on what I had heard him say, both in public and in private. We didn't tell embellished stories about him in those days. The first Gospels like mine were called Sayings Gospels because they were simply listings of teachings that J had spoken that were written down from memory.

The novels that became the Gospels were written later, from some twenty to sixty years after the letters of Paul, even though his letters appear later in the Bible. Because I was simply quoting the public and private J, my communications, including my Gospel, had more of an intellectual feel. However, many of the sayings in my Gospel were a lot more meaningful to the Middle East culture of that time than to the Western culture of today, so I'll only be explaining a few of what I consider to be the more relevant ones for you.

Being the provincial American that you are, you may have a hard time believing this, but back then the people of the Arab world were more advanced in many ways than the people of Europe or the Western Roman Empire. Because of your heritage, you think Europe was the be-all and end-all of intellectual accomplishment. Yet in the Middle East, the city of Petra made most of Europe look like a slum. The pyramids in Egypt looked nothing like they do today. They were completely encased in beautiful, smoothly polished limestone that could be seen shining across the desert from over a hundred miles away. The library they had in Alexandria, in Egypt, contained over *one million* documents, which included most of the sum intelligence and known history of the human race at that time. Until of course, it was partially ruined by the Romans upon their invasion and then subject to incredible neglect, pillage and a few fires after that.

I do not say these things to make the illusion real, or to wax lyrical about dreams in the night. I point them out only to show you what a warped view of history you have. You overlook the dark ages and think that Europe and the religion that came to be called Christianity were somehow superior to the rest of the world at that time. Yet it was the Europeans who were the worst barbarians of all, and it didn't matter whether it was a northern tribe, a Roman tribe or one of the later Christian tribes, as their many violent actions would prove so clearly. Unfortunately, their interpretation of our brother J was no better than most of their other endeavors. Yes, Europe eventually underwent a period of improvement while other areas went into decline or fell behind, but the Christian religion had been almost completely developed *before* that, and in fact acted as a force *against* the Renaissance, just as it actively opposes anything that doesn't fit the narrow confines of its ignoble theology.

GARY: You're not being very generous to Christianity. Most of the Christians I know are good people.

ARTEN: We're not saying there isn't some good in Christianity or that Christian people are not sometimes the salt of the earth. But their religion is a mixed bag, because the world that is a projection of the mind that made it is such a mixed bag. If the mind is going to be healed then it needs something that is *not* a mixed bag. In any case, don't be a dim bulb and assume you know what your history is, because you're only aware of a very small, distorted fraction of it.

> *Humans have built and destroyed many advanced civilizations on this planet. The same process is being repeated as we speak.*

Look at natural history. There is solid, scientific evidence of humans existing on the earth for much, much longer than most of your scientists would care to talk about in public because they fear it could ruin their careers. If they don't fit the accepted scientific models then their work can't get funding, and without money they're practically dead in the water. Don't expect to be better informed any time soon by the government and corporate-sponsored intellectual giants of your time, but the truth is that human types have built *and* destroyed many highly technologically advanced civilizations on this planet. The pattern of building and destroying civilizations has been repeated many times that you have no idea about. What you refer to as Atlantis is only one example, and the same pattern is being repeated as we speak.

The Great Soul, Gandhi, warned that there is more to life than making it go faster. But the world has learned very little, while thinking it has learned very much.

GARY: Something you said reminded me of a group of Biblical scholars I read about, who came to the conclusion that J probably only said about twenty per cent of the things the New Testament quotes him as saying.

PURSAH: Yes. Actually, the percentage is even less than that, and some of the things they think he said and didn't say they've got wrong. However, we didn't come here to attempt to make a contribution to Biblical scholarship which, despite its helpful contributions, is a flawed science.

GARY: How is it flawed?

PURSAH: One of its aspects is that the more times a quotation shows up in different sources the more credibility it's given. However, the Gospels of Mark, Matthew and Luke all copied from earlier sources, and Matthew and Luke also copied from one common source as well as from the Book of Mark which, even though it was written before the other three mainstream Gospels, appears second in the Bible — because the boys wanted to start off the New Testament with that unnecessary family tree business in Matthew that tried to trace J all the way back to King David in order to fulfill a prophecy, even though a purported virgin birth would nullify the whole thing anyway. Incidentally the old, original scripture just said that "a young woman shall give birth to him," meaning the Messiah. It never said that a virgin shall give birth. That was cooked up later, based on similar stories from other ancient religions.

GARY: People love prophecies.

ARTEN: You bet they do. Practically all of the Christian religion was borrowed from earlier stories and scripture including, but not limited to, some of the old copper Dead Sea Scrolls that didn't survive. By the way, we weren't very complimentary to the Essenes earlier, but they had a great talent for scribing and preserving scripture, which they were more devoted to than almost anyone.

GARY: You're not getting soft on people now, are you?

ARTEN: People are neither good or bad. You'll see. The point we started to make about the rules of Biblical scholarship is this: If Gospel writers copied from each other, which was not unusual at the time, and the scholars of today give credibility to stories and sayings based on how many different sources they are found in, then their findings will sometimes be erroneous — especially if the *original* source for the copying was incorrect in the first place *or* that original source was changed by the copier and then lost or destroyed.

GARY: So copying something doesn't make it true, and the fact that something wasn't copied very much doesn't make it false.

ARTEN: Yes. An exceptional student. Now I'll give *you* a prophecy. You're going to write a book about this, that will tell some people what we said.

GARY: A book? I have a hard time writing a check.

ARTEN: It will give you a chance to use that memory of yours, and those notes you're taking.

GARY: I don't think people would believe me if I told them you guys appeared to me like this.

ARTEN: Actually, some people would believe it and some people wouldn't, but how about this? I have a suggestion that will help you get going and be very peaceful. What if you don't *try* to convince anyone to believe anything? Start writing it like it's just a story — as though you made it up. Then tell people they made *you* up. It's *all* made up. That's the point, my brother.

GARY: I don't know. I probably wouldn't even be able to get the punctuation right.

ARTEN: What's the difference as long as people can understand most of it? Don't worry about the details; just write down what we told you. It's the message that matters, not the delivery. What you screw up in punctuation you'll make up for with substance and consistency. Besides, you might be surprised. Ask the Holy Spirit to help you and you'll do fine.

GARY: Doesn't this contradict what you told me before — about how I don't have to tell anybody anything if I don't want to, and how you're not gonna tell me about the future and stuff?

PURSAH: No. We're not going to tell you much about the future, and you *don't* have to write anything if you don't want to. Even if you do, you won't have to appear in public if you don't feel comfortable about it. You don't like to speak in front of a crowd, do you?

GARY: I'd rather stick broken pieces of glass up my butt.

PURSAH: I don't think that will be necessary. The point is, you're free to do whatever you choose — but you'll be wise not to do it alone. Let J or the Holy Spirit make your decisions for you whenever you have the time to ask. We have an advantage in talking about this because everything that's going to happen has already happened. It's not like we're giving you a special assignment; we're just telling you what's already occurred. We'll get into that eventually.

GARY: I feel a little uncomfortable not telling Karen about this. Would she be able to see you two if she were here?

PURSAH: Sure. The bodies we project are just as dense as yours, although our brains aren't. Just kidding. But anybody would be able to see us the same as they can see you. You may be doing Karen a favor by not telling her about us for a while, though.

GARY: How's that?

PURSAH: If you tell her about us now and she believes you, which she would, then it would alter her life and induce a series of events she doesn't need. It would be best for you to tell her later when our appearances are over. You're the only one we want involved right now.

GARY: Could I take pictures of you and record your voices?

ARTEN: You could, but I'll give you three reasons why not to. First, you'd be tempted to prove to people that we appeared to you. Yet any actors could have played us or our voices, so it wouldn't really prove anything. Second, this isn't about convincing anyone that you're right; it's about sharing ideas to help them along the path. Third, using our appearances as a means to induce anyone's belief in us wouldn't be in line with what we're teaching. We want to teach in a way that will induce the kind of practical application that leads to revelatory *experience*. That's what strengthens belief in a genuine way.

GARY: What if people reject what you have to say, or they just use it for a while but then give up and move on to something else?

ARTEN: Those are likely responses, but *some* people will stick with it and make the most of it. As we said, don't worry about the details. No learning is ever wasted. *Anything* that you learn stays in your mind forever. You can't lose it; even if you're not conscious of it, it's still there. That's why you shouldn't be overly concerned if you think you might not make it to Heaven in this particular lifetime. Learning is not linear. Not only does everything stay in the mind, but you can rest assured that any seemingly linear decision about reincarnation is *not* made by the human body or brain. That decision is made by your mind on a completely different level, depending on whether or not you have done your necessary part in helping the Holy Spirit heal your unconscious guilt.[8] As we said, no matter what appears to happen, your mind retains all information.

GARY: Cool. So none of us are as dumb as we look.

ARTEN: That's true. All ignorance is actually repression that exists in order to produce a particular effect for a specific reason, which we'll get into.

GARY: Huh. You know it's kind of funny, but a lot of the things you say ring true for me even though I haven't heard some of them before.

ARTEN: That's because during many of your past lives you have not been a stranger to theosophical instruction. During the last few years you've seen

> *Even on the level of form, Arabs and Jews, like Serbs and Muslims, are basically the same — which shows you how far people will go to be different.*

several images of what you've looked like in past lives. Seeing mystical images is a gift of yours. Part of the reason you've had so many spiritual experiences in this life — and why you will also take to many of these ideas like a duck takes to water — is because your combined lifetimes of learning are still within you.

GARY: Can you give me a short tour?

ARTEN: Very short. Remember, none of this makes you unique or special. Almost everyone ends up studying the same things eventually. At one time you were fortunate enough to be an enthusiast of the great thinker of the Kabbalah, Moses Cordovero. His famous formula, "God is all reality but not all reality is God," stated a very important point and also made a vital distinction between Kabbalistic mysticism and pantheism. At another stop on the wheel of time you were a Sufi Muslim.

GARY: That's funny. Jews and Arabs have often hated each other, yet in various lifetimes they *are* each other.

ARTEN: Good point. Even on the level of form Arabs and Jews — like Serbs and Muslims — are basically the same, which shows you how far people will go to be different. That's true of most people;

it's just that some examples appear to be more extreme. Today it is common for Jews, Blacks, and Native Americans to feel victimized by the past, but many of them would be shocked to learn that they have perpetrated victimization in their previous lives. By the same token, there are many victims of childhood abuse who become abusers in the same lifetime. Thus the victim-victimization dance of duality goes on, allowing everyone at one time or another to wear the blood-stained robes of righteous judgment.

As a Sufi Muslim you cultivated within yourself the thought of oneness, or monism, and made progress in experiencing each seemingly separate thing as an illusory veil over the eternal truth. You recognized the reality of God and the unimportance of matter, and one of the verses of the Koran that was the most dear to you was, "All things in creation suffer extinction and there remaineth the face of thy Lord in its majesty and bounty."

You also realized that an essential part of each illusion would be change, or as you learned to call it in a Buddhist lifetime, *impermanence* — which was unreal — as opposed to the goal of clear light. All of this learning was complimented very nicely by something that you studied in yet another lifetime — the teachings of Plato, who spoke and wrote about a perfect idea behind all of the imperfect things of this world. He called it "the Good," and described it as an "...eternal reality, the realm unaffected by the vicissitudes of change and decay..."

Six centuries later another one of your teachers, the neo-Platonist known as Plotinus, would borrow and expand on Plato's postulation that "the Good is One," and would attempt to define it as the ultimate Source of everything in the world. However, like almost all of the other great philosophers of history with the exception of J, neither Plato nor any of his successors understood where the world actually originated, or more importantly — why.

GARY: So Plato's popular pupil Plotinus was possibly a plagiarist of Platonist postulations?

ARTEN: One more outburst like that and you'll be punished. You know when we're kidding by now, right? Anyway, Plato would have liked Plotinus, and we want to emphasize that these are all lifelong paths. Our oversimplifications are only meant to point out to you that you *did* spend entire lifetimes on them.

The idea of a changeless reality is not an insignificant one. To see why, let's look at the notion of yin and yang, which you explored during several Taoist and Buddhist incarnations in the Far East.

GARY: Boy, I get around, don't I?

ARTEN: Everybody does eventually, but it really happened all at once. As Einstein noted, past, present, and future all occur simultaneously.

GARY: That Einstein was a really smart guy.

ARTEN: Yes, but he still had to learn it actually never happened at all. You'll see. Incidentally, when we leave here tonight it will feel to you like we've been here for a couple of hours, but only twenty minutes will have gone by on your watch.

NOTE: At this point I glanced at my watch and saw that even though Pursah and Arten had been speaking with me for what seemed like over an hour, only eleven minutes had passed.

GARY: You've gotta be kidding! My watch's second hand is still running normal, but there's some pretty unusual crap going on here.

ARTEN: Don't worry. We knew this would be the longest of our discussions, so we decided to play with time a little rather than keep you up late. We know you need a good night's sleep because you have work to do in the morning.

Time can be altered because even though your *experience* is one of being linear, you are actually a non-linear being. We don't usually play games, but we're also going to have a little fun with you on another occasion when we play with space. Not outer space, just space. You're not a spatial being, but a non-spatial one. Or as a physicist might put it, you're having a local *experience,* but you are actually non-local.

We said we were going to talk about yin and yang, and here we find the same kind of situation that exists with all the other famous philosophies and spiritualities of this world.

The original idea behind the yin, which is passive energy or chi, and the yang, which is active energy, is that they come from the Tao — which is absolute stillness. But since the Tao cannot perceive itself, then it decides to split into two and manifest eternally, giving rise to an ever-changing and seemingly infinite interaction of balancing forces. That's a very rough description, by the way. I'm not going to get into the development of Taoism, which was an extremely long process. But does the general idea sound familiar?

GARY: Yeah. So the New Age ideas are actually very old, and even Plato owed something to the teachers who came before him.

ARTEN: We all do. The idea of "the One" was not completely original, but Plato was still a great philosopher. Even J, although he was much more advanced, admired Plato's story of The Cave.

GARY: I remember that! My mother used to read it to me when I was a little kid. I remember thinking it was scary.

ARTEN: Why do you think your mother would do that, knowing that you couldn't really understand it very well?

GARY: Because she wanted to open up my mind a little, and let me know there were more diverse ideas available to me than the usual garbage society would lay on me.

ARTEN: Absolutely. She was an exquisite mother, and we'll talk a little about that story in a while. As we were saying, the idea behind yin and yang is not very different than many other philosophies. Unfortunately, it also contains the same basic error as the others. Yin and yang interact forever, and you find some yin in all yang and some yang in all yin, and meanwhile what the world laughably refers to as life goes on ad nauseam.

But the philosophy never really bothers to consider the lack of wisdom in all of this, except to *assume* that consciousness, chi, and perception are all very valuable commodities. By the time we're finished you will have an idea what they really are, and you also will have received your first overview of how to turn the tables on them. What you want to remember now is that because of their spiritual experiences, there was a sense among most of the originators of these ideas that the One was unchanging and eternal — and on that point they were quite accurate.

Another point many of them had right was that everything that was *not* the One was illusory. Even judgment in its most basic form, such as to label something as good or bad, would be to differentiate between things that are actually the same because of their unreality.

Thus it is not really valid to judge anything.

GARY: So it's the same kind of nonjudgment that the *Bhagavad-Gita* describes as "when suffering and joy are equal. . ."

ARTEN: Yes. Spoken like a smart Hindu, which you've also been. As a smart Hindu you had no use for politics, except for how it could be used by you to recognize illusion. But recognizing illusion is just a part of the process of forgiveness as taught by J, not all of it. The rest is coming. Before you know it, you'll be one with the J underground.

GARY: Would you care to explain that?

ARTEN: Well, I loved J. He was like a light leading the children back to their true home in Heaven. Once I was with him and I said something that was forgiving, and he said that I was now one with the J underground. He went on to say that this simply meant I was starting to think like him, sometimes right along with him. Only then, he said, could he come further into my mind and be even closer to me, because I was starting to see like him, thinking with the same inner attitude — which is what spiritual sight really is. As we already said, it has nothing to do with the body's eyes, although you may experience *symbols* of this inner attitude which can occasionally be seen with the body's eyes. Let us emphasize something: People shouldn't feel bad or slighted if they don't see any such symbols. They are *not* necessary. Some people have a gift for them like you, but some people's gifts are in other areas. The seeming effect is superfluous; it's the cause we're interested in.

Of course J so completely identified with the Holy Spirit that he was referring to me thinking with him as the Holy Spirit, not J the body. If people don't feel very comfortable with J, they can always think of the Holy Spirit. Because you think that you're a specific body or soul, it would be helpful for you to have someone who *you* think of as being specific rather than abstract to help you and lead you beyond all symbols.

GARY: Wouldn't Krishna or Gautama Buddha or Zoroaster or any of the rest of the gang suffice?

ARTEN: Yes, they would. But then you wouldn't be studying J. You think it's all the same, but to the trained eye there are important distinctions that make all the difference in the world. It is not our intention to put down anything else. Everyone will end up at the same goal eventually, and in fact they already have. That's a stretch you're not quite ready for. Just remember that if you choose to work with J then you can be certain he'll help you. A saying or two from Pursah's Gospel will illustrate that.

GARY: I've been waiting patiently.

ARTEN: I know, and we're just about there. To complete our short tour, you've had many good lives, and many others that were seemingly wasted. Sometimes you dream about them, bad dreams and good. Let me ask you something. Are you still having the dreams of being an American Indian at the city where the great rivers come together?

GARY: How did you know that? Oh, I forgot—you know everything.

PURSAH: Yes, but we remind you we can only work with you by using words and symbols you understand. You've experienced thousands of lives, including many Christian ones of various forms and many others that involved religions most people wouldn't even know about. For example, as an Aborigine your experience was that the spirit world, or Ika as you called it at the time, was every bit as real to you — or more real — than your so-called waking life.

Yet of all your lifetimes until now, it would be hard to pick a more rewarding one than the time you were a friend and a student of the marvelous American Indian spiritual teacher known as the Great Sun.

A thousand years ago, there was a city as big as a Boston or a Philadelphia of the early 1800s. This gathering place was all around what is now St. Louis, but its inhabitants included no white people. It had houses, not teepees. Teepees were used mostly by the tribes of the plains who traveled with the seasons. You were an Indian who lived in this city, and you knew the one who the people said had come down from the sun to mediate between the sky and the earth.

They called him the Great Sun. He rejected human sacrifice, taught most of the Ten Commandments and some of the wisdom of J, five hundred years before any white man ever brought a Bible to America. He was like a king or a pope, and he lived on top of an amazing man-made mound in a structure that the people had built for him as a sign of love and respect.

Although there was no written Indian language at the time, the pronunciation of the city would be written now like *Cahokia*, and the Great Sun was known and respected throughout the heart of the continent. The rivers connected the city to the different parts of the country, and you made a living by being a trader of furs. You always made it a point to share some of the teachings of your friend with the tribes you were doing business with. And you were always happy to get home and learn more from this man, who was an enlightened spiritual Being.

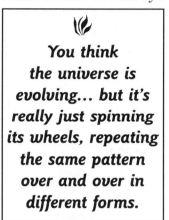

You think the universe is evolving... but it's really just spinning its wheels, repeating the same pattern over and over in different forms.

GARY: I have some pictures of that in my mind. Say, is this guy in the Book of Mormon?

PURSAH: No. Joseph Smith wasn't aware of him, nor would most white people be. American Indian history was an oral tradition. Smith was doing something else. He wrote down what he was supposed to from these metal plates he was translating. In any case, the Great Sun was very similar to J, only a thousand years later.

We're not going to give you a long story about that lifetime or your teacher. It's this lifetime we're concerned about. We're giving you some background to help prepare you for the newest and most advanced form of J's teaching, and that's why we want to caution you away from a minor mistake that was made by the Great Sun. Everyone makes mistakes, even enlightened Beings. The earth is not a place of perfection. Indeed, it is designed to be a place where true perfection is impossible. You think the universe is *evolving* into perfection. That idea is false. The universe is set up to *look* like it's doing that, but it's really just spinning its wheels — repeating the same patterns over and over in different forms. It's a trick you'll catch on to.

The difference between your mistakes and the mistakes of enlightened Beings rests in their ability to practice true forgiveness. They realize that if the mistakes of others should be forgiven immediately, then so should theirs. They also know it doesn't really matter what they do, but few people are ready to accept that. Most carry their mistakes and their guilt with them for eons, but there is no need for that.

GARY: So how did he screw up?

PURSAH: He didn't really. It was just a question of how he spent his time. He would have served people better by simply teaching them the truth. Whether then or now — north, south, east or west, the world needs help. It's full of people who are mentally attacking others and don't even know that they're attacking — they just think they're right, or cool, or some kind of a victim. The Great Sun allowed himself to get distracted from what was most useful. We've already told you that the truly enlightened seldom seek out leadership roles. Two thousand years ago, many of our people were hoping that J would be a Kingly Messiah instead of a priestly one. But he was happy just sharing the truth with people and giving them his experience. God's Love was his only concern.

The Great Sun, however, became very much like a pope. He ended up like most of the other conventional spiritual leaders, wasting his time with politics and dishing out spiritual platitudes in public instead of taking people up to a whole new level, which is what they really need. Leave politics to the politicians. Render unto Caesar that which is Caesar's. People need to be educated, but if you *really* tell them the truth, then you're bound to give up some popularity. You'll have to accept that — but those who have ears to hear, let them hear.

So the Great Sun became a big decision maker and people thought that was important. What was *really* useful was when he talked with people one on one, or in small groups, and told them all he knew instead of holding back out of concern about how they might take it. We've already said that you don't have to tell anybody anything if you don't want to. If you choose to teach occasionally then it's better to tell the truth, and have some people walk out on you, than to tell them only what they want to hear and have them stay.

Success in the world is about getting a lot of heads wagging in agreement, but the truth doesn't get people's heads wagging; it shocks them — or at least gets them questioning a lot of things. Eventually, the Great Sun wished he had done more of that and less of the public business, which took up more and more of his time. He knew at the end of his life that he was completely forgiven; he just

had that one small regret about not using his gift more constructively — a regret he then forgave. Obviously, we are bringing this up now
to help *you*. Don't try to become some kind of a big shot. Just tell people the truth and let the Holy Spirit take care of the rest. Most of your
time should be spent learning from Him, not trying to be a star.

GARY: You said I made a lot of progress in that lifetime?

PURSAH: Yes, but why do you think that was? You spent only small
amounts of time teaching, and most of your time listening to your
friend. You were fortunate enough to hear him in private, where he
was more open and detailed. In other words, you were a student. So
we give you this additional pointer, which is one you are already living but which you should always take care to remember in the
future. The biggest advances are not made by being a great teacher;
they are made by being a great student.

GARY: Did the Great Sun really come down to the earth from
the sun?

PURSAH: Never take publicity seriously.

ARTEN: In any case, your friend told you that he was born the
same as any man. Sometimes people insist on making a big deal out
of the trivial and paying no attention to what's important, like going
home — which is what we're here to help you with.

GARY: And J was conceived and born the same as any man?

ARTEN: That question could only possibly be of importance to people who think the body is important, and that J's body was *very*
important. Our future discussions will help you realize that the mind
is where the answers to your problems are; never out in the world or
in a body, *any* body — including J's. This is a major part of his message. Without understanding this, the rest is impossible to grasp. You
will get it, and you'll begin to realize how insignificant other bodies
are. Only then can you begin to experience how insignificant your
own is. How else can you be free? You will not break loose until you
realize that you yourself forge the chains that bind you.

GARY: You mentioned Paul rejecting the idea of resurrection being
of the mind and not the body. But one of the historical things I
remember him most for is talking the other leaders of the Jewish-
Christian sects into allowing people to convert to their faith by simply being baptized instead of circumcised.

ARTEN: I told you he was a real crowd pleaser. But don't get us wrong — we're not saying that Paul wasn't one of the most brilliant and influential men in history. Obviously, some of his writings are stunning in their eloquence. His spiritual experience of J on the road to Damascus was a genuine one. It's just that in the final analysis, many of the things he was saying are simply not what J was talking about.

You see, J taught the *whole* truth, and still does, while — as you may have gathered from everything we've been saying — others before and after him taught *parts* of the truth. People tend to take the parts that sound the same and assume that each one is saying the same thing in a different way. But J is unique.

GARY: J would agree with *some* of the same ideas that Krishna, Lao-tzu, Buddha and Plato expressed before him, but not all of them?

ARTEN: Yes, and he would also agree with *some* of the same ideas that Paul, Valentinus and Plotinus expressed after him. There are indeed some universal truths that J has in common with others. Once you understand what he's saying *in its entirety*, then he speaks for an original thought system that will lead you much more quickly to God, and is not really the same as any of the others.

PURSAH: All of which brings us to a position where we can begin to talk about what J *was* saying. As a small part of this, I'll tell you something of my Gospel. First tell me briefly what you know about it as a way of clarifying your own thoughts.

GARY: Well, I don't know much. Some guy accidentally found a copy of it in Egypt after World War Two along with a bunch of other Gnostic stuff, and the church said the sayings were made up by the Gnostic heretics. From what I've heard, some Biblical scholars have recently come to have a much higher opinion of it.

PURSAH: Yes. You haven't really read it, have you? Except for that time you browsed it in a bookstore — when you spent half the time looking at that beautiful woman down the aisle.

GARY: Is there a note of judgment in that remark?

PURSAH: No, but you couldn't read my Gospel very well while you were busy having all those superficial thoughts about her body.

GARY: That's not fair! I was also having superficial thoughts about her mind.

PURSAH: What did you think about what you *did* read?

GARY: It didn't suck too much. Would you care to give me a more educated overview, straight from the horse's mouth?

PURSAH: Yes, but I've already told you we're not going to dwell on it. You can do your own homework if you want to know more about it than I tell you. The discovery of my Gospel in 1945 marked the first time a complete copy of it had been seen by anyone in over a thousand years. The only other surviving parts of it were a couple of Greek fragments that had been discovered earlier.

You could write a book just about my Gospel, and some people have. I've already told you there are sayings in this copy, that were added on later, that J never said. You also have to consider the influence of about three hundred years of Egyptian culture and language and Gnostic philosophy on the Nag Hammadi version in order to account for some of its sayings. Also, it doesn't include everything J told me in private, partly because I was executed by a group of people at a time I least expected it. I was speaking to them of peace. A lot of people, including you, want peace. But let me tell you something, Gary. The people of the world will never live in peace until the people of the world have inner peace. Even though I didn't live that long, at least I got to be one of J's very first ministers. The Bible pretty much snubs people like me and Thaddaeus, but we were privileged to share J's teachings as spoken directly to us.

> 🔥
>
> *I got my head cut off in India. When you're in a body you just never know what kind of a day it's going to be.*

GARY: Quite an honor. Were you ordained?

PURSAH: I was pre-ordained.

GARY: Did you get crucified?

PURSAH: No. I got my head cut off in India. When you're in a body you just never know what kind of a day it's going to be. It wasn't a bad way to make a transition, actually; surprisingly quick. That reminds me of something I wanted to say about the act of crucifixion. It was strictly a Roman ritual. Nobody else practiced it. The writers of the later Gospels wanted to blame the Sanhedrin and the Pharisees, whom they hated, for J's death by describing a trial during Passover. But those groups wouldn't play a role in breaking Jewish law — not unless they wanted to incur the hatred of their own people by disobeying God. They were clever men. They wouldn't make a bonehead play like that — and the described trial wouldn't have met the guidelines of our law. It was later on that you had the specific, silly political feuds that led to the erroneous telling of that part of the story in the New Testament.

At the time of the crucifixion it was the Romans who exercised all civil power, and if there was *one* thing our people could find agreement on, it was in our disgust for the Romans. With a few exceptions, there were not many people lined up, taunting J. It was mostly the Romans who made fun of him. Most of the Jews along the way just saw him as another casualty of the Gentile Empire.

The next time you think about the people who supposedly killed your Lord, give the Jewish people a break. We were the objects of crucifixion, not the perpetrators of it. Judas didn't know J was going to end up on the cross. He simply made a mistake. Then he felt extremely guilty about it. That's why he hanged himself. Forgive him. J did, so can you. While you're at it, you can also forgive the Romans, who *did* kill the body of the one who they would later call their Lord. J could forgive them even while they were doing it, because he knew that what he *really* was could never *be* killed. Why do you think generation after generation of those who claim to follow him feel the need to assign some kind of guilt for this action to people who they don't even know?

GARY: I have a feeling you're gonna tell me. But I have a problem with your explanation of things. Didn't J talk about Judas betraying him with a kiss?

PURSAH: No. Before the supper, Judas was drunk and wanted money to buy more wine and a prostitute. A Roman officer who had seen him earlier with J spotted him again and asked for information. You see, Pontius Pilate was looking to make an example out of somebody as a way of exerting authority during the Passover. Pilate never washed his hands of the whole thing, he wanted it to happen. Judas told the officer where J and us were going to be that night in exchange for money. How many tragedies in your world are the result of someone doing something while under the influence of alcohol that they would never ordinarily do?

GARY: So Judas was half in the bag and looking to get, ah, some female companionship, and he didn't bother to stop and think about what the consequences of his actions might be?

PURSAH: Yes. A circumstance I believe you're familiar with. Except I'd say Judas was more like three quarters of the way in the bag.

GARY: You said earlier that J didn't suffer on the cross, which I find a little hard to believe. Are you gonna tell me how he was able to forgive everyone and not feel any pain during the crucifixion at the same time?

PURSAH: Absolutely, but not during this visit. By the time we leave you on our final visit, we will have given you a complete picture and started you on your way. The rest will be up to you, but we're not going to hold anything back. We're not going to give you that "it's a mystery" cop-out that your churches are so partial to. The thought system of the Holy Spirit doesn't leave you with a bunch of unanswered questions. There may be a couple of answers you don't *like*, but we told you at the beginning we weren't always going to tell you what you wanted to hear.

Now I'm going to be very honest with you about what my Gospel is and also about what it isn't. *The Gospel of Thomas* is not the Holy Grail of spirituality. It will not bring you salvation and it will not train your mind to think along the lines necessary for you to attain your salvation. It *does* however, perform three very important services for humanity.

First of all, despite what you and some others may think, my Gospel is *not* a Gnostic document. For those who care to see it, parts of it contain the scripture of the earliest form of Christianity, before there even was such a thing as a separate religion called Christianity. We were among the very first of the Jewish-Christian sects. Granted, there was diversity among the various sects, but we were not alone in our impressions of J. Why do you think the church was so desperate later on to label my Gospel as Gnostic and heretical? It was because they didn't *want* the members of the church to see what the earliest Christians were really like. Indeed, the church would do anything to hide the fact that some of its teachings are heretical to the historical J, not that he wouldn't forgive them.

There are already some Biblical scholars who realize that my Gospel is not derivative of the New Testament Gospels, and that it includes some sayings that are phrased in a more original and realistic manner than the similar sayings in the later, Synoptic Gospels. These scholars are right about that point, although some of the sayings they think are true are not, and then they are slow to approve of a few other, true sayings in my Gospel because they lack the confirmation that their rules call for.

Yet if J taught me something in private, or said something to a very small group of us disciples, why would you necessarily find it in the Books of Mark or Luke or Matthew? The authors of those books were not from our generation. Forty to eighty years later, they simply copied from earlier Sayings Gospels, kept what they liked and threw out what they didn't, and then added to the mix these attractive stories, rumors and speculation that fit in with their new religious dogma. The first Gospels, including mine, were written in Aramaic. Don't you find it a little strange that *not one complete original copy* of J's own words in his own language survived the rise of Christianity? Do you really think that was an accident?

Incredibly, even the later Gospels were changed over the next few centuries. The ending of Mark was completely changed. The changes in theology never stopped. You thought Arten was exaggerating when he said Christianity was still being made up. He wasn't. People didn't start praying to him — Thaddaeus — as Saint Jude, the patron Saint of desperate or impossible causes, until the eighteenth century. And as far as learning as you go along is concerned, there isn't anything wrong with continuous revelation, but Christianity has taken what is actually religious *art* — The New Testament — and attempted to falsely elevate it to the level of literal, absolute truth. There's nothing wrong with using art as a way of expressing what's true for the artist, but most people wouldn't go look at Leonardo Da Vinci's "The Last Supper" and take it to be an absolute, literal record and historical picture of our last get-together before the Passion.

GARY: What about you? Are *you* claiming to be telling me the absolute truth?

PURSAH: By the time we're finished with our meetings, we will have passed along to you some teachings that were given to us by J that do indeed express the absolute truth — which can be summed up in just two words — but only experienced by a mind that has been prepared for it. I already said those two words, but you didn't realize it. They speak the *absolute* and total truth. They are the correction of the universe. As we proceed, we will make no secret about what they are, and that they represent a choice. In order for you to competently make that choice, you will have to become much more aware of what you are really choosing between.

GARY: I guess that's fair enough for now. You may continue.

PURSAH: Thank you. I've already said that the surviving copy of my Gospel was changed over the years, but it still stands as a more realistic example of the kind of statements that were made by our leader. What I will affectionately refer to from now on as *Thomas* is a Jewish-Christian Sayings Gospel that predated Gnosticism. Gnosticism was a combination of many earlier philosophies mixed in with some of the things J said or that people thought he said. Yes, you could certainly say that J had what might be described as Gnostic tendencies, but they were not all new. Some of these traits go back to archaic forms of Jewish mysticism.

If you want to see some of the later Gnostic theology, you can always read the Valentinian *Gospel of Truth,* which is the finest of the Gnostic literature. You won't understand some of the terminology, but you'll get a general idea of what some of the Gnostic sects believed. J would even agree with *some* of it, most importantly that the world is very much like a dream and God did not create it. But *The Gospel of Truth* was written over a hundred and fifty years after the first version of my Gospel, which lists some of the teachings that were actually spoken by the historical J. I say *some* of the teachings, and call it the *first* version for the reasons I gave you earlier, but the implications of all this could not be more clear. The first service my Gospel performs is that the world can finally see *for itself* that as Christianity became Christianity, it bore less and less of a resemblance to the historical J — our Messiah wisdom teacher — and more and more of a resemblance to the made-up Apocalyptic figure of the later Gospel novels.

The second important service is in the general tone of the teachings themselves. J was from the Middle East, not Mississippi. His approach was much more mindful and eastern than the kind of running-away-from-the-mind, hard-core dualism of the West. These Western influences were brought in later.

The third service is in the meaning of some of the sayings themselves. I've already said we didn't completely get J's message at that time, but *Thomas* does give a more authentic representation of the kinds of things J would say than the other Gospels. I'll give you a sort of revised standard version of my own to help you understand some of it here. Please note that the sayings in *Thomas* are not in any special order. Also, I will choose only quotations that I actually heard J say. For the purposes of this discussion, I will only choose a few of them. Don't forget we have other, more important things to talk about. This is only meant to help prepare you.

Out of the one hundred and fourteen sayings in *Thomas*, J actually said seventy of them, or at least something reasonably close. The other forty-four are spurious, a word the church was once fond of using to describe the entire Gospel. The contributions of the scholars being what they are, the church doesn't talk as loud as it used to.

GARY: I'm sorry, but I'm bursting with one more question I have to ask.

PURSAH: Careful, kid. Too many interruptions and we may have to cook up Dante's *Inferno* for you.

GARY: I've always heard about this mysterious, hypothetical Q Gospel that scholars believe was used as a source by all three of the so-called Synoptic Gospels — Matthew, Mark and Luke. Supposedly, those three all copied from the same source, and I believe you used the word sources. Is your Gospel the missing Q document?

PURSAH: As we said, we didn't come here to attempt to make a contribution to Biblical scholarship — not that a scholar would listen to a source that can't be verified anyway. If you must know, I'll tell you exactly what Q was. The Gospels of Matthew and Luke did indeed copy from it, but Mark didn't. The writer of Mark had his own sources. And Q was not my Gospel, as scholars already know, but which you can be excused for not knowing.

GARY: What was it, then?

PURSAH: After the crucifixion, J's brother James, often called James the Just, was J's heir apparent in the eyes of many of the followers. They knew how much J loved him, and James was a sincere and steady man. However, he was also very conservative. *Conservative* is not exactly the word you would use to describe J, who was the radical of radicals — not in temperament but in his teachings.

For this reason there were three of James' followers who, although they respected him, decided to preserve for posterity the teachings they had personally heard J speak in public. They did not necessarily have faith in James or any other group to stick to some of the startling principles J had articulated, so they put together a Sayings Gospel titled simply *Words of the Master.* However, over the next forty years, as the original recorders of *Words* passed away, some distorted sayings that others, including John the Baptist, had spoken and that some followers *assumed* J believed, or falsely thought *he* had spoken, made their way into *Words.* The writers of two later mainstream church Gospels used this document, now referred to as Q — after a German word that means *source* — to copy sayings from so they could combine them with their stories. They also copied from Mark, the writer of which had used a consensus of sayings. The Gospel of John was written later, when the split between the newest sects and Judaism had become more obvious.

Interestingly, several copies of *Words of the Master* as well as *Thomas* survived in various places for longer than you might think. It wasn't until around four hundred A.D. that you had the new effort, directed by Saint Augustine, to wipe out anything that didn't fit in with the church's official beliefs. His book burning would have made the Nazis proud, but it was done in the name of God, of course. Even though *Words of the Master* and *The Gospel of Thomas* were not Gnostic, they were destroyed right along with virtually all of the existing Gnostic literature. After all, some of the sayings didn't sound very much like the church, so they must have been heretical! If it wasn't for the Nag Hammadi collection that was discovered buried near the river along with my Gospel, the world wouldn't have much to go on as far as alternative glimpses of J are concerned.

Now we'll proceed with *Thomas.* It begins,

These are the hidden sayings that the living J spoke and Didymus Judas Thomas recorded.

1. And he said, "Whoever discovers the interpretation of these sayings will not taste death."

I'll use the numbers now, although my version didn't have numbers, and this saying was numbered "1" later because people weren't sure whether I had said it or J did. I was the one who said and wrote it, and it was supposed to be a part of this brief introduction, not labeled as a saying of J. The word *hidden* simply means that many of these sayings were spoken by J, either in private or to a very small group of people. It does not mean that it was his intention to hide things.

One will not taste death because, as pointed out earlier, J was showing us the way to life; meaning that what we were experiencing here on earth was not life, even though we assumed it was. He was the living J because he had attained true enlightenment — his oneness with God. *Living*, in this case, does not refer to him being in a body, even though it appeared he was. It's a reference to the resurrection of the mind, as alluded to earlier — and also referred to a saying from my Gospel that I won't talk about until a later visit. Also, the word *living* here would have nothing to do with a resurrected body, even though J did appear to us after the crucifixion.

I want to give you a brief clarification now about names. For one thing, J's name was not really Jesus. His Hebrew name was Y'shua, although we seldom called him that. To us he was the master, not that he wanted to be called the master or anything else in particular, but because we were in awe of him at the time. The translation of his name to Greek and then English should have ended up as Jeshua, not Jesus. It doesn't really matter. What's in a name? Would not a Christ by any other name be as one?

GARY: If it doesn't really matter, then why do you call him J? Why not Jesus or Jeshua?

PURSAH: Why not cover both? You're not Jewish, but there will be some people who read your book who are. If they're ignoring J then they're missing a part of their heritage.

While we're on the subject of names, I was often called what is translated here as Didymus, which means *twin*. I humbly included that part of the name in the introduction so people would know who I was. I bore an uncanny resemblance to J. In fact, I was actually mistaken for him on a regular basis. There are those who believe I really was J's twin, but that's not true. My apologies to those I love who sincerely believe in the later written — and Gnostic — *Acts of Thomas,* which specifically says I was J's twin. Needless to say, some of the *Acts of Thomas* is true and some of it isn't, but a complete discussion of my lifetime as Thomas would take up most of our visits.

However, I'll tell you something else that only Thaddaeus or I could tell you. My likeness to J was so great that when I heard he was going to be crucified I wanted to switch places with him so he could go free. Thaddaeus and I tried to get close to him more than once — first while he was still locked up and again after the procession started. Sadly to us at the time, the opportunity to pull a switch never really presented itself. I would have gladly given my life for J. We didn't all run like hell out of town the way it's presented by people who weren't even there. It took me until J's appearance to us after the crucifixion to realize that the whole thing was a lesson he had *chosen* to teach. The world did not understand the lesson of the crucifixion at first, but J's process of being a teacher to the world was not over — which is something that you, my dear brother, will soon find out.

GARY: Ah, I have it in my notes here that you said earlier you and the other disciples made the error of attaching great significance to J's body. Later you said that you yourself thought resurrection was of the mind and had nothing to do with the body. Which belief did you really have? Or are you just jerking me around here?

PURSAH: Very good. We're challenging you, and there's nothing wrong with you challenging us once in a while. The answer is that at the time I had both beliefs. My mind was still split. We've also said we are speaking to you now with the benefit of subsequent learning. You will have a much better idea of what that means as we go along. Back when I was recording this Gospel I understood *intellectually* a lot of what J was saying about the importance of the mind, but my *experience* — and this was even more true of the other disciples — was that our bodies and especially J's body were very important.

The situation with me then was not much different than the

situation with you now. Today, you and your friends believe in the existence of a trilogy — body, mind and spirit. The "balance" of all three is important in your philosophy. But you will soon learn instead that the seemingly separated mind, which makes and uses bodies, must choose *between* the changeless and eternal reality of spirit — which *is* God and His Kingdom — or the unreal and ever-changing universe of bodies — which includes *anything* that can be perceived, whether you appear to be in a body or not. This is a cornerstone of J's message. He really did say, as it was recorded by me in what is now labeled saying number 47,

> **You must be vigilant only for God. This state of mind does not come all at once; it takes a lot of practice. You don't learn anything worthwhile overnight.**

A person cannot mount two horses or bend two bows. And a servant cannot serve two masters, or that servant will honor the one and offend the other.

GARY: Are you saying that giving equal value to body, mind and spirit actually *contributes* to me coming back here over and over again as a body, rather than being free?

PURSAH: Yes, but this doesn't mean that you should neglect your body. We're speaking of another way of looking at it. To finish the point about my past beliefs, my Gospel merely recorded things J had said. Unlike the writers of the later Gospels, I was not constantly inserting my opinion. Thus *Thomas* is not so much a reflection of my level of understanding at that time as it is a record of some of J's ideas. For example, these words are an excerpt from saying 61:

> I am the one who comes from what is whole. I was given from the things of my Father. Therefore, I say that if one is whole, one will be filled with light, but if one is divided, one will be filled with darkness.

In other words, to revisit an earlier point, you can't have it both ways. You can't be a little bit whole, any more than a woman can be a little bit pregnant. Your allegiance must be undivided. You must be vigilant only for God. This state of mind does not come all at once; it takes a lot of practice. You don't learn anything worthwhile over night. How long did it take you to become a good guitar player?

GARY: I thought I was good after a few years. After ten years I realized I was still improving.

PURSAH: Do you really believe that attaining the same level as J is an easier accomplishment?

GARY: I'm not afraid of practicing. I'd just like to be a little bit more certain that I'm on the right track.

PURSAH: Very well. Let's continue, and you can withhold your judgment until you have more information.

GARY: Sounds like a plan.

PURSAH: You cannot understand how much J, who is now totally Identified with the Holy Spirit, wants to completely join with you. That's why he said, in saying 108,

Whoever drinks from my mouth shall become like me. I myself shall become that person, and the hidden things will be revealed to that person.

The mystical joining J is talking about here is something that happens quite literally. The lessons of true forgiveness that allow this to take place are not for everyone all at once — they are for those who are ready to receive their individual instruction.

I shall choose you, one from a thousand and two from ten thousand, and they shall stand as a single one.

Of course, J chooses everyone, all the time. But how many are ready to listen? As this saying obviously foretold, the lessons of the Holy Spirit will not be listened to by the masses. But the ones who listen, who *are* the chosen ones, will surely stand as a single one — for that is what they are. God's Son shall return to the Kingdom whole and complete, and in the end there will be no one who does not stand with us. The J underground cannot lose.

In order to win however, you must — as saying number 5 puts it,

> Know what is in front of your face, and what is hidden from you will be disclosed to you. For there is nothing hidden that will not be revealed.

What is in front of your face is illusion, and God's Kingdom — which appears to be hidden — will be revealed to those who learn from the Holy Spirit the unique way of forgiving whatever is in front of them the way J did. Eventually you will be one with him, and there will be nothing left but your true joy in the Kingdom of Heaven.

GARY: That's all well and good, Pursah — but here in the kingdom of suckdom when the world really gets in your face, it can be a little hard to hang onto that Holy Ghost grin.

PURSAH: Tell me about it. I've been here a few times myself, remember? I promise we will not be giving you mere theories. You will learn very practical ways of dealing mentally with the situations that are apparently in your face. The result will leave you with the potential to attain the very same peace of God as J. Right now, you believe that certain things have to happen in the world in order for you to be happy. As you gain the peace of God, it will eventually result in the ability to reclaim your natural state of joy *regardless* of what appears to be happening in the world.

For as you can see from saying 113, J was teaching that the Kingdom of Heaven is something that is *present,* if not presently in your awareness.

> The disciples said to him, "When will the Kingdom come?" He said, "It will not come by watching for it. It will not be said, 'Behold here,' or 'Behold there.' Rather, the Kingdom of the Father is spread out upon the earth, and people do not see it."

J is not saying here that the Kingdom of the Father is *in* the earth. Indeed, he knew that the earth was in our minds. He was speaking about something that people do not see because the Kingdom of Heaven cannot *be* seen with the body's eyes, which are only capable of beholding limited symbols. Heaven does not exist within the realm of perception, but is the genuine form of life that you will eventually become completely *aware* of.

Like the caterpillar becomes the butterfly, you will become Christ — and be one with all of true Creation. The awareness of your one-ness with the Presence of God is yours because God gave it to you. You have forgotten it. Yet it is still there, buried in your mind.[9] There is a way to remember. And by remembering, you will reclaim what you really are and where you really belong. We have come to help you — and through you, help others as well.

> ## ✿
> *Like the caterpillar becomes the butterfly, you will become Christ — and be one with all of true Creation.*

There are some sayings in *Thomas* that are similar to sayings in the New Testament that J actually did teach us. I'll briefly speak a few of them for you.

26. You see the speck that is in your brother's eye, but you do not see the log that is in your own eye. When you take the log out of your own eye, then you will see clearly enough to take the speck out of your brother's eye.

31. A prophet is not acceptable in his own town. A doctor does not heal those who know him.

36. Do not worry, from morning to night and from night until morning, about what you will wear.

54. Fortunate are the poor, for yours is the Father's Kingdom.

Please note that those last two sayings are not to be applied at the level of the physical. They are about not being *mentally* attached to things. They have nothing to do with physically giving up anything. If you believe that you have to give something up, then you are making it just as real as if you covet it. That is also true of J's shortest saying of all,

42. Be passersby.

And I'll give you two more New Testament prequels from *Thomas.*

94. One who seeks will find. And for one who knocks, it shall be opened.

95. If you have money, do not lend it at interest. Rather, give it to someone who will not pay you back.

You will occasionally hear us make a reference to a saying from the New Testament that really was said by J, but the meaning will not always be the same for us as you are generally used to thinking of it. Now I will offer parts of a few more sayings from *Thomas* to give you a feel for the thought system J was expressing, which is the thought system of the Holy Spirit.

11. The dead are not alive, and the living will not die.

22. When you make the two into one, and when you make the inner like the outer and the outer like the inner, and the upper like the lower, and when you make male and female into a single one, so the male will not be male and the female will not be female... then you will enter the Kingdom.

49. Fortunate are those who are alone and chosen, for you will find the Kingdom. For you have come from it, and you will return there again.

Remember the story of the prodigal Son? You *will* return home again, but in order to do so you must re-trace your steps back to your original decision to be separate from God. For as J says next, the beginning and the end — which are the alpha and the omega — are really the same thing:

**18. The followers said to J, "Tell us how our end will be."
He said, "Have you discovered the beginning, then, so that
you are seeking the end? For where the beginning is, the
end will be. Fortunate is the one who stands at the beginning: That one will know the end and will not taste death."**

There is one more saying I must explain because it has been
the subject of much speculation over the years — not only for the
last fifty, but also the first four hundred years of the Gospel's existence. In saying 13, after speaking to a group of us, J asked me to
come with him...

**And he took him, and withdrew, and spoke three sayings
to him. When Thomas came back to his friends, they asked
him, "What did J say to you?" Thomas said to them, "If I
tell you one of the sayings he spoke to me, you will pick up
rocks and stone me, and fire will come from the rocks and
consume you."**

The fire in the last line is the wrath of God, and you should realize that stoning was the traditional Jewish punishment for blasphemy, even though it wasn't used as much as you might imagine. Many
people have wondered what J said to me then, even though the New
Testament writers — who felt like they were in competition with
my Gospel — portrayed Peter as being J's favorite student instead of
me. I told you they snubbed me. In any case, J was not concerned
about his own safety when it came to speaking blasphemy. The
reason he told me not to repeat these sayings was to protect *me*.
These are the three things he said to me that day.

**You dream of a desert, where mirages are your rulers and
tormentors, yet these images come from you.**

**Father did not make the desert, and your home is still with
Him.**

**To return, forgive your brother, for only then do you
forgive yourself.**

To say in public at that time that God did not create the world could have been fatal to me. That was then, this is now — and through your freedom of speech all of these principles will be amplified as we go along. The result will be a thought system that is not linear, but holographic — where the whole is found in each of the parts.

I could go on for hours about *Thomas,* but I will not. As I said, it is not the Holy Grail of spirituality. Yet right now on this earth, there is a spiritual document that comes as close as anything possibly can to expressing what J actually wants to say. There is an excellent reason for this. It is because he spoke it, word for word, to the person who took seven years of her life to write it down. There are no opinions in it from anyone but J. It was not edited to suit any religion, nor changed in order to appeal to a generic audience. Its final editing was directed by J through this woman. Unlike *Thomas,* it is a complete presentation as well as a comprehensive training. It is not meant to be the handbook of a religion or a code of moral behavior. It is a system of thought proposing that if you take care of the mind, all else will follow naturally.

Happily, this teaching, known as *A Course in Miracles,* is not designed to bring forth yet another organization obsessed with changing a world of dreams instead of the mind of the dreamer. It is a *self*-study, one-on-one metamorphosis into Christ that is done at the level of the mind between you and J, or you and the Holy Spirit, if you prefer to think of it that way. Either one will do. This puts you in the fortunate position where you can learn much more from the master than you could have two thousand years ago — if you are prepared to take advantage of it. And he really *should* be called a master. Many call themselves that, but you don't see them going around healing the sick and raising the dead.

There are things the people of the world are capable of understanding at the dawn of this new millennium that they simply were not capable of understanding in the past. J's message has not changed, but your ability to understand it has changed because of a broader picture of the world and the mind. J can only bring people along with him by using concepts they can comprehend. In the end, everything except for God is metaphor. But there is teaching and learning to do in the meantime.

I told you before that the people of the world will never live in peace until the people of the world have inner peace. Inner peace and true strength are major goals of *A Course in Miracles,* but it has a unique way of accomplishing this within you. The world will change as a result of it, but that is not what the Course is for. It is for you. It's a present. But it is also a challenge. You will sometimes hear people say that the Course is simple, but you will seldom hear anyone say it is easy. The world will appear to change for you at times because the Course handles the cause of everything, rather than effects. And what is the world but an effect? That is certainly not what the world believes — but this world is nothing to write home about.

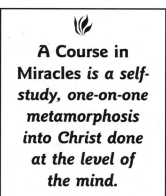

A Course in Miracles *is a self-study, one-on-one metamorphosis into Christ done at the level of the mind.*

ARTEN: Before we leave, we want to get you ready for the next three weeks. You will be guided as to what you should do, and you should remember to ask the Holy Spirit for guidance when you have the time. Be practical. You don't have to ask Him if it's all right to have a cup of coffee, unless that's an issue for you. But don't make important decisions on your own, unless it's an emergency and you don't have time to ask. Then you will be given guidance automatically if you need it.

As for our next visit, we'll be back in twenty-one days — and you have work to do in the interim. Please tell me briefly what you can recall from when your mother used to read you Plato's allegory of The Cave. Just give me a general outline of what you remember.

GARY: Well, it was pretty wild. Not as wild as *this,* but... I remember that there are men imprisoned in a cave, chained so tightly they can't move enough to turn their heads or even their eyes. All they can see is the wall of this cave in front of them. They've been there so long it's all they can remember; it's all they know. They can see these shadows on the wall in front of them and hear some sound. Because it's all they know, they *think* that what they're looking at is reality. It's all pretty dismal, but they're so used to it they think it's normal and they've become sort of comfortable with it.

Finally, one of the prisoners manages to break free, and he's able to turn around and see that he's in a cave. He can also see some light coming from the direction of the entrance. It takes a long time for his eyes to be able to stand the light, but when he makes it to the entrance he can see people walking by on the road outside, and it's their shadows that are being cast onto the wall inside the cave.

Realizing the prisoners inside the cave can't see that what they're looking at is untrue, the freed prisoner goes back and tries to share his knowledge with them. They're so used to their own way of thinking, they don't really want to hear what the free one has to say. In fact, it's just the opposite. They want to kill him. It's like what you've been telling me: People may *think* they want to be free, but they're not really willing to give up their own way of looking at things.

ARTEN: Thank you, Gary. Your mother is pleased. For Plato, the free one was his mentor Socrates — who was executed by being forced to drink poison. But you could fill in the names of numerous fine teachers who have challenged others to rise above the world. Many have had their bodies killed in the process, yet it doesn't really matter. For as Plato was trying to tell the world with that story, your reality is not at all what you think it is.

As great as Plato was, he didn't really know where the shadows were coming from. You will. Plato thought the light was coming from the Good, which was true symbolically. But he also thought that these shadows people see with the body's eyes all of their lives were being cast by perfect ideas of each thing. That wasn't true. J knew what was really causing the shadows — and exactly what to do about it. We will be sharing that with you.

It would be helpful for you to understand that J's *reality* is not the same as the world's reality. He is not here in the illusion. Just like when you wake up in your bed from a dream, you are no longer in the dream. At times you may have *experienced* the dream as being real, but it wasn't. You may long to bring J into your dream with you, but he has a better idea. He wants you to wake up so you can be with him. He wants you to be free — outside the dream completely. Outside Plato's cave. Outside all limits and beyond all boundaries.

You have often thought you had to try harder to be a more loving person, so you could exemplify the love of J. That's not true. If you really want to be perfect Love like him and God, then what you need to do is learn how to remove, with the Holy Spirit's help, the barriers that you have placed *in between* yourself and God. Then you will naturally and inevitably become aware of what you really are.

Your admirable determination to remove conflict from your life has put you in a state of mind where you are ready to move into the fast lane. State-of-the-art of spirituality is yours for the asking — as long as you continue to be willing to learn it. The teachings of J we will be sharing with you are not for everyone — at least not for everyone all at once in a linear illusion. But they are for *you*. You will know this by your own recognition. If you don't recognize it, then feel free to tell us anytime and we will stop visiting you. We are not bringing you orders from God. You may not want to believe this yet, but God does not make demands of people. You think it is God's Will that is being acted out here, but you and the world are wrong about that. It is something else that is being constantly acted out here — namely your seeming separation from God. We want to help you return to your reality *with* Him.

The seeming interaction between you and God is really an interaction within your own unconscious split mind — between the part of you that has forgotten your reality and the part of your mind where the Holy Spirit dwells. He has never left you. His Voice, which you will learn how to be vigilant for, is your memory of God — your memory of your true home. This Voice represents your long-forgotten reality. Now you must learn how to choose, like the prisoners in Plato's cave, something that you will have tremendous resistance to choosing. You must learn how to choose between the Holy Spirit, Who represents the real you, and the part of your mind that represents the false you. And you will learn how to do it in such a way that your long-imprisoned unconscious mind can finally be freed. It is literally impossible for you to do this on your own. You are certainly welcome to try. If you will let yourself be helped, then much time can be saved for you.

Then like us, you will be one with the J underground. You will seldom think of it that way, but it will be your real job. Anything else you do to get by in the world will just be a cover job. Your real job from now on is to learn, practice and eventually apply very skillfully the same art of advanced forgiveness that J did. That's how you will be brought by the Holy Spirit back to the Kingdom of God.

At this time, like the rest of the world, you believe that wisdom is having good judgment. During our next visit, we will tell you what wisdom *really* is. From now until our return, let the Holy Spirit direct your mind. Each day for at least a few minutes, think about God and how much you love Him. Then, just like before we made our first appearance to you, let your mind be still. You will find, my dear brother, that still waters run deep.

Like many people, there have been times in your life when you have been concerned about the possibility of going to hell. You didn't realize you were already there. There is an old Hebrew mystical tradition that says hell is distance from God and Heaven is closeness to Him — a thought that is quite valid. As your mind is guided into your new adventure, try to remember that everything you behold in the universe of perception has one of two purposes for you to choose from. One purpose will keep you a prisoner; the other will free you. If you choose the Holy Spirit's interpretation of what you are seeing, then you will find, as J teaches in the new scripture,

All that is given you is for release; the sight, the vision and the inner Guide all lead you out of hell with those you love beside you, and the universe with them.[10]

3

The Miracle

**Miracles fall like drops of healing rain from Heaven
on a dry and dusty world, where starved and
thirsty creatures come to die.**[1]

THE following morning I woke up feeling a little overwhelmed
by my long discussion with Arten and Pursah, but grateful for
the decent night's sleep I had received thanks to their alteration of
time. I sensed this was the most important thing that had ever happened to me, yet I also felt a sense of uneasiness because I didn't
know where it would all lead. Then I stopped and asked myself:
Have I *ever* known where it would all lead?

On Friday afternoon of that week I went to the movies, as I often
did, to take advantage of the bargain matinee price. On the way
home I remembered a little bookstore I hadn't thought of for several
months, called Holistic Books and Treasures. I felt impelled to turn
in that direction and pay a visit. As I walked through the door I realized I was having another experience of light flashing in certain
areas of my field of vision, and remembered that I'd meant to ask
Arten and Pursah about the meaning of these occurrences.

Then I walked over to a row of books and saw *A Course in
Miracles*. It had already occurred to me that this was probably why I
was being guided to go there on this particular day. After picking it
up and reading some of the pages I saw that it was actually three
books in one from the same Source — a Text, a Workbook For
Students and a Manual For Teachers. I was also drawn, for no
apparent reason, to another book lying near the Course called

Journey Without Distance, by someone named Robert Skutch. I soon learned that this book was a brief history of how *A Course in Miracles* had come into being. I asked the Holy Spirit what I should do and I heard the thought, "It won't bite you."

Late that night I read some of the Text of the Course and saw for myself that the "Voice" which had dictated the material, speaking in the first person, made no apologies about the fact that he was the historical Jesus, even going so far as to clarify and correct the Bible. I had mixed feelings about that. On the one hand, I was still skeptical of this really being J, who I had always thought would return in a body and not simply as a Voice.

On the other hand, there was something about the inspiring nature of the calm and certain Voice that rang true for me, although I couldn't quite put my finger on exactly why. I decided that evening, without asking the Holy Spirit, that I would do one of two things. If my future experience told me this really was J, then I'd make full use of the teachings. But if my future experience told me that things just didn't add up, then despite Arten and Pursah's appearances I would still do everything I could to expose *A Course in Miracles* as a fraud.

During these three weeks I did a crash course in learning what I could about the books so I'd be ready to ask Arten and Pursah some questions. I read the entire Text of the Course as quickly as I could and got a general idea of what the Voice was saying. I also learned that reading it so fast was not a good way to digest the principles of the Course. However, the ending of the Text, titled "Choose Once Again," left me shaken with the awesome statement of what it means to choose the strength of Christ. I couldn't recall reading anything else in my life that felt as real and true to me as this profound summary of exactly what J was asking of — and offering — his students.

I also went through *Journey Without Distance,* and familiarized myself with some of the history of where the Course came from and who the major players were in its scribing and dissemination. The more I learned, the more it looked as though my future would be spent as a student of the Course rather than a critic of it. From my experience, it already seemed plausible that this Course had not only come from J, but that it could not have come from anyone *but* him.

I also spent many hours scanning the Internet for information about *A Course in Miracles.* I was surprised to find out that this book, which was definitely not an easy read, had already sold over a million copies by word of mouth alone. There was clearly a large Course community that had sprung up during the time since it had been published. Yet for me, the beauty and genius of the Course was, as Pursah had emphasized, its *self*-study discipline, done completely between the reader and J or the Holy Spirit. Thus even if people were to disagree about what it means or what should be done with it, as long as the Course remained intact then it would always be there for the next person to come along and discover the truth about for him or herself.

Moreover, despite the apparently genuine humility of presenting itself as just one of many valid spiritual paths, I could also comprehend that the truth of the Course was absolute and unambiguous. According to its Source, the Course did not really need to be interpreted, it needed to be understood — as well as applied. Indeed, it was the student's insistence that he or she could interpret rather than understand — or lead rather than follow — that had gotten them into this world of trouble in the first place. Because of this, I was more than grateful that Arten and Pursah had said they would help me get off on the right foot with the Course.

I was also happy that instead of being a collection of books like the Bible, spanning hundreds of years and written by different authors with often conflicting teachings, this three-in-one book all came from the same Teacher. Any inconsistencies stemmed from the fact that the Course was speaking on two levels — one level being purely metaphysical instruction and the other being a more practical, everyday level of forgiveness practice — or as J had put it in *The Gospel of Thomas*, knowing what is in front of your face.

In any case, I was just beginning to realize that if all problems and issues were decided within the context of the Course's *larger* message of forgiveness — which was clearly not the same as the world's idea of forgiveness — then the problem or issue that needed to be forgiven would cease to be important in the mind of the student. That didn't necessarily mean that action might not sometimes be appropriate. Having made room for the Holy Spirit, the student would attain a state of mind wherein he or she would be much more likely to hear reliable guidance about what kind of action to take in any given situation.

Then one morning I awakened with an unusually clear mind. That was when I heard the Voice — from deep within me and all through me — say something with such perfectly clear authority that the Source of it was beyond any possible questioning. This is what I heard:

Renounce the world and the ways of the world. Make them meaningless to you.

Although visions of sacrifice danced in my head, I was still completely blown away. I intuitively said, "I'll do it. I don't know how, but I'll do it." The Voice answered with this reassurance:

I will show you how.

The impact of the Voice on my life was cathartic and immediate. I had never heard anything so amazing. The Voice was so full and whole, so complete — it was almost as though anything else I had heard in my life had something missing. From that day forward, I knew that J was both with me and aware of me, and ready to show me how to do whatever was asked of me. I wouldn't always *remember* that, especially when the world threw an unpleasant surprise my way, but the memory would always come back to me sooner or later. The sooner I remembered, the less I would suffer.

It would take me a long time to understand that I wasn't really being asked to sacrifice anything, but I was already thankful for Pursah's reminder that J wasn't asking anyone to give up anything on the level of the physical. I already had a good notion that J's instruction was to be applied at the level of the mind, or *cause*, rather than at the level of the world, or *effect*. The word that kept coming back to me from his message was "meaningless." I couldn't wait to talk to Arten and Pursah about my most recent experiences.

True to their word and without ceremony, Arten and Pursah made their third appearance to me twenty-one days after their previous visit. Their appearances always happened clearly and instantaneously, as did their departures. Once again, it was Arten who began the discussion.

ARTEN: You've had an eventful few weeks. Did you read it?

GARY: You mean the Course?

ARTEN: Yes.

GARY: No. I'm waiting for the movie.

ARTEN: God help us all. I'm just making conversation; I know you've already read the Text. You'll have to read it many times. The Workbook is designed to take one year, but it usually takes people longer than that. It will take *you* one year, four and a half months. The Manual for Teachers is the easiest part, except almost everyone forgets that to be a teacher of God means you practice forgiveness. As the Course says,

To teach is to demonstrate.[2]

Most students seem to believe that their teaching has to fit the traditional teacher-student format, but there is very little about the Course that is traditional. They would be a lot better off trying to learn the Course rather than trying to teach it.

GARY: Everyone wants to interpret scripture, I guess. It's a natural tendency.

ARTEN: If J meant for his Course to be subject to your interpretation rather than his instruction, then why give it in the first place? Why not just let you make up your own version of everything, which is exactly what you've been doing throughout your seemingly separate existence? The truth is that if you really understand *A Course in Miracles,* which is rare, then there *is* only one possible interpretation. If you change it, which is typical, then it is no longer *A Course in Miracles.* Do you remember from the Text what the first law of chaos is?

GARY: I think so, but I'd better look it up.

ARTEN: Good. Read the part that starts with, "Here are the laws..."

GARY: O.K.

Here are the laws that rule the world you made. And yet they govern nothing, and need not be broken; merely looked upon and gone beyond.

The *first* chaotic law is that the truth is different for

everyone. Like all these principles, this one maintains that each is separate and has a different set of thoughts that set him off from others. This principle evolves from the belief there is a hierarchy of illusions; some are more valuable and therefore true.[3]

> 🔥
> **The truth is the truth whether you agree with it or not. The truth is not subject to your interpretation.**

PURSAH: Everybody is trying to find and express *their* truth. Their so-called truth is actually designed to keep them stuck where they are. What J is teaching in his Course is that the truth is *not* different for everyone. It is *not* relative. He's saying the truth is the truth whether you understand and agree with it or not. The truth is not subject to your interpretation, and neither is his Course. He's the Teacher, you're the student. If that's not the case, then why do the Course? Do anything you want. Let your mind run wild. Get drunk.

GARY: So when you said in your Gospel, "he who finds the interpretation of these sayings will not taste death," you meant there was only one possible interpretation?

PURSAH: That's right — you're hot on the trail, brother. Remember, the Course is as advanced as it is because J took seven years of a woman's time, with her going through whatever it took, so he could tell you exactly what he wants to tell you.

GARY: I'll have to think about that. It sounds like the old literal translation of the Bible thing.

PURSAH: The Course is not the Bible, as you have already noticed. The parts of the Course that express non-duality *should* be taken literally, but the parts of it that seem to express duality should be taken as *metaphor*. There is no conflict in that, but without getting it, you'll incorrectly think the Course is contradicting itself. As I said before, in the end everything except for God is metaphor. You need help in your own language in order to *get* to the end. The Course is about the healing of your unconscious guilt by the Holy Spirit and your return to Heaven through the dynamic of forgiveness, which harnesses the tremendous power of your mind's ability to choose.

As J puts it,

This is a course in mind training.[4]

and

An untrained mind can accomplish nothing.[5]

GARY: I heard a teacher say once that you should follow someone who says they're seeking the truth, but run away from anyone who says they've found it.

ARTEN: That wouldn't serve you very well if you ever met someone who actually knows the truth, now would it? But it *would* keep you running for a long time. Well, J *does* know the truth, and how can either you *or* that teacher be trained if you insist on being the trainer instead of a student?

GARY: I see your point. Even in the movies they know the difference between the master and the student.

ARTEN: Yes, but they usually seek to use the power of the universe. We're interested in the power of God. I think we've already made it clear they're not the same thing.

GARY: How long does it take to become a master?

ARTEN: Everybody asks that, and nobody likes the answer at first. The answer is it happens when it happens. Still, the time comes *before* that when you're so happy that the question doesn't really matter anymore! In any case, since the Holy Spirit is your Inner Teacher, you should always expect to be a student as long as you appear to be in a body. This is a lifelong spiritual path for people who are serious about wanting to break free from the world and go home. That doesn't mean you always have to take things seriously. If anything, the Course is saying that the world *cannot* be taken seriously.

GARY: All right. But what if I don't want to have just one lifelong spiritual path right now? What if I want to dabble in other things?

ARTEN: You can stay in the spiritual buffet line as long as you want. Obviously, your mind cannot be trained without some willingness on your part. It's up to you. But remember, you always wanted to know what it was like to learn from J. Here's your chance.

GARY: I was gonna ask you about the people who were involved in the scribing of the Course.

ARTEN: We're not going to get into the story of the Course very much. You've already read one book about it, and there are a couple of others. You can read them on your own time if you're interested. For some people, the Preface of the Course alone will tell them all they need to know about the Course's history. What are your impressions of the whole thing so far?

GARY: I think it's all pretty interesting. I know that Dr. Helen Schucman, the scribe who wrote down what the "Voice" said, and Dr. Bill Thetford, who encouraged her to keep going, were a couple of research psychologists who worked together in the Big Apple and couldn't get along with each other. Then one day Bill said he wanted to find another way of dealing with their relationship.[6]

ARTEN: Sound familiar?

GARY: Sure. Like me, Bill's declaration represented a decision on the part of the mind to find something better.

ARTEN: Very good. That was the invitation for J to give the Course, or for you to find it. J didn't just give the Course for Helen and Bill, but it was meant for them as well as anyone else who was ready to listen. For Helen, it seemed to take forever to complete the job, and even though she was the scribe she never would have finished without Bill's support. He would type it out later when she read it to him from her shorthand notebook.

By the way, don't try to make them into saints. To repeat an earlier point, they were just people, like you. Even though their relationship improved, they still had times when they couldn't get along with each other right up until they retired and Bill left for California. They were human, but they were learning.

GARY: And the other original members of the Foundation for Inner Peace, the ones who joined with Helen and Bill and made the Course available to the world. You had Ken Wapnick, who was the next one to come on the scene and worked with Helen and Bill for a couple of years before the Course was published. He took on the job with Helen of organizing the Course into sections with chapter titles, using the right capitalization and punctuation. And Judy Skutch, who took the Course from Helen, Bill and Ken's hands out to all her friends and associates in the field of new thought. Then there was Bob Skutch, who I don't know much about because he doesn't elaborate in his book. Eventually, they were guided by J that the only way to publish the Course unedited and unabridged, and keep it that way, was for them to do it themselves. I take it these people were meant to be a kind of spiritual family, the real purpose of which was to practice forgiveness?

PURSAH: You've got it. As the Course says,

There are no accidents in salvation.[7]

Judy and Bob were absolutely indispensable in their roles of bringing the Course to the world. Ken was identified to the group by J as the one who would be responsible for teaching people what the Course means. He became very close to Helen. Today, whenever the Course is translated into a foreign language, it's Ken's job to make sure that the translator truly understands every single line of the almost thirteen hundred pages. That doesn't mean that Ken is the only teacher of the Course, but he will be viewed in the future as the greatest one. He's the one whom students and scholars will still be reading hundreds, even thousands of years from now. And you, bright student, will have the opportunity to learn from him in this lifetime if you choose to.

GARY: What do I need him for if I have you?

PURSAH: You *do* have us. But we're not always going to be making regular visits to you. We have places to go and minds to blow. You should continue to learn whether we appear to be here with you or not. I assure you, we will always be here with you — and so will J.

GARY: I'll have to think about who I want to study with when you're not around. Besides, I thought Marianne Williamson was the main teacher of the Course. I saw her on the Larry King Show last week and if I didn't already know better, I would have thought she wrote the Course.

PURSAH: No. Our sister Marianne, whom I call the holy rap artist, is just one teacher. Her gift for public speaking and her personality have put her in a position where she's been able to introduce more people to the Course than anybody else. However, it's still up to each individual to decide how far he or she wants to go with it after that.

GARY: You say the Course is being translated into other languages?

PURSAH: Yes. You're not bi-lingual, are you?

GARY: I have enough to handle with English.

PURSAH: As far as the translations are concerned, J's Course is actually spreading at a much faster pace than Christianity did. A hundred years from now, a significant percentage of the world's population will accept that the Course is really J speaking the Word of God. What good will that do if people don't apply it? That's why we want you to be clear about what the Course is saying, or at least get you in the ballpark.

> ## A Course in Miracles *is actually spreading at a much faster pace than Christianity did.*

That's not as easy as you might think. Since the Course became available to people in 1975, there has been an explosion of channeled writings, techniques from Course imitators and various teachings, many of whose followers say are the same as or just like the Course. But to the well-trained eye these other teachings are missing the most important parts of the Course — the parts that make it what it is. While you do not want to attack other teachers, that does *not* mean that a commitment to the integrity of the message of the Course should not be voiced.

It's all right to agree to disagree with other teachers. There are vital features of *A Course in Miracles* that make it original and represent a quantum leap forward in spiritual thought. Some of those features are virtually ignored by the overwhelming majority of Course students, teachers, and interpreters. As with J's teachings of two thousand years ago, the world is attempting to do its usual job of obliterating the truth by incorporating *parts* of it into its illusions and covering over the real message of the Holy Spirit. We won't leave out the ideas you don't like. If you resist them or don't want to accept them after you hear them then that's your decision, but at least it won't be because you weren't told.

GARY: You said before the absolute truth could be expressed in just two words. I've been reading and I think I know what those two words are, but I want to be sure. What are they?

PURSAH: Keep your shirt on, buddy. That's about five discussions away, when we talk about what enlightenment really is. I understand J had a little surprise for you the other morning, though.

GARY: You ain't kiddin'! It was great. My experience was that it was really him.

PURSAH: Yes, it was J's Voice; the Voice for God, the Voice of the Holy Spirit. And as you will eventually experience, it was also symbolic of what *you* really are. Ultimately however, as the Course explains about the Holy Spirit,

> **His is the Voice for God, and has therefore taken form. This form is not His reality, which God alone knows along with Christ, His real Son, Who is part of Him.**[8]

Thus the Voice is a symbol of the Holy Spirit, Who is always with you. As you could gather from what was pointed out earlier, the Holy Spirit is not male or female. Neither is Christ. J is using Biblical, metaphorical language in the Course in order to correct Christianity. God's Son, or Christ, is not a man or a woman; He is your reality. And you are not a person — you just experience that you are. It is at the level of your experience that your training must take place, but you will be led beyond your present experience. When the Course talks about you *and* your brother, it is speaking about the seemingly fragmented or separated parts of the collective prodigal Son, which are symbolized by the false images you presently see.

ARTEN: The Voice can speak to you in many ways, and you will not usually hear it in the manner that you did the other morning. Indeed, it is not necessary for people to hear the Voice the way Helen did, and most never will. Helen had a gift that had been developed during past lives that J was able to use with her permission, but he — or if you prefer, the Holy Spirit — works with people in many different ways. He can speak to you by giving you his thoughts. These thoughts may just come into your mind. Sometimes you will not realize they were given to you, but sometimes you'll notice that they seemed to come to you from someplace else — although there is not really anyplace else.

This Voice is also the Voice of Buddha and all ascended masters who eventually completed their part along with J. J and Buddha are not in competition with each other. Such fantasies are for members of religions, not them. Their Voice may also communicate with you in the dreams that you have in bed at night, not that those dreams are any more or less real than your daily projections. Relating to you in your nocturnal dreams is one of the Holy Spirit's favorite ways of working with people. But sometimes His Voice may simply come to you in the form of an idea from another person that rings true for you.

As for J's message to you the other morning, you were quite correct in eventually realizing that the most important word in his communication was the word *meaningless*. When people begin studying the Course they always mistakenly think they're being asked to sacrifice something. As the Manual For Teachers points out,

> **It seems as if things are being taken away, and it is rarely understood initially that their lack of value is merely being recognized.**[9]

The Course gives much instruction on that point and the meaninglessness of the illusory world. You see Gary, *everyone* wants their life to have meaning, but they're looking for it in the wrong place — in the world. People feel a deep emptiness somewhere, and then they try to fill in the hole with some accomplishment or relationship on the level of form. Yet all of these things, by definition, are transitory at best. Thus you need to realize, as J counsels very early in the Text,

> **A sense of separation from God is the only lack you really need correct.**[10]

The J of the Course is not the same as the version of J in Christianity, and the two thought systems are not compatible. For Christianity, their suffering image of J the body is extra special. He is different than you in the sense that he alone is God's only begotten Son. But the J of the Course informs you that because you and he are one, then you are equally God's only begotten Son or Christ — not any different than him — and furthermore, you can eventually experience this.

There is nothing about me that you cannot attain. I have nothing that does not come from God. The difference between us now is that I have nothing else.[11]

GARY: If the two thought systems don't fit together, then how can Christians do the Course?

ARTEN: Very easily, or at least as easily as anyone else. The Course is always done at the level of the mind, not out in the world. Going to church, or temple or any place of worship should be viewed as a social phenomenon. Some kind of public worship has always been an important part of society, and it is obvious that many of today's religious institutions are positive influences in their communities. But where you will *really* find salvation is in the mind. There is nothing inherently holy about any physical place or object. They are merely symbols. Thus it is possible to belong to any particular religion or organization, or do anything else you would normally do in life, and still practice the thought system of the Course at the level of the mind.

It is not necessary to proselytize for *A Course in Miracles* to others, although you can certainly tell people about it if you feel guided in that direction. But the point is you don't *have* to. Your epiphany could just as easily remain a private matter. It's up to you. The Course has absolutely nothing whatsoever to do with the physical world. Once again, it's about how you choose to look at the world.

GARY: So even Catholics could go to Mass over at Our Lady of Great Suffering and realize in their minds that J isn't really asking them to sacrifice anything.

PURSAH: Yes. It's not just Catholics, dear one. As you know, there are happy people as well as suffering bastards in every religion. Look at the way some individual Hindus choose to suffer in their worship of God. Even the happy members of different religions suffer eventually. It's built into the unconscious thought system. That's why Christians want to believe that J suffered and died for their sins. Don't you remember that pretty Southern Baptist woman who told you that you will never get past the gates of Heaven unless you have the blood of Jesus on you?

GARY: Oh yeah! I asked her where I could order a couple of pints.

PURSAH: Try to remember what we keep telling you. The Course is a mental process, not a physical one. Eventually you'll understand that *everything* is a mental process and not a physical one. Speaking of Catholics and Baptists, that brings up another important point about interpretations. Do you know how many different kinds of organized Christian churches there are in the world today, each with its own particular interpretation of Christianity?

GARY: I would imagine there must be hundreds.

PURSAH: There are over twenty thousand.

GARY: Jesus, Joseph and Mary!

ARTEN: It wasn't their fault. Let me ask you something else. If today you have twenty thousand churches that don't really understand J's message — and I assure you they don't — and if you have them all disagreeing about what J's message is supposed to mean, and in the meantime the world hasn't changed — not *really* — then do you honestly believe it will serve humanity if you end up with twenty thousand different interpretations of *A Course in Miracles*?

GARY: I take it that's a rhetorical question. Which is why you emphasize that if I really learn J's message as it's presented in his Course, then there is really only one possible correct interpretation. I think it's going to take some big people to be willing to give up *their* interpretations. But I also gather that there are inherent benefits in doing so.

ARTEN: Very perceptive, hotshot.

GARY: You're praising perception?

ARTEN: There is such a thing as true perception, as you will hear shortly. Since we're pointing out that you'll have to be willing to give up your own interpretation of the Course in exchange for the right one, we should also point out that in order for you to quote from the Course in your writing you'll have to be willing to note the various passages from it that we're speaking. You may not feel like doing that but trust us, it's part of the process of keeping the Course intact and not allowing it to be changed and its message lost. Two thousand years ago it wasn't possible to preserve the truth. Even today it will be very difficult to prevent J's message from being lost again, but there's nothing wrong with giving it a shot.

GARY: So two thousand years ago people started adding their own things to J's words and changing his message to conform with their own beliefs, and then before you knew it there wasn't any way to tell for sure which words were really his and which ones weren't?

ARTEN: Exactly. Do you really want that to happen again?

GARY: Not really, but what will prevent the Course from becoming like Christianity, with a central authority that has official churches laying down the law?

ARTEN: What will prevent that from happening is the nature of the Course itself. *A Course in Miracles is not a religion.* As you have already considered, as long as the Course stays in one piece and the integrity of its message is preserved as much as possible, then its self-study characteristics will always win out in the long run. The Course is actually ahead of its time. What's important now is that *you* do it.

GARY: Is it true that once the church was established then only clergy were allowed to read scripture, and the people were only able to hear what the church told them?

ARTEN: That's true. Most people didn't know how to read anyway. You take a lot for granted now, and you forget that the printing press didn't even exist until the 1450s. The church strictly controlled information, including all scripture. If the public only knows what they're told, then it's pretty hard for them to come to any conclusions other than what the powers that be want them to.

It wasn't until the 1700s that enough people were able to read and enough literature was available for it to make any difference in society. Today, people can read and think for themselves, and the information available is far more advanced. You may ask why J took so long to give the Course. Yet it wasn't until now that enough people would have been ready for it.

GARY: Hey, I don't mean to change the subject, but I really don't want to forget this time to ask you about these experiences I've been having with unusual flashes of light. I assume you know what I mean, since you seem to know everything about me. Are these light experiences associated with the Course?

ARTEN: Yes. Even though they started a year ago, they are connected to a decision made by you at the level of the mind which resulted in your study of the Course. Once again, most people don't have any such experiences, and they are *not* necessary for the Course to be effective. You haven't done the Workbook yet, but if you'd like to read the third paragraph of Lesson 15, you'll see J mention these kinds of manifestations. Do you want to read that now?

GARY: Yeah! Let me see here.

As we go along, you may have many "light episodes." They may take many different forms, some of them quite unexpected. Do not be afraid of them. They are signs that you are opening your eyes at last. They will not persist, because they merely symbolize true perception, and they are not related to knowledge.[12]

ARTEN: We'll be talking about the difference between knowledge and what leads to it, so be patient. We'll also talk more about your mystical experiences as we proceed, but I can tell that you still have another question in your mind.

GARY: Just to make sure I'm getting this, I have a question to ask about the Course and how it relates to Buddhism as well as Christianity. One of the main teachings of traditional Buddhism — and grant you there are other types of non-traditional Buddhism that don't have all the ritualistic trappings — is that people suffer because they have these raging desires that can't ever be fulfilled. Buddhists believe that the control of desire brings happiness and compassionate living towards others. You could look at that as another way of dealing with lack.

But you've already quoted the Course as saying, "A sense of separation from God is the only lack you really need correct."[13] Are you saying that Buddhism is *modification* of thought, as opposed to a healing by the Holy Spirit, and that Christianity and its approach is even one step further removed — being an attempt to modify the physical rather than the mental?

ARTEN: You're getting it. Once you really understand a couple of things we've already said to you, then you'll see that Buddhism is a step in the right direction because it doesn't run away from the mind the way Christianity does. That's why the Pope put down Buddhism in one of his books; he said that it seeks to transcend the world, but that in his opinion God must be found by doing certain things *in* the world. Not only has he got it backwards, whether you're looking for God or not, but Buddhism lacks God almost completely — depending on the individual teacher or interpreter. As we pointed out during our first visit, doing mental exercises on your own *cannot* heal your unconscious mind. As we proceed, we'll be giving you a good idea of J's thought system which, when done *with* him or the Holy Spirit, trains you to develop true perception. That will help the Holy Spirit heal you and lead you back to what you really are.

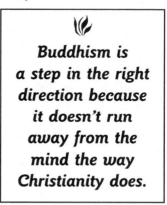

Buddhism is a step in the right direction because it doesn't run away from the mind the way Christianity does.

This brings up one of the interesting features of the miracle — a miracle according to the Course being a shift in perception[14] over to the *Holy Spirit's* way of thinking, and not merely a modification of your own thoughts, forms or circumstances. The Course says that the miracle can progress you much farther and faster along your spiritual path than would have otherwise been possible. For example, the Text says,

The miracle is the only device at your immediate disposal for controlling time.[15]

and,

The miracle substitutes for learning that might have taken thousands of years.[16]

J is not making outrageous claims here; he is simply telling you the truth based on the laws of the mind and the laws of God. We'll be concentrating on the Course's view of time during one of our visits with you.

In order for you to learn to save time, it would be very helpful if you approached the Course like the original thought system that it is, rather than seeing it as a continuation of Christianity, which it isn't. Please don't call it the Third Testament. It's not. It's the

Course. You get J without the religion. He'll tell you a lot of things that cannot be reconciled with the Bible. Don't waste your time *trying* to reconcile them. The Bible *begins* by telling you that, "In the beginning God created the heavens and the earth." He didn't! If you're going to understand what J is telling you, then you cannot compromise on these words from the Course.

> **The world you see is an illusion of a world. God did not create it, for what He creates must be eternal as Himself. Yet there is nothing in the world you see that will endure forever.**[17]

GARY: But what about energy? Isn't it true that energy can't be destroyed, only changed?

ARTEN: Energy cannot seemingly be destroyed on the level of form because it is not *really* energy, it is thought. Or more accurately, it is mis-thought, which *will* eventually be changed over to the eternal. In the meantime, there is a very simple criteria that the Course gives you to distinguish between the real and the unreal.

> **Whatever is true is eternal, and cannot change or be changed. Spirit is therefore unalterable because it is already perfect, but the mind can elect what it chooses to serve. The only limit put on its choice is that it cannot serve two masters.**[18]

So the fact that energy *can* be changed means that by its very nature it is untrue. It is not our intention to deflate the enthusiasm of your New Age buddies who are so ga-ga over energy. But energy is nothing. It's a waste of time, a trick, just another device for building your house upon the sand instead of on the rock. Sure, it may be a helpful idea for some people to be interested in the unseen instead of the seen. But we came to help you save time, so we need to say what we need to say. The good news isn't that *energy* can be changed, the good news is that the mind that made it can be changed.

GARY: I hear you. I was wondering something else. Do people *have* to believe the Course is really J and have a personal relationship with him in order for the Course to work?

PURSAH: No. It's possible to derive benefits from the Course and not believe it's J doing the talking. As we said, you could just do the Course with the Holy Spirit. Or you could do it as a secular person looking to learn about spirituality. Also, a Buddhist or a member of some other religion could substitute words and still do it. You could use the words Buddha mind instead of Christ Mind, or fill in your favorite. Feminists could and do substitute the word She for He.

While these people are doing these things, they should realize at some point that the fact they're doing it means they need to forgive something, because they wouldn't *have* to make the substitutions in the first place if they weren't attaching great significance to symbols and making them real.

Of course, any person who is capable of having, or already has a personal relationship with J should by all means continue to develop it. Eventually they will find the experience to be beyond this world, because where you join with J or the Holy Spirit, at the level of the mind, is also beyond this world. At first people always think of J as helping them *in* the world, but the Course will teach them to outgrow that.

Ultimately, each one will learn what you will learn: The Voice for God is *your* Voice; it's your real Voice, because you *are* Christ. There's no difference between the Father, the Son and The Holy Spirit in reality — but you don't live in reality. You live here. Or at least that's your experience. Until your mind has been healed by the Holy Spirit, you'll need the help that the symbols of the Course can give you.

For many people, when they first start studying the Text of the Course they think it may as well be written in a foreign language. This is because J presents the Course *as if* you already understand what he's talking about, even though he knows that on the level of form you do not understand a lot of it. Ideas are introduced, dropped, and then taught again later in more detail. The thought system builds upon itself in order for you to learn it. The learning of the Course must be seen as a process, not an event. Unfortunately, a lot of people study the Workbook, which is more approachable, and ignore a good deal of the Text except for when they go to their study group meetings. Yet if you don't really understand the Text, then you can't *really* understand everything the Workbook is saying either.

GARY: Do I have to go to a study group?

PURSAH: No. You can go if you want to, and I happen to know that you will. Study groups are not mentioned at all in the Course and, like going to church, they should be viewed primarily as a social phenomenon. They are not always the best source of information either, but if they are given to the Holy Spirit and used for forgiveness, then you can be certain He'll be happy to participate with you.

ARTEN: There are some people who will play down the importance of understanding what the Course means. They'll quote the first few lessons of the Workbook out of context, or the message that J gave you the other morning, Gary. They'll say that since the Course is making a *metaphysical* statement that everything is meaningless, then the Course doesn't mean anything either! Let's be very emphatic about something. The Course certainly *does* have meaning on the level where it meets you, and it is very important for you to understand it — or else it will be useless to you. That's because the Course is about reinterpreting the world and what you call your life. It's about giving up the meaning that *you* have given the world and switching over to the Holy Spirit's meaning for the world. This is absolutely necessary in order for the Holy Spirit to help you gently awaken from your dream. How can people think it's not important for students to understand precisely what the Course means if they've read the Introduction to the Workbook?

A theoretical foundation such as the text provides is necessary as a framework to make the exercises in this workbook meaningful.[19]

and,

You are merely asked to apply the ideas as you are directed to do. You are not asked to judge them at all. You are asked only to use them. It is their use that will give them meaning to you, and will show you that they are true.[20]

Let's forgive those who want to take the easy way and pretend the Course is saying the same thing as everything else, and move on to what the Course is teaching. It should be clear from what we've already said that when J told you to make the world meaningless to you, he was talking about giving up the *value* that you have given it, and accepting the Holy Spirit's meaning for it instead. For example, he says at the beginning of Chapter 24,

> **To learn this course requires willingness to question every value that you hold.**[21]

GARY: Surely he doesn't mean apple pie, family and motherhood?

ARTEN: We'll see. Pursah mentioned before that J's thought system is holographic. Once you understand it then you'll see it everywhere in the Course. To illustrate this, why don't we take a brief look at the Introduction. Not the Preface, the Introduction. Would you like to read that now, Gary? Afterwards, I'll give you a quick walk through it.

GARY: Sure. At least when I read out loud, it doesn't look so funny for me to be moving my lips.

INTRODUCTION

This is a course in miracles. It is a required course. Only the time you take it is voluntary. Free will does not mean that you can establish the curriculum. It means only that you can elect what you want to take at a given time. The course does not aim at teaching the meaning of love, for that is beyond what can be taught. It does aim, however, at removing the blocks to the awareness of love's presence, which is your natural inheritance. The opposite of love is fear, but what is all-encompassing can have no opposite.

This course can therefore be summed up very simply in this way:

> ***Nothing real can be threatened.***
> ***Nothing unreal exists.***

Herein lies the peace of God.[22]

ARTEN: Thanks, Gary. The Course is required because it express-
es the truth. I'm sorry if that sounds arrogant. It doesn't mean that
the Course is the only way for anyone to ever find the truth. The truth
is an awareness — not a book. But you can't find this awareness
alone. Can a sick mind heal itself? On the level of the world, the
answer is no. You need help. You need the miracle. The time that
you choose to learn and apply what the Course teaches is up to you.
You can delay as long as you want. The curriculum has already been
established. You can elect what you want to learn at a given time, but
you will eventually realize that there are really only two things to
choose from, rather than the myriad of choices you presently believe
are open to you.[23] The Course does not claim to be superior to any
other spiritual path, yet at the same time it doesn't make any secret
about the fact that it is ultimately, absolutely necessary for you to
learn it.

The meaning of love cannot be taught or learned. Love will take
care of Itself. *Your* job, as the Introduction says, is to learn how to
remove, along with the Holy Spirit, the blocks to the awareness of
the inheritance that you seemingly threw away. The opposite of God
and His Kingdom is anything that is not God and His Kingdom, but
what is all-encompassing — God — cannot *have* an opposite.

You have no doubt heard elsewhere that *A Course in Miracles* is
asking you to choose love instead of fear. That's true, but it's certainly not enough. A thousand writers have written about people
choosing love instead of fear since the Course came out in the 70s.
But if you tell people to choose love instead of fear, they'll think
you're telling them to choose *their* love, and that's not what the
Course is teaching. As you will learn, the love of the world and its
people is what the Course calls special love,[24] and the love of the
Holy Spirit is quite a different thing. The words *love* and *fear* in the
Course represent two complete and mutually exclusive thought systems, *both* of which need to be understood if you're ever going to
know what it really is that you're choosing between.

In fact, your unconscious belief system is held in place by *not*
looking at it.[25] What kind of a service are you rendering people if
you don't turn them on to the fact that the thought system of fear,
which they have denied and projected outwards,[26] must be closely

examined in their lives if they are to be free of it? What will you be bringing to the party if you fail to inform people that the solution to the problems of the world and its relationships will *never* be found at the level of the interaction between individual bodies?

Nothing *real* — which is your eternal and unalterable spirit that the Course's thought system of love will lead you to — can be the slightest bit threatened. Nothing *unreal* — which is everything else and has been produced by the thought system of fear — exists at all in reality. The peace of God is the goal of the Course because it *must* be attained in order to regain the awareness of your reality in the Kingdom.[27]

> 🖌
>
> **The words love and fear in the Course represent two complete and mutually exclusive thought systems.**

GARY: So all of this is done at a level beyond the body and the world, and a recurring theme of yours seems to be that J's attitude towards the body two thousand years ago was that it was totally insignificant to his reality. Also, it would seem you're saying that resurrection is something that takes place in your mind even though you still appear to be in your body, and it actually has nothing to do with the body at all. The ideas of physical resurrection and physical immortality are not only fantasies, but totally unnecessary.

ARTEN: Bravo! I knew there was hope for you. Reality and love are natural and abstract; bodies and fear are unnatural and specific. As the Course teaches,

Complete abstraction is the natural condition of the mind.[28]

We'll talk more about that during our next visit, when we discuss how you ended up thinking that you're a body — and where the universe came from.

GARY: I'm beginning to understand why you say the Course and Christianity don't fit together. The Course is saying that the body is illusory and is based on a thought system that is actually the antithesis of God, if there could be an antithesis of God. Christianity has served to *perpetuate* the thought system that results in a state of seemingly separate bodily existence by elevating J's body to one of extreme specialness — thus fulfilling the needs of people to validate their own experience of uniqueness and individuality.

ARTEN: Absolutely. The J of the Bible is an object in the world's dream of bodies, but the *real* J is absolutely free. As we've said, that's what he wants for you. In many ways you must continue learning to outgrow the thinking of religion. For example, throughout the Bible the Judaic-Christian tradition portrays God as *reacting* directly to sin as though it's a fact. In the case of Christianity, as we've already pointed out, God supposedly offers up J to suffer and die for your alleged sins in a sacrificial act of atonement. Some churches place such importance on this that they symbolically cannibalize J's body in the sacrament of the Eucharist and variations of that ritual. They believe that God has sacrificed his Son in the flesh to atone for their so-called sins of the flesh.

Yet God would not react to events in a dream any more than you would react to events in a bad dream your wife was having in bed next to you. In the first place, you can't even see the events because *they are not really happening.* Second, even if you *could* see them there would still be no need for you to react to them because, being untrue, they could not possibly affect you. The only logical thing would be to awaken your wife from her bad dream, but you would do it *slowly* and *gently*, so you wouldn't scare her even more. You wouldn't grab her and shake the hell out of her. Similarly, the Holy Spirit will gently awaken you. He is not a separate God reacting to your dream, but is actually the Voice for God that you still have *with* you in your illusory journey to this far country.[29]

One way the Holy Spirit will awaken you is to teach you that what you *think* is happening is *not* happening. Reality is invisible and *anything* that can be perceived or observed in *any* way, even measured scientifically, is an illusion — just the opposite of what the world thinks. But the Course is practical in more ways than one. You can use its thought system of true forgiveness to deal with what the body's eyes are telling you, and you can do it in such a way that allows you to function in society. One job in an illusion is no more inherently holy than any other job. Thus, while you are gradually learning that what you once thought of as sin, attack, guilt and separation are really something else, you can still live a relatively normal earthly existence and be awakened slowly and gently from your dream.

GARY: From what you've said — also from what I read in the Text where J talks about the real message of his crucifixion — even though it appeared to be a terrible attack, the crucifixion was really nothing to him, because he was so totally identified with the invulnerable Love of God, which he knew he really was, instead of illusions like the body. The fact that the crucifixion and J's supposed suffering for others on the cross are central ideas to Christianity is just an indication of how much his message was misunderstood and distorted.

ARTEN: Yes. Don't expect to attain the same non-suffering level of accomplishment as J in your first year doing the Course. It's an ideal that can only come with a great deal of experience. Yes, the time will eventually come when you will never suffer. That is one of the long-term payoffs of this spiritual path. Even while you still appear to be in your body, it's possible for you to attain psychological invulnerability. As the Course says,

The guiltless mind cannot suffer.[30]

But it takes the illusion of time for you to learn your forgiveness lessons and get to your goal.

GARY: That may be so, but I want to get there sooner rather than later.

PURSAH: Everybody wants that, and we're going to help you right now by passing along a major idea. This isn't the whole picture, but it's an important part of it. You might not agree with it at first, but think about it. We told you the last time that when we came back we'd let you know what wisdom *really* is. We'll be going into more detail about this, and you'll notice that our presentation will become more linear as we go along in order to help facilitate your understanding.

As far as wisdom is concerned, the world believes that wisdom is having good judgment and being right. That's not true. All being right will do is keep you stuck here forever. I'm going to recite what J says in the Course about wisdom and its relationship to innocence. By the way, this is also what it really means to be pure of heart.

Innocence is not a partial attribute. It is not real *until* it is total. The partly innocent are apt to be quite foolish at times. It is not until their innocence becomes a viewpoint with universal application that it becomes wisdom. Innocent or true perception means that you never misperceive and always see truly.[31]

GARY: Are you saying I'm gonna have to see *everyone,* no matter what, as being totally innocent?

PURSAH: That is correct. Once again, don't expect it to happen right away.

GARY: I don't know. How can a man like Hitler be innocent?

PURSAH: That's a typical question, and the answer doesn't have anything to do with Hitler. As one who remembers my Jewish lifetimes very well, I'm not exactly a fan of the Nazis, or skinheads, or the KKK or any of the other mentally injured groups. The reason they are innocent has nothing to do with the level of form. Hitler and everyone else in the world, including you, are equally innocent because *what you are seeing is not true.*[32] This is *your* dream. As the Course teaches, the dream is not being dreamed by somebody else.[33]

Hitler was an example of the thought system of fear being carried out to its extreme. You think the Holocaust was an unusual event, but it was unusual only in its size. The same kind of thing occurs all the time, all throughout history. If you'll think hard and do a little bit of research, you'll find that it has happened several times in this past century alone. You don't have to be Jewish, or Black, or an Indian or some other exotic color to be a victim. It would be hard to find *any* group of people that has not been persecuted. Even a white person, as long as he or she is a certain kind of white person in the right place at the right time, can be the victim of the year. Maybe they have to be a Catholic, or a Protestant, or an alleged witch. You were born in Salem. You know the story. How many people died during the Salem witch trials?

GARY: Around nineteen or twenty.

PURSAH: Yes. That was a classic example of the projection of unconscious guilt. Do you know how many people were killed during the witch trials that *preceded* that event in Europe?

GARY: I don't know. Hundreds?

PURSAH: Try forty thousand.

GARY: Forty thousand!

PURSAH: Yes. As a percentage of the population, that would be the same as if over a million people were killed today.

GARY: Wow! That would make the news — unless there was a big sex scandal somewhere.

PURSAH: All this is a result of a predicament where people have a deep, hidden need to project their unconscious guilt onto somebody else, and *any* excuse will do. We've been talking about extreme examples, but people do this in a thousand subtle ways. They don't know they need to, or why. If they did then they wouldn't do it. You'll be learning more about this situation, and you'll realize exactly why insane actions such as genocide are a routine part of the story of man's inhumanity toward man. You'll also learn that true forgiveness is the only way to break the pattern. As we said, you don't have to accept the idea that everyone is completely innocent, or any of the other Course ideas, right away.[34] But you'll see as you go along that forgiveness is immeasurably good for *you,* not just the images you are forgiving.

Incidentally, the thought system of fear and separation from God is given the name *ego* in the Course,[35] and this term shouldn't be confused with the term "ego" as it is used in traditional psychology. J always spoke to us in large, all-encompassing terms, and the Course use of the word *ego* is no exception. You should remember that no matter how large it may appear to be, the ego is just a thought — and thoughts can be changed.

GARY: I know you said you haven't given me the whole picture yet, but the forgiveness you're talking about sounds like a form of denial.

PURSAH: Once we've told you everything we want to tell you, then not only will you be able to see what's really happening with true forgiveness, but you'll realize that the thought system of love and the thought system of fear are *both* forms of denial. One of them, the Holy Spirit's teaching, leads to Heaven by uncovering and reversing the ego's denial of the truth. As the Course says about the peace that results from the Holy Spirit's teaching,

It denies the ability of anything not of God to affect you. This is the proper use of denial.[36]

Of the forgiveness that leads to peace, the Course says,

The crucifixion was an extreme teaching lesson. It is not necessary for you to go through it in order to learn from it.

Forgiveness then, is an illusion, but because of its purpose, which is the Holy Spirit's, it has one difference. Unlike all other illusions it leads away from error and not towards it.[37]

GARY: While I'm denying the ability of anything that is not of God to affect me, does that mean I should just let people attack me physically and not defend myself, or not go to the doctor if I'm feeling sick?

PURSAH: Absolutely not. We meant what we said about living a normal existence. You should never allow yourself to be harmed physically, or seek out danger or suffer in order to prove a point. The crucifixion was an extreme teaching lesson. It is *not* necessary for you to go through it in order to learn from it.[38] In most situations you will do what you would normally do, but try not to do it alone. Ask for guidance when you can. You will have the Holy Spirit's entire thought system, which J can articulate because he was the first one in the dream to complete his part perfectly,[39] to draw upon. In time, you too will become what this thought system represents.

Remember, the kind of forgiveness J used and his Course is teaching is not the same kind of forgiveness that Christianity and the world sometimes participate in. If it were, then it would be a waste of time. Christianity got J wrong. He is teaching true forgiveness in his Course, and we'll show you how to use it in specific situations so you can eventually apply it yourself in any situation. But remember that there is no substitute for studying and practicing the Course. We are learning aides. We're not doing our own thing, and you should not try to start *your* own thing. You've been doing your own thing for eons. It's like the old saying: *If you always do what you've always done then you'll always get what you've always gotten.* What you've always gotten is a return ticket to psycho planet, or someplace similar. It's time to get off the unmerry-go-round.

GARY: I think a lot of spiritual seekers are very interested in not reincarnating anymore. So that I'm clear about the miracle — not only does the Course sometimes refer to itself as the miracle, but a miracle according to the Course has nothing to do with the level of the physical. It's a shift in perception that takes place in the mind.

PURSAH: Yes. Very good. Then you're dealing with the cause. As the Course says,

This is a course in cause and not effect.[40]

and,

Therefore, seek not to change the world, but choose to change your mind about the world.[41]

GARY: If you watch carefully, you can see that most of the judgments people have don't really make them happy anyway.

PURSAH: That's very true. In fact, the Course asks you at one point,

Do you prefer that you be right or happy?[42]

GARY: I think most of us would *say* we'd rather be happy, but we *act* like we'd rather be right.

PURSAH: Yes. Part of the deception of the ego is that when people judge others and *believe* they are right, they sometimes feel good *temporarily,* because they've managed to project some of their unconscious guilt onto somebody else. Then a couple days later, without knowing why, their unconscious guilt — which, once again, they have no idea about — catches up with them and they have a car accident, or hurt themselves in any one of a thousand more subtle ways. Of course that's an illusory, linear example. The *whole* thing is really set up ahead of time, which we'll talk about later, but it's an example of one of the ways things play themselves out.

GARY: So people judge, feel good about it — or bad about it, depending on whether they're projecting their guilt outward or inward — and then they punish themselves. They think they've won, but then their karma runs over their dogma.

PURSAH: You're progressing quickly, but you still have a lot to learn. Remember, karma is just an effect. We're going to change the cause of *everything* by changing the mind. The effect on the level of the physical is not something to be concerned about, because it isn't real. The *real* things you should be interested in are inner peace and returning to Heaven. As far as temporal benefits are concerned, we'll address those things when we talk about the abundance that comes along with true prayer.

ARTEN: Also, let's point out that when the Course talks about not judging your brother, what it means is that you don't *condemn* him.[43] Obviously, you have to make judgments just to cross the street. We're not talking about abandoning that kind of judgment. Without it, you couldn't get out of bed in the morning. One thing the Course has nothing against is common sense.

GARY: For some people, common sense is a challenge.

ARTEN: Judge ideas, not people. Then accept the true ideas. As far as challenges are concerned, we have repeatedly told you we'd be challenging you. The time will come when your challenges will be over. As the Manual For Teachers says in referring to advanced teachers,

> **There is no challenge to a teacher of God. Challenge implies doubt, and the trust on which God's teachers rest secure makes doubt impossible.**[44]

But you, hotshot, are not there yet. It's time to get busy restoring your mind to its natural condition.

GARY: That's O.K. by me. As you said, it's not my mind anyway. One thing I find a little uncomfortable is the fact that you keep emphasizing differences and distinctions instead of unity.

ARTEN: I'm glad you brought that up, because the reason is important. It's because in the final analysis there are only two thought systems, and the Holy Spirit teaches you by contrasting them.

The miracle compares what you have made with creation, accepting what is in accord with it as true, and rejecting what is out of accord as false.[45]

PURSAH: People are not always going to agree on what is in accord with the miracle and the Holy Spirit and what is not in accord with Him and the Course. There will always be some disagreements among followers of spiritualities, and that includes Course students as well. That's what the world *does,* Gary. It divides like a cell under a microscope. It's built into the system, because the ego mind divides like a cell under a microscope, making seemingly separate minds — or what some people call souls. Don't worry about it or resist it. *Your* job is to go back to the source of the problem — the mind and *not* the world — and change your mind through forgiveness.

J doesn't expect his Course to live its life without controversy, whether in the Course community or outside of it. However, as he says in the Introduction to the Clarification Of Terms, which are words you could apply to any aspect of the Course,

All terms are potentially controversial, and those who seek controversy will find it. Yet those who seek clarification will find it as well. They must, however, be willing to overlook controversy, recognizing that it is a defense against truth in the form of a delaying maneuver.[46]

One such possible area of controversy, as you will see during our next discussion, is the idea that what is really driving this world is the unconscious guilt associated with sin — and that sin is just a false idea. You shouldn't make it psychologically real through condemnation.

ARTEN: Until we return, I want you to consider that spiritual paths are not the same, and that if you want unity, it is to be found in the *goal.* The goal *is* the same. All spiritual paths lead to God in the end.[47] But the paths are not the same. They go in different directions temporarily, until they all end up at the same place. There is no sadness in that. Indeed, it is quite necessary. In order to get the most out of any path, you have to understand and apply it. For how can you possibly apply it if you *don't* understand it? It would not generate any great disagreement if you said that Buddhism and Christianity are not saying the same thing. Why should it generate any great disagreement if you say that *A Course in Miracles* isn't saying the same thing as them?

The Course is not a movement; there are more than enough of those. You don't have to take over the world. It doesn't matter whether the Course is popular or not. J knows what he's doing. Those who are ready for the Course will find it. His Course is unique. It gives an individual a chance to learn that he or she is *not* an individual, and that they are never alone. It gives you the opportunity to commune with the Holy Spirit and ultimately, God. It accelerates your return to God by helping the Holy Spirit heal you. In order for that to happen however, it is absolutely imperative that you learn to understand statements like the following one J makes in his Course.

> It can indeed be said the ego made its world on sin. Only in such a world could everything be upside down. This is the strange illusion that makes the clouds of guilt seem heavy and impenetrable. The solidness that this world's foundation seems to have is found in this. For sin has changed creation from an Idea of God to an ideal the ego wants; a world it rules, made up of bodies, mindless and capable of complete corruption and decay. If this is a mistake, it can be undone easily by truth. Any mistake can be corrected, if truth be left to judge it. But if the mistake is given the status of truth, to what can it be brought?[48]

PURSAH: And so, dear messenger, it's time to renounce the mistaken values that *you* have given the world and begin to take on the Holy Spirit's meaning for it instead. His use for the world *has* meaning.

ARTEN: Continue your studies Gary, and during our next visit we'll begin to bring your mistakes to the truth, where they can be undone by the One whose function it is to free you.

4

The Secrets of Existence

There is no life outside of Heaven.
Where God created life, there life must be.[1]

I ADHERED to Arten's counsel and accelerated my studies. I began practicing the Course's Workbook lessons, one per day, sometimes spending two or three days on a lesson that I found particularly helpful. On rare occasions I'd take a day off, still mindful of the ideas I had been learning. I was now being trained in the art of true forgiveness, although this training would take longer than I thought. The first part of the Workbook was meant to begin the "undoing" of the way I presently looked at the world.[2] I didn't know Arten and Pursah were going to wait two months before returning in order to give me time to complete the first fifty lessons, especially designed to begin fulfilling that purpose. After a month or so I began to wonder if my friends, as I now thought of them, were going to return at all. Still, what I was doing was so interesting to me that I knew I'd continue my journey with the Course no matter what appeared to happen — or not happen.

One day I went back to the little bookstore where I had bought the Course and asked the woman who worked there if she knew of any Course study groups in the area. Maine is one of the quieter states in America, and hardly a hotbed of spiritual activism. Yet she was able to provide me with several phone numbers left by Course students just in case anyone else was interested in joining with them. After considering several and asking the Holy Spirit for guidance, I found myself driving up to a little town called Leeds, not far from the state capital of Augusta, where I found a group of people that I would happily study with for quite some time.

The facilitator of the group, who had been studying the Course for many years, offered to let me borrow two brief pamphlets — the only extensions of the Course spoken by J and scribed by Helen — called *Psychotherapy: Purpose, Process and Practice,* and *The Song of Prayer.* He also asked if I wanted to borrow some cassette tapes that were designed to help people appreciate what the Course is saying. I looked at the small tape set and saw it was an introduction to the Course called *The ego and Forgiveness,* by Ken Wapnick. The synchronicity of being offered these tapes so soon after Pursah had recommended Ken was not lost on me. I took the tapes home, although I'd procrastinate in listening to them.

By now, I was realizing that the Introduction to the Workbook meant what it said: the theoretical foundation of the Text was necessary to make the Workbook meaningful.[3] I picked up quickly on the idea that if students didn't understand the carefully detailed teachings J had set forth in the Text, then it would be extremely easy for them to misunderstand some of the Workbook lessons and occasionally quote them out of context to support their own beliefs. We students could *not* yet hear God's Voice clearly. In fact, the Course itself said, "Only very few can hear God's Voice at all...."[4] So instead of doing what I had already seen many students doing on the Internet — making pronouncements about what the Holy Spirit was guiding them to say and do — I was determined to do my best to understand and apply the Course's principles to everything I perceived. I wanted to help the Holy Spirit remove the blocks that usually prevented me from hearing God's Voice clearly.

I was just about ready to give up on the idea of seeing Arten and Pursah again when they surprised me one afternoon while I was watching a sexy movie I had rented at the local video store. Embarrassed, I grabbed the remote control and quickly shut off the scene of a man and a woman engaging in almost naked, heated foreplay. Pursah began the discussion.

PURSAH: Hey, what was that, Gary? It looked pretty interesting.

GARY: That was an experiment in duality.

PURSAH: Research. I understand.

ARTEN: You've been studying and applying the Course the best you can, which we appreciate. We wanted to give you some time. We neglected to tell you that it will be several years before our seventeen appearances to you are complete.

We're also happy you found a study group, although it will be a while before you recognize that study groups are not about joining with individuals on the level of the world, but for the sake of forgiveness that becomes possible through the relationships and the examination of your own ego. In study groups, or churches, or anywhere else in this world, it appears that there are multiple teachers and learners. But there is really only one Teacher of the Course — and only one student.

We'd like to begin this afternoon by pointing out something for you. Most of you Americans think it was TIME magazine in the 1970s that first said, "God is dead." But in the 1880s, Friedrich Nietzsche first made that famous statement. That's a secret wish of the ego — to kill God and take over His throne — but Nietzsche didn't know about that. While still in his forties, he collapsed into a state of dementia from which he never recovered.

People have always pondered the nature and origin of their existence. Many have assumed they found the answers, and have formed countless philosophies. Yet only one man, who is no longer a man, has been able to truly explain your origin. Now of course I do *not* say this to put down Nietzsche, who will find himself in God just as surely as everyone else will. I say it in order to emphasize the following words from *A Course in Miracles*.

There is no statement that the world is more afraid to hear than this:

I do not know the thing I am, and therefore do not know what I am doing, where I am, or how to look upon the world or on myself.

Yet in this learning is salvation born. And What you are will tell you of Itself.[5]

PURSAH: Let's talk about what you are and where you came from, and then you can decide how quickly you want to get to where you're really going. We'll begin by telling you a little story — courtesy of information in J's Course — that would have otherwise remained oblivious to you. Don't kid yourself; it's a privilege for you to learn these things. Without J they would remain forever unconscious. They will *still* be mostly unconscious even after you hear them. As we proceed, at least you're going to have a chance of finding your way — with the help of the Holy Spirit — through your veils of forgetfulness and back to where you really belong.

> 🔥
>
> **You have a chance of finding your way through the veils of forgetfulness, back to where you belong.**

Symbols cannot really express what appeared to happen just before the making of the universe. The magnitude of the trans-temporal mind is much too great to capture with words. We can however, give you a glimpse of what's really behind the so-called fall of man, and what many have called original sin. We can tell you what it was that resulted in the event you refer to as the Big Bang. No scientist will ever be able to trace anything back before that, except in theory. But it *is* possible to remember the very beginning — and to change your mind about it. It's not necessary, however, for you to remember the very beginning now, because you will really change your mind by forgiving the *symbols* of this beginning. Thus your salvation always has and always will depend on decisions you are making right *now*. Would you like to proceed, Arten?

ARTEN: Before the beginning, there were no beginnings or endings; there was only the eternal Always, which is still there — and always shall be. There was only an awareness of unflawed oneness, and this oneness was so complete, so awe-striking and unlimited in its joyous extension that it would be impossible for anything to be aware of something else that was not Itself. There was and is only God in this reality — which we will refer to as Heaven.

What God creates in His extension of Himself is called Christ. But Christ is not in any way separate or different than God. It is exactly the same. Christ is not a *part* of God, It is an *extension* of the whole. Real Love must be shared, and the perfect Love that is shared in God's Universe is beyond all human comprehension. Humans appear to be part of the whole, but Christ is all of it. The only possible distinction between Christ and God — if a distinction was possible — would be that God created Christ; He is the Author. Christ did not create God or Itself. Because of their *perfect* oneness, this doesn't really matter in Heaven. God has created Christ to be exactly like God, and to share His eternal Love and joy in a state of unencumbered, boundless and unimaginable ecstasy.

Unlike the concrete, specific world you appear to be in now, this constant and enthralling state of awareness is completely abstract, eternal, unchanging and united. Christ then extends Itself by creating new Creations, or simultaneous extensions of the whole, which are also exactly the same in their perfect oneness with God and Christ. Thus Christ, like God, also creates — because It is exactly the same as God. These extensions do not go inward or outward, because in Heaven there is no concept of space; there is only everywhere. The result of all this is the endless sharing of perfect Love, which is beyond understanding.

Then something appears to happen which, as in a dream, doesn't *really* happen — it just appears to. For just an instant, for just one, inconsequential fraction of a nanosecond, a very small aspect of Christ appears to have an idea that is not shared by God. It's kind of a "What if?" idea. It's like an innocent wondering in the form of a question — which unfortunately is followed by an apparent answer. The question, if it could be put into words was, "What would it be like if I were to go off and play on my own?" Like a naïve child playing with matches who burns down the house, you would have been much happier *not* to find out the answer to that question — for your state of innocence is about to be seemingly replaced by a state of fear and the erroneous, vicious defenses that this condition appears to require.

Because your idea is not of God, He does *not* respond to it. To respond to it would be to give it reality. If God Himself were to acknowledge anything *except* the idea of perfect oneness, then there would no longer *be* perfect oneness. There would no longer be a perfect state of Heaven for you to return *to*. As we will see, you never really left anyway. You're still there, but you have entered into a nightmare state of illusion. While you have traveled only in dreams,[6] God and Christ, Who are always One, have continued as they always did and always will — completely unaffected by what J refers to in his Course as the "tiny, mad idea..."[7] of separation.

In this cosmic instant of seeming individuality — and no matter how attractive you may think individuality is, it is nothing but separation — there seems to be a tiny aspect of Christ that is now aware of something else. That is duality. Now, instead of oneness, you have twoness. Before, there was the perfect oneness of Heaven and nothing else. That is non-duality, or non-twoness. That is still reality. There is not *really* more than one thing, but now something different seems to be going on for you. There seems to be God *and* something else. That is the illusion of duality, and the world of multiplicity and the endless subjects and objects you perceive in it are merely symbolic of separation. While you may still try to create, you cannot really create without the power of God, so everything you make eventually falls apart.

Each time a baby appears to be born into this world, it is merely reliving the time when it seemed to leave its perfect environment in God — where all was nirvana and it was completely taken care of and provided for — and then suddenly found itself slapped in the face by a seeming reality that was a living hell by comparison. You may think of birth as a miracle, but babies don't come into this world smiling, do they?

GARY: They come in crying and screaming.

ARTEN: Yes. The mind that is reliving the seeming separation has actually fallen asleep and is dreaming an idle, insignificant dream, or nightmare, because anything that seemed to be apart from Heaven would have to be symbolic of an opposite to Heaven. It would thus seem to include opposite characteristics. Once again, let's not get too far ahead of ourselves. We still have some explaining to do about your devolvement from a seemingly separate mind into a universe of bodies, and why it feels so real to you and appears to be.

GARY: There's no doubt we *believe* we're experiencing reality here.

ARTEN: Absolutely. You must be shown the way out of this experience. Your asleep-at-the-wheel mind doesn't know it, but it's going to wake up in the equivalent of a cosmic instant. That is because the Voice for God and Heaven, which we will refer to as the Holy Spirit, is still with you to remind you of the truth and call you to return.[8] This fail-safe memory of what you really are can never be lost, making an awakening to the reality of Heaven completely inevitable.

However, this memory can be seemingly delayed by unwise choices in the dream. Unwise choices have been made by you all along. You have the power to choose the memory and strength of God *or* something else instead, and if you really examine your thoughts you will find that you are usually choosing something else instead. That is what the part of your mind that chooses did immediately after the seeming separation. Out of shock, fear and confusion it made a series of unwise choices that resulted in you appearing to be here. You still don't realize that given the awesome power of the mind, certain choices made by you could end the seeming separation — and could have at any time. That doesn't mean that it's going to be easy at this point, but it *does* mean that you are capable of accomplishing it — with some help.

Make no mistake; in order to really accept God's helper, the Holy Spirit, you must begin to trust God. You cannot trust Him until you recognize that it is not Him, but you, who is responsible for your experiences. You will feel guilty until you understand that this world is not real, and that nothing has really happened. That doesn't mean you shouldn't act responsibly in the illusion. It means you must understand certain things in order to apply the true forgiveness that enables the Holy Spirit to help you the most.

God could not have created this world. It would not be in His nature. He is not cruel, and as J points out to you,

If this were the real world, God *would* be cruel. For no Father could subject His children to this as the price of salvation and *be* loving.[9]

Happily, this is not the real world, and God is not cruel. That's why we want to emphasize a vital point for students of the coming millennium, even if you think we stress it too often. Everything just described that was not the perfect oneness of Heaven, and anything that has appeared to happen since then, has absolutely nothing to do with God. The idea of separation, as well as your subsequent decisions, are things that God is totally unconcerned about. The events in a dream are of no consequence, simply because they are not really happening. Although it appears to you to be very real and often terrible, your universe is nothing but idle, miscreated thought — and energy is nothing but projected thought. I believe we have also made it clear that matter is just a different form of energy. Being without the power of God, all your mind can do is seemingly divide and subdivide and then attempt to glorify the result.

Yet to review, you are really still safe in Heaven, and because what you are seeing is not true, you are not really able to hurt yourself — even if you dream you are being hurt or even killed. In fact, you are able to awaken and continue with the perfect oneness of Heaven exactly as you did before. But your mind must be trained to be dominated by the thoughts of the Holy Spirit instead of your ego. This requires the ability to make decisions that reflect the Holy Spirit's thought system instead of your own. So we *must* make an enormous and firm distinction between *A Course in Miracles* and virtually every other spiritual thought system in existence — from pre-historic, to ancient Egyptian, to Lao Tzu, to aspects of Hinduism, to Zoroastrianism, to The Old Testament, to the Koran, to the New Testament and to other, neo-dualistic systems. Every one of them is a system of duality that has some kind of a Source — usually God or Gods — being the creator in some way of that which is not itself, and then responding to it or interacting with it.

Here in the 1990s, one of the most popular spiritual books ever written will have God Himself saying that He created fear! That is an inaccuracy so major we cannot stress too much how completely false it is. God does not create anything that is not the perfect oneness of Heaven. As J puts it very early in his Course when describing *anything* that doesn't reflect the thought system of the Holy Spirit,

Everything else is your own nightmare, and does not exist.[10]

And later on,

You are at home in God, dreaming of exile but perfectly capable of awakening to reality.[11]

Those are statements of non-duality. They are designed to save you time, and there are several thousand more like them in the Course just in case you don't hear J the first time — although it's apparent that even several thousand are not enough for many of your fellow students.

GARY: Is that because we're unconsciously afraid of its message?

PURSAH: Yes. It's not because of a lack of intelligence, but because of an abundance of unconscious resistance. We need you to help pass along some of the things people *don't* want to hear — the vital things that are being ignored by so many. It's a dirty job, Gary, but somebody has to do it. We're not calling on you to judge or attack other teachers or argue with people, because forgiveness and arguing are mutually exclusive, and forgiveness is *always* the way. But the world isn't all sweetness and light, and when it comes to your writing, staying in line with everyone else isn't what's needed from you. By having you emphasize that the Course is a self-study discipline, people are more likely to check it out for themselves and give the ideas a chance.

> *Forgiveness and arguing are mutually exclusive, and forgiveness is always the way.*

Don't hold anything back. Anybody can write what people already believe, but if you're going to pass along our words then what is needed is a willingness to say some things that people *don't* already believe. However, if you'll faithfully give our message then I promise that when we leave you in the end it will be on the most positive of notes. You will have learned about *true* joining, not with people on the level of bodies, but on the level of the mind — which is beyond all forms.

GARY: I take it there are important reasons why you keep pointing out the distinctions between duality and non-duality, and why you champion the real meaning of the Course?

PURSAH: Yes. It has to do with the laws of the mind and how true forgiveness works. Gary, the reason for understanding the Course is not merely for an intellectual comprehension! That plus a dollar will get you a cup of coffee. The reason it will be extraordinarily helpful for you to understand J's Course is so you can better *apply* it to the problems and situations that confront you in your alleged daily existence. It is the application of true forgiveness, along with J or the Holy Spirit, that will lead you to genuine happiness, peace — and eventually Heaven.

GARY: All right. I don't want to seem stupid, but to make sure I understand: You're saying the Course is purely non-dualistic, meaning that of the two *seeming* worlds, the world of God and the world of man, only the world of God is true and He doesn't interact with the false world — but the Holy Spirit is here to guide us home. When the Course makes statements about God weeping for His children and stuff like that, you have to take it symbolically as the Holy Spirit wanting us to choose His Voice instead of the ego's?

PURSAH: Exactly. Very good. You're not stupid, Gary — although your ego would like for you to be. The ego's entire world is a stupid idea, because it's based on a stupid decision. You just said something important, something that's very much in harmony with the right way of looking at the Course. Although you'd never know it by the way most people write and speak about the Course today, in the whole seven years Helen was scribing the Course, and during the eight years she lived after that, it never *once* occurred to her, or Ken — who was her best friend during those years, and whose tapes you should break down and listen to — that there could *possibly* be any other interpretation of the Course. But give the world a few years to screw up J's message and it's a wonder to behold. So let's continue our mission so you can hear the Course's explanation of what was really behind the creation, or more accurately, miscreation of your universe and the making of bodies.

ARTEN: We've already pointed out that in the beginning, a small aspect of the Christ mind...

GARY: Should I spell Christ mind with a big M in our book?

ARTEN: Don't worry about the details too much. The Course uses a capital M when talking about the Christ mind, but we're talking about the separation here, so you can use a small m or a big M if you want. You've started writing our book?

GARY: Not really. I'm still trying to think of a title for it.

ARTEN: Any ideas?

GARY: So far, it's between "Love is Letting Go of Beer" and "A Return To Beer."

ARTEN: Keep thinking about it. It's something Pursah said earlier; it'll come back to you.

So this small aspect of Christ has briefly dozed off and is dreaming a dream of separation and individuality. We'll explain the idea of briefly dozing off when we talk about time, which is a trick of the ego. As far as individuality is concerned, that's something else you mistakenly value very highly. Folks around this neck of the woods pride themselves on their so-called rugged individualism. You'll discover the roots of that nonsense shortly. At this point in our story you have the very beginning of consciousness — yet another thing you foolishly value highly. In order to have consciousness you have to have separation. You've got to have more than one thing. You have to have something else to be conscious *of.* This is the beginning of the split mind.

As the Course teaches in no uncertain terms,

Consciousness, the level of perception, was the first split introduced into the mind after the separation, making the mind a perceiver rather than a creator. Consciousness is correctly identified as the domain of the ego.[12]

The Course also says, just before that,

Perception did not exist until the separation introduced degrees, aspects and intervals. Spirit has no levels, and all conflict arises from the concept of levels.[13]

Thus, as mentioned earlier, you should try to remember that energy is not spirit — spirit being your *unalterable*, true reality. Energy, which changes and can be measured, exists within the domain of perception. As J also teaches,

Perception always involves some misuse of mind, because it brings the mind into areas of uncertainty.[14]

There is no uncertainty in Heaven, because there's nothing but everything. But here you have identities. People are born with special relationships immediately — first the ones with their mothers, and soon with their fathers.

GARY: You're making me a little uncomfortable.

ARTEN: Comfort is the goal, not necessarily the means. What is it, buddy?

GARY: Well, I miss my parents and I honor their memory. It feels a little strange to think they don't even exist except in an illusion.

PURSAH: That's understandable. Your parents are, along with spouses and children, the most fundamental of relationships. The Course refers to the relationships that are set up for this world as special relationships.[15] We'll be talking more about that and your resistance to giving up identities — whether yours or those of others — as we proceed. Remember, J loved his parents — Joseph the stonemason and Mary of Sepphoris — but he also loved everyone else the same. Special love is specific; the Holy Spirit loves everyone equally.

GARY: I thought Joseph was a carpenter.

PURSAH: No, but it doesn't matter. Do you believe J would have loved him any less if he was unemployed? The community would have loved him less, but not J. He loved us all — unconditionally.

GARY: Then he would have loved Saint Paul, too — even if his theology wasn't the same.

PURSAH: Of course. Paul, or if you will, Saul of Tarsus, is loved the same by J as the rest of us to this day. I remember I was speaking once in Parthia, which is now Iran, and the crowd tried to engage me in a discussion about various theologies. I told them that for J, it wasn't theology that mattered, but the truth — and the truth was the love of God — which is what J *is*.

Now, if you really *are* love, and not a person, then how can you love one person and not another? It wouldn't be possible. If you did that then you wouldn't *be* love, would you? You'd be something else. Yes, J loved his parents and so should you — but he was not willing to limit them, or anyone else, to false images of themselves. He knew his real home, and theirs, was in Yahweh.

GARY: Where?

PURSAH: Yahweh, E'lo-i, God, Adonai, Elohim, Kyrios — it's all Divine. Words and theology disappear in God. Nobody will be bringing their Bibles or Course books into Heaven with them. The Course is a tool; you use it like a ladder to climb up to where you're going. Once you get there, you throw the ladder away. It's no longer needed.

ARTEN: By the way, we mentioned special love earlier, but there are two kinds of special relationships — special love *and* special hate. We'll eventually explain more about both of them and their purpose — which is really the same — but right now we should continue with our story.

We've already talked about the first division in the mind, and along with it has come consciousness. Because of this, for the first time, you have a conscious *choice* to make. Before that, there was nothing to choose *between*. But now there are two possible responses to this idea of separation. That's what leads to the second division of the mind. We've already said the seemingly separated mind appears to divide and sub-divide. That symbolizes separation. But *all* the divisions are symbolic of the first few. Once you really understand the first ones, you will understand them all as the same, despite appearances to the contrary. You have to remember that after the first division, Heaven is just a memory.

GARY: What do you mean by that?

ARTEN: Consciousness is not of God, so now something *completely different* seems to be happening for you — an experience of individuality. Whenever the mind divides, its new condition *is* reality to it — and its former condition is denied and forgotten. A psychologist would call this repression, except the magnitude of what we are discussing is far beyond what any human could be aware of. However, the dynamic is the same in the sense that what has been repressed is unconscious. Incidentally, the unconscious is not a place — it's a device of the mind. It's still *possible* to remember what's been denied, but without help, it would be highly unlikely for you to remember that which you have dissociated.

Now, the *you* that we and the Course are referring to has nothing to do with you as a human being — it's the part of your mind that makes decisions. Even when you appear to be making a decision here in this world you are not really making it here, because you are not here. In our story this new, seemingly individual mind is going to make its very first decision.

At this point there are only two choices, and there will always be only two choices. There you have the second division of the mind.

> ❧
>
> **There will always be only two choices: your true home with God, and the thought of separation, or individuality.**

Now you appear to have a right mind and a wrong mind, each representing a different choice or a different response to the tiny, mad idea.

One choice is the memory of your true home with God, symbolized in the Course by the Holy Spirit, and the other is the thought of separation from God, or individuality, symbolized in the Course by the ego. J anthropomorphizes the Holy Spirit and the ego in the Course and talks about them as though they are individual entities, but he also makes it clear that

The ego is nothing more than a part of your belief about yourself.[16]

For J, the Course is a work of art, not a science project. It's a complete presentation given on different levels. You have to grant him some artistic license. Much of the Course is presented in Shakespearean blank verse, or iambic pentameter. Do you know why?

GARY: I have not a freakin' idea.

ARTEN: Not only is it beautiful, but it forces you to read the Course more slowly and carefully. Also, it tends to attract long term students who are serious about learning it. Obviously, the Course isn't for everyone. Or as we said before, at least not everyone all at once.

Once again, your mind has two choices to select from; we are now at a critical juncture in the seeming separation. The memory of what you are *is* both the answer to the separation and the principle of the Atonement rolled into one. As the Course teaches about the Holy Spirit,

He came into being with the separation as a protection, inspiring the Atonement principle at the same time.[17]

Obviously, the Course has its own meaning for various terms, including Atonement. As the Text explains, the Holy Spirit has always taught the Atonement.

He tells you to return your whole mind to God, because it has never left Him. If it has never left Him, you need only perceive it as it is to be returned. The full awareness of the Atonement, then, is the recognition that *the separation never occurred*.[18]

If, at the point where we find ourselves in our story, you had chosen to believe the Holy Spirit's interpretation, or response, to the separation instead of the ego's, then your little dream adventure would have been over. The ego had a selfish yet tantalizing response of its own. *If* you continue to believe in the separation, it offers you your own individual identity — separate from God, very special and uniquely important. As J puts it in the Text,

The ego must offer you some sort of reward for maintaining this belief. All it can offer is a sense of temporary existence, which begins with its own beginning and ends with its own ending. It tells you this life is your existence because it is its own.[19]

Of course, you have no idea what you're getting yourself into — and you make another numb choice. This is all new to you, and you're more than willing to give curiosity a chance to kill the cat. You choose with the ego so you can see what it's like to be special and apart. This in turn causes the third division of the mind.

GARY: When you say you, I assume you mean all of us as one.

ARTEN: Yes. I'm not putting you down personally; I'm just trying to help you take responsibility for the power of your mind. Even J was there. He just didn't really believe in it as much as the rest of us, which is the main reason he woke up before the rest of us.

GARY: So the first division in the mind is consciousness, which makes me *think* I'm separate from God, even though I really can't be. It's like being in bed and dreaming at night. I'm still in the bed, but I can't see it. In this separation dream you're talking about, it's the dream that's real for me and Heaven is forgotten. Just like when I dream at night, it's what's in the dream that I experience and react to, and where I really am is completely out of my awareness.

With the second division, I notice two ways of interpreting what's going on — one being the Holy Spirit, which is really my true Self, and the other being the ego, which speaks for separation and an individual self. Now there are two parts to the mind. I take it the third division was caused when I chose the ego?

ARTEN: Yes, but remember, once you make a choice at this level, then that's your new condition, and your old condition is completely forgotten — walled off in the mind. Once you choose the ego and cause the third division, it's the Holy Spirit that's just a memory. You are now totally identified with the ego. *However,* being holographic by the grace of God, even when the mind seems to divide, each part still maintains the characteristics of the whole — so you can't ever really be lost. Both the ego *and* the Holy Spirit are still to be found in every mind; it's just that the Holy Spirit is being drowned out by the ego's voice because that's what you chose to listen to — and what you really are has been pushed out of your awareness. We said before that you may have forgotten the truth, but it's still there — buried in your mind.

PURSAH: You have no idea how powerful the mind is, my brother. At the level we're talking about, still the metaphysical level, the entire tempest in a teacup you call the universe is about to be miscreated by just a few decisions on your part. The eventual result will be an alleged you who is now totally unaware of the real power that is available to you and instead, is virtually mindless and seemingly stuck in a body.

GARY: Does this answer the age-old question: If God is really all powerful, then could He create a rock that's so heavy He could not lift it?

ARTEN: Actually, it does answer that question about God — and the answer is no.

GARY: Why?

ARTEN: Because He's not an idiot.

GARY: And I am?

ARTEN: No, but you're having a dream that you are — and now you're starting to wake up. Getting back to the subject, listen to a little of what the Course has to say about the time you first substituted illusion for truth.

> You do not realize the magnitude of that one error. It was so vast and so completely incredible that from it a world of total unreality *had* to emerge. What else could come of it? Its fragmented aspects are fearful enough, as you begin to look at them. But nothing you have seen begins to show you the enormity of the original error, which seemed to cast you out of Heaven, to shatter knowledge into meaningless bits of disunited perceptions, and to force you to make further substitutions.[20]

GARY: Yeah, but don't you have the same problem with this story as with the Genesis story and God supposedly doing some of the things He did? I mean, why the hell would a part of Christ ever want to separate from God if everything was completely perfect?

ARTEN: First of all, in the Genesis story, God is responsible for the world you see and you are an effect instead of the cause. In the Course, *you* are responsible for the world you see and not a victim of it.[21] God and Christ are *still* perfect, as is Heaven, and the "you" that you *think* is in this world needs to learn, by listening to the Holy Spirit, how to awaken from your dream.

Now let's take a look at your other question. Is it really a question, or is it a statement? Aren't you saying that the separation from God really occurred? You can't ask how the separation could have happened unless you believe it did. Yet we have already said the principle of the Atonement is that it *didn't*. Then you ask how Christ could have possibly chosen with the ego when we have already said it wasn't Christ, but an illusory consciousness that appeared to do so. On top of that, you question how this stupid choice could have been made when here you are, making it again right now.

GARY: You're a smart ass, you know that?

ARTEN: Only for teaching purposes. Gary, we love you. I'll tell you, you will *never* get an answer within the ego framework to that kind of a question that will satisfy you *intellectually.* As the Course says,

> **The ego's voice is an hallucination. You cannot expect it to say "I am not real." Yet you are not asked to dispel your hallucinations alone.**[22]

The time will come when the answer to your question will be found outside the intellect, completely outside of the ego's system, and instead within the *experience* that you are still at home in God — which corrects the mistaken experience that you are not. As J puts it,

> **Against this sense of temporary existence spirit offers you the knowledge of permanence and unshakable being. No one who has experienced the revelation of this can ever fully believe in the ego again. How can its meager offering to you prevail against the glorious gift of God?**[23]

We'll talk more later about what revelation really is, as opposed to what most people think it is.

GARY: Just to make sure I'm picking this up, it's like when I wake up from a dream at night and I see that I never really left the bed. When I wake up from this dream of separation from God, I'll see that I never really left Heaven.

ARTEN: Yes, but you won't be seeing with the body's eyes. That's why in place of words like *consciousness,* which implies separation and is of the ego, the Course uses more abstract words like *awareness* when describing enlightenment — which we'll get to.

GARY: Even in the Introduction, it talks about removing the blocks to the awareness of love's presence, which is your natural inheritance.[24]

ARTEN: That's right, but before we try to get you back up the ladder, we have to finish our little synopsis of how you climbed down. It's important. Right now, the world has its head planted firmly up its butt looking for the light. There isn't any light up there, Gary. Your choice for the ego instead of the Holy Spirit, resulting in the third division of the mind, has made the Voice for God almost completely inaudible to you. Meanwhile, the ego is giving you its own version of what's happening — and here's where things really start to get nasty.

GARY: I'm sorry Arten, but I need to mention just one thing before we go on, or else I won't be able to concentrate.

ARTEN: I know. Make it fast, or we may have to bring out the thumbscrew.

GARY: I have a good memory, but I didn't know if I'd be able to remember our conversations well enough for our book, so...

Your choice for the ego instead of the Holy Spirit has made the Voice for God almost inaudible to you.

PURSAH: We know, Gary. You've been taping us all along — ever since the second visit. We told you not to tape us merely to prove to people that we appeared, but we didn't mean you couldn't tape us for your own personal use. We knew all along, even when you asked us if it would be a good idea, despite the fact that you were already taping us. All your mistakes are overlooked by those who judge truly with the Holy Spirit. We understood you needed to know you weren't going crazy, and that we were here talking to you for real — or at least as real as anything else. You wanted to know that you were really hearing our voices by listening to them again later on. No big deal. We'll explain more eventually about our bodies and our voices and what they really are. This will also explain the appearances by the Virgin Mary, and even angels.

ARTEN: Did you really think we didn't know you turn on that silly voice-actuated tape recorder in your stereo system every single time you come into this room, just in case we show up? Really, Gary! From now on, just turn it on when we get here.

GARY: I figured you probably didn't mind when you didn't say anything about it, but I wanted to be sure. How about if I trash the tapes when the book is done? That way I won't be tempted to use them for anything except the writing.

PURSAH: It's your property, but that's a good idea. The quality isn't anything to write to the record companies about anyway. It will be one less thing for you to think about.

ARTEN: So — in our story, you've chosen with the ego, and now you're identified with it. The first division made the awareness of your perfect oneness with God just a memory. The second division brought two parts to the mind. The third division has made the Holy Spirit just a memory, and the ego now has your attention. You look to *it* to explain to you what's going on, and the ego has a message for you. The message is this: *You'd better get the hell out of here, pal.* Then it proceeds to give you some reasons. In your confused state of mind, these reasons sound pretty damn convincing in their logic.

"Don't you know what you've done?"— the ego asks in our metaphorical story — "You've separated yourself from God! You've sinned against Him big time. You're in for it now. You've taken paradise — everything He gave you — and thrown it right in His face and said, 'Who the hell needs you?' You've attacked Him! You're dead. You haven't got a snowball's chance in hell against Him — He's awesome and you're nothing. You've ruined everything; you're so guilty. If you don't haul ass out of here right now, it's gonna be worse than death!"

"Oh my God," you think in response to the ego. "What have I done? You're right — I've ruined everything and attacked Heaven! But where can I go? What can I do? I can run, but I can't hide. There's no place I can hide from God Himself!"

"Well, that's not exactly true," says the ego, "because I'm here to help you. I'm your friend — and I have an idea. I have somewhere we can go together. You can be your own boss and not have to face God at all. You'll never see Him. He won't even be able to get into this place!"

"Really?" you ask. "That sounds pretty damn good to me. Let's go!"

"All right," says the ego. "Do exactly as I say."

PURSAH: Of course everything the ego is saying about God and what's happened is not true, for the ego is about as sane as Caligula Caesar. God would never do anything except love you. It's here that you need to know just a little bit more about how the mind works.

Because of the power of the mind, you need to appreciate the power of your *belief.* It was your belief in the idea you could be separate from God — your taking it seriously — that gave it so much seeming power and realism. As the Course says,

Freedom from illusions lies only in not believing them.[25]

You also have to realize that because you made duality by deciding to be a perceiver, everything you perceive will include characteristics that appear to be the *opposite* of that which you have apparently separated from. What you have seemingly separated from — Heaven — has one set of characteristics, and what you are perceiving as your reality has an opposite set of characteristics.

Heaven, although it is beyond all words, has these kinds of characteristics: It is perfect, formless, changeless, abstract, eternal, innocent, whole, abundant, complete Love. It is reality; it is Life. God and Christ and Christ's Creations are perfect oneness. There is nothing else. This is the domain of God's Will — the Knowledge of the Father. To describe the experience of your awareness of this perfect oneness is not really possible, but I assure you that you will *know* it when you have a temporary experience of it. It's not quite like *anything* else you are familiar with.

The domain of perception, on the other hand, being Heaven's seeming opposite, includes very different characteristics. Keeping in mind we are still speaking on a metaphysical level here, these attributes include: individuality, form, shapes, specifics, changes, time, separation, division, illusion, wishes, scarcity and death. *That's* why in the Book of Genesis 2:16-17, which comes right out of the writer's unconscious mind, it says, "You may freely eat of every tree of the garden; but of the tree of the knowledge of good and evil you shall not eat, for in the day that you eat of it you shall die." Good and evil are opposites, and once you have a seeming opposite to Heaven, you have death. But, as the Course consistently says in a thousand different ways, beginning right in its Introduction, "....what is all-encompassing can have no opposite."[26] Are you starting to get what that means?

GARY: Yeah, I think I'm beginning to get the magnitude of it. When is the artist formerly known as Christ gonna snap out of his coma so I can get back to the creation orgasm?

PURSAH: That's coming. We still haven't finished telling you how you appeared to get *here.*

Once you've chosen to listen to the ego's temptations to be a separate individual, your belief in the reality of the separation begins to cause some very serious problems for you. God now seems to be outside of you, and *everything* you experience tells you that you've separated yourself from Him. That's a problem you still have this very second, even though it's unconscious to you. Practically *all* of your mind is unconscious to you, just like almost all of an iceberg is underneath the surface of the water. As long as you believe in the reality of the physical universe Gary, then everything you perceive will be a constant, unconscious reminder to you that you've committed the act of separating yourself from God. As you'll see, that's an important point.

> ❦
>
> **Practically all of your mind is unconscious to you, just like almost all of an iceberg is underneath the surface of the water.**

ARTEN: Getting back to our little miscreation extravaganza, the ego-voice in your mind has told you some things about your condition and also about God that simply aren't true. You've bought it partly because you like the idea of being an individual with a seemingly separate will — even though that's not really possible. By taking the separation and the ego's voice *seriously,* that translates within your seemingly separated mind as a *sin against God.* Now if you've sinned, that means you're *guilty,* and on this metaphysical level you feel it — even though on the level of the world you will not always feel it. Being the guilty bastard you think you are, it means you think you're going to be punished, big time. Even on the level of this world, a psychologist would explain to you that guilt unconsciously demands punishment — and if you really think about that, it will explain a lot. On the metaphysical level we're talking about how you sincerely believe that you're about to be attacked and punished by God Himself!

The anticipation of this fate-worse-than-death kind of punishment from God creates *fear* — a fear so terrible you can't even comprehend it. Yet you've been running away from it for what seems like billions of years. So *now* we're at a point where we can tell you why your universe, your world and your body were made by the mind in the first place. They were really all made simultaneously, even though in a linear dream, things seem to happen separately.

There is no other spiritual discipline that understands and explains the motivation behind the making of this world, the same motivation that runs it today. That motivation is fear, always ultimately traceable to the fear of God.[27] The trans-temporal, non-spatial, seemingly separated mind is in a paralyzing state of fear because of a punishment you believe is coming from God. So the ego convinces you that you need a *defense,* without bothering to mention that the defense it offers is designed to insure *its* own survival through your individuality. In fact, if you look at the last four syllables of the word *individuality*, you will see that they spell *duality.* That's not just a semantic accident.

The ego's voice speaks to you as though it's your friend and is watching out for *your* best interests. You'll recall we've already said the ego has convinced you that God is going to get you and you'd better run for it to a place where you'll be safe. That place is this universe. As far as the ego is concerned, the best defense is a good offense. In fact, defense and offense are two sides of the same coin. In discussing how some of these concepts relate to each other, the Course teaches,

> The ego is the part of the mind that believes in division. How could part of God detach itself without believing it is attacking Him? We spoke before of the authority problem as based on the concept of usurping God's power. The ego believes that this is what you did because it believes that it *is* you. If you identify with the ego, you must perceive yourself as guilty. Whenever you respond to your ego you will experience guilt, and you will fear punishment. The ego is quite literally a fearful thought. However ridiculous the idea of attacking God may be to the sane mind, never forget that the ego is not sane. It represents a delusional system, and speaks for it. Listening to the ego's voice means that you believe it is possible to attack God, and that a part of Him has been torn away by you. Fear of retaliation from

without follows, because the severity of the guilt is so acute that it must be projected.[28]

So, believing that the separation has actually happened, and given your fear of God's punishment and retaliation that you desperately think you need to defend yourself against, you've already developed — by listening to the ego — a thought system that says you've sinned, you're guilty, and God's inevitable punishment requires a defense. You feel completely vulnerable, and the ego has told you it has an idea — a place you can go where God will never be able to find you. In your confused state, you are now a follower of the ego instead of God's Will, and you listen to the ego's brilliant but twisted idea to make you safe from that which you no longer remember is actually your own true reality — but which you now live in mortal fear of instead.

GARY: Just a second. I have one more quick question.

ARTEN: O.K., but I'm already visualizing duct tape over your mouth.

GARY: Are you going to tell me where all of these quotations are in the Course, since from what you said before, I assume I'll have to note them all?

PURSAH: Actually, no. We want you to find them yourself.

GARY: The Course has almost thirteen hundred pages! That sounds like work — which I'm generally opposed to, as a matter of principle.

PURSAH: Just think of it as studying. Remember, this message is intended for *you*. Learn it — then pass it along. Besides, the real work hasn't even started yet. That's in the application. As we've already asked you, how can you apply what you haven't learned?

ARTEN: So *now* the instant has finally arrived in our spectacular revue where the ego is about to give you its grand answer to your nightmarish but imagined predicament.

The awesome magnitude of the painful shame and acute guilt in your mind, resulting from what you *believe* you've done, appear to require an immediate and complete escape. So you *join* with the ego, and then the incomprehensible power of your mind to make illusions as a perceiver — rather than make spirit as a creator — causes the method of your escape to become manifest. At this point the ego, which you are now totally identified with, uses the ingenious but illusory method of projection to hurl the thought of separation *out* of your mind, and you — or at least the part of you that seems to have a consciousness — appears to be projected right along with it. This instantly causes what is popularly referred to as the Big Bang, or the creation of the universe. Now you appear to be *in* the universe, while you do not realize that you are actually quite literally *out* of your mind.

Now, the enemy you live in terror of, God, no longer seems to be in the mind with you — where you thought you wouldn't have had a chance against Him. Instead God, and for that matter everything else, is now apparently completely outside of you. The source of your problems, *including* your guilt, are now someplace else — even though we've already made it clear that there can't possibly *be* anyplace else. The making of the cosmos is your protection from God, your ingenious hiding place. At the same time, the universe itself becomes the ultimate scapegoat.

Now, both the cause and the blame for your problem of separation, not to mention the blame for *all* of your new, illusory replacement problems, can be found — if you look hard enough along with the ego — somewhere outside of you. Indeed, a *whole new level* has been made in which the thought system of sin, guilt, fear, attack and defense can be acted out in such a way as to protect your seemingly separated mind, which you presently think of as your soul, from your terrible, yet completely *unconscious* guilt and fear. To illustrate just how much the ego resists looking at this guilt in the mind, all you need to do is consider that despite the fact that *A Course in Miracles* is very much *about* the healing of this unconscious guilt, most of the teachers of the Course never even mention it.

Now, as the crowning achievement in its grand scheme, the ego makes — drum roll, please — the *body*. This allows the ego to permit into your awareness, almost exclusively, only those things which testify to the reality of its cherished illusion. Yet the body itself is just another *part* of the illusion, and to ask *it* to explain the illusion to you is no different than asking the illusion to explain itself — and of course the ego is more than happy to furnish you with its answers.

This universe, the world and your body give form to a defense structure in which you hide from your imagined sin, guilt and the resulting fear of God's vengeance. The ego has a method firmly in place to deal with this now-unconscious sin, guilt and fear — by projecting it onto others.

Once we explain to you, during our next visit, how this thought system is acted out on the level of this world, you'll be able to clearly observe it in action everywhere — in all of your personal relationships, the relationships of others, in international relationships, in politics and other professions, and anywhere else you care to look. Then you'll begin to see for yourself that the message of the Course is true. In discussing this, we're going to be telling you some things that are not for the squeamish. The ego isn't pretty. After that, we can start to have some fun.

When you're capable of observing the ego's thought system in action — which is certainly interesting enough to begin with — then we'll be able to explain to you how you can help the Holy Spirit turn the tables on the ego, hasten your own salvation at the same time, and eventually break the cycle of birth and death.

GARY: So I keep reincarnating because of this unconscious guilt and fear that's in my mind. You're saying if the guilt was healed, and I didn't have this hidden fear, then I wouldn't have any need for a body, the world, or even the universe.

ARTEN: Excellent. I knew you weren't a dumb bastard. I tried to tell J, but he wouldn't listen. Just kidding. After our next appearance, our visits to you will get shorter and sweeter. In order to really work with J or the Holy Spirit you must be able to *observe* the ego's thought system in action — which is the same thought system you've subscribed to for eons without being aware of it. You have to be willing to *look* at it with the Holy Spirit or J as your teacher.

As J puts it in the Course,

No one can escape from illusions unless he looks at them, for not looking is the way they are protected. There is no need to shrink from illusions, for they cannot be dangerous. We are ready to look more closely at the ego's thought system because together we have the lamp that will dispel

it, and since you realize you do not want it, you must be ready. Let us be very calm in doing this, for we are merely looking honestly for truth.[29]

PURSAH: All of the ego ideas we've talked about this time, and will discuss the next time, must be brought to the truth — which *is* J or the Holy Spirit — where you can surrender them in exchange for the Atonement. These thoughts have been very well hidden in your unconscious since the seeming separation. You don't know it, but you're very afraid of what you've forgotten or dissociated. *That's* why you don't really want to look at these things. Because of your hidden fear, you'll have tremendous *resistance* to approaching your unconscious. As the Course points out in the Text,

> *You're very afraid of what you've forgotten or dissociated. You'll have tremendous resistance to approaching your unconscious.*

Knowledge must precede dissociation, so that dissociation is nothing more than a decision to forget. What has been forgotten then appears to be fearful, but only because the dissociation is an attack on truth.[30]

And also in the Text,

Can you be separated from your identification and be at peace? Dissociation is not a solution; it is a delusion. The delusional believe that truth will assail them, and they do not recognize it is because they prefer the delusion. Judging truth as something they do not want, they perceive their illusions which block knowledge.[31]

GARY: Talking about the body made me think of the human body, but from what you've said, I assume the ego must have made all bodies — including my dog, Nupey and every other animal. If that's true, and if everything happened all at once anyway, then doesn't that mean evolution is also an illusion, kind of a smokescreen?

PURSAH: Congratulations to the one who knows that. Your generation worships evolution, thinking that you're on the way to creating some kind of new, hot consciousness. You value evolution almost as much as you value energy. What is called evolution was merely the ego separating all at once by seemingly dividing and sub-dividing cells over and over again in order to make bodies and brains that appear to be more *complex* — and thus more impressive. Yet *all* bodies are the same in their unreality.

Everything in your universe is set up to convince you of the uniqueness and reality of your body, and thus the validity of the ego's entire system. That's why the ego is always trying to make it look like God made the world, and have you continue to fear Him while also having Him be the alleged cause of your life. Related to the fact that the ego wanted to take over God's job anyway, it *wants* you to spiritualize bodies, like J's — even though it was meaningless to J — and it craves for you to spiritualize different places and objects. This makes some of them more special than others and thus *all* of them real. If God made the world and its bodies then *you* must be real. This legitimizes your alleged individual existence, and it also keeps you running away from your one real problem. Most importantly, it also keeps your attention away from the one real *Answer* to your problem — the Holy Spirit, who is *not* in the world but in your mind.

GARY: So the making of the universe was the fourth division of the mind, and that caused the Big Bang and what then appeared to be an almost infinite number of splits — or the world of multiplicity. As long as I believe in the reality of this universe then I will, by definition, also believe *unconsciously* that I'm separate from God, and that I'm one guilty son of a bitch.

ARTEN: Yes. You have a way with words, my brother. Everything you see, from the time you dream that you're born until the time you dream you die, and anything you dream in between, is all symbolic of the one thought that you have separated yourself from God. Heaven seems to have been completely shattered into an endless number of pieces and replaced by its opposite. Yet the history of the universe — past and future — is simply a script[32] that was written by the ego — the tale composed and glorified by mondo idiot —

which plays out, in every conceivable way, the act of separation.

GARY: What about joining on this level? People do get married; that's not separation. At least not right away.

ARTEN: You answered your own question. In this world, death makes separation inevitable. It's not a question of if — it's a question of when and how. Bodies cannot really join, although you've certainly tried, but minds *can* join — and they can join forever. The ego doesn't want you to focus on the mind. It wants you to focus on the body as your reality. Happily, the Holy Spirit also has a script,[33] and you can switch over to it anytime you want. The Holy Spirit's script is consistent. As the Course says,

Truth does not vacillate; it is always true.[34]

PURSAH: Once you begin practicing forgiveness with J, or the Holy Spirit, or both, or whoever you want to practice forgiveness with — although I would recommend that you do *not* do it alone — then you'll begin to realize that the Course can be very practical. It's written on two different levels — the metaphysical level we just talked about, and the level of the world, which we'll get into next time. We've already promised that we would *not* be giving you mere theories, and we've already pointed out that knowing this world is an illusion is not enough by itself. Without its practical method of forgiveness, the Course would be nothing but a beautiful and useless book — fuel for debate and the games of the ego. Fortunately, as J says in the Introduction to the Clarification Of Terms,

This is not a course in philosophical speculation, nor is it concerned with precise terminology. It is concerned only with Atonement, or the correction of perception. The means of the Atonement is forgiveness.[35]

You will find that the Course's idea of forgiveness is unique, and designed to undo the ego — not by attack, but through the power of choice. Your inner peace and the strength of Christ will be there, by forgiving the things you see right in front of you. They are your perfect opportunities that, when taken advantage of, will help the Holy

Spirit and the laws of the mind to lead you back to Heaven. While it will not always be easy, there will be many welcome times along your way when you will know that the Course is working for you. Until now, you've been locked into the script that repeatedly acts out the thought system of the ego. It's time for you to break free and start to follow a new script — the one that will take you home!

You might want to start writing, so you can share our message. Don't forget to have fun, even if you are grammatically challenged. How about this idea: Why don't you present our story in the form of a dialogue? That way you can copy most of it right off of your tapes, and you can use those notes you take. Our book would be almost done when we stop visiting you — if you get going and do it. Try it. It'll be fun.

GARY: Yeah, but what if I run out of crayons?

PURSAH: Must we have *all* the answers? Ask J for guidance!

ARTEN: While you're at it, remember this: the ego secretly *wants* you to be guilty by thinking you have separated yourself from God, but it's not true — despite all appearances and experiences to the contrary. We'll tell you more about how the ego seeks to accomplish its deceptions the next time we drop in. Between now and then, try to be honest with yourself when you consider the true nature of the universe and this world. J is very clear about what most people erroneously make out to be some kind of a beautiful, Divine Creation of God. To give you just one of many examples, in the Text he says of this world of false idols,

An idol is established by belief, and when it is withdrawn the idol "dies." This is the anti-Christ; the strange idea there is a power past omnipotence, a place beyond the infinite, a time transcending the eternal. Here the world of idols has been set by the idea this power and place and time are given form, and shape the world where the impossible has happened. Here the deathless come to die, the all-encompassing to suffer loss, the timeless to be made the slaves of time. Here does the changeless change; the peace of God, forever given to all living things, give way to chaos. And the Son of God, as perfect, sinless and as loving as his Father, come to hate a little while; to suffer pain and finally to die.[36]

GARY: I take it that was his Christmas message.

ARTEN: As you know, J does have some very beautiful things to say in the Course about Christmas and Easter. I commend you for reading the Text on a regular basis. It takes time for it to sink in, but it's good that you do it. Most students of the Course stick pretty much to the Workbook and the Manual For Teachers, which are important. But as Pursah pointed out earlier, they don't read the Text very often — except when they're taking turns reading it at a study group. They're really missing the heart of the Course by neglecting the Text.

PURSAH: I'm going to give you two final suggestions about your writing, and then we won't mention it too much — unless you ask us. From now on, that subject should usually be between you and the Holy Spirit. I want you to get used to working with Him. Ask Him what you should do when it comes to *anything* related to our mission. But these are the two things I want to say. First, don't bother describing Arten and I very much. The point is to teach people that they are *not* bodies. If they are not bodies, then our illusory bodies should certainly not be emphasized. The book shouldn't be about us — it should be about what we have to say. Second, you should do your writing completely free of guilt. The book is not your responsibility; it's the Holy Spirit's responsibility.

Now, we'll conclude our comments about the nature of this world, and we emphasize the *nature* of this world rather than the world itself because this dream of a world is not real. J briefly made reference to this world in my Gospel, when he said things such as in saying 40:

A grapevine has been planted outside of the Father, but since it is not strong, it will be pulled up by its roots and shall pass away.

And he said in the passage appearing in the Nag Hammadi version as number 56:

Whoever has come to understand this world has found merely a corpse, and whoever has discovered the corpse, of that one the world is no longer worthy.

And as far as Heaven is concerned, remember saying number 49?

> ❧
>
> *Even though
> the world is just
> as insane as it was
> two thousand years
> ago, it's now in a
> position to learn
> much more.*

Congratulations to those who are alone and chosen, for you shall find the Kingdom of God. For you have come from it, and you shall return there again.

In this saying, such people are alone because they know that there is really only *one* of us. Of course they are not really alone, because they have the Holy Spirit. As pointed out earlier, they are chosen because they choose to listen. The rest of the saying should be self-explanatory based on what we've been talking to you about here.

A Course in Miracles has been given by J in order to show you *how* to return to the Kingdom of Heaven. For as we've already pointed out, the world could only understand so much two thousand years ago. Today, even though the world is just as insane as it was back then, it's in a position to learn much more.

GARY: I guess this really *isn't* the same as anything else, including Christianity.

PURSAH: Not to belabor the point Gary, but Christianity was a continuation of the old scripture in a new form. All you have to do is read Romans, Chapter 1, to see that the future Saint Paul was endorsing the thinking in Leviticus, Chapter 20 for political reasons — in order to try to appease the suspicious James and the Jerusalem sect. Organized religion is politics, buddy. Look at how the Book of Revelation rips off the Book of Daniel. Christianity was the same old thing in a new package — except for the only Son of God being sacrificed and then worshipped routine. J, on the other hand, was and is *not* the same old thing in a new package — and neither is *A Course in Miracles*. A self-study Course does not require an organized religion, and as we said before, J was never interested in starting one.

ARTEN: As we take our illusory leave until the next time, start looking at the world more carefully, with the Holy Spirit, and you will have a very high standard — as high as J had — to help you choose between the Holy Spirit's thought system and that of the ego. As the Course puts it,

> The truth about you is so lofty that nothing unworthy of God is worthy of you. Choose, then, what you want in these terms, and accept nothing that you would not offer to God as wholly fitting for Him.[37]

Goodbye for now, Gary. Remember this with certainty. Whenever you are prepared to choose the Holy Spirit as your Teacher, J will be there with you. If you are not prepared, he will still be there with you. For as he tells you in the Text,

> If you want to be like me I will help you, knowing that we are alike. If you want to be different, I will wait until you change your mind.[38]

Arten and Pursah disappeared, allowing me to quietly consider the implications of our discussion — not the least of which was the fact that I did not really exist, except for my reality in Heaven — and to contemplate the motivation behind a world that appeared to me to be unchanged, but which I would never look at the same way again.

5

The Ego's Plan

Every response to the ego is a call to war, and war does deprive you of peace. Yet in this war there is no opponent.[1]

I WOKE up the next morning at about dawn and opened my eyes. To my surprise, I realized I couldn't see any separate images. All I could make out was what seemed to be a covering, like patches over my eyes. These patches were made of perfect, unblemished white light. This light was even more pure than the untouched snow I'd sometimes see in the field behind my house on mornings after a nor'easter had pounded the hardy Maine landscape.

When I closed my eyes, I saw something different. The beautiful white light that had occupied my field of vision was still there, but now there were large blotches of ugly darkness covering much of the light. Some of the light could still be seen, but a good portion of it — more than half — was obscured by this menacing blackness.

Disconcerted, I opened my eyes, and once again I saw only the beautiful and inviting white light. Upon closing my eyes, the blotches of sickening darkness returned. Not knowing what to make of this — and being the kind of a person who could sleep through a significant earthquake — I went back to my nocturnal dreams, not sure if this experience was a part of those dreams or not.

When I awoke again later, I remembered the experience and sleepily asked J in my mind, "O.K., I give up. What was that?" After trying not to think anything, I had this idea given to me: "Think about it along with me." Soon I realized that the pure white light represented the pure spirit that I really was, and would be again when

I *really* opened my eyes and woke up. The darkness was the deep, unconscious guilt buried in my mind. I reasoned, "This darkness is what needs to be healed by the Holy Spirit on the inside, while I forgive — along with Him — the corresponding symbols of my guilt that appear to be outside myself. When that job's finished, then the light will be all that's left."

With this experience, as well as the previous evening's discussion with Pursah and Arten fresh in my mind, I took a few hours that afternoon to listen to the tapes by Ken Wapnick that I had borrowed from my study group facilitator. At first I wasn't enthralled by Ken's style, which was very much like that of a college professor. After all, Ken was a scholar. As I continued listening, I realized that when it came to explaining the advanced metaphysical principles of the Course — as well as the everyday, practical applications of it — Ken was extremely helpful. Later that night, when I sat down and read a few pages of the Text, I was surprised at how much easier it was to understand *for myself* the exact meaning of quite a few of the lines I was reading.

In the weeks that followed, I also did my best to forgive, especially the times when Karen and I had trouble getting along. The Workbook Lessons helped, and I often used Karen to practice on. It was easy for us to get on each other's nerves, especially when money was tight and we felt under pressure. Karen was a good woman who loved and cared for me. We had been happily married for eleven years, but if there was one fault I would attribute to her, it was that she had more than her share of complaints and grievances. One of the reasons was that she had tried several careers, but had never found one she was happy with or that brought in a lot of money. The situation was exacerbated by the fact that I didn't bring in much cash with my own business.

One night when Karen was bitching and moaning about her job and money situation, I noticed with interest that I wasn't having my usual judgmental reaction to her negative monologue. Instead, I had two distinct and atypical experiences: The first was that Karen was calling out for love, which made her words sound different to me, like an innocent plea for understanding; the second new experience was that what I was seeing wasn't who she really was, but a figure

I had desired to have in my dream so I could blame her for creating a negative atmosphere — which I could then use as a convenient excuse for my own ineffectiveness.

These new experiences initiated a process of shifting the way I looked at Karen, making it more fun to talk with her (and more fun to go to bed). Even though I wouldn't *always* recognize my forgiveness opportunities, I was still learning quickly.

It was four months before I saw my ascended visitors again, and for me they seemed to be very long months. There were times when I felt annoyed, and other times when I felt downright abandoned — although I *did* catch myself making a special relationship out of the whole thing and attempted to forgive it. Sometimes I'd think, "Maybe it's all a test, to see if I can forgive." Then I did forgive — but not what Arten and Pursah were doing or not doing, which would only make an "error" real for myself. Because the world is only a dream, the Course implores its students to forgive their brothers for what they did *not* do,[2] and thus refrain from making error real to ourselves.[3] When I thought about things in those terms I found I was better able to experience myself as the maker of my dream, not the victim of it.

One evening when Karen was at a computer class and I was just about to drink the first of what I hoped would be several beers, Arten and Pursah appeared in my living room for the fifth time. The moment I saw their gentle smiles, I remembered how much I enjoyed their company and the honor of listening to them. I put down my beer, stepped over to the coffee table and picked up my notebook. I also started the tape recorder. In the past, I'd spent many nights taping my band during long performances, so I knew enough to use extra-length tapes so they wouldn't run out while my friends were still speaking. None of us would ever mention these tapes again — until our final get-together.

I surprised myself by being the one to start the discussion.

GARY: Hey guys; it's great to see you! Thanks for coming. I assume you know about my experiences of the last four months, and how grateful I am that you're helping me.

PURSAH: Of course. We're grateful to you as well. It doesn't do any good to teach someone or tell them anything if they're not going to take advantage of it. You, my brother, are using what we tell you — although, as you've already found out, it's not always easy.

As you learn more, you'll realize that we're teaching a purist, non-dualistic interpretation of the truth — the way the Course was meant to be understood. As time goes on, there will be more who teach the Course in this manner, although we're not as polite as most of them will be. Right now there's a tendency for people to borrow from the Course and then do their own thing. There will be many more purists in the future.

GARY: You say you're not as polite as them, so why *aren't* you more polite, my spiritual smart ass?

PURSAH: It takes one to reach one, hotshot. Besides, you're also a messenger, and it's about time somebody put the universe in its place.

There *is* something else you should be aware of, however. Once you have more experience with forgiveness — and we'll discuss an aspect of forgiveness in a minute before we look at the ego more closely — your forgiveness will eventually help you realize that you don't really need your satirical humor as much as you think you do. When *you* no longer need it, then *we'll* no longer need it in order to get through to you. The Holy Spirit speaks to people in many different ways. As they change — and I assure you that if they choose the Holy Spirit as their Teacher, they *do* change back toward reality, by undoing the ego's false changes — then the Holy Spirit can speak to you in a correspondingly appropriate manner. You think we're too hard on you, yet as you'll come to realize, it's really you who are much too hard on yourself. You don't really want to look at your hatred, but we're going to look at some of it during this visit.

You have also indicated that you believe we are too hard on other people. Yet we have repeatedly taught you that there is nobody else. There are no other people. So let's move on, and the time will come when you'll realize that our words are said in order to produce an eventual result — and certainly not to pass judgment on a world that doesn't exist.

ARTEN: Before we unmask your false amigo the ego, let's have you repeat one of the Workbook Lessons. We want to touch on the subject of forgiveness here because we're going to be pointing out some things about the ego that may disturb you a little, and just so you won't get too discouraged, we want to emphasize ahead of time that there are simple — not necessarily easy, unless you're an advanced teacher — but simple ways of undoing the ego.

You've been doing the Workbook for over six months now, and you're doing fine. When things happen fast in your world however, you still sometimes let yourself get away with condemning others. Almost everybody does, including experienced Course students. So we have a question for you. What if you refused to compromise on what you learned from the Course? I'm not just referring to the way you talk about the Course's principles to others. I'm talking about the way you practice what you preach — not that you have to preach anything. What would it look like if you actually followed a Workbook Lesson to the letter, and applied its principles every day the way J did when he appeared to be in a body?

> ❦
> *One of the goals of the Course is to train your mind so the time will come when instead of judging automatically, you will forgive automatically.*

GARY: What Workbook Lesson do you want me to repeat, and follow to the letter?

ARTEN: A very important one. I want you to read the first half of Lesson 68. Read through the third sentence of the fourth paragraph and then stop. You can do the rest of it later. While you're reading it, think of what it would be like if you always did it. Think of what it might do for your peace of mind and your psychological strength if you always did it. I'm not saying that many people always practice it. Most don't. I'm just asking, what if *you* did?

You see, right now your mind judges and condemns *automatically*. Most people's thoughts and behavior are really very predictable, no matter how cool and individualistic they may like to think they are. One of the goals of the Course is to train your mind so the time will come when instead of judging automatically, you will forgive automatically. The benefits to your mind from such a habit are immeasurable.

GARY: It's like one of the miracles principles early in the Text where it says, "miracles are habits?"[5]

ARTEN: Yes. You get so used to thinking the thought system of the Holy Spirit that His true forgiveness becomes second nature to you. So why don't you read that part of the Workbook Lesson. I know you've already done it, but be even more determined to do it this time.

GARY: All right, ascended Teacher guy.

Love holds no grievances.

You who were created by Love like Itself can hold no grievances and know your Self. To hold a grievance is to forget who you are. To hold a grievance is to see yourself as a body. To hold a grievance is to let the ego rule your mind and to condemn the body to death. Perhaps you do not yet fully realize just what holding grievances does to your mind. It seems to split you off from your Source and make you unlike Him. It makes you believe that He is like what you think you have become, for no one can conceive of his Creator as unlike himself.

Shut off from your Self, Which remains aware of Its likeness to Its Creator, your Self seems to sleep, while the part of your mind that weaves illusions in its sleep appears to be awake. Can all this arise from holding grievances? Oh, yes! For he who holds grievances denies he was created by Love, and his Creator has become fearful to him in his dream of hate. Who can dream of hatred and not fear God?

It is as sure that those who hold grievances will redefine God in their own image, as it is certain that God created them like Himself, and defined them as part of Him. It is as sure that those who hold grievances will suffer guilt, as it is certain that those who forgive will find peace. It is as sure that those who hold grievances will forget who they are, as it is certain that those who forgive will remember.

Would you not be willing to relinquish your grievances if you believed all this were so? Perhaps you do not think you can let your grievances go. That, however, is simply a matter of motivation.[6]

PURSAH: Do you remember when you quit smoking?

GARY: Yeah. It was hard after smoking for twelve years, but I had the motivation. I'd watched my parents die from the effects of smoking; they couldn't quit after forty years. So I did it for them *and* for me.

PURSAH: Your motivation for quitting grievances is just as important to your real life as quitting smoking was to your bodily one. All bodies die eventually, but your real life is in Heaven — and you can also achieve peace and joy during your temporary life here. Those are your motivations.

ARTEN: Sometimes those motivations won't seem like enough. Gary, what's going to happen is that when you try to forgive, sometimes you'll be able to. Yet if you're really trying to do this Course, then just as often you're going to come up against a lot of things that you *don't* want to forgive and you *don't* want to give up. That's how your resistance and your hidden, unconscious hatred shows up. Those are the things you're going to have to look at that you don't want to look at. What those things are made of can be understood by comprehending the ego's thought system and plan of attack.

GARY: I gather that the things I won't want to forgive, or even look closely at, are the secret sins and hidden hates[7] that the Course talks about, which are really symbolic of how I hate *myself,* except I've projected them, so they seem to be outside of me. The way to forgive myself and help the Holy Spirit take over my unconscious mind is to uncover and observe these things with Him, and keep on forgiving them. When I say the Holy Spirit will take over my unconscious mind, I remember that He's really me anyway, except He's my higher Self, or Christ, or you could even say the Truth.

I guess the material things and worldly desires I don't want to give up are the false idols that are really there as a substitute for the truth — so I can chase after them or worship them — and also to help convince me that it's all real.

ARTEN: Very good, Gary. That's why the Course wants to help people realize what's in their unconscious — so they can get rid of it. Most people, especially nice, spiritual people, don't know about the murderous thought system that runs this universe, or the hatred that's underneath the surface of their mind. Nor do most of them want to know. Most people just want everything to be hunky-dory.

You can't blame them for wanting peace, but *real* peace is found by undoing the ego, not by covering it over.

PURSAH: That's why you should remember the motivation of peace and joy in *this* life. Wouldn't that be better than suffering? People may think, "I'm not suffering," or "I don't feel guilty." Yet it's there in the mind, waiting to play itself out. Why wait for the inevitable when you can do something about it?

GARY: Because they're afraid and they don't want to.

PURSAH: Because the *ego* doesn't want to. When J asks you if you'd rather be right or happy,[8] he knows you really *don't* want to give up many of your grievances, idols and temptations.

GARY: I can resist anything except temptation.

PURSAH: Yes, but what *is* temptation, really? The Course is not the slightest bit vague about the answer to that question.

Temptation has one lesson it would teach, in all its forms, wherever it occurs. It would persuade the holy Son of God he is a body, born in what must die, unable to escape its frailty, and bound by what it orders him to feel.[9]

Why don't we look at the ego's plan and see how it tries to pull this off? We'll explain a lot more about true forgiveness the next couple of times. We already pointed out during our last visit that a *whole new level* of mind has been made in order for the ego thought system to act itself out through you, without you being aware of it. You're being used, and you don't even know it. You've been a robot. It's time for you to start taking your life back — your real life. In order to do that however, you have to know what you're dealing with.

The ego is quite a piece of work. We said already that the thought of separation from God has been projected seemingly outward from the mind — and you along with it — and that an entire universe that includes your body, as well as all other bodies has been made. By the way, your body seems to be attached to you, but it's actually outside of you[10] like everything else you perceive. Since everything that appears to be outside of you is equally illusory, your body should be regarded as no more real or important to you than anyone else's.

People are like ghosts, except on a seemingly different level. They think their bodies are alive, but they're not. They just see what they want to see. That's why J said, "Let the dead bury their dead." People need help in order to find the truth and be led home. They need the Holy Spirit's Help, but the Holy Spirit also needs *your* help in the form of your forgiveness of the images you see.

Obviously, this doesn't mean the body should be scorned. At the same time, you shouldn't be any more impressed with it than J is — like in this brief passage from the Course.

> *People are like ghosts. They think their bodies are alive, but they're not. They just see what they want to see.*

The body is the ego's idol; the belief in sin made flesh and then projected outward. This produces what seems to be a wall of flesh around the mind, keeping it prisoner in a tiny spot of space and time, beholden unto death, and given but an instant in which to sigh and grieve and die in honor of its master. And this unholy instant seems to be life; an instant of despair, a tiny island of dry sand, bereft of water and set uncertainly upon oblivion.[11]

GARY: The Text says the second of the four obstacles to peace is the belief the body is valuable for what it offers.[12]

ARTEN: Very good. That's directly related to your attraction to guilt and pain.[13] Read "The Obstacles To Peace" very carefully. You've got to understand that you're *attracted* to the whole ego system. You've confused pain with pleasure.[14] You're unconsciously attracted to sin, guilt, fear, pain and suffering. It doesn't make you any different than anyone else, except you'll be one of the people who is aware of it — so you can observe it, forgive it and eventually be free of it. Most people don't know they secretly go after that which will punish them somehow — not in every area of their life, but always in *some* way.

GARY: Like a moth to the flame.

ARTEN: Exactly. You may go to the head of the class.

GARY: I am the class.

ARTEN: Then don't fall behind. Remember, people believe unconsciously that they deserve to be punished for attacking God and
throwing away Heaven, and they play it out in many obvious and
dramatic ways. They also act it out in many not so obvious and
subtle ways — like you being a Red Sox fan.

GARY: Hey! Any team can have a bad century.

ARTEN: Do you have any other questions before we move along?

GARY: Well, I don't know. If I ask another question will there be
any divine retribution?

ARTEN: No — nor has there really ever been any in the history of
the universe.

GARY: Just one thing, then. I was starting to write down some of
what you've said, and even though I know you guys are cool, some
of your statements look a little arrogant. I mean, I can see your faces
and hear your voices and get your attitude. For people who can't,
some of the things you say might seem a little different in print than
in person. Is there anything I can do about that?

ARTEN: Sure. Explain it like you just did. Also, people should
remember that I said we were going to be blunt — but let me make
these two points about what we *haven't* said. We've never said that
A Course in Miracles is the only way to God, and we've never said
that our words are the only way to *A Course in Miracles*. Ours is one
approach. It's for some people — not for everyone. Having said that,
let me remind you that we've come here to help you save time. If you
really want to know God, then we want you to find the way to your
experience of the absolute truth as soon as possible. As touched
upon earlier, the Course teaches that "The miracle minimizes the
need for time."[15] Our goal is to help you understand the miracle.

We'll talk about the Holy Spirit's purpose for the universe later
— giving you no less than the answer to what you call life. As we
said, everyone wants to have meaning and purpose in their lives.
The Course isn't mysterious about what the answer is to that quest.
First, let's look more closely at the ego flame on the level of the
world, and see why the moth is so attracted to it.

PURSAH: We've already established that the universe you see is symbolic of the one thought that you have separated yourself from God —
presented in many forms — and that you feel secretly terrified and

enormously guilty over the separation. On this new level of the world of bodies, the thought of separation has been projected, seemingly outside yourself. Now the substitute causes of sin, the projected responsibility for guilt and the many imagined reasons for fear of any kind can be found somewhere outside of you — and of course, other people see everything as being outside of them.

Once you understand that, it isn't too hard to see the acting-out of separation and the projection of unconscious guilt at work in the world every day. The ego has set up people and groups against each other for its entire script of the history of the universe — guaranteeing the acting-out of separation in individual relationships in some way. Only when everyone has awakened from the dream will the thought of separation be over.

Even in joining, there is still separation in this world. To bring this about, the ego made *special relationships.* As mentioned before, with duality you have special love *and* special hate. Love is now selective rather than all-encompassing, and so it is not really love, but passes for it. When you appear to enter an incarnation, you are immediately part of some kind of family — which means you are *not* a part of other families, economic classes, cultures, ethnic groups and countries. You are already different than others in many ways. You even have competition between families, parts of families and individuals within families.

The special relationships within your family, whether biological, adopted, or in a foster home, may be good or bad, loving or hateful — resulting in either special love or some kind of victimization. Everyone who dreams their way into this world sees themselves as a body from the beginning, and thus a very special body indeed. Thoughts of victim and victimization cannot help but be seen from this point of view, resulting in the *unaware* projection of your sin and guilt — which are hidden by walls of forgetfulness — onto someone or something.

Now all the secret sins and the hidden hates you have about yourself are seen elsewhere; the fact that you are experiencing an unreal dream projection from your own forgotten mind is completely shut off from your awareness. Other people and outside events, or your own body and brain's misguided and thus seemingly guilty actions, are the perceived cause of the endless series of fears and situations — big and small — that you call your life. As J teaches you in the Course, while comparing the dreams you have in bed at night with the dreams you have during the day,

> It is the figures in the dream and what they do that seem to make the dream. You do not realize that you are making them act out for you, for if you did the guilt would not be theirs, and the illusion of satisfaction would be gone. In dreams these features are not obscure. You seem to waken, and the dream is gone. Yet what you fail to recognize is that what caused the dream has not gone with it. Your wish to make another world that is not real remains with you. And what you seem to waken to is but another form of this same world you see in dreams. All your time is spent in dreaming. Your sleeping and your waking dreams have different forms, and that is all. Their content is the same.[16]

GARY: So in the illusion people project their denied guilt onto others. Not only are they unaware that they're doing it, but on top of that — because there's really nobody out there anyway — what they're really doing is recycling the guilt within their *own* unconscious mind, keeping it and the ego intact. I take it that's what J meant when he said, "Judge not, that ye be not judged; for with the judgment you pronounce you will be judged, and the measure you give will be the measure you get." That's true because people are really judging and condemning their own images of themselves. This leads to a continuation as a seemingly guilty ego from lifetime to lifetime, because what caused the dream is guilt — and the need to escape it.

PURSAH: Superb, my brother. Don't forget, the ego adds the sly trick of having just as much projection in special love relationships as special hate relationships, thus helping to insure the continued dynamic of recycling guilt. If you'll look hard enough, which most people won't, then you'll see that love in this world is always qualified in some way. If those qualifications are not met, watch out.

ARTEN: Now we come to another one of the ego's favorite devices for maintaining its vast illusion. Tell me Gary, since you have a show business background; what does an illusionist do to trick the audience at a magic show?

GARY: One thing is to hide the illusion by diverting the attention of the audience someplace else while the trick is being done.

ARTEN: Yes! The ego is a master illusionist, and one of the ways it diverts your attention, from the moment you're born, is by giving you — and this calls for another drum roll, please — *problems*. These problems are usually right in front of you, and the *answers* to these problems have to be found out there in the world and utilized. It doesn't matter if it's your own survival that's the problem, or something as seemingly

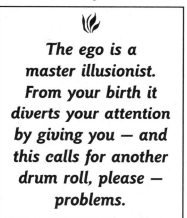

The ego is a master illusionist. From your birth it diverts your attention by giving you — and this calls for another drum roll, please — problems.

lofty as attaining world peace. The problems and the answers are always somewhere *out there* in the world or the universe. "The truth is out there," says your generation. It doesn't matter if they're talking about extraterrestrials, or any of the ego's other substitute mysteries and problems. For the *real* truth is *not* out there — because the real problem is not out there.

But you keep looking out there, never realizing that, as the Course says about the ego,

> Its dictates, then, can be summed up simply as: "Seek and do *not* find."[17]

While you are seeking, the more things change for you, the more they stay the same, and your buried globs of guilt over the seeming separation remain in place. I understand you actually got to see your own unconscious guilt symbolized for you one morning, when the Holy Spirit made that adjustment on your eyes while you were in bed.

GARY: Yeah, that was pretty far out. It wasn't very encouraging, but the light behind it was — and I know now that I'm being healed. *That's* encouraging.

Just so I know I'm getting the Course's teachings here — the first, or metaphysical level that the Course is given on, which you were talking about during your last visit, involves perception. The second level, or level of the body, world and universe that you're talking about now *also* involves perception. One of the main differences between them is that this second level I'm experiencing now is an end result of the collective denial and massive projection that took place on the first or metaphysical level — which resulted in the universe of time and space that I now see as being outside of myself, in order to have a defense against my hidden guilt, my fear, and of course God — of whom I'm erroneously terrified, and trying to run away from. Except I'm not in touch with that because it's unconscious.

The seeming causes of my fears, like pain and death, are now seen as things outside of me — although the fear is still in me. In fact, you could say the contents of my own mind are now perceived symbolically as being all around me, instead of inside me. That's why I'm mindless — because my memory is lost. The ego's plan to keep itself going is through blame — both subtle and obvious — attack, condemnation and the continuing projection and recycling of my guilt. This in turn tricks me into thinking I'm getting rid of guilt when what I'm really doing is holding on to it — keeping it in my own unconscious, keeping the whole vicious cycle going.

PURSAH: You said a mouthful accurately, my brother. We should get a gold star for your forehead.

GARY: Would the star have five points or six?

ARTEN: Knock it off. Religious jokes are our job.

PURSAH: The good news is, the Holy Spirit's dynamic of forgiveness undoes the ego at *both* levels. The Atonement principle undoes denial and projection at the level of your mind by forgiving what you perceive, and the Holy Spirit undoes the denial and projection at the metaphysical level of your mind at the same time — as well as undoing the whole idea of separation right along with you. *You* must practice forgiveness on the level where your experience is. Yes, you have to understand the metaphysics of the Course in order to understand what you're doing. But your *forgiveness* is done here, which means you should be practical — and respectful of other people and their experience. In other words, when you're living your everyday life, be kind. Your job isn't to correct others. Just help the Holy Spirit clean up *your* wrong mind by switching to your right mind, and then leave the rest to Him.

GARY: So, on this level, when I'm thinking with the ego that's wrong-mindedness, and when I'm thinking with the Holy Spirit, that's right-mindedness.

PURSAH: Yes. The *you* who is doing the thinking is you-as-mind — not as a human brain or body. The Course is addressed to the part of your mind that needs to choose between the ego and the Holy Spirit. We'll talk more about that the next couple of times so you can learn how to do it right — and save yourself a few thousand years of trial and error, and all the corresponding incarnations. You'll be amazed at how simple it is once it all becomes a part of your attitude.

We'll be breaking it down temporarily into steps, but eventually the steps merge into one attitude. The end result is the peace of God. We've already emphasized that everyone, and thus your self, is innocent because what you are seeing is not true. How can what you're seeing be true if the separation from God never occurred? If the separation never occurred, then how can what you are seeing have any more of an affect on you than it had on J?

ARTEN: Something you should always try to remember is that by keeping you looking outside of yourself, the ego prevents you from really looking at its thought system. As we already said, the Course teaches that illusions are protected by *not* looking at them.[18]

We're going to take a brief look at the nature of the ego thought system, not to scare you, but just so you'll understand that although it may be ugly, it is *not* you. The way to get this is by looking at it with the Holy Spirit. The ego doesn't want you to look at it. The ego is afraid of your power to choose against it. If you're looking at it, then you *must* be doing it with the Holy Spirit. If you're joined with Him, then you're no longer in your wrong mind, but looking at things with your right mind. You're no longer an effect instead of a cause. You're no longer alone as a guilty individual, but reconnected to your Self.

Look at the ego without judgment or fear. If it's not real, then it's not something to fear. But it *is* something to forgive. Thus in order to forgive yourself as well as others, you're going to have to be willing to look at the ways you use people and kill them off in your mind. That's not really you, but it is a part of the system you unconsciously *think* is you.

Incidentally, when it comes to the illusion of time, you should understand that sin equals the past, guilt equals the present, and fear equals the future. Of course it could be the very immediate future or the distant future. It really doesn't matter. As examples, say you're being robbed at gunpoint and you think you might be killed. Or maybe you're worried about your retirement twenty years from now. Those things are different in form, but really the same. The real reason you're fearful is because you believe you've sinned. If you didn't believe in the ego system, you couldn't *be* afraid. You may think that not being afraid would be bad for your effectiveness and survival. Yet when is it that you're more effective — when you're afraid or when you're not?

You should also recognize that fear, sin, rage, guilt, jealousy, anger, pain, worry, resentment, revenge, loathing, envy and all other negative emotions are versions of the same illusion. That's why the Course taught very clearly, before all the borrowers came along, that

Fear and love are the only emotions of which you are capable.[19]

People who borrow from the Course instead of teaching it generally make one of two mistakes. Either they try to make up a secular version of the Course, which doesn't work because when you leave out God, you're ignoring the one real problem — the seeming separation from Him — or they make up a version that includes God, but is a dualistic system. This *also* fails to solve the one real problem because of the very nature of duality. How can you undo the separation from God by believing that God created and acknowledges separation? Thus they end up wasting a lot of time by reinforcing the seeming separation rather than correcting it.

PURSAH: So what *is* the nature of the ego that you carry in your unconscious, and that it doesn't want you to look at?

GARY: I thought you'd never ask.

PURSAH: Wise guy. Its nature is hatred. Even if they see the hatred, which most people rationalize or gloss over, they still don't realize —

as you've already astutely pointed out — that it's really *self* hatred. So you and others see people in the world who hate, attack, and even kill each other, and who would hurt or even kill you if they got the chance. The variations of this are endless. It can be as simple as being made uncomfortable by people you disagree with, personally or politically. It can show up in the form of people at work who try to make your life difficult, or relatives who don't encourage you. Or there can be situations that are more physically threatening.

But always it's a case where you took the hatred you have for yourself — for throwing away Heaven — and made up a world where the reasons for this hatred, your guilt and lack of peace could now be seen outside yourself, almost always connected in some way to other beings. Now the guilt is not in you. It's not *you* who took the peace of God away from you, it's *them*. Of course nobody can really take the peace of God away from you except by your own decision; that's just as true today as it was at the first instant of the seeming separation. You've bought into the apparent trueness of it all, and in order to deal with it, you have it all wired up so that the responsible parties are now out there — exactly where you wanted them to be.

GARY: The people who give me trouble — I *want* them to show up?

PURSAH: Make no mistake, you want them to be there, without exception. They're your scapegoats. If you could just remember that fact the next time some apparently real flamer pushes your buttons, then you could hold your tongue, think with the Holy Spirit and change your mind. You want them to be there, all right. Always. You need it. That's how you trick yourself into thinking you're not guilty, or at least not terribly guilty, so you can cope most of the time — for the guilt is somewhere else. As long as you're stuck in the maze, you can't see that the whole thing is unnecessary, because you were never really guilty in the first place. The whole maze is an illusion to defend yourself against an illusion.

Don't forget — you believe you really are guilty on a much deeper level than you realize. You need your defense because the *alternative* is unthinkable to your ego — that you might actually look upon your own guilt — the horror of which is presently covered over by the world. The ego has you convinced that to look upon the hideousness of this guilt is the equivalent of death. To avoid the viciousness that goes along with the entire can of worms, you project it outward, forgetting that what goes around comes around — because it never really left in the first place:

> Who sees a brother as a body sees him as fear's symbol. And he will attack, because what he beholds is his own fear external to himself, poised to attack, and howling to unite with him again. Mistake not the intensity of rage projected fear must spawn. It shrieks in wrath, and claws the air in frantic hope it can reach to its maker and devour him.
>
> This do the body's eyes behold in one whom Heaven cherishes, the angels love and God created perfect.[20]

ARTEN: To continue with the Course's teaching along those lines, the ego is always trying to find ways to prevent you from closely examining its thought system.

> Loudly the ego tells you not to look inward, for if you do your eyes will light on sin, and God will strike you blind.[21]

As J explains, this is not what the ego is *really* worried about.

> …Beneath your fear to look within because of sin is yet another fear, and one which makes the ego tremble.
>
> What if you looked within and saw no sin? This "fearful" question is one the ego never asks. And you who ask it now are threatening the ego's whole defensive system too seriously for it to bother to pretend it is your friend.[22]

PURSAH: Don't let that last statement scare you, by the way — for that is never J's intention. The ego already hates you. If it gets vicious, so what? It would have eventually, anyway. The weird thing is that now when you think about it, you realize that whatever it is that hates you is not really on the outside, it's on the inside — right along with you. The murderous thought system of the ego can no longer be denied and projected. Your only way out is to undo it.

GARY: Now wait a minute. If the contents of my mind, including my own hatred and guilt, are symbolically all around me, then how can I really look within when I'm all wired up in a body and a brain that can only perceive outward?

ARTEN: Exactly! That's how the ego set you up. Everything you experience testifies to the reality of the illusion, and then you judge it and make it real to yourself — keeping the whole system intact. The answer to the question you just asked is the answer to life. The way out is the Holy Spirit's alternative — the law of forgiveness. You have to learn how to turn the tables on the ego. The *only* way to forgive what is within is to forgive what *seems* to be without. Our next two visits will explain these things, and it will be fun — or at least the result is. We want to make sure you understand up front that you will *never* be able to find your way out and experience your own innocence and Divinity until you learn how to forgive everything you see around you. Until then, real escape is impossible. You think people who want to escape the world are weak; actually, they have the right idea. They just don't know how to do it right.

> *You have to learn how to turn the tables on the ego. The only way to forgive what is within is to forgive what seems to be without.*

What is everything you see around you anyway, except a series of pictures or images; a movie of your own hatred and guilt? Yes, you have some seemingly good experiences mixed in that are designed to mask things, but that's just duality. On this level, the duality that is perceived in the universe simply reflects the duality of your own split mind, symbolized as opposites and counterparts. So you have good and bad, life and death, hot and cold, north and south, east and west, inward and outward, up and down, dark and light, left and right, sickness and health, rich and poor, yin and yang, love and hate, wet and dry, male and female, hard and soft, near and far, and a thousand other polarities and dual forces — all of which have nothing to do with God, Who is perfectly whole and complete and would never create anything that isn't. All splits are merely symbolic of division and separation, and designed to keep you chasing after the supposedly good things, so you won't ever find out that the good and the bad are equally untrue. That way your attention is continuously fixed on the ego's tricks instead of the Holy Spirit's answer.

The ego has tricked you into fighting a battle that is continuously seen outside yourself, where the thought system of sin, guilt and fear is projected in a way that is certain to make sure this battle is always fought where the answer *isn't*. The answer, the Holy Spirit, remains within the split mind, along with the ego mind that is projecting the universe. Your job now is to stop fighting the battle where you can't win, and turn to the decision-making power of your mind, where the Holy Spirit is.

Remember, the Holy Spirit is not in the world. How can He be in a world that isn't there? He is in your mind. That's where both the problem *and* the answer are. Switch to the Holy Spirit's thought system and you can't lose. Remember, we're not talking about winning and losing in the world. That's not what the Course is about, although it does teach you how to receive true guidance through inspiration, which we've promised to cover.

Right now, when things go bad instead of good, *that's* when you really experience your unconscious guilt. You experience it as actual physical pain, or psychological suffering, or both. This makes the separation seem real to you. What you have appropriately dubbed the kingdom of suckdom is merely your own unconscious guilt coming to the surface, causing you to suffer. Yet, as we have already said, the Course teaches that the guiltless mind *cannot* suffer. What remains for you then is to let the Holy Spirit teach you of your absolute guiltlessness.

Indeed, if it weren't for the Holy Spirit, your situation would be hopeless. Your hatred and guilt would remain forever trapped in the depths of your unconscious. Happily for you, the Holy Spirit is no fool — and the ego is no match for Him. When you join with the Holy Spirit's forgiveness, the ego is no match for you either. On some level, the ego knows this — and is always in fear for its purported existence. So are you, but only when you identify with your ego instead of the Holy Spirit. J eventually Identified *completely* with the Holy Spirit, and now he is exactly the same as Him.

GARY: And you are too? I'm asking for the benefit of my future readers.

PURSAH: Yes, but it's not necessary for your readers to believe in us. Our words can benefit people whether they have trust in us or not. It's the Holy Spirit's message that matters — not those who appear to be bringing it. If *we* don't believe in our own projected bodies, then why would we be upset if someone else didn't?

GARY: Is our book gonna be a hit?

PURSAH: Don't worry about that. Whatever happens, don't make a big deal out of it. It's nothing. Think of it this way. If what the Course is saying is true — that everyone who comes to this world is delusional or else they wouldn't think they were here in the first place — then if you have a hit book, all it means is that you are admired by a large group of disturbed people.

GARY: That *was* a joke, right?

PURSAH: Yes. Don't worry about the reactions of people who take jokes like that seriously — *whoever* they may be. Don't be defensive and walk on eggshells. Just put it out there. If somebody doesn't like you because of it, forgive them.

GARY: There was a time, in the very recent past, when I would have used another *f* word.

PURSAH: Now you have the new *f* word. Forgive them. After we leave this time, you're going to have five months to work on that "Love Holds No Grievances" idea until we come back. You should keep doing the rest of the Workbook too, and keep reading the Text, but you should throw in the "No Grievances" idea during key situations when you remember it. Everyone has certain phrases and ideas from the Course that work the best at reminding them of the truth. That's one of yours.

GARY: Why so long before you come back, guys?

ARTEN: We've stressed all along this isn't an overnight thing. We'll actually be going to eight months between visits after that. When we said it would be several years before our visits to you were complete, we meant a total of nine years — with our last few visits being a year apart.

GARY: Nine years! What am I, in the slow group or something?

ARTEN: No, but this is a serious, lifelong path — if you're still interested. Your genuine transformation is about to begin. Work at it, and don't worry about time. It's nothing. Your mind is ageless, because time isn't real. Just enjoy the results when you experience them. Not only are the results fun, but practicing forgiveness is interesting enough to be fun a lot of the time, too — although you might not always want to do it.

Don't forget, as we've already emphasized, the Course teaches that you don't have to change anybody's mind and you don't have to change your world. All you have to do is change *your* mind *about* the world. For example, don't worry about world peace. The best way for you to help bring world peace is to practice forgiveness yourself, and share the experience with people. When the people of the world finally seek real inner peace by understanding and correctly applying the law of forgiveness, then the seemingly outer peace *must* follow. But that's not the focus of J's Course. The focus is on changing your mind about your dream.

GARY: Speaking of dreams, I never had any nightmares before I started doing the Course, but recently I've had some pretty bizarre, and what *should* have been horrifying images, in my dreams. For some reason I'm not scared when I see these things, and I'm not scared when I wake up. It's like these things are being deliberately shown to me — these terrible images of murder and shame and hellish figures.

ARTEN: Yes. As a comparison, you've seen some of the old religious paintings in books that suggest what hell is supposed to look like, right?

GARY: Yeah. Some of them are pretty graphic.

ARTEN: Yes, a lot of them are quite horrifying. It doesn't show up in the same way for everybody, but what's going on in those paintings, and in your dreams, is your unconscious guilt coming to the surface, being shown to you and, in your case, being released. In the example of the artists, their fear is being symbolized in the paintings. In the case of your dreams, your no-longer-unconscious fear, guilt and self-hatred are put into images. Then, because you are practicing forgiveness by applying the Workbook lessons, this old thought system is being forgiven and released to the Holy Spirit. That's why you're not afraid of it, even though it looks horrible. J is there, looking at it with you. Your right mind knows he's there. There's a part of you that knows it's just a dream and there's nothing to fear.

That's what your waking life will be like someday — when all your secret sins and hidden hates have been forgiven. No matter what you see, or what appears to happen to you or anyone around you, you'll know there's no reason to be afraid. The details of these pictures are different for everyone, but as you are well aware, the images in what people call their real, waking lives can also be hellish at times. Yet it's all just symbolic of the ego thought system of fear, guilt and death — and it's not real. So why fear it? All images are just images, no matter where or when they appear to happen.

PURSAH: These images you've seen in some of your nightmares are very typical of the nature of the ego thought system on the level of your unconscious. You see, the unconscious is much *more* horrible than what's above the surface. This is how the ego hides itself and its plan. The conscious projection you see all around you is an entire level removed from the unconscious mind. So while at times the universe you see can be horrible and frightening, it's nothing compared to the awful thought system it springs from. In fact, because the projection you see is a defense, you could say that the universe exists *because* it is tolerable to you *compared* to what's in your unconscious mind. The world may not always be tolerable to everyone — often resulting in murders and suicides — but it's still a walk in the park compared to the deep, vicious crap that's underneath the surface. You've seen some of your guilt symbolized in different ways, now. What would you say it's like?

GARY: Oh, the words *ugly, monstrous, demonic, savage, ghastly* and *tormented* come to mind.

ARTEN: There you go. You just gave a decent description of what the unconscious is like for everyone, although they don't know it — and how it will remain until it's released to the Holy Spirit. It's so terrible because of what it represents: no less than the separation from God and the attack on Him, and the death penalty for His Son who thinks he committed the crime — and whose horrific guilt demands that he suffer. The world you see can certainly be disgusting at times, but incredibly, it's actually an escape from a seemingly worse fate — the guilt in your own mind that you didn't even know about.

GARY: It's not much of an escape for those people who kill others or themselves. Doesn't that make them even more guilty?

ARTEN: No. Remember, guilt is just a thought in the mind, and no consequence can really be created by an action in the world. Acts like murder and suicide do recycle the guilt that everyone unconsciously thinks is real, and keeps it going. People who kill others or themselves see death as an escape. Those who murder really hate themselves, although they've projected this hate onto others, and killing is a convoluted attempt to destroy themselves. As we've said, your hate is really self-hatred. Every criminal secretly hopes to get caught and to be punished. Remember, although much guilt is projected onto others, it is also projected onto your own illusory body which, as we've already said, is projected outside of your mind.

> *Those who murder really hate themselves, and killing is a convoluted attempt to destroy themselves.*

There are many other variations, like the suicide-by-cop strategy, where people open fire on the police because they know it will probably result in their own death. Those who commit suicide, in any manner, seek to end the intolerable psychological pain of their guilt and suffering. Since their unconscious guilt remains intact, they merely end up reincarnating and keeping the problem unresolved. Death is not a way out. True forgiveness is the way out. As the Course teaches,

> **The world is not left by death but by truth, and truth can be known by all those for whom the Kingdom was created, and for whom it waits.**[23]

PURSAH: Not only do you have this tremendous resistance to facing what you think is your awful guilt underneath the surface, but simultaneously, your ego is terrified that to do so successfully, and change your mind about it, would result in losing its identity as a separate individual. It's going to take some willpower on your part to admit to this thought system within yourself as you observe it in action, and then allow the Holy Spirit to undo it as you forgive the symbolic images of it that you see outside of you.

GARY: And you're gonna tell me how? The Workbook obviously does that, but you're gonna give me some more help?

ARTEN: Everything we'll be giving you is in the Course. We'll just be taking some things from all of the books and putting them together in a way that will help you apply it more effectively for yourself. We said we wouldn't just give you theories, but a way to deal with what's in front of your face.

GARY: Well, I hope so, 'cause sometimes I think I'd have to be a freakin' saint to do all this. I mean, *never* hold a grievance against anyone? Never judge, condemn or attack? Never have any bad thoughts without noticing them and forgiving? And *never* believe my anger is justified? It's impossible, man.

ARTEN: You *are* a saint, Gary; you just don't know it yet. As far as it being impossible to do the Course, you're wrong. As you pointed out yourself, the Course says that miracles are habits. You will experience more and more that the Course is right when it says,

> **Anger is *never* justified. Attack has *no* foundation. It is here escape from fear begins, and will be made complete.**[24]

Why are these things important? Because, as the Course also teaches, whether you are attacking others with your own thoughts, or somebody else appears to be attacking you, verbally or physically,

> **The secret of salvation is but this: That you are doing this unto yourself. No matter what the form of the attack, this still is true. Whoever takes the role of enemy and of attacker, still is this the truth. Whatever seems to be the cause of any pain and suffering you feel, this is still true. For you would not react at all to figures in a dream you knew that you were dreaming. Let them be as hateful and as vicious as they may, they could have no effect on you unless you failed to recognize it is your dream.**[25]

Whenever you judge the dream figures and thus make your dream real, you fall right into the ego's trap — whether you believe that you must atone for sin, or that others must atone for *their* sins, or that they deserve your condemnation.

> **You cannot dispel guilt by making it real, and then atoning for it. This is the ego's plan, which it offers instead of dispelling it. The ego believes in atonement through attack, being fully committed to the insane notion that attack is salvation.[26]**

As the Course goes on to say,

> **...In the ego's teaching, then, there is no escape from guilt. For attack makes guilt real, and if it is real there *is* no way to overcome it.[27]**

GARY: So God doesn't have to forgive me; I need to forgive myself by forgiving others instead of attacking them. Even if it's just a mental judgment and I don't say or do anything, an attack thought is still an attack thought. That's why I have to monitor my thoughts. Whether I attack *or* forgive, I do it to myself because these people aren't real anyway — they're just symbols of what's in my mind, just as I'm a symbol in the collective mind. The world doesn't need God's forgiveness; people need to forgive themselves by forgiving the images they see.

ARTEN: Yes. Absolutely. The Course couldn't be any more clear about that.

> **God does not forgive because He has never condemned. And there must be condemnation before forgiveness is necessary. Forgiveness is the great need of this world, but that is because it is a world of illusions. Those who forgive are thus releasing themselves from illusions, while those who withhold forgiveness are binding themselves to them. As you condemn only yourself, so do you forgive only yourself.**
>
> **Yet although God does not forgive, His Love is nevertheless the basis of forgiveness.[28]**

Even though you don't need God's forgiveness, because He has never condemned you, you *do* have access to His Voice, the Holy Spirit, who handles guilt in this way:

The Holy Spirit dispels it simply through the calm recognition that it has never been.[29]

We'll talk more about that during our coming visits.

PURSAH: Perhaps you don't yet fully understand that the benefits of true forgiveness are for *you*. You don't have to — nor will you — always forgive immediately. Occasionally you'll have to forgive something that happened a half an hour ago, or two days ago. That's the way it goes. Nobody's perfect, and right now there's an epidemic of anger going on in the world, making it even more difficult for you to not respond. Even two thousand years ago, J was tempted to identify with the body at times, but because he was a master, he forgave and got over it *very* quickly. In your case however, since time isn't real — and because memory is just as much of a perception as any other image — you can forgive a past event at any time, even if the person who is associated with your forgiveness is no longer seemingly living in a body.

GARY: Any unresolved things I may have with my parents can still be forgiven — including forgiving myself for something I may have said to them or done in the past?

PURSAH: Absolutely. You must forgive yourself as surely as you must forgive others, or else you're not yet really getting the insignificance of the body. As we said, your body is no more real or more important than any other body.

Speaking of the body, we should emphasize something about the subject of reincarnation. We talk about it as though it actually happens. Yet just like everything else, it's only a dream. Yes, it *appears* that you incarnate into a body, and your experience is that you are a body — but as we like to point out, the Course says that what you are seeing is not true. You, dear brother, are not completely unfamiliar with the concept of your experience being a dream.

NOTE: When Arten had first mentioned the idea of the universe being a dream, I had balked at it because it ran contrary to my experience. Yet as both Arten and Pursah knew, I had read Shirley MacLaine's eye-opening book, *Out on a Limb*, back in the 1980s, and one of the most interesting quotations she had used was from Leo Tolstoy's *Letters*. It was a rhetorical question that rang true for me, and although I didn't realize it at the time, it could just as easily have been posed by a Valentinian Gnostic: "... now our whole life, from birth unto death, with all its dreams, is it not in its turn also a dream, which we take as the real life, the reality of which we do not doubt only because we do not know of the other more real life?"

GARY: It's not that the idea is completely alien; it just doesn't *feel* like a dream very often, although I have had those kinds of experiences.

ARTEN: Yes, and you'll have more of them — but forgiveness is where it's at if you want to make those experiences more the norm rather than an occasional thing.

GARY: Could you just tell me a little bit more about how the ego's plan shows up in the world so I'll know more about what to look out for. I mean, you said it's all a set-up, right?

ARTEN: Yes. The ego believes in the separation from God, and the seeming separation that is being constantly acted out here was a very upsetting thing for you, to say the least. You'll experience thousands of times in your life when things seem to be going good, just fine, and then suddenly something will happen to upset you. It may be something you think is big or small. It doesn't matter. If it disturbs your peace of mind even in the slightest, it's symbolic of the separation. Whenever it happens, in all its different forms, it's always a way of repeatedly living out that first time when you were perfectly happy in Heaven and then suddenly you were very upset — that first time you thought you were separate from God — which is what all the other upsets in this world are based on. In your ordinary dream of life, the causes for the upsets seem to be happening to the specific identity you have as a body, which is itself a false idea of separation.

GARY: It's like The Poet said: "We are symbols, and inhabit symbols."

ARTEN: Why, yes. I believe that's from *Essays: Second Series (1844),* The Poet. You know you're very sophisticated, considering your immaturity.

GARY: Thank you. I'll put that on my resumé.

ARTEN: During our next visit you'll learn in more detail about how, as the Course teaches, there is really only one problem, and one solution — which is the Holy Spirit's. As far as the ego's plan is concerned, your seemingly multiple problems show up in this world in an attempt to get you to *react* — to feel bad, or guilty, or mad, or defeated, or bored, or scared, or inferior, or self-conscious, or annoyed, or lonely, or superior and condescending. It's all some kind of a judgment, regardless of the form. As soon as you make that judgment, you give validity to the ego's world and reinforce the seeming reality of the separation and everything that goes with it.

Within its script, which includes all of time — a subject we'll talk about later — the ego has *every* possible variation of separation scripted out in such a way as to insure perpetual conflict. This is mixed in with your good times in order to make them seem more real, except that this mixture is really just another example of duality. Even though what you *really* are — spirit — cannot *be* divided, we'll give you a few more examples right now of how the ego tries to suck you into the belief in division.

PURSAH: It is by your responses and reactions to what you see that you make the experience of separation from God seem real. The details of what you are making real show up in your relationships, and in the predicaments that have been scripted out for you. It's not always about things that appear to happen to you. It can be about events you are observing as a spectator — in the relationships of others, or even on the news you watch or read on the Internet.

For example, if people die in a plane crash, what could be more symbolic of the fall of man? Or when a baby leaves the paradise of its mother's belly and gets shoved out into the world, what else could it symbolize except the separation from God? When a bullet, knife, laser beam, arrow, spear, or crown of thorns pierces someone's skin, what does the skin do?

GARY: It separates.

PURSAH: During an earthquake, what happens to the ground on which you've built the foundation of your illusory life?

GARY: It separates.

PURSAH: If someone is abandoned as a child or infant, that's obviously separation — not to mention an excellent opportunity for the child or infant to blame its birth parent or parents who abandoned it, and thus project its unconscious guilt onto them and preserve its ego-itis. The examples are infinite, but once again. . .

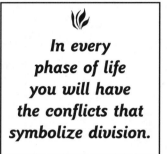

*In every
phase of life
you will have
the conflicts that
symbolize division.*

GARY: They're really all the same.

PURSAH: In sickness, the attack thoughts in the mind — often unconscious — may become symbolized by cells in the body attacking each other as cancer, or show up in the form of countless other ailments.

In every single phase of your life — your childhood, your schooling, all the participatory activities you engage in over the decades, and different careers that feature their own variations of Machiavellian bull, you will have the conflicts that symbolize division. If you're lucky, your country *won't* go into that most special of all conflicts, war — but you can't count on that. Never mind the countless opportunities for violence that are there from cradle to grave, whether or not you are living during what is ironically referred to as peacetime.

Aside from these special hate relationships, which may simply show up in the form of your not approving of someone, you will also have special love relationships. Yet how could this be possible without bodies? We have already quoted the Course teaching that the body is the thought of sin made flesh and then projected outward, producing what seems to be a wall of flesh around the mind, keeping it prisoner![30] Is this the kind of love you would have? The Holy Spirit's love says that bodies cannot keep you apart. Rejoin with yourself through forgiveness, that you and your brothers and sisters may be one and unlimited. Then, if you should choose to join with bodies on the level of form after that, you are simply doing what you're supposed to do — the same things you would have done anyway. Now you do them with forgiveness, and the Holy Spirit is with you.

In your personal relationships, Gary, what happens symbolically when you have a falling out with someone?

GARY: You separate. All right; I hear you. It's not contradictory to say there's nobody out there and then turn around and say the only way home is to forgive what's out there, because you're only forgiving what *appears* to be out there — which is symbolic of what's in your own mind.

PURSAH: Yes, and we'll get more into how to do that. Also, as we said before, our visits will be getting shorter. One of the reasons is because the Holy Spirit's Answer is a lot less complicated than the ego's seemingly multiple problems. Indeed, one of the reasons that *A Course in Miracles* is so long is that, even though the truth may be simple and consistent, your ego is not — and it needs to be undone gradually.

GARY: I can understand that, but I was also wondering about how this seemingly enormous script of ours gets translated from an invisible idea into a visible manifestation. I mean, if everything is all mapped out ahead of time, then how does everything that's supposed to happen in the universe go like clockwork — just the way it's supposed to?

PURSAH: You've asked a complicated question, but it's interesting that you used the word *clockwork*. The universe is very much like a big wind-up clock, or better, a wind-up toy. Let's use your solar system as a microcosm, and we'll use just one of the so-called forces of nature as an example. This doesn't explain the entire picture, but it will give you a taste of the ego's ingenious ways of illusion.

Even though energy, which I'll call *chi*, is an illusion, it's very much a part of how the ego takes the script that's in the mind and transmutes it from invisible thought into invisible but measurable forms, and then into the visible manifestations you see and experience. This really happens all at once, but it's necessary to be linear so you can better understand it.

For instance, let's say you could look at your planet from outer space, from half the distance to the moon, and that you could see chi.

You'd then be able to see that the earth is completely encased by electromagnetic chi that's carried to it, and past it, in the form of a huge flow of radiation from your sun. This flow of chi is constantly changing, with yin and yang going in and out of balance and everywhere in between balance. The changes in the chi are caused, in turn, by the constantly changing radiation on the sun.

Now, if you could look at the sun close up from space, you'd see what could be described as *enormous* swirling oceans of gas. What few realize is that these oceans of gas behave in a similar fashion to the oceans of the earth. Just as the tides of the earth's oceans are subject to the movements of your moon, the tides of those solar oceans of gas are subject to the pulling and pushing of the total interaction of all of the planets in your solar system, and even the universe beyond it — which of course is all connected. This causes different gaseous tides, sunspots and other solar events — which in turn regulate the changes in the flow of the radiation while it's carried to the earth as particles via the solar wind, or directly by sunlight.

This changing radiational flow, regulated by the movement within the entire solar system, including the earth and its moon, causes corresponding changes in the chi surrounding your planet and sends electromagnetic fields onto every inch of it. You can't see these chi fields with the body's eyes, but they're everywhere — and you've been walking right through them every day of your life. They regulate everything about you, including your decisions and resulting movements. They are actually *thought* from a completely different level, transmuted into the form of chi, telling you what to think on this level. Everything you do follows from what you think, and sometimes it follows instantaneously, like a reflex. This is true of every animate and seemingly inanimate object you behold.

As one simple example, how do you think a tiny bird like a swallow can be flying in South America, then all of a sudden know it's supposed to make a turn and begin a flight of thousands of miles that will result in it arriving in California within the same general time period every year?

GARY: Some people would say it's because of God, and some people would use words like instinct, or nature — but you're saying the bird is run by remote control?

PURSAH: In a sense, yes. And so are you — keeping in mind that the word *remote* is a relative term, and we're actually talking about decisions that are coming from a totally different level of the mind, which is a non-spatial thing. Your *experience* is that your decisions are made here, but that's not true. Decisions aren't made by the human brain any more than they're made by that little bird's brain. When we said you've been very much like a robot, we weren't kidding. But the programmer isn't somebody else. There isn't anybody else. We're talking about *self* pre-determination. Your fate on this level was sealed by your deal with your ego, not God — who makes no deals. Your *entire* ego mind is the programmer that sends signals to your brain. Your brain is just part of the hardware. It forwards the signals telling the body, or computer unit, what to do, see and feel.

Your experience is that you are here on the computer screen — separate from God, separate from your brothers and your sisters, and acting out the thought of separation and the conflict that goes along with the duality of your split mind. Your brothers and sisters are doing exactly what you want them to do. We've already quoted the Course teaching that you do not realize that you are making them act out for you.[31]

Changes in the electromagnetic fields even regulate how you see things. To say that something is visible to you simply means that it is situated in the region of the electromagnetic spectrum that is perceptible to human vision.

GARY: Huh?

PURSAH: The important thing is that your decisions are not really made by you here. They were made on a totally different level when you agreed to the ego's plan, and the only way out of the whole can of worms is to return to your right mind and choose the Holy Spirit's alternative interpretation of what you see instead of your ego's interpretation, which keeps you trapped in the script. It might help if you try to remember that the whole business is just a recording playing itself out. For example, how are computer records and information stored, even on floppy discs?

GARY: On electromagnetic strips?

PURSAH: A very versatile thing. As we said during our first visit, inventions on this level usually mimic some aspect of what the mind

does. You may think you have free will here and that you can determine what's going to happen to you, but the truth is it's all happened
already. You're just playing the tape, watching and listening —
thinking it's all real and a result of your own volition or chance on
this level, rather than a set-up from another level.

GARY: Why should I bother to do anything, then?

PURSAH: Two reasons. First of all, even though it's a closed system, there are different scenarios open to you in each lifetime.
Making a different choice that doesn't involve the Holy Spirit within the dream won't undo your unconscious guilt and get you out of
the system, but it can result in a temporarily different experience.
It's like a multiple choice script, where if you make a different decision, then a different scenario will play itself out. If you make one
decision, you get the girl and have a good time — but if you make
another decision, you blow it and end up with depression. It's even
possible to live the same lifetime over again, with a different set of
earthly results. Once again, none of that will get you where you really want to be. It will just keep you stuck here, attempting to achieve
temporary happiness.

The other, far more important reason why you should be engaged
in your decision-making is to return to your right mind and choose
the Holy Spirit instead of the ego, which *will* get you where you
really want to be. Forgiveness has its fringe benefits in the dream,
some of which are not always obvious to you. For instance, let's say
a man murders his wife, or a woman murders her husband. One of
them is dead, and the other spends the rest of their life in prison or
gets executed. But what if they had learned to forgive, and there was
no killing? Would that change things on this level?

GARY: It would change everything, and people probably wouldn't
even be aware of it.

PURSAH: Yes. That's an extreme example, but there are thousands
of scenarios where even on the level of form, forgiveness has results
— and you often don't realize how much better off you are than you
would have been if you didn't forgive. That's why you want to develop a trust for the Holy Spirit. He really does know what's best for
you. So don't think it's not important for you to take charge of your
own mind from this level. Indeed, it's what the Course is training

you to do. Control of your mind even gives you the power to stop pain in your body — but more about that later.

GARY: You know, I was driving the other day, and this guy was right on my ass. I mean, he was practically touching my bumper. That really pisses me off. I'm not about to speed up, 'cause we're in this neighborhood where the kids play in their yards. I was just about to give this asshole the finger, when I thought about the Course. So I didn't do anything, and then he made a left turn a few blocks later, and that was the end of it. After that I was thinking, what if I'd given him the finger and he had a gun? Then we'd have had a case of road rage, and I could have been road kill.

ARTEN: Yes. Remember that your brother in that car was symbolic of what's in *your* mind, including the impatience that you exhibit in other areas of your life, symbolized by his impatience. You know as well as us that you'd probably be rich by now if you could display more patience in your trading. You and your brother are impatient because you've made the separation real, and you think you have to strive to get somewhere so you can overcome God and prove yourself right.

So you saw your faults and your guilt in your brother instead of in yourself. Fortunately for you in this particular case, you made the right decision — both on the level of the mind and on the level of form. You can't go wrong by breaking out in peace, unless you must defend yourself from bodily attack and possible death — in which case you have permission to kick ass, or better yet, to think of a way out.

GARY: I guess I shouldn't have thought of him as an asshole, though?

ARTEN: That's correct, your assholiness. As J counsels you in the Course, "As you see him you will see yourself."[32]

GARY: I hear you. Oh, before I forget, what you said about the solar system and the chi would explain why astrology works sometimes.

PURSAH: Yes, but astrology isn't precise, and what we're describing is always precise, because it corresponds exactly to cause and effect on the level of the universe in accordance with the ego's script. It's true that astrology, numerology and many other things will occasionally *correlate* to the script, but they're hit or miss — because a part of the script is that the script itself will *never* be completely predictable, or else you wouldn't have the appearance of chance. Chance helps to maintain the inevitable shock, chaos and fear that will always show up in the script.

GARY: It's built into the system.

PURSAH: Yes. The ego's chaotic nature also insures that there will never be a unified theory of the universe that will hold up over time, because the universe isn't really based on the thought of unity — it's based on the thought of separation and division. However, it includes fascinating and ingenious patterns that help to give it the *illusion* of unity.

That's why you shouldn't be impressed by every new discovery or theory about the universe. So what if superstrings can make gravity work at both the Newtonian and sub-atomic levels? An illusion is still an illusion. We're not saying you shouldn't do research or analysis, if that's what you do. Go for it. Just try to remember that you're doing it during a pre-programmed dream script.

GARY: Not to mention the fact that you're a freakin' robot.

PURSAH: Only temporarily. You're *not* a robot once you get in touch with your power to choose. It's independence day, Gary. You'll never be the same once you know how to forgive.

ARTEN: The process Pursah has been describing gives you one example of how the universe follows a script that was made in a holographic way but appears to play out in a linear manner, like a movie that's already been filmed. The whole thing has already been written, and so has your life story. Even the day your body will die has already been determined. The only *real* freedom you have is to choose to return to God by listening to the Voice for Him, instead of continuing indefinitely within a fixed system that has nothing to do with Him. Your brain isn't hard wired to know God; your mind tells your brain what to do! Be glad the universe and your brain have nothing to do with God, and that there's a way to return to *His* Universe.

You think your universe is impressive because it's all you can remember. You think it's big, but it's not. What you've done is make yourself look and feel small, like one little piece of the puzzle. You're like a child with little toys you don't want to give up. Yet what you *really* are cannot even be contained by your universe.

GARY: This universe as a wind-up toy — can that idea be demonstrated scientifically?

PURSAH: Some of it can be, and some of it can't be. You cannot measure thought. You can measure changes in the magnetic field, but you can't prove what is *causing* electrical changes in the brain. You can document the resulting chemical and hormonal reactions in the body, but once the brain has gotten the signal what to do, it's all effect. It's set up so you'll think the body is independent. But as the Course teaches right in the preface,

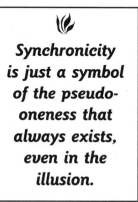

Synchronicity is just a symbol of the pseudo-oneness that always exists, even in the illusion.

> **The body appears to be largely self-motivated and independent, yet it actually responds only to the intentions of the mind.**[33]

ARTEN: Of course your body, your world and your universe are *all* responding *simultaneously* to the intentions of your mind. That's because there is actually only one thing, or one ego mind, that *is* the one thought of separation. Playing it out leads to all kinds of fascinating discoveries that serve, like a carrot and a stick, to keep you interested. Synchronicity, for example. That's just a symbol of the pseudo-oneness that always exists, even in the illusion. Remember, the ego wants you to think that the illusion is spiritual and that what *it* made is holy.

By the way, even though there's only one ego mind, just like there is only one Son of God — and you're It — we'll remind you that we've pointed out how this one ego-mind is split into both a right mind and a wrong mind, which you must choose between. You're observing everything, and you've got to choose whether you want the ego to be your teacher as you observe everything, or the Holy Spirit. When we or the Course talk about the ego, we're almost always talking about the wrong part of the mind, and not the right mind where the Holy Spirit abides.

GARY: O.K. So if I can just gather some of my thoughts here, and I don't mean to be repetitious, but...

ARTEN: Let me tell you something, buddy. Repetition is not only perfectly all right, it's mandatory. That's the only way you can possibly learn a thought system, have it become a part of you and get to the point where you apply it automatically — eventually without even thinking about it. That's why it's called *practicing* forgiveness. You practice over and over, until it becomes second nature. You'll see.

GARY: All right. I'm thinking that the ego thought system and script would explain an awful lot, like why some children are born sick or deformed. It makes me feel better just to know that God doesn't do that. It would explain why children are in conflict almost from the time they lay eyes on each other, fighting over toys and all that, and why children in school tease and torment each other, form cliques and project their unconscious guilt onto each other — to make the other ones wrong, and thus make them the guilty ones.

People always end up taking sides in one way or another, so all through your life you have victims and victimizers. There are all these differences that seem to make some people better than others, make some people feel superior and other people feel worthless. We see opposites everywhere that people take for granted, like health and sickness, beauty and ugliness. Yet the only thing that *tells* you that something is beautiful or ugly is your body — so it's all subjective and made up from scratch, but you just accept it 'cause it's all you know.

And you have special love as well as the perpetual conflict of special hate. The people you love can often do no wrong in your eyes, and even if they do it's easy to forgive them. The people you hate can do no right, and no matter what they do, *they're* not forgiven. So you have all kinds of rivalries throughout life, and all kinds of business and corporate competition, all following the same ego patterns. A lot of people pursue careers where they try to gain power over other bodies, which is really just a pathetic imitation of power. These careers are full of unconscious projections of guilt, although we don't know it. In some of the most obvious examples, the lawyer who wins the case is the clever one who most successfully makes the other side sound wrong, and thus gets the members of the jury to project their unconscious guilt onto that side.

The politicians who win elections are the ones who are best at blaming the other side, getting people to think that side is responsible for their problems, which is the cosmic equivalent of blaming that side for the separation from God, and all the pain and unhappiness that goes along with it. *They're* the guilty ones, not us. Both sides often sincerely believe they're right, but neither one is right, because what they're seeing is not true — and as soon as you react and take sides you become part of the problem instead of part of the solution. All the while, people who don't forgive don't realize that all they're doing is reacting to a self-directed set-up and getting sucked into the ego's plan.

When we have a problem, we attack it. We have a war on poverty, a war on cancer, and a war on drugs and a war against everything — and none of them work. Even our sports, from childhood through adulthood, are fought like wars.

When you think about it, the ego's script also explains why people who are into religion usually believe it takes sacrifice, or suffering, to get to God. Christianity has J suffering and dying for everybody's sins. Yet sacrifice is an ego attribute, and has nothing to do with God. That's why I assume J actually did say, as the Gospels reported, "And if you had known what this means, 'I desire mercy, and not sacrifice,' you would not have condemned the guiltless."

All people seem to know how to do is condemn their special hate objects in one way or another. Even if they don't do that very much, they find some other way to suffer and act out the ego system, through accidents and sickness and a hundred other ways — because you can project the guilt onto your own body as well as others, since all hatred is actually self-hatred anyway.

We see all of this in our lives every day, and on our talk shows, on the news and in the rest of the media. Unfortunately, the eventual, logical extension of this projection is violence against the ones who are being made wrong in the mind — regardless of the form the violence takes. So you may have hate crimes, or on an international level, wars. On the domestic level, you have political struggles that result in people attacking others verbally or, depending on the place and time, you could have a political argument that results in an all out civil war — as it did, even in America.

It's all duality, which is symbolic of the conflict of the split, ego mind — in everything from the forces of nature to economic expansion and contraction — both on an individual and macro level. I could go on forever.

ARTEN: You already have! What you say is true, my brother. And true forgiveness can change the world, for the world is merely a symbol of the collective or the one ego mind. To put it even more emphatically, forgiveness is the *only* thing that can *really* change the world, and that isn't even the purpose of forgiveness! The real benefits of true forgiveness go to the forgiver.

GARY: I take it the benefits also go to the receiver simultaneously.

ARTEN: Yes, but that's the Holy Spirit's job. He'll make sure you're both taken care of. Your job is to faithfully handle your part. When you appear to choose forgiveness on this level — and I say you *appear* to choose it here because you're not actually here — as you make your choice here, the Holy Spirit then gets the message to your *entire* mind. It doesn't matter that you can't see it. You're being healed on a larger level whenever you choose the Holy Spirit's alternative instead of the ego's plan. You've been programmed to play out the ego's script, but you can and will break free of that program.

GARY: From what I recall in the text, the Holy Spirit or J will adjust the script for me?

ARTEN: Yes, and you'll be learning more about the subject of time. For now, remember we've already said there are two scripts — the ego's and the Holy Spirit's — and that one of the purposes of the miracle is to save you time. If you choose forgiveness instead of the ego, then J has made the following promise to you.

When you perform a miracle, I will arrange both time and space to adjust to it.[34]

He's not talking about changing time here, so much as taking out the parts you don't need in your future anymore, because you've already learned those particular forgiveness lessons. He says,

The miracle shortens time by collapsing it, thus eliminating certain intervals within it. It does this, however, within the larger temporal sequence.[35]

But more about time later.

PURSAH: We'll begin to sum things up now; when we return we're going to start focusing more on the right mind instead of the wrong mind. That will be more fun. We told you our visits would get shorter and sweeter. That's true, but don't ever forget what you're up against. We've refused to be nice about the nature of this world and gloss over J's message. There are numerous passages in his Course about your world that are just as scathing in their opinion as would be expressed by any caustic Gnostic. When we say you should be kind to others, it doesn't mean you should be in denial about the ego thought system. But don't try to change others; change your own mind instead.

Never forget that your fear of losing your individual identity will cause resistance, sometimes serious resistance, to the practice of forgiveness. Sometimes it will prevent you from even wanting to look at the ego, either in the world or in yourself. You're secretly afraid of what's in your unconscious. That's why you have to be vigilant. There is hatred in your mind underneath the surface, but it can be released simply by noticing it when it does surface, and then taking the Holy Spirit's hand instead of the ego's. We'll be a lot more specific about how to do that two visits from now, and we'll share some actual examples with you.

Do you have any other questions you'd like to ask us right now?

GARY: Yeah. Since we're on the subject of how the universe works, are there extraterrestrials out there, and if so, do they have to learn forgiveness lessons too?

ARTEN: In the illusion, yes, there are beings who live on other planets, and some of them do visit Earth. Yes, they do have their own forgiveness lessons to learn. They are not *really* out there, because the universe is in your mind. To believe that beings are necessarily more spiritually advanced than you just because they are more technically advanced would not always be true. What's important is that whether they are compassionate or not, and whether they are humanoid or not, they are your brothers and sisters in Christ — and that is how you should see them.

GARY: Cool. Also, I was wondering, do you know what's causing all these crop circles? Some of them are really intricate.

ARTEN: Sure. Some of them are hoaxes, made by silly people who secretly hate themselves. They're forgiven, but they can't possibly know that until they start practicing forgiveness. Most of the crop circles are authentic — especially the ones that are very complex. One of them is actually the mathematical symbol for the duality of order and chaos! There's a picture of it available. Like the others, it was made with electromagnetic chi directed from the level of the unconscious. It's just another way of throwing an interesting mystery onto the pile of mysteries, in order to keep people looking for answers out there in the world. They are actually being made by the unconscious mind.

> ❧
> **Crop circles are a way of throwing another mystery onto the pile of mysteries, in order to keep people looking for answers out there in the world.**

GARY: All right, I've got one for you. Who murdered President Kennedy?

ARTEN: If you knew, would you forgive them? That's the real question. We didn't come here to get you chasing shadows in the world, brother.

GARY: You can't blame a guy for trying. Oh, before I forget, I thought of another oxymoron for you.

PURSAH: Let's hear it.

GARY: Smart bombs.

ARTEN: Very good. I agree.

GARY: Let me see, what else? Oh yeah, I saw Marianne Williamson on TV again. She has her second book out, and it seems to be mostly about feminism. I saw her give a speech on another network where she said, "What the world needs is more fierce women." Now, I love Marianne, but I was wondering, would you say *A Course in Miracles* has feminism in it?

PURSAH: Marianne is certainly entitled to teach feminism, if that's what she wants. There's nothing wrong with it, but it shouldn't be confused with the Course. The Course doesn't need women teachers to teach other women how to be better women. There are thousands of teachers doing that, and they're welcome to. What the Course needs is women teachers who are willing to teach other women that they are *not* women — because they are not bodies. That would make a unique contribution, if the point was made in no uncertain terms.

ARTEN: Gary, I should point out that you'll be in the same situation we are when it comes to people reading your spoken words without being able to see your facial expressions and hear the tone of your voice and get your attitude. People might not know from the words you've spoken so far that you actually have a good attitude toward women. In fact, haven't you always considered them to be more intelligent than men?

GARY: I think it's pretty clear they are. They're less violent, more nurturing and they vote more intelligently. A lot of us men are just macho dick brains.

PURSAH: You're not — entirely.

GARY: That's right. I stand as a glorious and inspiring example for all of the world to emulate.

ARTEN: We've created a monster! Incidentally, you'll soon be entering a phase of your earthly life where you'll begin to be a little less concerned with bodily adventures and a little more concerned with accomplishments — in your case, spiritual accomplishments. Many men are preoccupied with physical pleasures in the earlier part of their lives, but as they begin to get a little older, their pursuit of sex is replaced by something else.

GARY: Erectile dysfunction?

ARTEN: No. It's something called maturity. We already know you're a lot more mature than your ego defense system would care for you to act. But you're beginning to snap out of it. As the body ages, you tend to be less ruled by your hormones. That's just one of the reasons why people who are a little older tend to do better with *A Course in Miracles*. In general, they're not quite as obsessed with the body, although health does become a concern — but it's not as *driven* a concern. It doesn't take much observation to notice that your society is sex crazed. Physical pleasure is just one of the ego's ways of making people think that bodies are valuable, but we'll talk about sex on another occasion.

GARY: Should I bring anything?

PURSAH: Yes. Forgiveness. It should be pointed out that people who are not as successful in the world have a tendency to get more out of the Course than highly successful people. Some of the people who appear to have it made in the world, and who are relatively satisfied with their lot in life, are actually falling into a trap. The ego sucks them into thinking the world is a good place. What's really happening is that they're living one of the few lifetimes where good karma is called for in the script, so they have a good time. Maybe they have an easy job, and it makes them rich and they appear to have all the luck.

GARY: You mean like Vanna White?

PURSAH: Exactly. How do you know in her next lifetime she's not going to be born starving to death in Africa?

GARY: I wish her nothing but the best in every lifetime. Besides, I heard she's kind of spiritual.

ARTEN: You see? You're catching on. You just wished *yourself* nothing but the best. On a related subject, in the near future we'll be instructing you on the art of forgiveness. As you forgive, you may find yourself to be more at a loss for words than you used to be. Don't worry about that. This isn't about looking smart; it's about being healed by the Holy Spirit. This process is already accelerating within you. As the Course says, you are no longer wholly insane.[36]

GARY: You'll have to excuse me if I *don't* put that on my resumé. But I like the idea of not being a body, being free, not being controlled by magnetic storms changing the earth's magnetic field and so on.

ARTEN: Yes. That kind of thing isn't limited to the earth's magnetic field. It applies to any magnetic field, anywhere in the universe — and it works on any kind of a being. That's because it's really the unconscious mind directing the acting out of a script, and what appears to happen is merely the effect.

GARY: So there are robot bodies being manipulated all over the universe, except they don't know it because they think they really are bodies.

ARTEN: Sure. As just one example, you could say that on any sun, no matter where it is, you have sunspots and sunspot clusters, which are less hot places on the sun's surface caused by a concentration of temporarily distorted magnetic fields. They in turn trigger these huge eruptions, or flares, that shoot up into that sun's atmosphere — sending clouds of electrified gas at a planet or anywhere in that solar system. That type of action is universal, and it controls the thoughts and movements of everything there. Your scientists assign separate causes to everything and reinforce people's illusion of being separate from the so-called forces of nature, as well as being separate from the mind. People are actually being controlled by the collective mind, which then translates its thoughts from the invisible into visible manifestations.

GARY: What you're saying about the resulting script that's acted out, the karma and everything — when people are having one of those good lives where they think they have the world by the balls, don't they use that as an excuse to think they're better than other people, and thus not the guilty ones?

ARTEN: Yes, but don't make them wrong for it. They may think they're more enlightened because of their good karma, or that God has smiled upon them, or that they're just plain better than other people, but everyone participates equally in the script and ends up with just as many so-called good lives and bad lives as everyone else. That's why we emphasized before that how much money or success you get has absolutely nothing to do with how spiritually enlightened you are. There's a danger of thinking you're better than other people if you're doing well, even if your feeling of superiority is a subtle one — but that's just a form of the projection of your unconscious guilt. On the other hand, the people who are having the seemingly less successful lifetimes feel guilty because they're not doing better! Remember, guilt can be projected onto yourself as well as onto others. In any case, the roles people play are reversed in different lifetimes.

GARY: All this is just another way of escaping our own unconscious guilt?

ARTEN: Yes. Remember, the guilt in your unconscious is more terrible and even more acute than what you see and feel on the surface.

GARY: Why is that again?

ARTEN: It's because of your *proximity* to it — if you're in your unconscious. That was the reason for the whole miscreation of the universe in the first place, remember? The need to escape your guilt and your terrible, misguided fear of God. Now you have a world of bodies where the contents of your mind, including the thought of separation and your own unconscious guilt, are seen symbolically as being outside of you, in the world and in other people. You get to be the innocent victim of the world rather than the maker of it. Thus the world and other bodies are the cause of your problems, and even if you feel guilty it's still not your fault. Not *really*. There's always an exterior reason or contributing factor to explain your condition. Get it?

GARY: I think so. I just don't want to, right now.

ARTEN: That's O.K. It's been a long visit for you. Our next one won't be. As we said, the truth is more simple than the ego. Besides, your resistance doesn't make you unique. As we've already indicated, it's very necessary for us to repeat these kinds of ideas in order for them to sink in. Overall, you're doing well, and the Course is here to remind you that instead of being a robot, you have a mind — and that you can change it. It doesn't matter if you have different forces of nature pulling at you, electromagnetic chi telling you what to do, gravity pulling you one way and dark energy pulling you the other way, and allowing the universe to expand at the same time — and a thousand other forces that all work together to cover up the mind during the dance of duality. No matter what appears to be happening, you *can* outmaneuver the ego simply by remembering there are really only *two* choices, then forgiving the contents of your own ego mind. You were being trained in the art of true forgiveness the second you started hearing these ideas — because from that moment on you were looking at the world differently.

To emphasize an important point, you still believe you have a thousand different problems, but the Course knows you have only *one* problem — the seeming separation from God.[37] During our next visit we'll discuss the one real answer to that problem — the Holy Spirit's Answer. After that we'll get more specific about using it to undo your ego.

PURSAH: It's been said by brilliant people, mostly Buddhists, for the last 2600 years, that there are three great mysteries in life. To a fish, it's the water. To a bird, it's the air. To a human being, it's himself. We've said there's nobody out there. Soon, you'll be able to start acting and feeling that way.

GARY: I've heard people say before that there's nobody out there. They didn't really tell me what to do with what I *am* seeing in a satisfactory way, though. Anyway, until you come back, when the world gets in my face and I observe the pecking order of life, and I get not so nicely reminded of where I am in the food chain, I'll try to remember that it's all there merely to facilitate projection. I'll assume that when the Course talks about images, it applies to any perception, including memories, sights, sounds, ideas — anything. Even a blind person would have images in the mind, and they would be just as real or unreal as any other person's images. It's all just a recording that's already been made. While I'm at it, I'll try to apply the "Love holds no grievances" idea any time I remember to. It's not easy to be consistent, but I'll go for it.

> *Never forget the ego is a killer, so it wants you to think God is a killer and fear Him.*

PURSAH: Excellent. A luminous student. Never forget the ego is a killer, so it wants you to think God is a killer and fear Him. The very best way to keep itself going is to suck you into reacting to the script so you'll make it real in your mind. The ego wants conflict, and if you react with any negative emotion, that's conflict. It's your judgment that keeps the ego system alive, but your forgiveness will free it. So you have to be on your toes.

To forgive means *to give ahead of time*. In other words, your attitude is that you're ready to forgive, no matter *what* it is that comes up in your awareness. At first, that seems like a tall order. Yet I promise you the day will come when you'll be capable of laughing at anything the ego throws at you — just like J could, and just like we did eventually. The day will come when you'll be ready to be like us and leave the script, and serve as a light for others to follow out of the dream.

GARY: Sounds good to me. I might try to start our book, too. I promise to labor for long minutes between numerous breaks.

PURSAH: Good. I wouldn't want you to change your lifestyle; it's very becoming. Becoming what, I'm not sure.

GARY: Say, I just thought of something. Since you have a tendency to repeat things, will I have to do it too, or should I edit out things I think are redundant? I wouldn't want people to think you didn't realize that you repeat ideas.

ARTEN: We want you to arrange our conversations into a presentable format. Repeating ideas is an essential part of our teaching style. Reading or hearing spiritual ideas just once is *not* enough. I told you at the beginning we'd be repeating ideas enough for you to learn.

GARY: All right. I'll do my best.

PURSAH: Yes, you will. Don't forget, you're living at a very unique point in history and you have a chance to make a contribution. My Gospel as well as some others were rediscovered in late 1945, and the Dead Sea Scrolls soon after. For 1600 years before that, the church had strictly forbade any questioning of scripture or church theology. Then suddenly in the 1960s, all that changed. The 2ND Vatican Council reversed the policies of many centuries of intellectual repression — when it had been considered heresy even to question the church's assumptions about J. It was in the historic year of 1965 that the Council issued its encyclical, *The Church in the Modern World*. There was finally freedom of inquiry into theology, the Bible, the nature of J and the church's place in the world. These things were now open to honest study and intellectual analysis. Scholars were actually encouraged to investigate everything. I assure you it was no accident that J started dictating the Course to Helen that very same year.

ARTEN: You think the Course is part of the New Age movement, but it's not. Don't limit it. Yes, it's good that some people are more open-minded and ready for new ideas. Remember the Course is unique because it's J explaining what he really wants to say. Remember that this is his *only* Course. There are other things that have come out since the Course was published that people have said came from him. Yet they don't really teach the same thing as the Course. I ask you, would J contradict himself? I don't say that to put anybody down. Obviously, we are not angry at people who we disagree with. We say these things merely for your clarification.

PURSAH: During the next few months, don't just hide out and study. Interact with people. Experience them and forgive them when you should. Consider it to be an opportunity. Illusions must be for-given on the level where they are experienced. For you, that means living a normal life and interacting with society. Remember, the Course wasn't given to a solitary person on a mountaintop some-where. It was given in New York City — the epitome of complexity.

ARTEN: When we return, we'll talk about your Helper, the One who has been with you for an eternity, but whose Voice you're just beginning to really hear. The Holy Spirit's Voice will lead you home. At first, He's like a whisper in your dream. But then, as you keep practicing forgiveness, His Voice gets louder and clearer. He can show up for you in many different ways. One way is in a book. In our case, He may be an irreverent whisper — but only because that will be helpful in its own way. We are reverent only to God and spirit, and perhaps that will help you cut to the chase.

Until we come back, remember that when you forgive, you shouldn't fall for the ego's brand of forgiveness — which is the world's ineffective and traditional way of forgiving others. As the Course tells you,

> The ego, too, has a plan of forgiveness because you are ask-ing for one, though not of the right teacher. The ego's plan, of course, makes no sense and will not work. By following its plan you will merely place yourself in an impossible sit-uation, to which the ego always leads you. The ego's plan is to have you see error clearly first, and then overlook it. Yet how can you overlook what you have made real? By see-ing it clearly, you have made it real and *cannot* overlook it.[38]

Your brothers and sisters — which includes your mother and father — haven't really done what you think they've done, and remembering that fact is vital.

PURSAH: We'd like to leave you with a thought from the Course you may want to remember when you're tempted to judge someone. Whether you're driving down the street, working with people, social-izing, watching television or reading something on your computer, if you feel the addiction of judgment assert itself, remember J's words from the section in the Text called "The Self-Accused":

...Learn this, and learn it well, for it is here delay of happiness is shortened by a span of time you cannot realize. You never hate your brother for his sins, but only for your own. Whatever form his sins appear to take, it but obscures the fact that you believe them to be yours, and therefore meriting a "just" attack.[39]

You judge only yourself, and you forgive only yourself. We wish you success, and we'll be sure to pop in sometime.

And then they appeared to be gone, but I sensed I wasn't alone.

PART II

Waking Up

6

The Holy Spirit's Alternative

The ego made the world as it perceives it, but the
Holy Spirit, the reinterpreter of what the ego made,
sees the world as a teaching device for bringing you home.[1]

F OR the next several months I was excited about the five visits I
had received from Pursah and Arten, but I also felt like the rug
had been pulled out from under me. I'd gotten used to learning spiritual and self-improvement programs that were designed to help me
better the experience of my everyday life. Now I was attempting to
apply a thought system designed not to improve my life, but to wake
me up from what I *thought* was my life. This was a whole new
approach. Ironically, the training I was now embarked upon would
also raise my quality of life, with an emphasis on living for peace
instead of strengthening myself to win conflicts.

In taking a closer look at my everyday life, I was shocked to see
how automatic my judgments often were. I made gains in observing
this kneejerk tendency, detaching myself from it and taking the
charge out of my grievances. That wasn't all the way to forgiveness,
but it helped me become more aware of my ego's thought patterns. I
realized that even in my discussions with Arten and Pursah, my
smart-ass defense against shyness would dominate my personality
and make me say things I probably wouldn't say if my ego wasn't
running the show. I wondered if Arten and Pursah were just trying
to make me feel comfortable by speaking to me in my own language;
I realized that if I changed my style a little, they probably would too.

As I practiced the Course's Workbook Lessons, I was being steadily trained to choose to think with the Holy Spirit in my right mind instead of the ego in my wrong mind. This resulted in some wild and joyous light episodes during the day as well as bloody and horrific nightmares while in bed at night. I would have never believed such ugly images could be in my unconscious. I was sure that such nightmare images didn't show up for everyone who did the Course, but here they were, reflecting the awful and insane self-image that was buried in the depths of my ego — and now being shown to me in order to be forgiven and released to the Holy Spirit in peace.

It was disconcerting to remember that my thinking wasn't really being done on this level. The mind was signaling to my brain what to see, hear, think, do and experience. My brain was simply the programmed hardware that ran and regulated my body, relaying to me a movie that could be called "Life of Gary."

The mind was like a programmer that told me, through my brain and body, what to experience and how to respond. I had been controlled like a robot, told what to do, and programmed to think it was really me making these decisions on this level. Just as a human being could build a computer, program it and tell it what to do — or could direct a virtual reality figure to do things within an environment that didn't truly exist — the programmer mind was directing me to move within and experience a world that didn't truly exist in order to convince me I was a body. That body was sometimes getting what it wanted, but usually missing out on something, whether physical or psychological. This sense of lack was symbolic of being separate from God. The specific reasons for my problems were shown to me as external to myself, operating in a universe that was never really there, in order to serve as a scapegoat for my hidden unconscious guilt over that very same separation.

I realized that even though this unconscious mind that was calling the shots seemed to be outside of me, it really wasn't. The mind issuing the directives of the ego thought system was within me, not without, which also meant that the universe was in my mind, not without. I had to turn the tables on it; Heaven was also here and was, in fact, all that really existed. There was no place else — but I had made an illusion that seemed to replace Heaven and then tucked that illusion in between myself and God in an effort to escape an imaginary punishment which I now secretly and erroneously believed I deserved. Like everybody else, I would find a way to punish myself for this imagined guilt. Yet all the while, God was merely waiting to welcome me home — as soon as I was healed by the Holy Spirit and ready to return to reality. We would then celebrate for all of eternity. Until now, I hadn't had a clue about all this.

Being aware of these things made me begin to appreciate the magnitude of my mind. I knew that all the decisions for illusion had been made unconsciously, and then the corresponding symbols of those decisions were acted out in the false universe. The decision to be separate and guilty came first, and then the universe had instantly put up its smokescreen. This all seemed so real to each individual observing from his or her particular point of view in the dream that it would take training to forgive what they thought were authentic happenings and think with the Holy Spirit instead.

What I was learning changed the way I looked at my relationships. For example, my in-laws — whom I saw as hard, judgmental people — did not seem to be changing, but now I could back off a little and understand that their reactionary ways symbolized how I reacted to some of the people and problems that came up in my life. Whenever I realized that I condemned my in-laws for my own "sins," presented to me in a deceptively different form, it became much easier for me to be forgiving of them and myself.

Another example was the way I thought of the brokers whom I made trades with over the phone, in the financial markets. Several of these people had the most rude, self-centered and destructive personalities I had ever encountered. Although many brokers sincerely tried to be helpful and professional, there were others who seemed to take a perverse pleasure in the difficulties and occasional losses of a customer, sometimes acting more like enemies than friends. Now I could see their hostility as a symbol of the ego thought system being acted out in a world that waited for my forgiveness rather than my retaliation. In turn, the hidden, dark cornerstones of my unconscious mind were surely being forgiven and healed by the Holy Spirit at the same time. I became more peaceful, and I began to take the occasionally inappropriate behavior of others in stride.

I realized that if I was to continue on this path then I'd need a lot of help in forgiving the very realistic images that were being shown to me, and were designed by the ego to get the better of me on any given day. J was the one I would ask for that help. I could have asked Arten and Pursah, to whom I was deeply grateful, or I could have prayed to them as Thaddaeus and Thomas. Or, as most Course students did, I could have emphasized my relationship with the Holy Spirit, Who was wisely referred to in the Course not as *the* Voice of God, but the Voice *for* God.[2] But I had already established a relationship with J, and I was more than happy to continue to develop it. From what I had learned and experienced, I knew the instant I took J's hand the separation was over.

Of course this would also be true if I took the "hand" of the Holy Spirit. In fact, any symbol of God would do; this was a personal decision. What mattered was that a person had such a symbol and could join with God through this symbol with no sense of distance or separation. With J's Course, God was no longer a removed concept, but right here and right now. I found that the spirit of this feeling, as well as an important part of the message of the Holy Spirit, which J had lived, was beautifully articulated at the beginning of Workbook Lesson number 156:

I walk with God in perfect holiness.

Today's idea but states the simple truth that makes the thought of sin impossible. It promises there is no cause for guilt, and being causeless it does not exist. It follows surely from the basic thought so often mentioned in the text; ideas leave not their source. If this be true, how can you be apart from God? How could you walk the world alone and separate from your Source?[3]

Thus was the Holy Spirit consistent in teaching the principle of the Atonement my teachers had quoted from the Course, that the separation from God never occurred. But I knew there was more. I believed that what Arten and Pursah said about true forgiveness being the way home was true. How else could J have been able to forgive people when they were destroying his body? I practiced the Workbook Lessons faithfully, but also looked forward to Arten and Pursah's explanations of the Holy Spirit and true forgiveness.

I especially made it a point to remember the "Love holds no grievances" idea whenever I could. This had a way of stopping my judgment right in its tracks. How could I complain about a situation, or judge a sister or brother, or wish for a different outcome if I was Love, and if Love holds no grievances? My attitude and my mental processes were changing.

For instance, Karen's personality and mine often seemed like oil and water. When I wanted to be quiet and think, she wanted to talk — constantly. I explained to her many times that I needed to concentrate when I was in the room we used as our office, but it didn't do any good. I felt like I may as well have been talking to a brick wall.

When I thought about the situation using the Course principles I had learned so far, I remembered that I was the one who decided to get married. I certainly wasn't a victim. Also, what was her resistance to honoring my repeated requests except a form of sleep or denial — and wasn't this really symbolic of my own denial of numerous things, including the entire thought system of the ego?

One night when Karen started talking up a storm while I was trying to work, I finally remembered to use the "Love holds no grievances" idea in this particularly difficult circumstance. Suddenly I felt different. I wasn't trying to apply love, I *was* love! I could then see this problem as an opportunity to choose what I wanted to be by seeing Karen through the eyes of the Holy Spirit's unconditional love. Soon after, I started doing most of my work when she wasn't home or after she went to sleep. That way I could take the time to listen, and also find the time to concentrate on my work.

Then on December 21, one year to the day since Arten and Pursah had made their very first appearance to me, they showed up in my living room for the sixth time.

GARY: I knew you'd come today! It's our anniversary.

PURSAH: Yes. We came on this day just for you. Dates aren't important, but we knew you were looking forward to it.

GARY: Just because I had it marked on my calendar doesn't mean I was looking forward to it. Sorry, I'm trying not to be as big a wise ass.

ARTEN: Don't try to change all at once, dear brother. You might explode.

PURSAH: That notwithstanding, we're here to help you accelerate your progress even more. The past is prologue. Everything we've said up until now was just to help prepare you. Our style was designed to get you to pay attention. But it's not the first day of school any-more, and it's time for you to *grow up*. If you walk with J or the Holy Spirit then it means you think like them. Let's talk about how they think. In order to do so, we'll compare the Holy Spirit's attitude to your ego's frail ideas.

ARTEN: The ego believes in opposites — things like pleasure and pain. The Holy Spirit says there are no opposites, and that your *true* joy can have no counterpart. As the Course puts it,

> **How else can you find joy in a joyless place except by real-izing that you are not there?**[4]

The ego wants and believes in complexity. The truth of the Holy Spirit is simple — not necessarily easy for you to accept, but simple.

The ego says you are different than others. The Holy Spirit says that in reality, everyone is the same — and you must feel that way in order to see like Him. For the Course tells you,

> **The difference between the ego's projection and the Holy Spirit's extension is very simple. The ego projects to exclude, and therefore to deceive. The Holy Spirit extends by recog-nizing Himself in every mind, and thus perceives them as one. Nothing conflicts in this perception, because what the Holy Spirit perceives is all the same. Wherever He looks He sees Himself, and because He is united He offers the whole Kingdom always. This is the one message God gave to Him and for which He must speak, because that is what He is. The peace of God lies in that message, and so the peace of God lies in you. The great peace of the Kingdom shines in your mind forever, but it must shine outward to make you aware of it.**[5]

Of course God gave that message to you in Heaven, and the Holy Spirit is your memory of that message. Now, in order to remember Who you really are, you must share the message of the Holy Spirit with those who you see in your mind.

The ego says you've suffered a terrible loss, and loss is now a part of what you call life. The Holy Spirit says there is no loss in reality, and that God's child cannot lose. The Workbook says,

> *The ego says you've suffered a terrible loss, and loss is now a part of what you call reality. The Holy Spirit says there is no loss in reality.*

Forgive all thoughts which would oppose the truth of your completion, unity and peace. You cannot lose the gifts your Father gave.[6]

and, a little later in the Workbook,

You but receive according to God's plan, and never lose or sacrifice or die.[7]

The ego says others are guilty, because it secretly believes you're guilty. It uses anger and righteous indignation, or even laughing at others, to put distance between you and your guilt. You think only animals and children are innocent, because that's where you've chosen to see your own seemingly lost innocence. The ego has to put the idea of innocence *somewhere*. But the Holy Spirit says everyone is completely innocent, because He knows that you're completely innocent.

Think of yourself as being self-accused. For as the Course puts it,

Only the self-accused condemn.[8]

You've accused and convicted yourself. But now, think of the Holy Spirit as being like a Higher Court, as the Course describes with these great words:

You need not fear the Higher Court will condemn you. It will merely dismiss the case against you. There can be no case against a child of God, and every witness to guilt in God's creations is bearing false witness to God Himself. Appeal everything you believe gladly to God's Own Higher Court, because it speaks for Him and therefore speaks truly. It will dismiss the case against you, however carefully you have built it up. The case may be fool-proof, but it is not God-proof. The Holy Spirit will not hear it, because He can only witness truly. His verdict will always be "thine is the Kingdom," because He was given to you to remind you of what you are.[9]

The ego attempts to convince you that you have a personal story that is obviously real. The attitude of the Holy Spirit though, can best be summed up in just three words: *It never happened.*

The ego would be ecstatic if you continued to believe there is a world out there that existed before your life began, and will go on without you after your body dies. The Holy Spirit's response, as outrageous as it may seem to your ego, is this — as quoted from the Workbook:

> ...There is no world! This is the central thought the course attempts to teach. Not everyone is ready to accept it, and each one must go as far as he can let himself be led along the road to truth. He will return and go still farther, or perhaps step back a while and then return again.
>
> But healing is the gift of those who are prepared to learn there is no world, and can accept the lesson now. Their readiness will bring the lesson to them in some form which they can understand and recognize.[10]

GARY: I wish people could hear you when you quote from the Course; it's really beautiful. You're right, though — some of what the Course says is really outrageous to the ego and hard to believe sometimes. If someone is mad at me, it seems the Course is saying that what I'm seeing isn't a real person, but a symbol of my *own* anger, presented as being external to me. So it's actually my own hatred and insanity I see out in the world, even on the news. That's pretty far out. Yet within the model you've explained, it makes sense.

ARTEN: Yes, and the ego would say the angry person you see outside of yourself is a threat that needs to be taken care of in some way. The Holy Spirit sees the angry person as a suffering person who is calling out for help. Since the Course teaches, as we've already quoted, that you have only two emotions, love and fear, then the Holy Spirit sees everything in the world as either an expression of love or a call for love.[11]

Now if someone's *expressing* love, what would be an appropriate response from you?

GARY: Love, of course.

ARTEN: Excellent, Gary. That high school diploma is finally starting to pay off. And if someone is *calling out* for love, then what would be the appropriate response from you?

GARY: Love, wise guy. Under the Holy Spirit's thought system, the proper response to any situation is always love. When you think with the Holy Spirit, you're consistent in your attitude, which is love.

ARTEN: Beautiful. I'll make a love-inspired deal with you. I'll stop being a smart ass if you will. It's not as much fun when you're on the receiving end, is it?

GARY: I see what you mean. Anyway, I'm cutting down. I get the idea about the consistency of love.

PURSAH: Very good. If the Course is saying there is no world, then there are not really any people out there who are smarter or more gifted than you. There are not really any people out there who are richer than you, or any who are more famous than you, or getting more sex than you, or doing whatever is necessary to make you feel angry, inferior, or guilty. There's not really anyone coming after you for whatever reason. There's no world for you to conquer, like adults playing King of the Mountain, trying to push each other off the top, which is merely symbolic of the ego trying to overthrow God. There are no problems or threats that can harm what you really are in any way. It's only a dream, and it's actually possible for you to have the kind of peace of mind and lack of fear that would accompany the conviction of that truth. As J asks you so pointedly in the Text,

...What if you recognized this world is an hallucination? What if you really understood you made it up? What if you realized that those who seem to walk about in it, to sin and die, attack and murder and destroy themselves, are wholly unreal?[12]

The Holy Spirit knows that the images you see are just that — images and nothing more. By taking Him as your Teacher, you can learn to experience this through the power of His forgiveness, which is *your* power when you join with Him and think like Him.

ARTEN: The ego says you're a body. The Holy Spirit says you are not a body; you are not a person, you are not a human being — you are like Him. The ego says your thoughts are quite important. The Holy Spirit knows that only the thoughts you think with God are real, and nothing else matters. In Heaven, you don't have to think at all. In fact you are thought *by* God. On this level, the Course considers the thoughts you think with the Holy Spirit to be your real thoughts. Moreover, it could be said that the Holy Spirit *is* the only truth on the level of the world. Review Workbook Lessons 35 and 45, among others.

The ego calls for sacrifice. In contrast, the Holy Spirit says there is no need for sacrifice of any kind. During our next visit, we'll talk about the real meaning of the crucifixion and the resurrection.

The ego says, "The Lord giveth and the Lord taketh away." The Holy Spirit knows that God only gives, and *never* takes away.

The ego reverently proclaims death is real. The Holy Spirit says nobody is dead, and no one can ever really die.

The ego judges something as good or bad; the Holy Spirit says it is neither, because it isn't true. Thus all things on the level of form are equally untrue because of their illusory nature.

The ego assigns specific, different identities. Both its "love" and hate are directed at specific individuals. The Holy Spirit thinks of everyone as being the same and totally abstract. Thus, like J, His Love is non-specific and all-encompassing.

The ego devises clever reasons why you should continue to listen to its selfish counsel, but the Holy Spirit is certain that at some point you'll turn to Him, and ultimately go home with Him — as the law of forgiveness and the laws of the mind dictate. For as the Course teaches, if you really learn how to forgive and actually do it, your return to God *must* eventually follow.

> Salvation is nothing more than "right-mindedness," which is not the One-mindedness of the Holy Spirit, but which must be achieved before One-mindedness is restored. Right-mindedness leads to the next step automatically, because right perception is uniformly without attack, and therefore wrong-mindedness is obliterated. The ego cannot survive without judgment, and is laid aside accordingly. The mind then has only one direction in which it can move. Its direction is always automatic, because it cannot but be dictated by the thought system to which it adheres.[13]

PURSAH: The ego loves it when you regret your past. "Would have, could have, should have," and, "If only I had done this instead of that," and "If only I knew then what I know now," are some of the ego's favorite numbers. Not only does this make your past real to you, it makes you feel bad at the same time — all to the ego's delight. The Holy Spirit knows that with the exception of forgiveness, it doesn't matter what you do. To the ego, this is heresy. But the Holy Spirit wants you to be healed, and knows that the unconscious guilt in your mind would have played itself out in some way eventually — even if you did take a different turn along the road.

ARTEN: In connection with that, the ego wants *what* you do to be important. As a way of intruding on your spirituality and delaying the truth, it tries to make what you do in *that* area important and special. Yet to the Holy Spirit, what you do for Him, or for Jesus or for God are not important. How can anything that occurs in an illusion be important if you actually understand it's not real? Only forgiveness and your healing matter. True, that kind of a teaching may not be the basis for a popular religion that takes over the world and tells everybody else how they should be living their lives — but it is definitely the truth.

GARY: So it doesn't really matter if I write our book or not — or how long it takes me?

ARTEN: That's correct. We're happy to be here with you and teach you Gary, but it's not important. It's not important that you *do* anything. You don't have to establish your worth with us or with God. That was done in God's Mind when He created you. Nothing else that appears to happen in the universe of perception can change that — except in your mistaken dreams. As the Course helps you to remember,

You dwell not here, but in eternity.[14]

and,

> ❧
> **You don't have to create your worth with God. That was done in God's Mind when He created you.**

Whenever you are tempted to undertake a useless journey that would lead away from light, remember what you really want, and say:

The Holy Spirit leads me unto Christ, and where else would I go? What need have I but to awake in Him?[15]

GARY: I *am* Christ in reality, and so is everybody else, and we're all one. Like you said earlier, on this level we all see the same dream, but from a different point of view. I think Freud said everybody in your dreams at night is really you, so day or night it's always a symbol of me over there who's seeing my own dream from a different vantage point. My job is to rejoin with myself through forgiveness and become whole again.

PURSAH: Not bad for a male of the species. You know, when we first came here, you didn't like to talk very much.

GARY: I still don't, but I guess I'm different with you 'cause I know you won't judge me — not *really.*

PURSAH: All you have to do is remember there's not anybody out there to judge you, and what you really are can't be affected by what the world thinks. As the Course tells you,

> ...You cannot be hurt, and do not want to show your brother anything except your wholeness. Show him that he cannot

hurt you and hold nothing against him, or you hold it against yourself. This is the meaning of "turning the other cheek."[16]

ARTEN: While the Holy Spirit teaches you of your true strength, the ego tells you and your fellow macho men, and all the liberated women, that they have to be tough and learn how to kick ass in the rat race or someone else will get their cheese. All this does is prove how fearful they are, because if they weren't afraid then they wouldn't have to *be* tough. They're really calling out for love without knowing it.

PURSAH: The ego tries to convince you that your problems are the problem, but the Holy Spirit knows it's the well-hidden, unconscious guilt which makes you need to dream a world of separation in the first place that's the problem. Of course, the world doesn't think that. The world doesn't even know about it! As the Course makes sure to remind you late in the Text,

> ...Of one thing you were sure: of all the many causes you perceived as bringing pain and suffering to you, your guilt was not among them.[17]

ARTEN: We've already quoted the Course as saying the guiltless mind cannot suffer. So when the Course says you cannot be hurt, it means that practicing the kind of forgiveness which knows you cannot really be hurt will eventually result in the same ability as J had, not to suffer or feel pain. How significant will your problems be then? To amplify something we said before, the ego wants J-the-wonder-body to be much different than you and very special, which is a very clever way of keeping everyone different and special. The Holy Spirit knows you're really the same. As the Clarification of Terms at the end of the Course says about J,

> The name of *Jesus* is the name of one who was a man but saw the face of Christ in all his brothers and remembered God. So he became identified with *Christ*, a man no longer, but at one with God.[18]

That's what He wants for you. We're getting close to the point now where we're going to get a little more precise about how you can have the attitude that will help you see the face of Christ — which is really *your* face — in everyone. It might help you to remember that *you're* the one whom forgiveness helps. You don't always have to care personally about the person you're forgiving. Your job is simply to correct your misperceptions, and it isn't against the rules to know that you can't help but benefit because of it.

GARY: So just because I'm forgiving someone, that doesn't mean I have to hang around with them.

ARTEN: That's right. This isn't about being a do-gooder, not that there's anything wrong with doing good deeds if it turns you on. The Course is about being a right *thinker*. A lot of Christians ask nowadays, "What would Jesus do?" There's only one correct answer to that question, and it would always be the same. He'd forgive. Forgiveness has to do with what you think. What you do isn't the important thing, even though it's a result of what you think. It's what you think that will either keep you dreaming or help get you home, not what you do.

GARY: You mean J never said to you, "Go therefore and make believers of all nations?"

ARTEN: I'm glad you're kidding.

PURSAH: Speaking of nations, remember that they're not important either. What you really are is eternal. The United States isn't.

GARY: Blasphemy!

ARTEN: Thomas Jefferson, considered to be the greatest thinker among your forefathers and the author of your Declaration of Independence, was also an expert on scripture. Over the years of his life he edited the Bible in order to make his own personal Bible. Of course he couldn't make it available to the public at that time without being accused of terrible things, but it will be made available soon for those who want to see it.

To summarize, he left out the old scripture — what you call the Old Testament — completely. He didn't leave in anything about J being God in the flesh. He didn't retain anything about J performing physical miracles. He left out almost 200 pages of the New Testament, leaving only 46. But he kept in *everything* about forgiveness and healing and how you think. If the conservatives in your country want to dismiss *A Course in Miracles* as being too radical, perhaps they should listen to the visionary genius behind your nation's roots, rather than wasting their time blindly defending the corporate-owned mockery of democracy it has become.

GARY: So Thomas Jefferson was able to cut through the religious and dualistic bullshit and get to what's important. At the same time, I should remember that a lot of people need the bullshit until they're ready to give up the unnecessary stuff and cut to the chase. There's not really any sense in putting them down or trying to take the ideas they need away from them.

ARTEN: Very good, Gary. A radiant student. But watch your language. Just because a lot of those movies you like are rated "R," it doesn't mean our book has to be.

GARY: I've been trying to mind my manners.

ARTEN: We know. You haven't used the *f* word once. We've also noticed you're not drinking much lately. Such discipline is surely indicative of a future master — providing you continue with your training.

GARY: It occurred to me that I drink because I think I'm guilty, even though I'm not really guilty, and I'm afraid of God, even though my fear shows up as worry about other things.

ARTEN: Yes, but that doesn't mean that people who don't drink, smoke or use drugs aren't afraid. They just find other ways of dealing with it or denying it. Forgiveness is the only way out for everyone.

PURSAH: Which brings us close to the end of our brief discussion about the Holy Spirit. The Course says He recognizes your illusions without believing in them.[19] So listen to Him, that you might see like Him. The Course says later, in the Workbook,

> ...The Holy Spirit understands the means you made, by which you would attain what is forever unattainable. And if you offer them to Him, He will employ the means you made for exile to restore your mind to where it truly is at home.[20]

GARY: So He takes the same illusions or images I've made and uses them to get me home. That's perfect, like turning the tables on the ego by using the same stuff the ego made to undo it. In order for that to happen, I have to do something you quoted the Course as saying earlier; I need to bring my illusions to the truth instead of giving truth to my illusions. The Course also says J is a Savior because he saw the false without accepting it as true.[21] If I do that, then not only will I be a Savior like him, but my mind will be healed by the Holy Spirit at the same time.

PURSAH: Yes. J was able to tell the story of the prodigal Son so well because he *was* the prodigal Son, just like you. He listened to the Holy Spirit; that's how he was able to see the false without accepting it as true. By listening to the Holy Spirit, you can become like J and be totally identified with Christ. As the Course says about your Helper,

The Holy Spirit abides in the part of your mind that is part of the Christ Mind.[22]

In one of the Course's references to the prodigal Son story, connecting the Holy Spirit to it,

...He seems to be a Guide through a far country, for you need that form of help.[23]

ARTEN: If you're really going to turn the tables on the ego and achieve the thought reversal[24] that the Course talks about, then you have to remember what we discussed last time. The ego has tricked you into thinking you're getting rid of your unconscious guilt when you project it onto others by making them wrong, or condemning them or blaming certain circumstances for your problems or the world's problems, or whatever. Instead, what this really does is cause you to hang on to your unconscious guilt forever. Are you beginning to understand how important forgiveness is for you?

GARY: Believe it or not, I think I really am. The Workbook is helping me a lot.

ARTEN: Yes. By our next visit, you will have completed it. You'll be in an excellent position to practice true forgiveness.

GARY: Then I can be a T.O.G.

ARTEN: Which is?

GARY: Teacher of God.

ARTEN: I like it. You may not have a PH.D., but you can still be a T.O.G. That's your real job now, buddy. All the rest is superfluous. The Course is very poignant about how important your real job is.

...Is not the escape of God's beloved Son from evil dreams that he imagines, yet believes are true, a worthy purpose? Who could hope for more, while there appears to be a choice to make between success and failure; love and fear?[25]

True forgiveness is the real purpose of life, but you've got to choose it in order to make it yours.

GARY: Yeah, I guess I couldn't hope for any more than that. I think the Course also says the Atonement is the natural profession of the children of God.[26] I guess if I'm gonna do it, then I might as well be good at it — forgiveness I mean.

PURSAH: Yes. True forgiveness is the real purpose of life, but you've got to choose it in order to make it yours. Remember, practicing real forgiveness can't help but lead you home. The J underground cannot lose, for J doesn't compromise — because the Holy Spirit doesn't compromise. This is not a revolution of the physical, it's a reclaiming of the mind — ushering in a new way of thinking. When it comes to the Course's advanced form of forgiveness, you *will* be good at it. That will be the focus of our next visit, although it will be a recurring theme through all of our remaining visits. The holy instant will be yours for the asking, my brother.

GARY: Could you briefly clarify for me exactly what the holy instant is?

PURSAH: Yes. As a Course student you'll hear about it a lot. Even though the holy instant actually takes place outside of time and space, you appear to choose it here. The holy instant is simply that instant when you choose the Holy Spirit as your Teacher instead of the ego. As the Course says,

Against the ego's insane notion of salvation the Holy Spirit gently lays the holy instant. We said before that the Holy Spirit must teach through comparisons, and uses opposites to point to truth. The holy instant is the opposite of the ego's fixed belief in salvation through vengeance for the past.[27]

This happens anytime you choose forgiveness — thus acting in both you and your forgivee's best interest, which are really the same, even though on the level of form it may appear that you have separate interests. Your common self-interest is to return to Heaven.

GARY: Are you sure *forgivee* is a word?

PURSAH: It is now. Of course the forgivee is really you; it just doesn't look that way. What you're really accomplishing is the forgiveness of the symbolic contents of your own mind.

GARY: I always forget to ask the questions I want to until after you leave, so do you mind if I ask you something while I'm thinking about it?

PURSAH: What do you think, Arten?

ARTEN: I won't say anything. I promised him I'd stop being a smart ass if he would.

GARY: O.K. You don't have many of the sayings from the Sermon on the Mount in *The Gospel of Thomas*. I was wondering if J really said some of the things I like the most in the Gospels like, "Do not lay up for yourselves treasures on earth, where moth and rust consume and where thieves break in and steal, but lay up for yourselves treasures in Heaven, where neither moth nor rust consumes and where thieves do not break in and steal. For where your treasure is, there will your heart be also."

PURSAH: Yes. As I said before, my Gospel doesn't contain everything he said. I never even got to finish it. He did say something very similar to that, although he was a little more graphic than you might think. For example, he didn't use the word *rust*, he used the word *worm* and made the saying more of a choice between the body and spirit. The Sermon on the Mount is actually a composite of sayings. J didn't go up on mountains and give long sermons to the adoring masses below. He did say things that are reasonably close to some of the sayings in the Gospels, and once you understand his thought system, which is the thought system of the Holy Spirit, then you should almost be able to pick out for yourself the kinds of things he would say compared to the kinds of things he wouldn't say.

For example, he says something similar in the Course to the saying you just referred to in regards to the importance of what you treasure. No matter how he says it, the choice is always between two things: the ego's world of the body, or the Holy Spirit's world of spirit and God.

> ...Faith makes the power of belief, and where it is invested determines its reward. For faith is always given what is treasured, and what is treasured is returned to you.[28]

GARY: Some Course students I've talked to seem to think God created the good parts of the world and not the bad, and that the Course is trying to get us to give up our bad perceptions, but keep the good ones.

ARTEN: Yes. We've already said enough about perception and consciousness being of the ego, but there will still be those who try to tell you what you just described. Let's be very clear again; God did not even create *part* of the world. We just quoted the Course as saying there is no world! How could God have created part of it if there isn't any? It's not the Holy Spirit's intention to do *anything* except wake you up from *your* dream that there *is* a world! That's true whether it seems to be temporarily good or bad.

Ultimately, the truth is not temporal; it is plenary, absolute, total. Yet on this level, the healing of your perception by the Holy Spirit is a temporary process leading to an absolute solution.

GARY: Another question. Why the emphasis on mind and spirit being different?

ARTEN: It's simple. The ego, or wrong mind, makes *everything* that appears to happen on the level of form. Spirit makes *nothing* happen on the level of form, which is why you shouldn't spiritualize events or objects in the universe. The right mind gives the Holy Spirit's interpretation of the level of form, leading you — and by you we mean that observatory part of the mind that has identified with and thus bound itself to the ego — back home. Home is unchangeable spirit.

GARY: It may be simple for you, but I think I get it.

ARTEN: Good. Even though the Holy Spirit doesn't do anything in the world, His interpretation of the level of form can help you see more clearly what you should do here. That's just a fringe benefit of choosing Him as your Teacher, not the main reason, which is salvation.

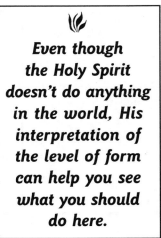

Even though the Holy Spirit doesn't do anything in the world, His interpretation of the level of form can help you see what you should do here.

GARY: Next question. I've known for a long time that separation isn't real, even on the level of form. If the physicists are right and you can't even observe something without affecting it at the subatomic level, then if I look at a star that's billions of light years away, I cause it to change instantly. It doesn't matter how far away it is, because it's not really out there; it's in my mind. If a lot of things in the universe mimic aspects of the truth, does the fact that most of the universe is hidden from us correlate to the fact that most of the mind is unconscious?

ARTEN: Aren't we in a profound mood today? Ninety-five per cent of the universe is dark, or hidden from you. Not only is it correlating to the unconscious, it's also set up that way so you can continue to make discoveries about it and look for answers in the universe instead of in the mind, where the answer really is. You must also remember that the ego uses smoke and mirrors, like a great illusionist, to hide the translation of its unconscious directions into illusory sensory manifestations. For example, are you beginning to get that you don't actually see with the body's eyes?

GARY: I think so, but that's kind of scary. I mean it's like the mind is seeing, and the body doesn't really do anything.

PURSAH: Good. We'll leave it right there. There's no need to go too fast. As you said, it can be scary. Do you remember in my Gospel when J said, "Have you discovered the beginning, then, so that you are seeking the end? For where the beginning is, the end will be"? Well, as J says in the Course,

...As you approach the Beginning, you feel the fear of the destruction of your thought system upon you as if it were the fear of death. There is no death, but there *is* a belief in death.[29]

As I said, there's no hurry. The Holy Spirit knows you're afraid of your unconscious. The purpose of the Course is peace, not to scare the hell out of you. The more prepared you are, and the better you do your forgiveness work, the less scary your journey with the Course will ultimately be.

We're going to take our illusory leave, but we'll be back in eight months. The Holy Spirit will be with you, offering you His Alternative at all times. Between now and the time you see us again, finish the Workbook, and have fun. We love you, Gary.

GARY: I love you too, guys.

ARTEN: In four days it will be Christmas. This year, instead of making the holidays the usual orgy of capitalism, make them what they should be. Think about God, and about what you and your brothers and sisters really are. Remembering that the word *light* is synonymous with *truth*, think about these beautiful words that J gave as a present to all those who love his Course.

The sign of Christmas is a star, a light in darkness. See it not outside yourself, but shining in the Heaven within, and accept it as the sign the time of Christ has come.[30]

7

The Law of Forgiveness

Fear binds the world. Forgiveness sets it free.[1]

THE path I had chosen was not fast-food spirituality, and the Course's Workbook was no piece of cake. After a year and four months of almost constant dedication and attention, I managed to complete all 365 of the Workbook Lessons. Although the Course's theory is set forth in the Text, it is greatly elaborated in the Workbook. Both are necessary to understand and apply the Course; neither is complete without the other. The Workbook, however, has a more practical feature to it. Its exercises, which are applied to students' personal relationships and to any situation they find themselves in on any given day, are designed to bring about the *experience* that what the Course is teaching is true.

Indeed, Arten and Pursah had already emphasized that the real Answer to the ego's world would not present itself in the form of an intellectual answer, but as an experience of God that would in effect render the experience of separation meaningless. For me, there were also the occasional and welcome experiences of peace that were present, instead of my usual and habitual upsets. That alone was enough to make me thankful for the direction my life had taken.

For example, instead of being habitually upset that Karen wasn't very "spiritual" and didn't seem to care as much about my sacred path as I did, I decided to follow Arten's advice and just let her learn whatever she should learn at the time. As I forgave her, I felt more peaceful about the fact that I almost certainly didn't meet all of her hidden expectations, and I allowed both of us to simply be the way we were.

Much to my amazement, Karen soon became a "part time" student of the Course, occasionally coming to our study group meetings and even completing the Workbook, which was no small accomplishment. Although she wasn't into the Course as much as I was, she believed what it was saying and made much progress in shifting from a state of conflict to one of peace.

One of the necessary changes in my thinking along the road to the ultimate experience was the acceptance of the idea that the mind projects everything, observes its own projection from a different and seemingly separate point of view, and then interprets that perception as an external fact. The body, being itself an idea of separation, existed only in the mind as a way to experience separation! All my life I had assumed that my eyes saw the world, my body felt it and my brain interpreted it. The Workbook was helping me comprehend that it was silly to think the body's eyes could really see, or that the brain could think or interpret anything.[3] The mind told my body what to see and feel, and how to interpret what I was seeing and feeling. The body was simply a trick, a device within the ego mind that was designed to convince me my worldly life was the truth. The Workbook not only taught the opposite of Newtonian science, but also gave me experience at accepting the Holy Spirit's interpretation of everything, thus facilitating the beginning of the end for my ego.

I was quite annoyed by the first sentence of the Workbook's Epilogue, but not by the second one. "This course is a beginning, not an end. Your Friend goes with you."[4] I knew by now that my Friend, the Holy Spirit, was really my own higher Self. Yet it was very helpful for me to use the Course's soothing and artistic metaphors, and think of myself as being helped by another. In fact, this was very necessary. I still had the world in my face, and the Course was always practical: "This course remains within the ego framework, where it is needed."[5]

As far as observing the world was concerned, the Course explained everything in it without exception. I could look at my entire life, as well as the present, and understand the cause of all human behavior. For example, in school the bullies who had made other students' lives miserable might as well have been saying, "We're cool, you're not. *You're* the guilty and wrong one, not *us*."

The "good" students who could see the injustice in this, as well as the ludicrous nature of many other things in the world, were simply playing their own part in the victim-victimization cycle by seeing guilt in the perpetrators of the injustice instead of in themselves.

And what were most members of various extreme religious sects really saying while proselytizing? Perhaps something like: "You're the guilty ones, not us. *We've* got God! Not *you*. We're going to Heaven and you're going in the fire." What were the insane terrorists of the world really saying when they took away the lives of innocent men, women and children? How about: "*You're* responsible for our problems. You're the guilty party, certainly not *us*." Human beings tend to blame each other for their lot in life, but what we all do is blame each other for our seeming separation from God, resulting in the loss of peace that feels like a permanent fixture of our existence.

The variations are endless. Whether in a close personal relationship or a distant one, someone or something else can always be found to be the cause of the problem — excepting those tortured souls who project all guilt within, consciously blaming themselves for their own unfavorable circumstances. Yet is this really different than blaming another body?

I often felt encouraged by the way I was thinking and the way it made me feel. There were other times when the Course actually seemed to make things worse. With my long denied ego thought system being raised to my awareness, the guilt that kept it denied was also being raised to the surface — sometimes resulting in a greater self-expression of fear than would normally have occurred.

As one example, I had noticed a pronounced increase on television in the previous few years of right-wing political propaganda, especially since the Federal Communications Commission had repealed its "fairness doctrine" and the "equal time rule." Now the powers that be could put out all of the one sided conservative misinformation they wanted to through their networks without having to give fair and equal time to an alternate point of view. A practice which had worked fairly well during the previous thirty years was now abolished, and even though I should have known better, I sometimes found myself becoming more upset than ever by the nonsense I was seeing and hearing on my television screen. I'd sometimes use a raised voice to ask questions like, *Are people really so out of it that they'd believe this crap?* Unfortunately, the answer was often yes.

Despite my occasional lapses, I was still able to practice the Course's principles a good deal of the time. My natural stubbornness was paying off, not in a constant flow of happy experiences but in a new way of looking at the bad ones, thus dramatically shortening the duration of their effects.

By August, I was very excited because eight months had gone by since I had last seen Arten and Pursah. By now I trusted them to keep their word and appear to me again at the end of that interval. Then one afternoon, Pursah showed up, but Arten didn't.

PURSAH: Hey, teacher of God. What's up?

GARY: If I told you, you'd slap my face.

PURSAH: Did we forget to take our anti-smart ass pill this morning?

GARY: Just joking. It's great to see you, but where's that Arten guy?

PURSAH: He's on business.

GARY: Where, or should I say when?

PURSAH: Another dimension. It's not really a different place, because there aren't really any different places, and I think you're starting to get the metaphysical picture. Arten is working with you right now in another one of your lifetimes, and you don't even know it! Sometimes people don't know an ascended master is around. That's why I told you we like to fit in wherever we go. Arten is actually here, too. An ascended master is everywhere. You just can't always see them. We seldom project more than one bodily image of ourselves at one time, and it's always for teaching purposes. The teaching isn't always traditional. Sometimes we interact with someone or do something somewhere that will help facilitate forgiveness in that particular dimension. Most of the time we don't appear at all; we just give people our thoughts.

GARY: I don't suppose you're gonna tell me about the lifetime Arten is helping me in?

PURSAH: Let's work on this one, hotshot. When you forgive in one lifetime, you help the Holy Spirit heal all of them. The forgiveness you've been doing for the last few months is having an effect on you in other dimensions of time. Arten will show up with me again next visit. This time, just focus on talking with me. We're going to discuss forgiveness — true forgiveness. I want you to be even better at it, O.K? The Course is enough, but you're fortunate to have good help in understanding it. For most people, that kind of help is absolutely necessary.

GARY: As Benjamin Franklin said, "Necessity is a mother."

PURSAH: Let's hope you quote the Course more accurately. The Workbook has helped you tremendously. You can read parts of it again anytime you want, but you don't have to do the exercises again. Some people do the exercises in the Workbook twice; some people do them every year. It's an individual thing. In your case, just reading and applying the Workbook ideas the same way you do with the ideas in the Text and the

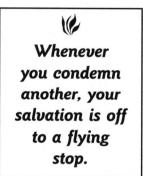

Whenever you condemn another, your salvation is off to a flying stop.

Manual will be enough from now on. As for this discussion, let's get to work.

The Course teaches that your sole responsibility is to accept the Atonement for yourself.[6] You've already accelerated a process where you forgive others instead of judging them. Having completed the Workbook, you finally understand that whenever you condemn another, your salvation is off to a flying stop. You've also had more experiences that the world is a dream, nothing but illusion.

GARY: We had a guest at our study group meeting a couple of weeks ago when somebody mentioned something about the world being an illusion, and this guy was really pissed. He said, "What's the point?" I knew the answer was that you have to understand the world's a dream in order to comprehend forgiveness and salvation, but I didn't explain it very well.

PURSAH: Yes. We said earlier it's not enough to say the world is an illusion. The *point* is that you have to learn how to forgive in order to get home. Understanding the metaphysics of the Course is required in order to understand forgiveness, but it may be helpful to some people if you stress forgiveness first, then bring in the dream-like nature of the world and other features of the truth gradually.

That's just the opposite of what we did with you, but there's a big difference between a book like the one that's going to result from our visits and the kind of personal interactions you'll have with most people. You're not going to teach anybody the whole Course. That means people will only stay with it if they hear something that rings true for them, or piques their interest. Don't try to control that. Just be yourself and let the Holy Spirit work with people. Yes, ask for guidance and share your experience if you want, but don't try to change the world or anyone in it. Just forgive — silently. Don't go up to people and say, "I'm forgiving you now, you know." Which brings us back to the subject at hand.

Tell me something you remember from the Course; anything that comes to mind — quickly.

GARY: O.K. This is one of my favorites.

I am not a body. I am free.
For I am still as God created me.[7]

PURSAH: Good one. That's from the Workbook, which also says,

...The ego holds the body dear because it dwells in it, and lives united with the home that it has made. It is a part of the illusion that has sheltered it from being found illusory itself.[8]

Now, if you thought you were a body before you had the Course, then you can be certain other people definitely think *they* are bodies. An important component of your forgiveness is that you want to teach people, silently, that they are not bodies. That's how your mind learns for certain that *you* are not a body. As the Course puts it,

As you teach so shall you learn.[9]

As we go along, try to remember that. As we've said, when you forgive others, it's really you yourself who is being forgiven.

I'm going to talk about components of forgiveness. That's because, as we've said, forgiveness is an attitude. Everything you learn becomes incorporated into that attitude until forgiveness happens automatically. For most people, especially during the first few years, forgiveness requires that you think about it. You become a master by having *forgiving thought processes*. These right-minded thoughts eventually dominate your mind instead of the ego. A situation occurs or someone comes along whom you need to forgive, and following the lead of the Workbook, you've learned to have right-minded thoughts about the person or situation. Using your understanding of the Course's entire thought system, including the Text and the Manual, contributes to and strengthens your attitude of forgiveness.

These forgiveness thoughts of yours won't usually be linear. Everyone has certain ideas that work best for them. It helps tremendously that the Course is holographic in nature, each thought being related to all others. In fact, you could say that like a hologram, the whole of the Course's thought system is found in all of its sections, or that each part contains the whole. I'm going to give you a few of the Course's ideas that will be especially helpful in building a strong forgiveness attitude. This will free both you and the images you see from the prison they appear to be in. First, let's talk a little bit more about the situation you're faced with, and why the Course is not just abstract, but very practical on this level.

GARY: One important question, please.

PURSAH: All right. You've been good.

GARY: What about people who don't seem to have any fear when they commit horrendous acts? There are people who strap bombs to their bodies and kill themselves along with many other victims, believing that martyrdom will guarantee them a place in Heaven. In America, mass killers tend to prefer automatic weapons to blow away dozens of people without batting an eyelash. Either way, these killers are so cold and methodical — like they don't have any fear. Sometimes they're even smiling. What's the difference between that lack of fear and what you're teaching?

PURSAH: That's a decent question, and the answer can be found in many of the things we've already told you, because they are all part of the same thought system of love. We've already said that the Course teaches that the direction of the mind cannot help but be determined by the thought system to which it adheres. The thought system of the Holy Spirit is guided by love; the thought system of the ego is guided by fear and hatred and will always eventually result in some kind of destruction. Suicide bombers and other murderers may *appear* to be fearless, but their psychotic fear has merely been denied and projected outward. The appearance of peace is not always true inner peace, and it cannot be stated too often that the people of the world will *never* live in peace until they have inner peace, the inevitable result of true forgiveness.

> ❧
>
> **Forgiveness is where the rubber meets the road. Without forgiveness, metaphysics are useless.**

We've also said that what you do is a result of what you think. That doesn't mean you're always going to behave perfectly. Indeed, when the Course talks about a teacher of God becoming perfect here, it is referring to perfect *forgiveness*, not perfect behavior. True peace will come from true forgiveness. And violence — which is the acting out of one's own self-hatred *seen* as being outside of oneself — will *never* come as a result of the thought system of the Holy Spirit, who teaches only love and forgiveness. The metaphysics of the Course are built around the reality of God and the unreality of the separation, and are essential to know. But forgiveness is where the rubber meets the road. Without forgiveness, metaphysics are useless. That's why we say the Course is practical. In the end, there are really only two things you can do. As the Course teaches,

He who would not forgive must judge, for he must justify his failure to forgive.[10]

Your job is to teach forgiveness. We've said the Course tells you that to teach is to demonstrate. It also says,

I do not call for martyrs but for teachers.[11]

Forgiveness will never result in violence, but judgment will always result in some kind of negative effect on the level of form, even if the effect is just on your own health. Violence is the ultimate and illogical extension of fear, judgment and anger. The delusional thought system of the ego will always lead to some form of violence and murder eventually, because it requires that people see their enemy — or the perceived cause of their problem — as being outside of them. So do you, but you have found the way out. By reversing the ego's thinking, your fear will be released, not projected.

With salvation there is no one out there to blame for your one real problem, of which all the others are symbolic. The cause, which is the decision to believe in the separation from God, and the solution, which is the principle of the Atonement, are both in your mind — where you now have the power to choose the Holy Spirit's Answer.

Let's examine the components of forgiveness. Learn and remember them well, dear student. If you can remember them when you are confronted by the ego's constant temptations to regard yourself as a body, you'll go into the forgiveness hall of fame. These ideas are the way of salvation, and your ticket home — if you get to the point where you apply them regularly.

GARY: I take it that thing about the forgiveness hall of fame is a metaphor, since I'm a baseball fan, huh?

PURSAH: You see? You can already tell the difference between what should be taken literally and what should be taken as metaphor.

GARY: All right. Let's get to it. I'm used to working for nothing, so tell me about the forgiveness gig. You know I'm kidding, right? I know Heaven could hardly be called nothing.

PURSAH: That's correct. And you don't have to wait until your experience of enlightenment before you enjoy the benefits of forgiveness. As the Course tells you,

A tranquil mind is not a little gift.[12]

With that in mind, a component of practicing forgiveness when you're confronted by an opportunity would be to *remember that you're dreaming*. You authored the dream and made the figures in it act out for you, so you could see your unconscious guilt outside yourself. If you remember you're dreaming, then there's nothing out there but your own projection. Once you believe that — and belief only comes from practice and experience — then there's no need for what you're seeing and now forgiving to have any impact on you. As the Course puts it,

> The miracle establishes you dream a dream, and that its content is not true. This is a crucial step in dealing with illusions. No one is afraid of them when he perceives he made them up. The fear was held in place because he did not see that he was author of the dream, and not a figure in the dream.[13]

That quote was from the section of the Course called "Reversing Effect and Cause," which also says,

> **The miracle is the first step in giving back to cause the function of causation, not effect.**[14]

GARY: So now it's *my* dream, not somebody else's, because there's only one of us. There's not really anybody or anything besides my projection, which I'm now "re-calling" by taking responsibility for it.

PURSAH: Yes. Remember, that doesn't mean there aren't seemingly separated minds who think they're really there, but like you, they have to learn the truth in order for the entire mind to be one again. As we say, this will all become part of your attitude, but it's helpful at first to think of it as being made up of different components. Once you're the cause and not the effect, another component of forgiveness would be to *forgive both your projected images and yourself for dreaming them.*

You already know the Course tells you to forgive your brother for what he *hasn't* done. That would be true forgiveness because, as the Course also says, you're not making the error real. You're not giving truth to your illusions; you're bringing your illusions to the truth. Now it's time to forgive yourself for dreaming this whole mess in the first place. If nothing's happened — and if the Course teaches *anything*, it's that nothing's happened — then you're innocent. Thus as you forgive your brothers and sisters, your mind realizes simultaneously that you are forgiven. Remember, we've also quoted the Course as saying that as you see him, you will see yourself.

GARY: If nobody's there, and if I believe the Course, then what is really out there is Christ. If that's what I choose to see, instead of the images my body's eyes show me, then that must be what I am.

PURSAH: Very good. You see? The components of forgiveness all fit together. If the people you see are Christ, then so are you. If you respond with the judgment of the ego and give reality to the dreams of others that they too are egos, then that's what you'll think you are. It's true that there's nobody out there. To repeat an important point, the people you see think that they are out there — just like ghosts. As the Course says, from the section called "The Greater Joining,"

Join not your brother's dreams but join with him, and where you join His Son the Father is.[15]

And in the next section, "The Alternate to Dreams of Fear,"

You share no evil dreams if you forgive the dreamer, and perceive that he is not the dream he made. And so he cannot be a part of yours, from which you both are free.[16]

GARY: Doing this forgiveness will cause me to gradually wake up from the dream?

PURSAH: Yes. If you woke up all at once I assure you it wouldn't be pleasant. You have to be prepared for a different form of life. Even in this life, where people think they are bodies, change is not really welcome — even if people want to pretend it is. We said that J admired Plato's story of the Cave, the one your mother used to read to you. He makes reference to it in this quote from the Course, which points out that both you *and* your brother will have conscious and unconscious resistance to the truth. It also advises that you shouldn't expect everyone to agree with you in this lifetime.

Prisoners bound with heavy chains for years, starved and emaciated, weak and exhausted, and with eyes so long cast down in darkness they remember not the light, do not leap up in joy the instant they are made free. It takes a while for them to understand what freedom is.[17]

Your job is to forgive, not to beg for the agreement of those seemingly separated minds you are forgiving. As another way of looking at this same component of forgiveness, remember this paragraph from the Workbook.

There is a very simple way to find the door to true forgiveness, and perceive it open wide in welcome. When you feel that you are tempted to accuse someone of sin in any form, do not allow your mind to dwell on what you think he did, for that is self-deception. Ask instead, "Would I accuse myself of doing this?"[18]

Instead of accusing yourself, remember that their call for love is your call for love. You should be grateful to them; you need them as much as they need you. Without those images you see and the miracle, you'd *never* be able to find the way out. These images are symbolic of what's in your unconscious mind and without them, your unconscious guilt would be forever hidden from you — there would be no escape.

The Holy Spirit takes the very device the ego made to protect itself and uses it to undo it. His devices can *only* be used for good. Don't worry about results that may or may not be seen on the level of form. Be grateful for what forgiveness and the Holy Spirit are doing for you. By forgiving your brothers and sisters in the manner just described, you are rejoining with what you really are. You're telling the world and the bodily images you see that their behavior can't have any effect on you, and if they can't have any effect on you, then they don't really exist separately from you. Thus there is no separation of any kind in reality — which brings us to the final major component of the attitude of forgiveness: *Trust the Holy Spirit and choose His strength.*

The peace of the Holy Spirit will be given to you if you do your job. He will heal the larger, unconscious mind that is hidden from you, and give you His peace at the same time. This peace may not always come right away, and sometimes it will. Sometimes it may surprise you in the form of something happening that would usually upset you — except this time it doesn't. All this will lead you to the Kingdom of Heaven, for along with the Holy Spirit, you are doing the work that leads to the condition of peace — which is the condition of the Kingdom.

Forgiveness is actually preparing you to re-enter the Kingdom of Heaven! As the Course says,

> ...The ability to accept truth in this world is the perceptual counterpart of creating in the Kingdom. God will do His part if you will do yours, and His return in exchange for yours is the exchange of knowledge for perception.[19]

It may look like people aren't accepting your forgiveness. That doesn't matter.

This knowledge, which is not traditional, technical knowledge, but the experience of Heaven — similar to the original idea of Gnosis — is everyone's right. The Course is not neo-Gnosticism; it is unique. The Gnostics did understand some things correctly, particularly the second century Valentinian School in Rome. We mentioned *The Gospel of Truth* earlier. That was written by a student of Valentinus.

GARY: Is that like the cheat notes of Gnosticism?

PURSAH: Sort of, although some of the terms would confuse you. It was a popular Gospel for a while. There's nothing wrong with being a popularizer, Gary — as long as you do a good job, further a general understanding of the subject matter, make your own contributions and also remember to give credit where credit is due. As far as the Gnostics and most of the other spiritual seekers who came before you are concerned, they didn't have access to most of the information about forgiveness that you are privileged to be learning now. So their minds couldn't really be prepared for Gnosis. Since you *do* have access to it, you should trust that the Holy Spirit is doing His job to make you prepared for Heaven, and don't worry about how things appear on the surface.

It may look like people aren't accepting your forgiveness. That doesn't matter. The Holy Spirit will hold your forgiveness in their minds until they're ready to accept it. It doesn't even matter if the person is still "alive" in the body or not. The Holy Spirit will bridge the gap that seems to be in between the different aspects of your mind and make you whole again. For as the Course says about you and your forgivee,

> **The Holy Spirit is in both your minds, and He is One because there is no gap that separates His Oneness from Itself. The gap between your bodies matters not, for what is joined in Him is always one.**[20]

GARY: Cool. If I've got this straight in my notes, these are the major components of forgiveness: I remember I'm dreaming, I forgive both my projected images and myself for dreaming them, and I trust the Holy Spirit and choose His strength. My dream that the separation from God is real is the cause of the problem, and the Holy Spirit's forgiveness is the solution.

PURSAH: Very good. That's an outline; a companion to the Course's formula of forgiveness, which says,

a) that the cause should be identified,

b) then let go, and

c) be replaced.[21]

That's the way to remember God. The Course also says that the first two steps in this process require your cooperation. The final one does not.[22] In other words, the Holy Spirit's part is not your responsibility. That's why I say you have to trust Him.

Still, it's helpful to think of yourself as choosing His strength, because ultimately you are exactly the same as Him and Christ. There is no real separation in the Holy Trinity. That was just a theological device to help people understand some Christian ideas. Through true forgiveness, you are becoming aware that you are the same as J and the Holy Spirit — One with God and Christ.

There will be no recognition of differences in Heaven, for there are none. There is, however, a perpetual high that will blow away anything you can experience here, because it is beyond all highs. Transcending any description, it is a shared Oneness and joy that you can receive glimpses of, even in this lifetime. Arten and I will talk a little bit more about that when we catch you next time.

After that, our visits will be quite short at times, and they'll be designed to help you look at different topics and situations with the thought system of the Course. Over the next several years, we're going to help you grow in your application of forgiveness in all aspects of life. But you'll be the one who will be doing most of the work. The day will come when you *will* awaken from the dream.

GARY: When? When?

PURSAH: Let's just say it will be a hell of a lot faster than it would have been if you weren't prepared to accept the Course. Eventually the Course's thought system will be second nature to you, and you'll be able to apply it with less and less effort. Sometimes there's no thinking at all; it's just a way of being. Other times you will have to think about the Course's ideas, which reinforces your forgiving attitude. It takes the illusion of time and a lot of practice to get to the point where the thought system of the Holy Spirit is just the way you are, and ultimately *what* you are. But it will come, and you'll know the Course viscerally as well as intellectually. That's a marvelous experience.

GARY: That would be like the Zen concept of knowing as unarticulated truth.

PURSAH: Pretty good, hotshot. But this is about experiencing what you *really* are, not what you thought you were. I'm going to give you an example of a forgiveness thought process shortly that you'll find helpful. Make this thought process an integral part of your thinking — along with the major components of forgiveness, the entire thought system of the Course that we've been explaining to you, everything you study and all of the quotes I've been speaking. That should keep you busy the next few months. The more you know the more likely you are to remember the Course's thought system when you need it the most, which is when things seem to be going badly.

GARY: You mean when life sucks ferociously.

PURSAH: Ferociously, mildly, it doesn't matter. It's just as important to forgive the little things as the apparently big things. Anything that disturbs your peace of mind is disturbing your peace of mind, and that's *not* the peace of God. You have to be willing to forgive everything equally. That's why the Course says miracles are all the same.[23] Eventually, you'll see the equality of the things that aren't important to you and the things that are important to you.

GARY: Like Hawaii?

NOTE: Ever since I was a teenager and had seen movies and television shows filmed in Hawaii, I had dreamed of living there someday. I'd visited only once, which was one of the happiest times of my life. I hadn't been disappointed by what I found, and desired more than ever to find a way to move there without struggling financially. Hawaii is expensive; it takes moola to hula, and I knew that many of the people who made the move there were forced to give up and return home within the first couple of years for financial reasons. I was more determined than ever to live there, but I also wanted to create the conditions that would make me successful. There was nothing in my life that I coveted more.

PURSAH: Yes. As we've pointed out, forgiveness doesn't mean you have to give up anything on the level of form. Your psychological attachment to Hawaii is one of the ways your ego clings to the body and the world. That *will* need to be forgiven. It masks your unconscious resistance to the truth that there is no world. Like you, most people don't want to hear that their dreams and passions are really false idols — a substitute for God and Heaven. You've even chosen a place they call paradise! Hear this: There's nothing wrong with your dream if you understand it and forgive it. Forgive — and then do what you and the Holy Spirit choose to. And have fun!

GARY: You know, I really love having you here, but I kind of miss Arten.

PURSAH: He's helping you right now; you just can't see it. But remember something. When Arten said last time that *we'll* talk about certain things with you next visit, he meant that very literally. His Voice and mine are the same Voice, Gary. We appeared as a man and a woman because we knew that would be helpful to you, but the time will come when you'll hear us as just one Voice. There *is* only one of us — the Voice of the Holy Spirit. You'll understand that more and more as we go along.

GARY: Say, I was wondering. J let you touch him so you could know he was real when he came to you after the crucifixion, right? So I was wondering, can I touch you just to see if you're real?

PURSAH: Yeah, right. Where would you like to touch me, Gary?

GARY: Are you flirting, or is it me?

PURSAH: It's you. I was referring to that secret fetish of yours. Most women you've met didn't realize you'd get a bigger thrill out of touching them someplace that most people wouldn't even think of as being sexual.

GARY: You really do know everything about me, don't you?

PURSAH: Don't worry. I won't tell anyone. Maybe we can talk some more about that when we discuss sex with you, but let's stick to the subject of this visit. Go ahead, touch my hand and my arm, the way I touched J when I was Thomas and he freaked us out by appearing to us after we knew his body was dead.

NOTE: I walked over, sat next to Pursah on the couch and touched and held her hand and her arm, which felt as real to me as any flesh I had ever felt. Then I said thank you and walked back to my chair.

GARY: You're the real deal, girl.

PURSAH: As real as anything else, but it's all in the mind. I appreciate you not indulging your fetish. That brings up something, though. You've experienced wet dreams in your lifetime, right?

GARY: Getting a little personal, aren't we?

PURSAH: Just for a minute — to make a point. When you were in those kinds of dreams that seemed so real, where were you feeling the woman?

GARY: You mean what part of her body was I feeling?

PURSAH: No. *Men.* I mean, where were you *really* feeling her?

GARY: In my mind?

PURSAH: Excellent. *This* dream, which you take as your real life, is no different. Yes, it feels very real to you, yet you can have the same experience in a dream in your sleep at night. Your body even responds to it as though it's real. Your heart pumps harder; you breathe harder, and I won't mention what else gets harder.

GARY: I see what you mean. As the Course says, all my time is spent in dreaming.

PURSAH: Yes. Let's continue our discussion and help you wake up, although you may not always want to, and perhaps we'll talk about some of your other dreams — sleeping or waking — later on. Remember always: bodies are like figures in a dream, nothing more.

GARY: If I'm taking all of this in, then my attitude is that I look at the dream figures and I think, "The guilt I thought was in you isn't in you; it's really in me, because there's really only one of us, and you're just a figure I made up for my dream. I can forgive myself by forgiving you, and only by forgiving you, because you're symbolic of what's in my unconscious mind. If you're guilty then I'm guilty, but if you're innocent then I'm innocent."

Then, through true forgiveness — forgiving "both" of us for what we haven't actually done — my mind starts to know it's really innocent. The conflict diminishes as I keep doing it. It doesn't even matter if I appear to be forgiving the same images over and over, because they may look the same, but it's really just more guilt that's being forgiven and released. As peace returns, the laws of the mind say that my mind's direction is determined by the thought system it follows, and of course there are *really* only two thought systems, even though there may appear to be many.

If I'm doing my forgiveness homework, which means I forgive whatever comes up in front of my face that pisses me off on any given day — or even just bothers me a little — then I must be going with the Holy Spirit toward Heaven. I help release my images so they can go too, but the Holy Spirit will take care of that kind of stuff.

PURSAH: You're learning well, dear student. Of course you're really already in Heaven, but you don't know it. Your mind is not aware of it. You never really left God or Heaven. If the separation from God never occurred, then that would have to be true, wouldn't it? That's why J said about the Kingdom of Heaven, as recorded in my Gospel, "It will not come by watching for it. It will not be said, 'Behold here', or 'Behold there.' Rather, the Kingdom of the Father is spread out upon the earth, and people do not see it." As he asks you in the Course,

Why wait for Heaven? Those who seek the light are merely covering their eyes. The light is in them now.[24]

You have work to do along with the Holy Spirit to uncover your eyes and get your mind into the condition where you can awaken from the dream and become aware of what you really are, and where you really are. No matter how hard it may be for you to believe in your present condition, all your lifetimes have been just one big, gigantic mind trip going nowhere. To get to the point where that truth becomes your experience, it takes work.

So do it. Think forgiveness; don't say it; forgiveness is done silently. Do the Course, Gary. Don't dumb it down. Don't fall into the trap of thinking you can just pray to God and everything will be hunky-dory. That's a myth. The Course says of the words, "I want the peace of God,"

> ❧
> ***Don't fall into the trap of thinking you can just pray to God and everything will be hunky-dory. That's a myth.***

To say these words is nothing. But to mean these words is everything.[25]

Later, in that same Workbook Lesson,

To mean you want the peace of God is to renounce all dreams.[26]

Thus you demonstrate that you mean you want the peace of God *not* with your words, but by your forgiveness. If you really want to pull the plug on psycho planet then you need to do your forgiveness homework which, as you just said, means you practice the Course's true forgiveness on whatever comes up in front of your face on any given day. Those are the lessons the Holy Spirit would have you learn. You won't always do them perfectly, or even well. Sometimes you'll have to do them later. No problem; a memory is just as real an image as any other image. They're all the same. Forgive them and be free — and save the world at the same time. We said during our first visit that you save the world by concentrating on your *own* forgiveness lessons, not somebody else's. The law of forgiveness is this:

Fear binds the world. Forgiveness sets it free.[27]

The world feels solid to you because fear binds it. It doesn't feel solid to me because I have forgiven the world, so its touch is no more solid than your dreams are for you at night. Yes, I feel *something* — but only enough to be able to function while I appear to be here. It's very gentle. *That's* why the nails didn't hurt J as they were being driven into his flesh. Being guiltless, his mind could not suffer — and someday you will attain the condition where you cannot suffer. That is the destiny the Holy Spirit holds out to you when you forgive the episodic fantasies of your bodily addicted ego.

The message of the crucifixion has been interpreted by the world as a message of sacrifice. That is not the lesson J intended it to be. I didn't understand that until after he appeared to us and spoke of his lesson as being one of resurrection rather than crucifixion. He said there was no death, and that the body was nothing. Some of us, and later the church, confused the manner of his death, *which didn't matter*, as a call to sacrifice and suffer for God. That was incorrect.

We've already said it is not necessary for you to repeat the example of the crucifixion. Remembering that, all you need to do is understand the real lesson of it and apply it, through your forgiveness attitude, to your own body and your own personal life's circumstances. Here is part of what J says in the section titled "The Message of the Crucifixion." You will never find a more striking example of refusing to compromise on the truth.

> **Assault can ultimately be made only on the body. There is little doubt that one body can assault another, and can even destroy it. Yet if destruction itself is impossible, anything that is destructible cannot be real. Its destruction, therefore, does not justify anger. To the extent to which you believe that it does, you are accepting false premises and teaching them to others. The message the crucifixion was intended to teach was that it is not necessary to perceive any form of assault in persecution, because you cannot *be* persecuted. If you respond with anger, you must be equating yourself with the destructible, and are therefore regarding yourself insanely.**[28]

He goes on to say in that same section,

The message of the crucifixion is perfectly clear:

Teach only love, for that is what you are.

If you interpret the crucifixion in any other way, you are using it as a weapon for assault rather than as the call for peace for which it was intended.[29]

GARY: Jesus, Pursah.

PURSAH: No, I was Thomas.

GARY: I know. I've read that section on the crucifixion before, but I guess it didn't really hit me. I'm gonna have to think about this stuff, and I'm either gonna have to quit, or turn it up a notch. I don't really emulate J.

PURSAH: Such determination is admirable, my brother. Remember, J is calling for teachers, not for martyrs. I did not seek for my death as Thomas consciously, nor did I have much time to think about it when I was killed in India.

GARY: Your old alma martyr.

PURSAH: Cute. The point is you shouldn't feel bad when you're not up to J's standards right away. It's an ideal. It takes practice, and not just a little.

GARY: Then I *will* practice.

PURSAH: I know. We didn't choose you foolishly. You're stronger than you know, and wiser than you think. It takes wisdom to choose the right Teacher, and you're getting more and more into the habit of doing so. Don't sell yourself short, to use one of your investment terms; just do your homework. Forgive, and it must follow, as the night the day, that you will experience love as being what you are. Maybe not that same minute, but it will be more and more in your awareness. Here's a pointer that will help you remember to forgive — and remembering is the hardest part! You love J, don't you?

GARY: Yes.

PURSAH: Well, what if you treated *everyone* you came across on any given day as though they were him? Would that help you remember to do forgiveness thoughts?

GARY: Yeah! I think it would. I'll try it.

PURSAH: What is the Course teaching except that everyone is the same, and that we are all Christ? That idea will at least help you think about people the way you should, and remember that if they're not expressing love then they must be calling out for it. Even that won't always stop you from reacting to people and situations in a judgmental way, because the ego is very clever. Except in the case of a "slow burn," where you have an ongoing situation that upsets you, most of the things that bother you happen suddenly. The ego loves unpleasant surprises, because that's what the separation was. When the next rude awakening comes your way, here's another tip that might help.

Any kind of an upset, from a mild discomfort to outright anger, is a warning sign. It tells you that your hidden guilt is rising up from the recesses of your unconscious mind and coming to the surface. Think of that discomfort as the guilt that needs to be released by forgiving the symbol you associate with it. The ego is trying to get you to see the guilt as being outside of you by projecting the reason for it onto an illusory image. The ego thought system is trying to put some distance in between yourself and the guilt, and any suitable object or person who comes along will suffice.

Projection always follows denial. People have to project this repressed guilt onto others, or correctly forgive it. Those are the only two choices that are available, no matter how complex the world may seem. If you want to outplay the ego and successfully turn the tables on it, you have to be alert for that warning sign of discomfort or anger, and then stop reacting and start forgiving. That's how you'll win.

GARY: And remember it's just a dream.

PURSAH: That's the backdrop; the prevalent attitude. People won't agree with you on that if they're not ready to forgive. People always resist the truth; the ego wants what it made to be real. Forgive those who think you're a moron for not buying into the system, and stick to your principles. Don't forget, the Course isn't saying you can't be successful in the world, but it *is* saying you shouldn't believe it's true. Your real success is with God, because with Him you can't ever lose. However, if you stick around psycho planet long enough, then eventually you *have* to lose!

Lucky for you, the Course turns you on to the fact that it was only a dream. The universe itself and everything in it, including all the idols you covet, were projected by you from another level — just as surely as you engage in projection on this level. As J informs you,

> ...You choose your dreams, for they are what you wish, per-
> ceived as if it had been given you. Your idols do what you
> would have them do, and have the power you ascribe to
> them. And you pursue them vainly in the dream, because
> you want their power as your own.
>
> Yet where are dreams but in a mind asleep? And can a
> dream succeed in making real the picture it projects outside
> itself? Save time, my brother; learn what time is for.[30]

The purpose of time is to forgive. That is the only viable answer to life. Act accordingly, child of God.

GARY: So as long as I remember to forgive, I can still go about my business. While I'm busy reversing the thinking of the world, I don't have to neglect my personal life and the things I want to accomplish. By knowing these things are idols, or substitutes for God projected into a dream script, I can forgive them at the same time.

PURSAH: You've got it. You'll have bodily concerns as long as you appear to be here. Money won't buy you happiness, but it *will* buy you food, shelter, clothing, methods of communication and a lot of other things that aren't bad. There's nothing wrong with making it big either, but why make it real — especially now that you know what's going on? It's fun to know the truth! You don't have to take everything so damn seriously. Why would you be envious of those who don't know the truth? The President of the United States thinks he really *is* the President of the United States. As long as he buys into the dream, it will have the power to hurt him, or someday — her.

GARY: You said you'd give me examples of applying forgiveness.

PURSAH: Yes. I'll give you an example from my final lifetime, although I won't say exactly when in your future it was, and Arten will give you an example during some other visit. Mostly we want you to give us examples from this lifetime. Time is over; you just can't see it. The way to experience the truth is to forgive what's in front of you *now*.

You've got to understand that if the Course is teaching there is no hierarchy of illusions, and if a miracle is a shift in perception where you switch over to the Holy Spirit's script, then one miracle is no less important than another. In what you would call my last lifetime, because that's when I experienced my enlightenment, I learned it was just as important to forgive a cold as it was to forgive a physical assault, and just as important to forgive a subtle insult as it was to forgive the death of a loved one. If you think that sounds heartless, you're wrong. It hurt when my parents died, and it hurt when my husband died. Yet what is perceived as a tragedy can be forgiven just as quickly as you're willing to recognize that the separation from God never occurred, so it's only a dream and nobody's guilty — including you.

> *It is just as important to forgive a cold as a physical assault, and just as important to forgive a subtle insult as the death of a loved one.*

In that lifetime, I was a woman who happened to be an American citizen. Miracles know no borders, and it doesn't matter where you're from. I only mention it because my parents had immigrated here from Southern Asia, which explains to you my name. I was a professor at a fine university, and I enjoyed being one very much. I didn't have a lot of friends because I was quiet, but I was very good at what I did. I also loved *A Course in Miracles*, and I was grateful that J had given something that was obviously designed for highly intelligent people to help them achieve enlightenment in a world where ideas of any nature, including spiritual ones, are aimed at the common masses.

That's not a putdown. In the 21ST and 22ND centuries, the truth is that *A Course in Miracles* will not meet the spiritual needs of the masses — only a small minority. The Course will be much better understood five hundred years from now than in the next couple of centuries. Yes, it will be acknowledged by the public that the Course is J speaking the Word of God sooner than that, but having it meet the public's ritualistic spiritual needs is a different matter entirely. Christianity has nothing to fear from the Course. All the world's major religions will still be here a thousand years from now.

During my final lifetime I practiced the Course for forty-one years, from the age of forty-three until my transition at eighty-four.

However, my enlightenment, or resurrection, came eleven years before I laid aside my body. I can't tell you how permanently blissful those last eleven years were, when time had ceased to be relevant, and how wonderful it is to have your reality remain that way forever. That was the result of practicing forgiveness as an almost constant habit for many consecutive years. It's been said that life is just one thing after another. Life with the Course should also just be one thing after another, except that when one of the things calls for forgiveness, you do it. Once again, you don't have to try to be loving. If you forgive, then love is revealed naturally, because that is what you *are*.

GARY: Forty-one years seems like an awful long time to study the Course.

PURSAH: You're looking at it wrong. I would have lived those forty-one years anyway! How would you rather spend the second half of your life, being peaceful or not very peaceful?

GARY: That makes sense.

PURSAH: At the age of fifty, I had been a professor for over eighteen years at this prestigious university when a male student failed a class of mine. This young man, who was mentally unbalanced and feared the reaction of his family to his poor grades, came to my office and told me to change the grade or else he would accuse me of demanding that he have sex with me in exchange for getting a good grade. He said that unless I passed him, he'd tell everyone that he had refused my sexual proposition and that I failed him for that reason.

Even though I had all the evidence I needed to justify failing him in the form of his work and his tests, when I refused to change his grade, this sick but convincing man went public. He had no trouble finding a willing reporter who was looking for career advancement. The story was repeated in other media. Then two other students who had bad grades, one female, came forward to say similar things.

Public perception and enrollments are very important to certain universities. Despite my innocence and my tenure, a legal loophole was found to force me out, wrecking my career.

I couldn't believe it. For a while, I was devastated. It seemed as though everyone in the academic community had abandoned me. The truth didn't even matter. Decades of study and work went down the drain. I had done nothing wrong, but I was as good as finished. I'd never get another job in that lifetime that was as prestigious or as high-paying.

Fortunately, through perseverance, I did eventually find a job that was satisfying, and I ended my career feeling as though I had made some kind of a contribution. Needless to say, what that young man and the other people did to me was one of the most important forgiveness lessons of my final lifetime. I had established a way of life, and they took it away from me.

GARY: That really blows. How'd you deal with it?

PURSAH: Even with a "slow burn," or a series of related, progressive images, you don't do it any differently. You still handle one image at a time. Fortunately for me, I had the Course and I understood it pretty well when this whole thing started, so my feeling of being devastated didn't last. That's one of the best things about *A Course in Miracles*. Even if you get broadsided and you're hurting, if you're willing to forgive then the pain doesn't last anywhere near as long. That alone would be worth doing the Course!

If you know it's your dream, then there's a part of you that knows there's not really any such thing as injustice.[31] You made it all up, and you got what you wanted for a reason. You got to keep your individuality and project the guilt for it onto someone else at the same time. How convenient! I knew better. When I say it was a "slow burn," yes, I had a series of upsets to forgive, because a lot of different things happened one after another — but I was able to forgive them, one thing after another.

You see, I was already in the habit of *remembering* it was my dream, and that the dream figures were acting out for me. I'd been practicing for seven years, and I had the conviction that these people didn't really exist, and neither did their abandonment, the reasons for my embarrassment, or the seeming injustice of it all. As soon as I remembered that, then it would have to logically follow that these people weren't really guilty. If they didn't exist, then where could the guilt be but in me? But if the separation from God never occurred, then I wasn't guilty either.

It was hard, but I was able to forgive whatever situation or person was in my thoughts or in front of me and forgive myself at the same time. Now instead of seeing the other person as guilty, I could see *both* of us as innocent. How could they be guilty if it's a dream I made up, and they're a symbol of what's in my unconscious? When you really get that there's nobody out there but Christ, then you can give the other person the gift of forgiveness and innocence. Then, as the Course teaches you, that's how you'll think of yourself:

To give this gift is how to make it yours.[32]

Then after forgiving, I trusted J, who I knew was also the Holy Spirit. I tried to remember that it didn't matter if I could see results or not. If you work with J or the Holy Spirit and practice forgiveness, then you always have an impact. As the Course says, right in the first fifty miracle principles,

A miracle is never lost. It may touch many people you have not even met, and produce undreamed of changes in situations of which you are not even aware.[33]

GARY: You mean like where Arten is right now?

PURSAH: Yes; not only does the miracle have effects on your own dimension of time, but it also affects other places and times, including your past and future lives.

GARY: That's excessively cool. You've given me the nuts and bolts, but I have a feeling it's not as simple as you're making it out to be.

PURSAH: Oh, it *is* simple, Gary, but I never said it was easy. In fact, I said it was hard, and remembering to do it when you're caught up in things is the hardest part. Sometimes it will seem impossible, but it's not. It's doable, and well worth it. The example I just gave you had to be forgiven over a period of months. Sometimes I'd still think of it years later, and parts of it would have to be forgiven again. That's the way it is with the hardest forgiveness lessons in your life. Yet at the same time, you learn it's just as important to forgive the seemingly little things as you go along. Eventually you begin to understand that they're really all the same.

The more you practice, the better you'll get at it, and it *will* seem easier to you at times. The key is doing it and not giving up.

Now, I'm going to give you some good news and some bad news. Which do you want first?

GARY: I could use some good news. You know how positive I am.

PURSAH: All right. On this level, when the Course asks, "Why wait for Heaven?" it means that you can experience the peace of God *now*. We've said the Course teaches you that joining with the Holy Spirit and using your right-mindedness is the perceptual counterpart to creating in the Kingdom. You don't have to wait to feel good. There will be many experiences of peace when you choose the holy instant. It takes many such experiences to produce the ultimate holy instant of enlightenment.

> ❦
>
> **This is a lifelong spiritual path with numerous rewards along the way — but they happen within a difficult process.**

So now the bad news. It's not really that bad. If I told you it would take quite a while for you to be completely enlightened you'd be disappointed, wouldn't you?

GARY: Hell, yeah.

PURSAH: I'm not going to say exactly how long it will take, at least not today. Let me ask you a very serious question. How enlightened will you be X number of years from now if you *don't* practice the Holy Spirit's forgiveness?

GARY: I see your point. If it's a choice between being enlightened much sooner or not being enlightened much sooner, then the choice is obvious.

PURSAH: Very good. A brilliant and timeless student. Now, when we told you we were going to be visiting you for nine years, you asked if you were in the slow class.

GARY: I remember.

PURSAH: We said no. The Course is a *process*. It's that way for everyone, unless you're a spiritual genius who is practically enlightened already, and there are only about twenty of them in the world. The bad news is that for everyone else, including you, this is a process that takes time and work. That's why we emphasized that it's a lifelong spiritual path. There are numerous rewards along the way, some of them beautiful and quite unexpected. But they happen within a difficult process. In the Manual For Teachers, the Course talks about a period of unsettling:

> ...And now he must attain a state that may remain impossible to reach for a long, long time. He must learn to lay all judgment aside, and ask only what he really wants in every circumstance.[34]

Only after that can you attain what the Course calls the "period of achievement," which is "the stage of real peace."[35]

GARY: A quick question, before I forget. One of the things that really bothers me isn't just when I judge others, it's when they judge *me*.

PURSAH: Ah, but you see Gary, their judgment of you is really your own *self*-judgment that is seen as being outside of you. They're not even there. You keep forgetting that. Yes, it looks like they're really there and the judgment is outside of you, but it's not. When you forgive the other, you're really forgiving what's in your own mind. Their call for love really *is* your call for love.

GARY: Do I always have to do these forgiveness thoughts just right?

PURSAH: No.

GARY: I don't have to get the words right in my mind?

PURSAH: No. You don't have to get all the details right. Once you really understand all this — which is why we expect you to continue and deepen your studies — then it will become a permanent part of you. If these kinds of thoughts become dominant in your mind, then it can't help but mean the Holy Spirit is taking over.

Think of these pointers as being meant to help you save time and make you as effective as possible. The truth is, whenever you think *any* of the thoughts I've talked to you about today, it means you've chosen J or the Holy Spirit as your Teacher, which *is* the holy instant. When you remember to do that and forgive — in the quantum rather than the Newtonian sense — and you see your brothers and sisters as innocent like you are, then that *is* the miracle. And rather than the ego's special relationship, when you join with your brothers and sisters as one in Christ, then that *is* the Holy relationship. If you employ the Course's thought system, you can't miss. The Holy Spirit knows what your intentions are without you spelling it out just right. But you've got to have the ideas in your mind in order for them to *become* dominant. Use the ideas I've been talking about today and they will.

With that in mind — and to summarize — here's an example of a forgiveness thought process. Remember that it helps to be on the lookout for the ego's surprises. It takes a sharp mind if you're going to do what the Course says and be vigilant only for God and His Kingdom.[36] As the Course informs you,

Miracles arise from a miraculous state of mind, or a state of miracle-readiness.[37]

In this thought process, the words *you* and *you're* can apply to any person, situation or event. It's all right to improvise while maintaining the basic ideas. Also, please note that the Holy Spirit will remember to remove the unconscious guilt from your mind and perform His healing of the universe when you forgive, regardless of whether you remember to ask Him. That's His job and He's pretty good at it. You have to remember to do *your* job — if not immediately, then later on. If you completely forget, then you can be confident that the ego's script will eventually provide you with a similar opportunity that will do just as well.

TRUE FORGIVENESS:
A Thought Process Example

You're not really there. If I think you are guilty or the cause of the problem, and if I made you up, then the imagined guilt and fear must be in me. Since the separation from God never occurred, I forgive "both" of us for what we haven't really done. Now there is only innocence, and I join with the Holy Spirit in peace.

Please feel free to use this example of a forgiveness thought process as much as you want in order to help get into the habit of forgiveness.

GARY: I like that. Now all I have to do is remember to think like that when the battle is raging.

PURSAH: Relax, Gary; the war's over — whenever you remember the truth. I'm going to take off now, but I know you'll forgive me. In fact, J says in his Course that he knows you'll eventually listen to him and practice true forgiveness.

And thus will all the vestiges of hell, the secret sins and hidden hates be gone. And all the loveliness which they concealed appear like lawns of Heaven to our sight, to lift us high above the thorny roads we travelled on before the Christ appeared.[38]

In the weeks following this extraordinary learning encounter with Pursah, I noticed my increasingly negative reaction to a member of my study group. This guy, who I regarded as a friend, was a very loud and aggressive speaker, and he often dominated the time spent discussing the Course at our meetings.

His knowledge of the Course was impressive; I don't know if I've ever met someone not known publicly as a Course teacher who knew more about it than he did. The problem was, he used his technical knowledge of the Course to make himself right and others wrong — instead of using it to forgive. This is a pitfall the ego can employ to ensnare any intelligent Course student, resulting in an attitude that says, *Look at me. I know so much more than you I must be very enlightened!*

My friend's behavior in the group drove home for me the fact that it's not just what you know, it's what you do with it. Indeed, just knowing how to forgive wouldn't get me home if I didn't really do it. And who could provide a better opportunity for applying my new knowledge than my friend, whose abrasive teaching style took up so much time at our meetings?

What could his loud pronouncements be but a call for love? And what was the surest way to experience love but by removing everything in the way of that love, via forgiveness? I considered the possibility that Pursah and the Course were right; as I watched and listened to my friend at our meetings, I tried to comprehend that he wasn't really there. I was only dreaming, and he was a figure I had made up so I could identify him as the problem causing my lack of peace (i.e., my annoyance with him). In my ego's script he was the guilty one, not me — but now I could change my mind. It didn't really matter if I got in touch with the form of my own guilt that he was symbolizing for me. All that mattered was that I forgive. The Holy Spirit would take care of the details.

Without separation, this guy couldn't exist apart from me — and if our separation from God was an illusion, then neither one of us could possibly exist as individuals. *What I was seeing wasn't really there.* I could now perceive innocence, or true perception, by having the *attitude* that he was entirely without guilt. I could forgive him for what wasn't really happening. In that view, my own sins of which I covertly accused myself were also forgiven. I released my brother to the Holy Spirit in peace, and thus I was released as well.

I knew this episode was just one step; along the way ahead there would certainly be resistance to forgiving many more "difficult" people and unpleasant circumstances. Miracles were all the same to the Holy Spirit, but definitely not to the ego. I wouldn't always want to look at my ego as projected onto others. Noticing that very resistance was an essential part of doing the Course.

In fact, forgiving myself when I *didn't* do the Course very well was a major part of the process. My ego couldn't be forgiven and undone without looking at it first — and how did it show up most dramatically except in the desire *not* to forgive? True, I had resistance, but also persistence. Sometimes it would take me a second, a minute, a half-hour or a day, but whenever I felt the pitchforks of judgment rising up within me, ready to condemn something or someone who appeared to be outside of me, I would always change my mind, forgive, and remember Who my brothers and sisters really were. Then, as it must certainly follow, I would remember Who I was.

Perhaps this is how an ordinary life can become a great one, without the world even knowing. For when I practiced true forgiveness, it didn't really matter to me what the world thought it knew.

8

Enlightenment

Enlightenment is but a recognition, not a change at all.[1]

FOR the rest of 1994 and the early months of 1995, I practiced forgiveness every chance I got — and there was no shortage of chances on a daily basis. I'd also be reminded by recent memories of things I should have forgiven but hadn't; then I would forgive these things as well. When memories from my more distant past came up, I'd have to forgive these mental images in the same manner. Last but never least, there were my concerns about the future. Yet the Course taught me that all of these concerns were just illusory rabbits from the ego's magic hat.

Whether they were recent or distant recollections, I could see that my ego had a never-ending list of bad memories for me to choose from in order to guard against the possibility of present happiness. Whether I regretted my own actions or resented others for theirs, bitter memories could always show up when I least expected them. The ego didn't really want me to be happy, and it was now my vocation to bring my illusions to the truth. The Holy Spirit *was* the truth, and He was more than prepared to throw out the cases I had built up against myself or any of my brothers and sisters.

I knew from my previous, multi-year spiritual search that discipline is doing what *doesn't* come naturally. Eons of habitual reactions and thought patterns are not changed easily, but my recent experiences were telling me that they *could* be changed.

I was glad I had been taught so forcefully the concept of the dreamlike nature of my world, which was articulated in great detail in the Text of the Course, because everything I read in the Workbook supported the idea without always mentioning it. The simplicity of seeing the universe as a dream, and forgiving the images my body's eyes were apparently showing me, was well summed up in one of the Workbook's explanations of forgiveness.

> **Forgiveness recognizes what you thought your brother did to you has not occurred. It does not pardon sins and make them real. It sees there was no sin. And in that view are all your sins forgiven.**[2]

I had also been taught that the Course's idea of sleep was roughly the equivalent of denial or repression. On a grand scale, projection followed denial, which meant that all of the objects in my dream, whether they be animate or inanimate, were equally untrue. Certainly there were times when that was a little hard to swallow, even for a metaphysically inclined guy like myself. Yet if I believed what the Course said about the ultimate reach of forgiveness, it would have to be true. *My life was a dream.* Reality was still here, but I was not aware of it. So my forgiveness homework — the only way to undo my unconscious projections of guilt — was done at this level, while the Holy Spirit took care of the part of the job I couldn't see.

Since Pursah had mentioned enlightenment in her last visit, I began to look up the subject in the Course. I wanted to talk more about it the next time I saw my teachers. I had a sneaky motive; I didn't want my enlightenment to take a long time, and I had to see if there was any way I could speed up the process even more.

When April and a welcome spring had arrived in Maine, it was time for Arten and Pursah to return. I knew they would, and one weekday afternoon they reappeared for me.

PURSAH: Hey forgiveness guy, how's the world holding up?

GARY: It's holding, but no thanks to me. I've been busy trying to free it.

PURSAH: You remember Arten, who was more than your equal in the domain of smart-ass enlightenment.

GARY: I thought you looked familiar. Did you help the Holy Spirit heal my mind in another dimension?

ARTEN: We tried, but the damage was just too much. I'm kidding. Time and space have been adjusted for you, thanks to your forgiveness. There are situations and events that will never occur because you no longer need to learn from them. Also, there will be times when you make decisions which save you from punishing yourself. Usually you will not even be aware of it.

GARY: Can you give me an example?

ARTEN: Sure. You went to the movies three weeks ago, but you had a hard time deciding which movie to see, and you didn't like the one you chose.

GARY: I remember. I wasted two hours of my life watching that piece of crap — which of course I forgave immediately. Well, almost immediately.

ARTEN: They can't all be gems. Afterward you asked yourself, "Why didn't I go see the other movie? It would have probably been a lot better."

GARY: Yeah. Wasn't I right? I saw it a week later and it was good.

ARTEN: Maybe you were right about the quality of the films, but your judgment, like that of other people, can be very myopic. If you went to that better movie the week before, it would have gotten out at a different time. On the way home, you would have been in a bad car accident, and you would have been seriously injured.

GARY: You're kidding.

ARTEN: I don't joke about things like that. I know things that appear to happen in the world are not true, but I still don't joke about some of them.

Your forgiveness has made your mind start to suspect you're not guilty, and there will be times you don't punish yourself when you may have otherwise done so. And you won't even know about it! You thought you made a bad decision going to a certain movie, and that your decision didn't work out for you. That can be true about important decisions, as well as small ones. You may not be able to see that a setback could have actually saved your life, or at least helped you — although usually the effects involve extending forgiveness to other minds, including your other lifetimes. With God all things *are* possible — on the level of the mind, that is.

GARY: That's incredible. It seems trivial to ask this now, but I've always wanted to, so I'll do it before I forget. If the mind is so powerful, then why *not* perform miracles on the level of the physical?

ARTEN: That's a pretty tough row to hoe, Gary. Sure, physical miracles are *possible,* because the mind makes everything. All psychic phenomena are possible, because "minds are joined."[3]

But why waste all that time and energy working on the illusory effects when you can go right to the cause and just take care of the mind? It's a question of how fast you want to get to where you're going. Why delay yourself? It's like people who waste their lives fighting the battle of "good versus evil," when what they're really seeing out there in the world is merely symbolic of the conflict between right-mindedness or good, and wrong-mindedness or evil, that is occurring within their own split minds. Save your airfare and forgive. You'll get to Heaven a thousand times faster in the process. *After* you forgive, if you feel guided by the Holy Spirit to have a job aiding people in the world, go right ahead. While you're doing it, you can continue to practice forgiveness at the same time.

Which almost brings us to the subject we *know* you want to talk to us about this time — your enlightenment. First, a quick advisement: We're not going to be covering every topic or piece of information you could when one is teaching the Course. We don't want you to write a 900-page epic. Your studies should always continue, even after we're apparently not visiting you any more.

GARY: No problem. I already paid for the Course book. Why do you have to stop appearing to me? Does it really make any difference if you talk to me as the Holy Spirit or appear to me this way?

PURSAH: No. It's your dream, Gary. If you really want us to appear to you after our scheduled visits are complete then we will. Indeed, we wouldn't be very kind if we didn't. But you need to understand that it's not important. Getting back to the subject, since you paid for the Course book and even read it, then you should know that while you've been asleep, J teaches you that

...Your other life has continued without interruption, and has been and always will be totally unaffected by your attempts to dissociate it.[4]

When you really wake up, what appeared to be real before is now *recognized* as the idle dream that it is. Then it is forgotten, or at least rendered meaningless. There are dreams you had last night that you can't remember. Your present lifetime and all of the others will disappear, and when everyone reaches the same state of enlightenment, the universe will disappear — leaving only God's Universe of Heaven. One thing we want to stress right now is that enlightenment has nothing at all to do with seeming near-death experiences.

We've already told you the Course teaches that consciousness was the first split introduced into the mind after the separation. Consciousness is another way of saying split mind. When the body is finished functioning, your consciousness continues. That's another reason why you shouldn't fear death. People either hear or find out for themselves how beautiful the near-death experience can be, but they don't understand that it's temporarily beautiful only in *comparison* to life in the body. When you are free of all the body's pain and restrictions and become temporarily aware of the larger split mind, it can be awe-inspiring. But people can't tell you the whole experience, because if they *could* then they would have had the whole experience, and they'd be dead! Of course it's their body that would appear to be dead, and they'd be moving on to the next illusory lifetime.

What happens is that the awe eventually wears off because the unconscious guilt that is still within the mind starts to catch up with you. This causes you to reincarnate as a way of escaping your guilt and your fear of God. This *always* happens to you eventually, unless your mind has been completely healed by the Holy Spirit. Some Buddhists try to avoid reincarnating by practicing lucid dreaming while they're in bed at night — a state where you're conscious of the fact that you're dreaming — in order to train their mind so that when the death of their body comes they can simply decide not to reincarnate.

That's very clever, but it doesn't work unless there's a total absence of unconscious guilt. If their unconscious guilt was completely healed they'd be enlightened while still appearing to be in the body, not just afterwards. In any case, what we want to stress is that you shouldn't confuse the very transitory joy of reported near-death experiences with enlightenment. Enlightenment happens *during* one of your illusory lifetimes. The body is laid aside once and for all only after your mind awakens from the dream.

I told you during our second visit that I'd mention a saying in my Gospel that relates to this.

GARY: I thought you forgot.

PURSAH: If I forget something it's on purpose, hotshot. The saying in question was listed in the Nag Hammadi Version as number 59.

> **Look to the living One as long as you live. Otherwise, when you die and then try to see the living One, you will be unable to see.**

In this saying, the "living One" is the Holy Spirit, who speaks for Christ and God on this level. You look to Him to attain your salvation while you are still seemingly in the body. If you don't, you're not going to find enlightenment somewhere on the other side afterwards. In other words, you have to forgive and make your progress *now*. Heaven is not a reward that is bestowed on you by an outside force for good behavior or clever metaphysical musings. The symbols that give you your opportunities for enlightenment are all around you — if you accept the Holy Spirit as your Teacher in forgiveness.

GARY: All right. You're saying St. Paul was wrong when he trashed the idea of resurrection being of the mind rather than the body?

PURSAH: Yes. Unfortunately, Paul's letters were eventually taken quite literally as Gospel. One of the reasons he thought the way he did was because he believed in the old scripture. We've stressed that Christianity was a continuation of the old deal in a new package. If you were to read Chapter 53 of Isaiah, especially Verses 5 through 10, you'd see the attitude of Christianity in a nutshell! How could Paul think resurrection was of the mind and not the body if he thought this way? Resurrection has nothing to do with the body, and believing it does makes the body very important — the exact opposite of J's real message. As his Course clearly teaches you,

> **Salvation is for the mind, and it is attained through peace. This is the only thing that can be saved and the only way to save it.**[5]

, The Course also teaches that you attain this peace by forgiving your illusions.

> **...And what they hid is now revealed; an altar to the holy Name of God whereon His Word is written, with the gifts of your forgiveness laid before it, and the memory of God not far behind.[6]**

It may be helpful to remember that the words "heart" and "mind" meant the same thing two thousand years ago. When J said, "Look into your heart," he meant your whole being. He wasn't referring to how you feel about worldly behavior or current theology. He was telling you to examine your mind, forgive your brothers and sisters and remember God.

> **Your resurrection is your reawakening.[7]**

So, enlightenment or resurrection is waking up from the dream and recognizing the truth that has always been and always will be.

GARY: And true forgiveness can't help but lead to this?

ARTEN: That's right, brother. Keep doing what you've been doing lately and in the long run, you can't miss. You're worried about how long it will take, but you've got to give that up, Gary. As the Course says,

> **Now you must learn that only infinite patience produces immediate effects.[8]**

GARY: I'm working on it. I take it that with enlightenment you experience the *absolute* truth. You told me a while back that during the visit about enlightenment you'd tell me the two words that speak the absolute truth. I think I know what they are, but I'd like to hear it from you.

ARTEN: Actually, you can also get a glimpse of the absolute truth through the experience of revelation, where God Himself communicates to you in a way that reflects communication in Heaven.[9] God does *not* speak in words — ever — and those who think they are hearing His Voice are usually hearing the Voice of the Holy Spirit mixed in with their own thoughts. That's normal for spiritual seekers.

The experience of revelation, where God Himself silently communicates His Love to you, is beyond this world and cannot be captured with words. This experience sometimes happens to people before they are enlightened, but it doesn't always happen, and people shouldn't feel slighted if it doesn't. Each one's path is unique, but the way to God always comes back to practicing forgiveness.

> *The experience of revelation is beyond this world and cannot be captured with words.*

GARY: And the two words I asked you about?

ARTEN: Your persistence will now be rewarded, dear brother. The Workbook puts it this way.

...We say "God is," and then we cease to speak, for in that knowledge words are meaningless. There are no lips to speak them, and no part of mind sufficiently distinct to feel that it is now aware of something not itself. It has united with its Source. And like its Source Itself, it merely is.[10]

GARY: God is. So that's the absolute truth. J used to say that to you sometimes in the old days?

ARTEN: Yes. Of course the phrase "God is" must be taken in the light of pure non-dualism. God is, and *nothing else* is. It's easy enough for people to get the first part of that statement, that God is. It's very difficult to accept the second part, that nothing else is. That's why we cease to speak, because there *is* nothing else.

Do you remember the old Zen koan they used to ask in the *est* training, "What is the sound of one hand clapping?"

GARY: Yeah. They never gave us the answer. Zen koans don't always have an answer. They're supposed to help you break free of your old way of thinking.

ARTEN: That's true, but this one does have an answer in terms of God. What do you think it is?

GARY: I don't really know.

ARTEN: Think in terms of God is, and nothing else is. What is the sound of *one* hand clapping?

GARY: Nothing! The answer is nothing.

ARTEN: Outstanding, Gary. That's the correct answer. The sound of one hand clapping is nothing, because there is no sound with true oneness, which is outside the universe. With twoness you have interaction and conflict, but with genuine oneness there can be only God, who has no parts. God is, and there is nothing else to *be* aware of. How does it feel to know the absolute truth?

GARY: Pretty cool. Does this mean I'm enlightened?

ARTEN: No. When you're enlightened, you will completely awaken from the dream. Even though you'll still appear to be in a body, you'll see what the Course refers to as the real world.[11] You will only "see" it when you have completely forgiven the world, because the real world has no projections of unconscious guilt upon it. You'll see only innocence everywhere, because it's your own innocence — the innocence of Christ. That is what J saw, and what he teaches you now to see.

GARY: I like that — but speaking of innocence and forgiveness, couldn't some of the blissful experiences of near-death, not to mention some of the good mystical experiences I have while still appearing to be in a body, be symbolic of forgiveness?

ARTEN: An excellent point; the answer is yes. Your split mind is being forgiven and healed by the highest part of your mind, where the Holy Spirit dwells. It is indeed likely that many experiences you have, including seeing us, would be symbolic of forgiveness even before your enlightenment has occurred. But enlightenment is beyond the split mind. You *will* get there, and it's not our purpose to belittle the experiences people have on the way to enlightenment. We just want you to stay focused on the goal whenever you can — so you can get there more quickly. The Course says,

> ...A universal theology is impossible, but a universal experience is not only possible but necessary. It is this experience toward which the course is directed.[12]

That universal experience is the Love of God. While the Course is *directed* toward experience, it takes the wise intellectual choices of a trained mind to bring about that experience. That's why we're always encouraging you to continue to study the Course and do your forgiveness homework. As a musician, you know the importance of having good chops. Although most people don't realize it, spirituality is no different. You've got to have the technical knowledge in order to make the most of your natural ability and play your best.

GARY: Then I want to make sure I'm getting the big picture here. I know a lot of these terms are almost synonymous, and since time isn't real these things really happen all at once, but it's helpful to be linear in order to understand it better.

It *always* starts with forgiveness and choosing the right Teacher. I jotted down the pages of a couple of quotes I wanted to read here.

> When you unite with me you are uniting without the ego, because I have renounced the ego in myself and therefore cannot unite with yours. Our union is therefore the way to renounce the ego in you.[13]

So instead of using illusions to defend my illusions against other illusions, I just forgive. That leads to Heaven; it's a factoid. It's like you're replacing the dream that leads away from truth with the dream that leads *to* truth, 'cause as the Course says about salvation,

> ...What could it be except a happy dream? It asks you but that you forgive all things that no one ever did; to overlook what is not there, and not to look upon the unreal as reality.[14]

The happy dream is necessary because if the rug of time and space got pulled out from under me suddenly, it would be too much for me to handle. The dream of separation seems too real for me to wake up suddenly without crapping a brick. Like the Course puts it,

> ...So fearful is the dream, so seeming real, he could not waken to reality without the sweat of terror and a scream of mortal fear, unless a gentler dream preceded his awaking, and allowed his calmer mind to welcome, not to fear, the Voice That calls with love to waken him; a gentler dream, in

which his suffering was healed and where his brother was his friend.[15]

He's my friend because, for one thing, I can't get home without him! Forgiving the images I see as my separated brothers and sisters, which are really symbolic of myself, is the only way out of this hell hole. Like the Course asks,

...Can you to whom God says, "Release My Son!" be tempted not to listen, when you learn that it is you for whom He asks release?[16]

If you put enough holy instants together in the happy dream of forgiveness, then you can't help but get your ass saved, or at least the mind that made it.

ARTEN: Pretty good, Gary. You should write a book — if you ever get around to it. Since we're on the subject of your resurrection, let *me* briefly recite a couple of things the Course says about it. In fact, I'll give you a very short rundown of the Course's description of the disappearance of the universe; although as you said, these things will really happen all at once. I'll give you a few passages from the Manual for Teachers on the resurrection.

Very simply, the resurrection is the overcoming or surmounting of death. It is a reawakening or a rebirth; a change of mind about the meaning of the world.[17]

It goes on to say,

The resurrection is the denial of death, being the assertion of life. Thus is all the thinking of the world reversed entirely.[18]

When you have completely awakened from the dream of death and attained your resurrection,

...Christ's face is seen in every living thing, and nothing is held in darkness, apart from the light of forgiveness.[19]

Once you have seen the face of Christ,

> Here the curriculum ends. From here on, no directions are needed. Vision is wholly corrected and all mistakes undone. Attack is meaningless and peace has come. The goal of the curriculum has been achieved. Thoughts turn to Heaven and away from hell. All longings are satisfied, for what remains unanswered or incomplete?[20]

The time will come when each seemingly separated mind has attained its enlightenment or resurrection. When everyone — not every*body*, mind you — but every mind that has dreamed thousands of lifetimes has reached this state of awakening from the dream, *that* is the Second Coming of Christ. As the Course teaches,

> The Second Coming is the one event in time which time itself can not affect. For every one who ever came to die, or yet will come or who is present now, is equally released from what he made. In this equality is Christ restored as one Identity, in Which the Sons of God acknowledge that they all are one. And God the Father smiles upon His Son, His one creation and His only joy.[21]

GARY: That's beautiful. We left as one, and we'll return to Heaven as one.

ARTEN: Yes. Of course you never *really* left, because you can't help but be safe in God no matter what you're dreaming. When the entire Sonship is ready, then God will give His Last Judgment. As J informs you,

> This is God's Final Judgment: "You are still My holy Son, forever innocent, forever loving and forever loved, as limitless as your Creator, and completely changeless and forever pure. Therefore awaken and return to Me. I am your Father and you are My Son."[22]

GARY: Cool. You know, if I ever have a choice between being

judged by God or being judged by people, I'll take my chances with God any day.

ARTEN: You *do* have a choice, and the decision you described is a wise one. Extend the same forgiveness to your brothers and sisters that God extends to you. That's how you make it yours. When everyone has completed their forgiveness lessons, God Himself will take the last step and welcome the collective prodigal Son home into the oneness that you have never truly left.

...When you perceive yourself without deceit, you will accept the real world in place of the false one you have made. And then your Father will lean down to you and take the last step for you, by raising you unto Himself.[23]

Extend the same forgiveness to your brothers and sisters that God extends to you. That's how you make it yours.

GARY: That'll be awesome. What about the ones who get enlightened sooner? Do they have to hang around for millions of years waiting for the others?

ARTEN: No! Once you attain your enlightenment and lay your body aside, then you're awake and *outside* the dream — which means that you're actually outside time and space. While it may appear to others that many, many years are passing, for *you* the end of time has already occurred, and the "waiting" for when everybody "else" is enlightened is only an instant. Of course you can choose to help J help the others like we have, and I assure you it's not a burden.

GARY: The experience of being enlightened and being outside of time and space must be practically the same as Heaven anyway.

ARTEN: Would you like to comment on that, Pursah?

PURSAH: Certainly, but why not let the Course tell Gary what Heaven *is*? You want to remember that Heaven is *real* oneness, unlike the idea of being one with the universe, or even one with the mind that is outside of time and space that made the universe. Those ideas are still seemingly outside of God. With true oneness there is *only* God, and there cannot ever *be* anything else. That's why God

Himself takes the last step, and it is also why no compromise on this idea is possible. The Course's idea of God is as lofty as it can possibly be, because it is the truth. Oneness cannot be perfect if there is anything else to be aware of.

> ...Heaven is not a place nor a condition. It is merely an awareness of perfect oneness, and the knowledge that there is nothing else; nothing outside this oneness, and nothing else within.[24]

GARY: If there is nothing else, then there are no obstacles, and no friction to impede your extension?

PURSAH: I knew you were deep! Quite correct. In Heaven there *are* no obstacles and it's joyous; where on Earth, what is referred to as life is little more than a constant obstacle course.

Consider these ideas from the section in the Course called "The Gifts of Fatherhood."

> ...There are no beginnings and no endings in God, Whose universe is Himself.[25]

> ...The universe of love does not stop because you do not see it, nor have your closed eyes lost the ability to see.[26]

> God has given you a place in His Mind that is yours forever. Yet you can keep it only by giving it, as it was given you.[27]

GARY: I think I'm getting the distinctions.

PURSAH: Yes you are, and it will help you hasten your experience of the awareness of love's presence.

ARTEN: We told you some of our remaining visits would be quite brief. Today, we've been discussing something that can't really be put into words, so we merely did the best we could. The Course is directed toward the experience of true oneness that we have described, which can be summed up in just two words — two words that do indeed express the absolute truth. Keep your mind on the goal as you forgive the world, and always remember what the Course is leading you to.

> ...God is, and in Him all created things must be eternal. Do you not see that otherwise He has an opposite, and fear would be as real as love?[28]

PURSAH: You know the Course is telling you the truth, Gary. You've been around the block a couple of times. All that's left is for you to keep doing what you're doing, and the goal will ultimately become your reality. We'll be back in December. In the meantime forgive, and remember What you really are.

> Oneness is simply the idea God is. And in His Being, He encompasses all things. No mind holds anything but Him.[29]

Then Arten and Pursah disappeared, and I forgave them.

9

Near Life Experiences

The universe is waiting your release because it is its own.[1]

AFTER almost three years of doing the Course, my occasional nocturnal nightmares had abated. The murderous thought system of the ego was still present in my mind, but a layer of it had disappeared and the dreams that symbolized it had gone as well. The sun that was the Holy Spirit, which had been so long obscured by the ego's clouds of guilt, now shone more brightly for me. Those clouds that remained still cast shadows in the form of a symbolic world of bodies at the conscious level, and a world of fear and guilt on the unconscious level. Now I knew for sure that the shadows were not real, and that the light they appeared to hide could be covered over, but never extinguished.

This process of waking up was so intriguing and inspiring to me that I began writing, as Arten and Pursah knew I would. I even borrowed from Shakespeare to express the idea:

What truth, what light through my mind's window breaks?
It is the east, and the Holy Spirit is the sun
Arise my Friend, dissolve the ego moon
who is already sick and pale with grief
that thou the truth art far more great than he
Oh It is the Christ Child, yes It is my Love
and if I knew What I was, the brightness of my mind
would shame the stars as daylight does a lamp

My Mind in Heaven would through the unseen regions stream
    so bright
the world would sing and knoweth not the night

This was a process I intended to see through until the end, no matter how fearful it might prove to the sick and pale ego I sometimes identified with. Maybe on the illusory level of *form* my body was just a robot being manipulated by the ego mind, yet at the same time my mind was being freed by the Holy Spirit as I forgave each seeming happening. There was no turning back for me now.

The symbols my teachers were using were surprisingly worldly, but the Course itself said they had to be if I was going to share their message with others:

> It would indeed be strange if you were asked to go beyond all symbols of the world, forgetting them forever; yet were asked to take a teaching function. You have need to use the symbols of the world a while. But be you not deceived by them as well. They do not stand for anything at all, and in your practicing it is this thought that will release you from them.[2]

It was now my job to teach through forgiveness, and also to share the message of the Course in ways that my brothers and sisters could relate to.

> Thus what you need are intervals each day in which the learning of the world becomes a transitory phase; a prison house from which you go into the sunlight and forget the darkness. Here you understand the Word, the Name Which God has given you; the one Identity Which all things share; the one acknowledgment of what is true. And then step back to darkness, not because you think it real, but only to proclaim its unreality in terms which still have meaning in the world that darkness rules.[3]

So I started to write the book Arten and Pursah had said I would, misspelling words, using incorrect punctuation and persevering throughout a task that wouldn't be completed for over six years.

In the meantime, I was making the choice for God. Now I understood why my friends had emphasized the distinctions between *A Course in Miracles* and other paths. How could I be vigilant only for God and His Kingdom when I was fooling around with ideas that dealt with evolution, the power of the false universe and other such stuff as dreams are made of? The Answer was *never* in the dream, only outside of it, where the truth was and where I really was. There *was* nothing else; the truth was taking over, and I would look constantly toward the light of the Holy Spirit, who represented the Atonement — the one answer to my only problem. The Course said,

> **You cannot cancel out your past errors alone. They will not disappear from your mind without the Atonement, a remedy not of your making.**[4]

This explained why so many other approaches didn't work — because they lacked God or the Holy Spirit. But I also knew I had to do my part and choose forgiveness. Vicarious salvation that was magically brought to me by an outside force or figure could not work. Nobody else could wake up from the dream for me. Indeed, there *was* no one else to wake up from the dream. That's why the Course said, "My salvation comes from me."[5] It was up to me to change my mind about the world and choose the miracle.

On a metaphysical level, I was beginning to think of myself not as a *body* — or even as *spirit* in the way the world traditionally thought of it — but as *mind*. Yes, my Source *was* spirit, and that was the reality I would return to. But I had to use my mind to rediscover my sinlessness.

> **What has been given you? The knowledge that you are a mind, in Mind and purely mind, sinless forever, wholly unafraid, because you were created out of Love. Nor have you left your Source, remaining as you were created.**[6]

And there was a way of life that could bring me back to the awareness of my reality.

There is a way of living in the world that is not here, although it seems to be. You do not change appearance, though you smile more frequently. Your forehead is serene; your eyes are quiet.[7]

When Arten had first told me it would be entirely possible for me to practice the kind of spirituality we'd be discussing without anyone else ever knowing it, I had doubted it. After all, didn't everybody proselytize for their religion or spiritual path? Yet I knew now that Arten was right. If I didn't *choose* to tell people about the Course, I could still practice it and never say a word about it. As the Course said about the people my mind was showing me through my eyes,

...You walk this path as others walk, nor do you seem to be distinct from them, although you are indeed. Thus you can serve them while you serve yourself, and set their footsteps on the way that God has opened up to you, and them through you.[8]

I did this through forgiveness, so I didn't need to be distinct or special. My brothers and sisters were returning to God just as I was. Some of them knew it at the moment and some of them didn't, but the result was as certain for any one as it was for all.

One of the things that continued to blow my mind was the variety of mystical experiences I had while doing the Course. I had experienced such things many times in previous years, and now I knew they were symbolic. I had also learned that the *real* test of whether or not one was progressing on their chosen spiritual path had nothing to do with "spiritual experiences." Indeed, the real questions one should be asking were: Am I becoming more loving? More peaceful? More forgiving? Have I taken responsibility for my life? Do I understand the folly of judgment? *That* was how to tell if a path was working for someone. Still, my particular mystical experiences were giving me joy, especially because I had learned they were symbolic of my mind being forgiven — as a result of forgiving the world.

Now instead of the little white lines I used to see around various objects, sometimes I saw a person's head completely replaced by beautiful white light. Then there were the times when J seemed to be gently playing with me, as on one occasion that I remembered from doing the Workbook. While eating breakfast one morning I felt a beautifully loving, warm and very gentle touch upon my shoulder; a touch I would have sworn must have come from an angel, or Divine Being or J himself. After breakfast I read that day's Workbook Lesson which included the sentence,

Christ's hand has touched your shoulder, and you feel that you are not alone.[9]

I just kept saying, "Thank you" over and over again, almost beside myself for knowing I wasn't really alone.

A few months after that I was walking in the back yard with Karen, picking up some large branches that had blown off the trees during a rough windstorm. As I turned around to look at her, I was taken aback to see not Karen, but a large column of light extending from the ground all the way up to the Heavens, as far as my eyes could see. I stared at the wonderful sight for several seconds before looking away and then looking back again. This time I saw only Karen's body. She asked, "What are you gawking at?" I just said, "I don't know," lost for words in utter amazement. The experience was beatific, and I remembered later from my readings of the Text exactly what I must have seen.

As the ego would limit your perception of your brothers to the body, so would the Holy Spirit release your vision and let you see the Great Rays shining from them, so unlimited that they reach to God.[10]

So I became less interested — if not totally disinterested — in bodies, and looked with greater consistency to the light beyond the temporary shadow.

I discovered one source of fun and experimentation in the images I'd see before I fell asleep or just before awakening. With my eyes shut I'd often see moving images in color like a movie, sometimes even with sound. These images sometimes had predictive value in regards to what the script had in store for me that day. Many of these images were archetypal, residing in the collective unconscious and having been traced back by researchers of dream dictionaries for many centuries.

For example, the right hand, mine or someone else's, seemed to be positive and the left negative, a mythical correlation that went back as far as ancient Greece and Rome. Calm waters were positive and rough ones were not. Some images belied the obvious; for instance, being struck by a blow was a good sign where hitting someone else was not. Most of the omens were straightforward. Positive and smiling faces or friendly animals were obviously good omens and unpleasant ones weren't, and they seemed to foreshadow the pleasant or unpleasant surprises of the day ahead. These "movies" helped convince me of the truth of a collective mind, as well as the fact that the images in my dreams were really symbols of myself — and that Arten and Pursah were absolutely correct when they said everything in my life that was going to happen had already been determined.

Still, I tried not to get too sucked into all this. Yes, I could probably find some clever ways to use and even profit from such information, especially in the investment business. Yet at the same time I knew it wouldn't always be reliable. I had already been told by my teachers that some degree of unpredictability was built into everyone's script. I also knew that the most famous predictive tool in history, the Oracle of Delphi, had at times *deliberately* deceived people! The ego was still in control of part of my mind, and I knew there was nothing it wouldn't stoop to in order to mess me up and cause me to suffer, always tempting me to believe I was a body. In the end, only my forgiveness would get me home. As a friend and student of J, my newest psychic ability would remain a source of interest, but not the false idol I almost certainly once would have made it.

As for the idea that the events in one's life are already determined ahead of time, I realized there were people who hated the concept. For some, existentialism offered more hope than predestination because it gave them a reason to try to change things, both in their personal lives and the world in general. Yet the Course offered higher forms of hope — the hope of going home in the long run as well as attaining peace at any given instant, not to mention being able to avoid countless bad experiences by learning forgiveness lessons and rendering them unnecessary in the future. On top of all that, while changing one's mind about the world and practicing forgiveness, any seeming individual could *still* seek solutions to problems that would seem acceptable in the illusory world — as long as they didn't chain themselves to the level of perception through the burden of belief.

Then one night, a couple of weeks before Arten and Pursah's next visit, something happened that was quite unlike anything else I had experienced. I was sitting alone reading a magazine in a chair when I was suddenly overcome by an overwhelming sense of awareness. The universe momentarily disappeared, and I just sat there alone in a stupor of awe. I felt *totally* safe and *completely* taken care of, within the knowledge of a Presence that, until that moment, would have been unimaginable.

Revelation unites you directly with God.[11]

Although the experience of revelation can never be translated into words, there is one quality of it that is so unique it clings to the memory. It happens in an instant where one is given an experience of being outside time and space, and even beyond that. You become one with something so big it's beyond size. The clearest quality of it that's completely unlike anything of this universe is that it is *constant.* There is no change or interruption in its limitless power; it doesn't shift or waver. It gives you a taste of something that can be relied upon; something real — the joy of which is beyond belief. I knew then that I had been communicated to by God.

Revelation is not reciprocal. It proceeds from God to you, but not from you to God.[12]

I didn't do anything else that night. I just continued to sit there in my state of awe and gratitude.

Awe should be reserved for revelation, to which it is perfectly and correctly applicable.[13]

There was nothing for me to say, or any need to.

Revelation is literally unspeakable because it is an experience of unspeakable love.[14]

I knew I would never be the same. As time went on I'd remember that this experience had happened because I was ready for it through my practice of forgiveness, making me even more excited about continuing on my chosen path. As my visitors had already said while reciting the Course to me, no one who has experienced the revelation of this kind of permanence and unshakable being can ever fully believe in the ego again.[15] I was preparing to return to God.

…Healing is of God in the end. The means are being carefully explained to you. Revelation may occasionally reveal the end to you, but to reach it the means are needed.[16]

After this complete but temporary suspension of doubt and fear,[17] I knew I wouldn't mind always being that way. Although I felt like I had very little fear most of the time, my shyness and discomfort would still show up in my interactions with strangers or new acquaintances. I wondered if that would ever go away, and also what my visitors would have to say about my many experiences during their soon expected return. When they showed up, Pursah was smiling brightly.

PURSAH: Hey, Gary. How does it feel to have a taste of Heaven?
GARY: Absolutely amazing, but I feel too stupid to put it into words.
PURSAH: Don't try. I was just offering you my congratulations.
ARTEN: Me too, Gary. Now that you've had a sample of permanence, you'll be less impressed by the impermanent, which will make it even easier for you to forgive.
GARY: You mean like yesterday at the corner store?

NOTE: The previous day, I had gotten stuck in line waiting for a cashier who was talking on the phone. There were several people in front of me and the cashier kept talking, making me and the others stand there for several minutes. When I started to feel a little anxious, I remembered my training and the fact that I was making the whole thing up, like a director of my own movie. Then I forgave the cashier for what he wasn't really doing, and thus myself at the same time. The cashier then stopped talking on the phone, and it seemed like I made that part up too.

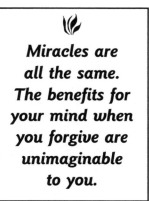

Miracles are all the same. The benefits for your mind when you forgive are unimaginable to you.

ARTEN: Yes. Miracles are all the same. The benefits for your mind when you forgive like that are unimaginable to you. A couple of years ago you probably would have gotten angry and expressed it in some way, even if it was just with a dirty look. You're doing well. You don't *always* do well, but keep working at it. As far as revelation is concerned, now you know what it really is. It will happen again sometime. Keep using the means, and let the end — as well as some glimpses of it — take care of themselves.

GARY: I've felt peaceful and joyous at other times, too. They don't all have to be peak experiences, I guess. Just feeling good is fun.

ARTEN: Oh, you mean like last summer, when you were circling around on your riding lawnmower within earshot of your conservative neighbors and screaming at the top of your lungs, "The Son of God is free! The Son of God is free!"

GARY: Yeah, that was me.

ARTEN: Do you have any questions before we proceed?

GARY: Yeah, which really *did* come first, the chicken or the egg?

ARTEN: Obviously they were both made simultaneously, along with the rest of the universe. Within the illusion they appear to be separate, even though they're not. Let's move on.

PURSAH: You've had many experiences that could be described as psychic, although revelation is not one of them because it comes from God. Most experiences, even spiritual ones, do not come from God Himself, but rather spring from your own unconscious mind. They *can* be symbolic of what's in your right mind. Let's put some of these other experiences into perspective.

As the Course says in the Manual,

> Certainly there are many "psychic" powers that are clearly in line with this course.[18]

It goes on to say,

> The limits the world places on communication are the chief barriers to direct experience of the Holy Spirit...[19]

and

> Who transcends these limits in any way is merely becoming more natural.[20]

Keeping in mind, however, that there's only one of two things you can do — make something real or forgive it — then any new abilities that come your way should be given to the Holy Spirit and used under His direction.

The Manual also says no one has any powers that are not available to everyone.[21] The Holy Spirit would certainly remind you that you're not special, and you shouldn't try to convince yourself or others that you are.

> Nothing that is genuine is used to deceive.[22]

Be mindful of your goal. Heaven is permanent, and nothing you seem to do outside of Heaven is permanent. How can it be important? You want to keep things in perspective. As you practice forgiveness your awareness increases, and as the Manual says of any such student,

> ...As his awareness increases, he may well develop abilities that seem quite startling to him. Yet nothing he can do can compare even in the slightest with the glorious surprise of remembering Who he is. Let all his learning and all his efforts be directed toward this one great final surprise, and

he will not be content to be delayed by the little ones that may come to him on the way.[23]

GARY: Thanks, and of course I mean thanks to J, too. That does put things in perspective, especially now that I've had a taste of that one great final surprise.

ARTEN: Very good. Now, we want to prepare you for receiving brief visits from us with many months in between. We'll be coming in order to encourage you to continue practicing, and while we're here we'll talk about various subjects and answer any questions you might think of. Mostly we want you to concentrate on working with the Holy Spirit and practicing forgiveness. Don't be disappointed when we don't stay a long time. You're a big boy. Besides, I assure you we are *always* aware of what's happening with you, and we always will be.

GARY: I believe you. By the way, I've started writing a little, as I'm sure you know, and I was wondering if you have any advice for me on how to proceed?

PURSAH: Of course. We knew you'd break down and write something eventually. You're slow, but you're not hopeless. Just kidding. Considering the fact that you're a little overwhelmed, we're happy you're going for it. Don't let the fact that you're starting from scratch intimidate you. Remember, the purpose of writing is to communicate. That Shakespeare thing was cute, and what it said was true. If you're good at communicating then you're an effective writer. Don't worry about the rules too much. Just between you and me, English is kind of a silly language anyway. But far be it for me to judge anything.

GARY: Yes. To do so might suggest you ain't got no culture.

PURSAH: Perhaps — just as our book might suggest you don't speak no good English.

GARY: You're saying I shouldn't worry about what some English teacher might think about my writing style?

PURSAH: Exactly. I'm glad I wasn't misconscrewed.

GARY: I love it when you talk dirty.

PURSAH: Once again, I think we'd better move on. Remember this: if someone thinks badly about what you write, or even if they're just not positive about it, forgive them. Always remember what your number one job is, no matter what you may appear to be doing.

ARTEN: Also, as you put the book together you have permission to expand the dialogue and make it into a more linear and complete presentation. Of course your narration is your own. Just make sure it's all based on our visits and that it's consistent with our talks.

GARY: What should I do with the book when it's finished?

PURSAH: You could always follow *The Gospel of Thomas* model. What you do is bury your book somewhere in Egypt. If someone digs it up after fifteen centuries, you'll be famous.

GARY: Funny. Any advice for my current lifetime?

PURSAH: Yes. Don't worry about it. We'll tell you what to do off the record, but it's a little early.

GARY: Well, you'd better tell me, or I won't have a clue. I don't even know if I'm good enough to write the book, but I'll give it a shot.

ARTEN: We know, so you don't have to worry about being good enough. Just do it. Now, do you have anything else you'd like to ask us at the moment?

GARY: I don't know. I'm pretty high from everything that's happened.

ARTEN: Yes, you can be excused for being all agape, considering your recent experiences. But you must have some other questions.

GARY: All right. You said a while back you'd explain more about your bodies and your voices and what they really are — and that you'd explain the appearances by angels and the Virgin Mary. Now, when I was doing the Cracille somebody gave me this picture of Mary as a present that was taken at the church in Medjugorje where she was appearing in the 1980s in front of those visionary children. Given my experiences, I feel a bit of an affinity for those children. As I'm sure you know, I went to see Ivanka — one of the children who is grown up now — when she gave a talk at a Catholic church here in Maine. I got the impression, even though she used a translator, that her experience was genuine and she was telling the truth.

On the program for that event there was a picture of the Virgin Mary based on *another* image she left on this guy's cactus shirt when she appeared to him some 460 plus years ago at what is now Our Lady of Guadalupe church in Mexico. Scientists say that shirt should have decayed and disintegrated after just a dozen years or so, but instead it's still intact and on display at the church, and has been there going on five centuries now! So here I've got these two images of Mary that were made about 460 years apart. One of them is an actual picture. And the incredible thing is, they look the same! What's going on there?

ARTEN: We've said that all bodily images are made by the mind. These images can be symbolic of the right mind and the Holy Spirit, or the wrong mind and the ego. That image of Mary is in the unconscious mind and can be projected either by individuals or the masses. The image you speak of has a Western look to it; it's not really the face of a Jewish woman from two thousand years ago. It's a composite of what's in the mind, just as the image people have of J in their minds is not really how he looked, but *is* representative of the collective mind.

In the appearances by Mary, which are usually more detailed if they take place before just a few individuals because they're so focused, she looks the same because the image is archetypal — a concept you've become familiar with. What happens in these appearances is that the love of the Holy Spirit is the content behind the appearance. The mind, whether that of an individual or a group, gives that love its form.

GARY: You're saying the love of the Holy Spirit is real, but the form comes from us?

ARTEN: Precisely. Pursah told you anything that takes on a form must be symbolic of something else. The Holy Spirit doesn't do form; He does love. It's possible for the love of the Holy Spirit to shine into your universe and then be given a specific form by your right mind. The form itself is a projection of the mind, but the love behind it is real. That explains appearances by Mary, angels and all ascended masters. It also explains how J appeared to us after the crucifixion two thousand years ago. Our minds were ready to experience his love, so his love appeared to us in a form we could accept and relate to at that time, just as our love is appearing to you now in the form of bodies and voices that *you* can accept and relate to.

Once again, we're not talking about the brain making these forms; it's the entire mind that makes specifics. We've also said there is only one mind, so on this level it would be literally impossible for each thing that is made not to be a product of the one split mind. While our love is real, our bodies are as illusory as yours — like figures in a dream. When we said to you early in these conversations that *we* made these bodies, we were referring to our love. That's also what Pursah meant when she said J made another body to communicate with us after the crucifixion. His love was the genuine content behind the illusory form, but it's minds that are asleep and projecting that make *all* forms and give them shape and details.

PURSAH: Since people are enlightened before they leave the body, obviously it must be possible for enlightened Beings to *appear* to be functioning in this world. Yet they know they're *not* really in the world, and that there's no need for them to return here except as a way of letting their love help others. To repeat, it is their love that the seemingly split minds give form to in the illusion. There's really no need for masters to make any form after they're enlightened.

GARY: That's really interesting, but you know that some people will say you came out of *my* ego.

ARTEN: Let them think what they want; they will anyway. While they're at it, let them answer these questions: Would the ego teach people how to undo the ego? Would the devil teach people how to escape from hell?

GARY: An excellent point. What you're really doing is trying to educate the ego to choose against itself?

ARTEN: Superb. Such an inspired student!

GARY: I guess what you said about the appearances of divine symbols also explains how that farm woman in Georgia can have the Virgin Mary appear to her and leave messages, except the messages sound just like they're coming from a farm woman in Georgia. Mary may really be appearing to her, but the messages are in the form she can best relate to.

ARTEN: Very good. That woman is sincere. The messages, simple though they may be, are meant for those who can benefit from them the most.

GARY: How about something that isn't such a pleasant subject, like that crazy bastard who blew up the Federal building in Oklahoma City? It's so easy to get sucked into projecting my hidden guilt onto him. We've already said it's my own insanity I see out there in the world. I still think people are gonna have a hard time — just like I do — believing that we've chosen to see our hidden thought system in this nutcase. You're asking us to believe that no matter how sick the crime, the criminal is just a convenient scapegoat we use to see our unconscious guilt as outside us. That would mean we have to forgive him for what he didn't really do if *we* are to be free.

ARTEN: Yes, the ego's very good at setting you up, but let me make a couple of points. When it comes to what seems to be a terrible tragedy, it's *very* easy to get drawn into it. Yes, you have to forgive, but you also need to be aware of a couple of things in such a situation. First of all, choosing to recognize the unreality of the dream doesn't mean you shouldn't be sensitive to the needs and the feelings of people who are involved in a nightmare like that. You've gone through the death of

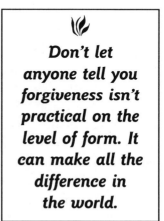

Don't let anyone tell you forgiveness isn't practical on the level of form. It can make all the difference in the world.

loved ones. How would you have felt *at that time* if some jerk came up to you and started telling you how it was all just an illusion so you shouldn't feel bad? It would just make you angry that your pain wasn't being respected.

You can't expect bereaved people to do anything except grieve. Always allow the feelings and beliefs of others. That's what we meant when we said the Course wouldn't meet the social needs of most people for a long time. Let them have their weddings and funerals and church services and court trials. Those things are necessary for society. The Course is not a rite of passage, it's a way of thinking. Second, it would be equally insipid to tell people at a time like that it's all a script they chose to experience. Let people learn the truth when they're pursuing the truth, not when they're grieving for their friends or relatives.

Obviously, if that bomber had learned how to forgive instead of how to hate, then the whole thing never would have happened in the first place. Don't let anyone tell you forgiveness isn't practical on the level of form. Indeed, it can make all the difference in the world. Choosing true forgiveness and the Holy Spirit as your Teacher is *not* a part of the ego's script — it's a decision *you* have to make in order to be free of the ego's script.

GARY: If someone wanted to have the Course read at their wedding or funeral you should allow that too, right?

ARTEN: If that's what they want, absolutely.

GARY: I take it any explosion involving death like the one in Oklahoma City would be symbolic of the separation, the Big Bang and Heaven being seemingly destroyed?

ARTEN: Very true, although most people wouldn't have the background to think of it that way. Any other questions?

GARY: Yeah. I first did the *est* training back in 1978, and they taught this technique, or formula called, "Be-Do-Have," which has been copied by other spiritual teachers since then. It taught how to be and get what you want. Basically, the idea is that instead of *trying* or struggling to be, say, a great musician, you should just *Be* a great musician, *Do* the things that great musicians do and then you'll *Have* the things that great musicians have. Werner Erhard, the founder of *est*, was a great teacher, despite his attackers, and he was very helpful to me at the time — although my success has a tendency to come and go. I was wondering, how do you feel about things like the "Be-Do-Have" process?

ARTEN: We're not saying you can't use such techniques, but when we talk about abundance we mean a way of joining with God so you can be naturally *inspired* as to what you should be, do and have. Why don't we wait for *that* conversation and see if it answers any questions you have about success and abundance? Incidentally, one of the things great musicians do is practice a lot — and for a long time. I doubt if you found a way around that.

GARY: Your point is well taken, but it would still help one feel better about it if the underlying attitude is that of already being a great musician.

ARTEN: That's true. Anything else?

GARY: Yes, Arten. Pursah gave me a forgiveness example that helped her tremendously in her final lifetime, but you haven't. What's the deal? Are you failing to fulfill your holy obligation to me at the risk of incurring the wrath of the Lord our God?

ARTEN: Don't be judgey. I learned that word in my final lifetime.

Sure, I'll give you an example. But one of the things I want you to know is that when you achieve mastery, you really understand the whole idea of the world being *your* movie. Let me ask, even though we've touched on this before — when you're asleep in your bed and dreaming at night, or in your case, sometimes even before you go to sleep and you have your eyes closed, you see moving pictures with sound, right?

GARY: Yeah, and when I'm asleep my dreams can seem every bit as real to me as you do right now.

ARTEN: All right, but most people don't stop to think and ask, exactly what are you seeing those dream images *with?* Your eyes are closed! If your eyes are closed then it certainly can't be the body's eyes you are seeing with. That's an important point.

GARY: All right, I'll grant you that. I must be seeing with my mind.

ARTEN: Yes, and you've already had a sense of that before in your waking life; you said it was kind of scary. The truth is that when you are apparently awake during the day and you have your eyes open, it's not really the body's eyes you are seeing with any more than when you're asleep at night. It's *always* your mind that is seeing. It's *always* your mind that is hearing and feeling and doing the other things you give the body's senses credit for. There is no exception to this. The body itself is just a part of your projection.

As you attain mastery you know the movie you're watching is *all* your projection; it's not coming from someone else's mind because there *is* only one mind. That's why all judgment is folly. Yes, the projection you call the universe is coming from a different, split-off *level* than the one you are currently experiencing. That's why it seems real if you let it be real. On this level the body *appears* to be experiencing something outside itself, but what appears to be outside you is merely a macro view that is being projected by your own mind, and your experience of it here is merely a micro view that is being projected by your own mind! It's absolutely true to say that only your interpretation of it — your judgment or forgiveness — makes it real or unreal.

Now, as you become accomplished in the application of forgiveness, your pain and your discomfort will lessen and sometimes disappear. Notice I didn't say that the *apparent* cause of the pain and discomfort would disappear. It would be theoretically possible for a master to die of cancer, or be murdered like J, and not feel the pain associated with such events. If your pain is gone, and your suffering along with it, then does it really matter if the illusory cause of the pain still *appears* to be there?

> ❧
>
> **The ego's script doesn't always change when you want it to. But you can end all the suffering called for by the ego's script. That's the Holy Spirit's script.**

GARY: I never thought of that. The world would judge the situation by the appearance, but it would be possible for a master not to suffer regardless of what appeared to be happening, and to even be quite unconcerned about it. The world would say, "That person died of cancer; some enlightened Being!" Yet it could have been a forgiveness lesson that was accepted by that person and done very successfully.

ARTEN: Which is just one more reason why you should never go by appearances. If there is no effect, or pain, then there is no cause. Not *really*. Whatever appears to be causing your pain, whether it's a circumstance or a relationship or both, may or may *not* disappear when you practice forgiveness. The ego's script doesn't always appear to change when you want it to. But it *is* possible to end all the suffering that's called for by the ego's script and have peace instead of fear. *That's* the Holy Spirit's script.

Remember, just like you choose which movies you go to see at the local theater, you also chose this movie you call your life, as well as any other life movie you attend. It's always a case of *self* pre-destination. Your lifetime movie's already been filmed, Gary — just like your bargain matinees. You know it, so why fight it? Remember, we didn't say you shouldn't have your personal interests. You wouldn't have them in the first place if they weren't part of the script.

So yes, develop your abilities. Trade the markets if you want to, as just one example. Use technical analysis. Get excited when you see a divergence on your stochastics — although a simple trend-following method would be smarter. While you're doing things like that don't forget that the body's eyes see nothing, and you're really just experiencing your own movie. By the way, it doesn't matter if you like the ending or not, because it's *never* really the ending — just a new beginning until there's no need for any more beginnings or endings. When that time comes, they'll be nothing but true joy — and Heaven's seeming opposite will disappear.

Another thing you should remember is not to be distracted by teachings that may serve others and help them feel temporarily better, but are not part of the path you've chosen. There will be those who tell you that when you have a problem, person or object to deal with you can say, "I am that," and it will disappear. Becoming one with something in your projection only makes it real for you, and will not undo the guilt in your mind that you *can't* see. Only true forgiveness can do that. There will also be those who tell you that observing and being aware of your emotions will free you from your compulsions. Yet even though you've seen for yourself that observing your feelings can lessen their impact, it is still not the same as forgiving them. Only the true forgiveness of your relationships, and thus the healing of the unconscious guilt in your mind, can really free you from your compulsions or anything else.

Finally, you may hear from those seeking balance: the balancing of body, mind and spirit, or balancing dual forces like yin and yang, or balancing "the force" itself. Balancing illusions is not forgiving them. Concentrate on the path that was meant for you. Others will follow that same path during different lifetimes. Don't forget, the Course is a very new thing. Rock'n'roll is twenty years older than the Course! Be grateful you got to play both, and give this new spiritual path a chance to find those it's meant to find.

Nobody knows how to forgive at first. It takes time to learn. People don't know what they're doing to their own minds when they judge and condemn others. Even us, J's own disciples, didn't really understand it at first. Sure, we thought we knew a lot at the time. Everybody does. Yet as J says in the Course, in regard to the derivative teachings of the New Testament, some of which originated with and were handed down by certain disciples,

As you read the teachings of the Apostles, remember that I told them myself that there was much they would

understand later, because they were not wholly ready to follow me at the time.[24]

I hope that will help put an end to the myth that the disciples were ascended masters. That includes Pursah and myself. Some people may not want to know it today, but *all* of the disciples had at least twenty more lifetimes to go through and more lessons to learn before they attained their enlightenment. We certainly *did* learn a lot from J in that lifetime though, because we couldn't help but be struck by his belief in the one *Great Commandment* of the God of Israel: "The Lord our God, the Lord is one, and you shall love the Lord your God with all your heart, and with all your soul, and with all your might." J had the kind of humility that said, "God, I just want *you*." How many people are ready to say that and mean it? Are *you* ready to go for the end-game?

During my final lifetime, I was in my sixties by the time I met Pursah. It would be the final lifetime for both of us. Her husband had passed on a couple of years before that, and my wife had made her transition also. Pursah and I recognized quickly that we belonged together. Not only did we have the Course and our personal understanding of it in common, but we sensed we had known each other in previous lifetimes. In fact, we were able to help each other remember many events from previous incarnations. We lived together in that last lifetime but didn't marry. It was our way of honoring our spouses and yet having each other at the same time.

GARY: You rascal.

ARTEN: We won't give you personal details, nor do we expect you to reveal intimate details about your life. Some things are best forgiven in private. Pursah and I were about the same age, and I'll tell you what was unique about our relationship. We loved each other very much, but we released each other to the Holy Spirit. We didn't make any demands or calls to sacrifice. Just as the world confuses pain with pleasure, it also confuses sacrifice with love. Yet what is sacrifice in the final analysis but a call for pain? Is that what you really want for the ones you love?

Your special loves are simply idols in which you seek to get what you feel is lacking in yourself. Romance is a vain attempt to fill an imagined emptiness — a hole that doesn't really exist, but that you experience as a result of the separation. That sense of lack can really only be healed by the Atonement and salvation, leading you to the wholeness of your oneness with God. Pursah and I were fortunate enough to have learned that by the time we met. We didn't demand the fulfillment of special love bargains. We let each other be the way that we were, and we were free to love each other without demands, but as an expression of our oneness as Christ and with God.

Pursah became enlightened before I did. We had been together for about eight years when we knew it had happened. There's no explanation of what it was like that would do her experience justice; we just knew it. I didn't worry about the fact that she was a little ahead of me because I knew that we were on the same path and on pretty much the same level. The next decade after that was wonderful.

GARY: That's great, but what's your forgiveness lesson you said you'd tell me? Wait a second, I'll show you some infinite patience and maybe you'll give me some immediate results.

ARTEN: Good. It's really very simple. It's not always rocket science, Gary. What happened was that Pursah laid her body aside. She made her transition without me, and I was left seemingly alone to live the last few years of my life without her. *That* was a big forgiveness lesson for me — and as it turned out, the last one I needed before my own enlightenment. After a couple of years I remembered Who I was and completely regained my memory of God.

That final lesson helped me to learn once and for all the meaninglessness of the body. Pursah was not well for a couple of days before her body stopped, but she explained to me it doesn't matter whether your body is healthy or not. *It's not you.* How can it matter unless it *is* you? Health and sickness are also two sides of the same illusory coin. Neither one is true, and Pursah knew this. She knew her body was dying, but instead of letting her ego run amok there was only peace. Part of my job was to understand that her giving up her body didn't mean she wasn't with me. I sensed she was with me, and I was aware of her presence many times those last few years. I'd think of something she used to say to me, "Don't be judgey," and it was like she was still there. I forgave the world, even though I thought I already had, and I was soon able to leave my body aside and become one with Pursah, Christ, and God.

I couldn't have gotten to that point without many, many years of practicing true forgiveness. So I give you this humble bit of counseling when it comes to all of your relationships in this world, whether they were founded on special love *or* special hate. Why don't you stop worrying about whether or not people love you and just love them? Then it doesn't matter what they think about you. You can just *be* love. It's so simple! And guess what? It will ultimately determine how you feel about yourself!

GARY: I don't know if I can handle that. I think I have fear of joy. Can you give me a quick rundown of your attitude in practicing true forgiveness, like Pursah did?

ARTEN: Sure. It was all from the Course; you can even find it summarized in the Introduction. It's your continued study and diligent application of it that gives you an advanced understanding and makes it real for you. It's very much in line with the forgiveness thought process Pursah gave you sixteen months ago. If I made up this world then it means there's nobody out there. I was the one who conjured up all those people I was seeing as the cause of the problem. Nothing unreal exists, remember? I could really understand that there's nothing to fear and then deny the ability of anything *not* of God to affect me. I could forgive my brothers or sisters and myself simultaneously. Then I could experience more and more that my house was built upon the rock. As I'm sure you recall, nothing real can be threatened. The ideas all fit together — and lead to the peace of God.

GARY: Once again, it's simple but it's not easy. Especially when the crap hits the fan.

ARTEN: The more you do it, the more you begin to see the crap coming through the fan as an opportunity. You're getting it; your persistence is quite interesting. Hang in there.

GARY: I can dig it. I think it's really cool that you and Pursah knew each other as Thomas and Thaddaeus, and then you also got to spend the final part of your last lifetimes together. That's really interesting.

ARTEN: Oh, there are some *very* interesting things to find out, Gary — as you'll see for yourself.

PURSAH: Now, it's about time for us to hit the road — metaphorically speaking of course. It's not an accident that we visit you on this date in some years. Not only is this day related to me as Saint Thomas, which I'll let you figure out sometime if you can, but it gives us a chance to do a little holiday joining with you and encourage you to take advantage of your forgiveness lessons in the new year to come.

NOTE: I eventually found out that December 21ST is the date of the religious feast for Saint Thomas, although it is July 3RD in the Syrian church, where Thomas is also still revered.

We'd like you to join in your mind with all the people of the world at this time of year. It doesn't matter what holiday they celebrate, or whether they admire J or Judah Maccabee.

GARY: Who?

PURSAH: Look it up, but you may have to look under Hanukkah. You'll learn something about that holiday, too.

GARY: I just found out about Kwanzaa, so I might as well make it an international thing.

PURSAH: Everybody celebrates this time of year. If they could bring their peace into the new year then it would *really* be something. Christmas, Hanukkah, Kwanzaa, Ramadan, Gita Jayanthi — they are all symbols of the acknowledgment of something bigger than the individual realm.

GARY: Gita Jayanthi is the celebration of the *Bhagavad-Gita?*

PURSAH: Yes.

GARY: How about the Wiccan festival of the Yule?

ARTEN: Pagans don't count. Just kidding! This is a great time of the year for everyone. As you know, the church ripped off the time of the Christmas holiday from a pagan festival. It's interesting what people will do when they think they're in a competition.

GARY: You mean J wasn't born in a manger on December 25TH?

PURSAH: Moving along, this is a time of peace and renewal. As the Course teaches you,

It is in your power to make this season holy, for it is in your power to make the time of Christ be now. It is possible to do this all at once because there is but one shift in perception that is necessary, for you made but one mistake.[25]

Home is where the heart is, Gary. If your heart is with God, then you're already home. Renounce the world, not physically but mentally.

This world you seem to live in is not home to you. And somewhere in your mind you know that this is true.[26]

That attitude will make it ten times easier for you to forgive. The next time it hits the fan my friend, remember God and forgive — for if you forgive then you *will* remember God.

God loves His Son. Request Him now to give the means by which this world will disappear, and vision first will come, with knowledge but an instant later.[27]

Forgive your world. Release each illusion equally, for they are equally untrue. As J advises you in his Course,

Make this year different by making it all the same.[28]

ARTEN: Love and forgiveness; that's what J was all about — always. Happy holidays, Gary. Forgive your brothers and sisters, for you are one — and thus are you made whole again.

...Now is he redeemed. And as he sees the gate of Heaven stand open before him, he will enter in and disappear into the Heart of God.[29]

10

Healing the Sick

*The acceptance of sickness as a decision of the mind,
for a purpose for which it would use the body, is the basis
of healing. And this is so for healing in all forms.*[1]

I HAD become interested in spiritual healing, and during the next few months I studied what the Course had to say about it. *A Course in Miracles* doesn't use the term spiritual healing, because it says that all sickness and healing is done by the mind. The term itself is a valid one because it can refer to what the mind chooses to identify with. I didn't feel that spiritual healing was one of my particular gifts, and I had no specific intention of trying to heal illnesses. Yet the subject still fascinated me, and I knew I'd want to talk to my teachers about it when they returned. Then, on a hot and breezy August day in Maine, Arten and Pursah were in my living room once again. I laughed with joy to see them appear.

ARTEN: We're going on a brief excursion. We played a little time trick on you during our second visit. Today we're going to have a little fun with space. Are you ready?
GARY: Ready for what?

NOTE: That very instant, I was shocked to see I was someplace completely different than my living room. Instead of sitting in my chair, I was now sitting on some cement stairs in front of a building. I immediately recognized I was in Portland, on the seacoast some thirty miles from my house. I had walked in the city with Karen several times in the last few years. Arten and Pursah were sitting on either side of me. They got up and motioned for me to follow.

ARTEN: Quite a mind blower your first time, isn't it?

GARY: You've got to be kidding me. Are we really here? I mean, it sure seems real.

ARTEN: There's a quote from the Course we paraphrased earlier, "You travel but in dreams, while safe at home."[2] Well, that's true of *all* your travels. They're all a projection of the mind, just like everything else. It's all a dream, and that body you usually appear to travel with is no more real than this historic little city.

NOTE: We walked for a while, which helped me adjust to the surprise of this sudden, incredible experience of mind-transport. Then Pursah began the conversation again.

PURSAH: Actually, we didn't come here to talk about time or space. We know what you want to discuss with us today. There's an interesting connection between our present location and the subject of healing.

On this very street in 1863, a suffering woman whose name was to become Mary Baker Eddy was carried up a flight of stairs and into her hotel room. Mary had an awful spinal malady and she had been sickly much of her life. She came to Portland because she'd heard something through the spiritual grapevine about a gentleman named Phineas Quimby, a brilliant but obscure pioneer of the mind. The combination of probing questions and hypnosis Quimby was using wasn't that different than the cathartic method used later by Sigmund Freud and his partner, Josef Breuer, before Freud went off on his own and developed the method of free association, which was the beginning of psychoanalysis.

Quimby turned Mary around, opening her eyes to the fact that all sickness is of the mind and has nothing to do with the body. Unfortunately for Mary, Phineas was near the end of that scheduled incarnation and soon passed away. She then had a relapse, but the seeds had been planted. She later went on to become the founder of Christian Science. She also realized that sickness has nothing to do with God. One of her favorite quotes from the Bible was, "The same fountain cannot bring forth both sweet and bitter water." In other words, only good can come from God, and everything else is of your own making — although contrary to popular myth, that making is not really done on this level.

Let's add another wrinkle to the fact that your life is self-determined. *Sickness isn't personal.* You may find that hard to believe, but sickness is not made by you at *this* level. That's just another reason why no one should feel bad about it if they get sick. You don't choose cancer on this level any more than a baby chose to be deformed on this level. Illness was made by your mind at a larger level, and is being acted out here in a pre-determined way. You *can* get in touch with your power to choose and thus have an enormous influence on whether or not you feel pain, and sometimes lessen or eliminate your physical symptoms.

> ❦
> **You don't choose cancer on this level any more than a baby chose to be deformed on this level. Illness was made by your mind at a larger level.**

I say sometimes because unless you're a master then you won't always be successful, and if you are successful it doesn't necessarily make you a master. Besides, it's the changing of your mind and its result on the way you feel that's the most important thing. Just for fun, we'll also talk in a little while about the effect you may have on others, but first let's head back to your place.

NOTE: We were there in an instant, and my mind was buzzing.

PURSAH: You O.K?

GARY: Yeah! That was incredible! That's the wildest ride I ever had, and it was instantaneous.

PURSAH: You'll have plenty of time to think about it. Every location of time and space that you behold is projected by the mind that is outside of time and space. It's possible to get in touch with that mind. The best way to do it is to eliminate the barriers that block your awareness. All aspects of healing contribute to removing those barriers. So today we'll talk about sickness and healing.

ARTEN: Remember, we're talking about levels here. We're not saying you're not responsible for your experience or that you didn't choose the script on another level. We're saying you've got to get in touch with your power to choose from where you presently think you are. That's also true when you're healing "others." You never join with their bodies, and you never ask the Holy Spirit to heal the body. The body, sick or well, is just a dream. As the Course teaches you in regards to all aspects of joining with the dreamer of that dream,

> ...Choose once again what you would have him be, remembering that every choice you make establishes your own identity as you will see it and believe it is.[3]

Now I'm going to give you the number one rule of all time when it comes to spiritual healing:

It's not about the patient.

All healing is a result of some kind of forgiveness, and all forgiveness leads to self-healing.

GARY: So even when it comes to healing the sick it's really about forgiving my own dream, and forgiving myself for dreaming it.

ARTEN: Yes. As the Psychotherapy pamphlet puts it while talking about how the Course looks at healing in psychotherapy,

> ...The process that takes place in this relationship is actually one in which the therapist in his heart tells the patient that all his sins have been forgiven him, along with his own. What could be the difference between healing and forgiveness?[4]

GARY: O.K. So when J told that paralyzed man in the Book of Mark, "Your sins are forgiven you," and the guy got up and walked, J was demonstrating that healing and forgiveness are the same.

Of course people freaked out and took it to be J doing something that only God was supposed to be able to do, namely forgiving someone his sins. They missed the point.

ARTEN: Very good.

GARY: So I should see another person's illness as my own call for help?

ARTEN: Yes. You have a chance to be healed in your mind by forgiving that person.

GARY: It seems a little selfish to use another person's difficulties as my way to get home.

ARTEN: It may *seem* selfish, but it's actually selfless.

GARY: How do you mean that?

ARTEN: Ultimately, forgiveness is saying that *neither* you or the person who appears to be sick really exists separately from God. Thus are you *both* free. Furthermore, it's the *only* way for you to be free! It's all right to want freedom, and the way out is to see both of you as guiltless.

GARY: You could say that a great spiritual healer, like Joel Goldsmith for example, must have gotten in touch with the idea that people think they're guilty or unworthy in some way, and that the way to healing is through forgiveness.

ARTEN: Yes. All spiritual healers may not articulate it the same way, but the holiness that comes from unconditional love and forgiveness is essential. In some cases it triggers something in the unconscious mind of the patient — a recognition that they're really innocent and forgiven by God. Of course the mind of the healer is being healed simultaneously because there *is* really only one mind. There *is* no patient. Not *really*. The dream is not being dreamed by someone else, remember?

GARY: Oh, yeah.

ARTEN: By the way, J really did heal that man as described in Mark. After he said, "Your sins are forgiven," he also said, "that you may know the Son of man has authority on earth to forgive sins." He didn't just mean that *he* had that authority, he meant that *you* also have that authority. Do you not appear to be a Son of man on this level? Yet you are really Christ.

Of course there really isn't any such thing as sin, and J did *not* pardon sins to make them real. His attitude was that everyone in the dream is equally innocent because it's just a dream.

GARY: Why didn't he just say there's no such thing as sin because this isn't real?

PURSAH: You had to be there. People could only take so many blasphemies in one day. He had to bring them along gradually by talking to them in a way they could take, or at least sort of accept. He did tell me in private about the whole game being just a dream, which I found startling. As I told you before, to say certain things in public at that time could have quickly led to the death of my body. J was already being accused of blasphemy as it was!

ARTEN: I wasn't kidding you during our first visit when I said there are more advantages to being a student of his today than there were back then. You don't know how lucky you are. You already know a lot more about his thought system, the thought system of the Holy Spirit, than we did in those days. You should be very grateful.

GARY: I am. I just forget sometimes.

ARTEN: We're not going to cover everything about spiritual healing that we could. It would be very easy to do an entire book on this subject alone. We're going to touch on some basics and then you can take it from there. Sooner or later, it always comes down to some kind of forgiveness and how willing you are to do it. How willing are you to accept that it's all *your* dream? How willing are you to release your dream and choose God? You know J plays a little trick on you in the Course. Most of the time he says it takes a little willingness. But that's not for advanced students. In the Manual For Teachers he says it takes *abundant* willingness.[5]

GARY: The old bait and switch, huh?

ARTEN: Whatever it takes to get a lazy guy like you moving. Just kidding.

GARY: Yeah; keep it up, Arten. I could write some unflattering things about you, you know.

ARTEN: I stand corrected with my head lowered in silent humility.

GARY: That's better.

PURSAH: There are certain things you've got to understand when it comes to doing spiritual healing, whether it's with a patient or with yourself. We've said it's not about the patient. Now here's the second biggest rule of all time when it comes to spiritual healing:

Pain is not a physical process.
It is a mental process.

We talked briefly about Georg — that's spelled without an 'e' on the end — Groddeck. Dr. Groddeck understood what I just told you. In fact, he used to ask some of his patients what they thought the purpose of their illness was! Why would he ask someone who was in pain such an irritating question? It's simple. He was immediately shifting their mind from effect to cause. He knew that the "It," as he called it, which was roughly equivalent to the Course term "ego," had made the body and was using it for its own purposes. His questioning of his patients was designed to get them to give up their ideas about being a victim and look at their own decision — made on a higher level, although he didn't tell them that — to be sick.

Sometimes when they thought of their pain as being a decision of their own mind rather than a bodily function they got well. Of course, nothing works on the level of form all the time. If it did then the universe would be predictable. The ego is very complex and highly individualized. I assure you the universe would have it no other way. Still, the principles of healing as known to a limited extent by Groddeck, and articulated much more completely in the Course, are sound ones. Healing requires a shift in perception, and as the Course asks and answers for you,

What is the single requisite for this shift in perception? It is simply this; the recognition that sickness is of the mind, and has nothing to do with the body. What does this recognition "cost"? It costs the whole world you see, for the world will never again appear to rule the mind.[6]

GARY: We've talked about the idea that the guiltless mind can't suffer, but you seem to be saying that even people who still have some guilt in their minds can control their pain and sometimes get well.

PURSAH: Yes. A completely guiltless mind would *never* suffer pain, although it could choose any number of lessons to teach. It's possible

for people who are not masters to alleviate their pain and do countless remarkable things with their minds on the road to becoming
masters. As J says in that same section of the Manual about a spiritual healer's patient, or for that matter any kind of a patient,

> ...Who is the physician? Only the mind of the patient him-
> self. The outcome is what he decides that it is. Special
> agents seem to be ministering to him, yet they but give form
> to his own choice. He chooses them in order to bring tangi-
> ble form to his desires.[7]

Once the patient or the healer accepts the Holy Spirit's forgiveness, then this is his attitude:

> ...The world does nothing to him. He only thought it did.
> Nor does he do anything to the world, because he was mis-
> taken about what it is. Herein is the release from guilt and
> sickness both, for they are one.[8]

GARY: It's an advanced variation on forgiveness, but still the same.

PURSAH: Exactly, cool student. Within that forgiving shift in perception lies your own freedom, as well as that of your brothers and
sisters. For as the Course elaborates,

> ...What you behold as sickness and as pain, as weakness
> and as suffering and loss, is but temptation to perceive your-
> self defenseless and in hell.[9]

As J goes on to say, there's an immeasurable reward for those who
refuse to buy into these images they see — and instead choose the
Holy Spirit's forgiveness and healing.

> ...A miracle has come to heal God's Son, and close the door
> upon his dreams of weakness, opening the way to his salva-
> tion and release.[10]

Who is being healed — the patient or the healer? The forgiver or the forgivee? The answer is both, for they are one. You can get into the habit of always having a forgiving attitude.

> …And thus are miracles as natural as fear and agony appeared to be before the choice for holiness was made. For in that choice are false distinctions gone, illusory alternatives laid by, and nothing left to interfere with truth.[11]

GARY: So if you're a master like J then you don't have to be healed, but you can still act as a reminder to the mind of the person you're healing that they're really Christ and that they're innocent — and *any* teacher of God can fulfill that function and also be healed by the Holy Spirit at the same time. The day can't help but come when you end up like J, and you'll be like a light of truth. Either way, you represent the truth to the unconscious mind of others.

PURSAH: True, indeed. The Course says of the patients who are seen by right-minded healers,

> To them God's teachers come, to represent another choice which they had forgotten. The simple presence of a teacher of God is a reminder.[12]

ARTEN: Remember, the words aren't important; it's the attitude. I used to think as I looked at a patient, "You are Christ, pure and innocent. We are forgiven now." You'll think whatever feels right for you after you ask the Holy Spirit for guidance. Remembering that any form of sickness is just a dress rehearsal for death, the Course says this of God's healers:

> …Very gently they call to their brothers to turn away from death: "Behold, you Son of God, what Life can offer you. Would you choose sickness in place of this?"[13]

GARY: That quote about how outside agents seem to be ministering to him reminds me of what the Course calls magic, or using illusions as solutions to problems, including sickness, instead of using the right mind. There's not really anything wrong with that. In fact, it might help people accept a healing without fear.

ARTEN: Very important, Gary. Being right-minded doesn't necessarily mean throwing away your medicine or refusing to see a doctor or therapist. That's been an error of many Christian Scientists. They've made a system of behavior out of what's supposed to be an exercise in the power of the mind. If taking a certain medication makes you feel better it's because your unconscious mind finds it acceptable. In other words, you can accept that particular remedy without fear.

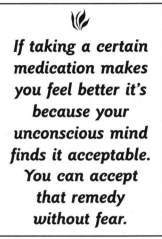

If taking a certain medication makes you feel better it's because your unconscious mind finds it acceptable. You can accept that remedy without fear.

That's true of anything that seems to work, even though anything except salvation only works temporarily. In most cases it's better to allow the patient, and yourself for that matter, to use a combination of right-minded healing and some form of magic — whether it's from the traditional health industry or from other forms of health care. That way the mind can handle getting well without the fear that might accompany a sudden and spontaneous healing. When there's that kind of a healing, the entire unconscious belief system of the patient can be called into question. Some people can handle that and some people can't. Occasionally it can trigger great fear on the part of the ego.

Don't begrudge people their various healing methods and don't put anybody down for using them. In many cases they are still a necessary part of the healing in terms of the mind being able to cope. Just use right-minded healing at the same time, because practice makes perfect. While you're practicing, remember that the world's magic is not evil. That would make it real. As the Course tells you,

> …When all magic is recognized as merely nothing, the teacher of God has reached the most advanced state.[14]

GARY: At the same time, while an advanced teacher of God wouldn't condemn illusory remedies, he'd also know what the Course says is true:

Only salvation can be said to cure.[15]

ARTEN: Precisely. That's an important Workbook lesson. The Course also says in that same lesson,

...Atonement does not heal the sick, for that is not a cure. It takes away the guilt that makes the sickness possible. And that is cure indeed.[16]

Those last two statements plus the next two are like cornerstones of J's entire attitude about healing.

...Being sane, the mind heals the body because *it* has been healed. The sane mind cannot conceive of illness because it cannot conceive of attacking anyone or anything.[17]

He goes on to say,

...The ego believes that by punishing itself it will mitigate the punishment of God. Yet even in this it is arrogant. It attributes to God a punishing intent, and then takes this intent as its own prerogative.[18]

GARY: Very clear, man. One thing I'd have to remember is that I shouldn't join with their body because I'm *not* one with the body. Instead, I should join with them through the Holy Spirit and be of one mind.

ARTEN: Excellent. Here's another quote from the Course; one that captures that principle:

...Your minds are not separate, and God has only one channel for healing because He has but one Son. God's remaining communication link with all His children joins them together, and them to Him.[19]

And that communication link is?

GARY: The Holy Spirit. It's a good thing I knew, huh? I would have flunked out.

ARTEN: Fortunately, you can't flunk the Course. The worst that happens is you get to stay here, or so it appears.

GARY: Some people wouldn't think that was such a bad thing.

ARTEN: We've covered that. The time will come when they'll want out — in the positive sense of the word.

PURSAH: Those are the basics, buddy — straight from the Course's mouth. The truth *is* the truth, but your healing style will be your own. Never forget, *all* healing is spiritual, not physical. *A Course in Miracles* is always done at the level of the mind, with some form of forgiveness always being the Holy Spirit's tool. What you do is think right-minded thoughts with the patient or even yourself, if you're the one who's hurting, and sometimes the symptoms will disappear. You can get better and better at making pain disappear. Now here's the third biggest all-time, perhaps hard to believe yet absolutely true rule, when it comes to spiritual healing:

**Ultimately, the universe itself
is a symptom that will disappear.**

GARY: You guys are so far out! I've been to the Unity Church, but even they're conservative compared to you.

PURSAH: Yes. Charles and Myrtle Fillmore were marvelous people. They were somewhat influenced by Mary Baker Eddy, and their love for J and their loyalty to the more loving and forgiving aspects of Christianity were obvious. Still, they made every cell in the body real. Although the Course has often found a friend at Unity churches, and people can obviously do both at the same time, the two still shouldn't be confused with being the same.

GARY: You know, it seems people have always been aware of the struggle of good against evil and then made it real.

PURSAH: Sure. Sometimes the idea of wrong- and right-mindedness has been spoken about profoundly. What the Course would call the wrong mind, at least on this level, Carl Gustav Jung called your "shadow"; and what the Course would call right-mindedness, Abraham Lincoln referred to as "the better angels of our nature." Only the Course puts everything in perspective.

GARY: It explains why people usually end up hurting themselves.

PURSAH: That's right. People always do things, big and small, that they know will hurt them. Often they're even conscious of it. Like you. Why do you always eat those chocolate bars at the movies even though you know they'll make your face break out?

GARY: Because a man's gotta do what a man's gotta do.

PURSAH: You're so butch.

GARY: Isn't that old-fashioned gay and lesbian language?

PURSAH: Yes. You don't have anything against gays and lesbians, do you?

GARY: No. Most of my relatives are gays and lesbians. Just kidding; only some of them are.

ARTEN: Not to break up this witty repartée, but you should try eating the candy bars without guilt. Then you won't break out. Now, it's time to take off. Any quick questions, fine student?

GARY: Sure. I could heal people in my mind in Hawaii just as easily as I could here, right?

PURSAH: Yes. I believe the last time we consulted the oracles, there were people in Hawaii. More Buddhists than Christians, by the way — and of course, Huna.

GARY: No wonder most of the people there are nicer than the people on the mainland. While we're talking about healing, this whole discussion highlights the idea that everything is caused by the mind — not just sickness, but also miraculous healings.

ARTEN: Yes. *All* things, seemingly good and bad, from miraculous healings to AIDS to anorexia to spontaneous human combustion to stigmata, are done by the mind. Every single disease you know of, and each one to come, is made by the mind. What is bacteria but a projection? What is bi-polar disorder but a form of duality, proclaiming the separation to be real?

GARY: The AIDS epidemic is just a newer form of the same old thing, then.

ARTEN: If it wasn't AIDS it would be something else. In the 14TH century the Black Death killed over forty million people. The death toll from AIDS is nothing in comparison when you take it as a percentage of the population, although AIDS deaths will eventually pass the forty million mark. Since the mind makes all illness, what happens is that when one disease is eradicated the mind simply makes another one. This gives the illusion of progress and hope while masking the fact that people die just as horrible deaths from disease as ever.

GARY: What about the studies showing that when people pray for someone who's sick or being operated on, the person seems to do better as a result?

ARTEN: Since minds are joined, prayers *can* temporarily help — but they are not a cure in themselves. Only true forgiveness can remove unconscious guilt from the mind. If you will think of the things the Course says about healing, you'll see that they are really true forgiveness being applied to sickness.

GARY: I had this dream the other night that was really clear, and I noticed that I had absolutely no fear in the dream; none whatsoever. I woke up and I wished I could be that way all the time. In the old days they used to advertise horror movies by saying, "You'll have to keep telling yourself, it's only a movie. It's only a movie." Sometimes I tell myself during the day, "It's only a dream. It's only a dream."

ARTEN: Yes, and it really *is* only a dream. Sometimes you'll wonder why you can't just feel that same complete lack of fear all the time during the day. Yet I promise you the time will come when it *will* be that way for you all the time. Indeed, it is that way for you much more often now, but you have a tendency to take the peaceful times for granted and notice the unpeaceful times more. Fortunately for you, you'll continue to do your forgiveness homework, and when your mind has been completely healed by the Holy Spirit there will be no such thing as fear for you.

GARY: I've tried to heal people before and they haven't gotten well. Does that mean I suck?

ARTEN: Yes. Just kidding. The truth is you can't go by results because you can't see the mind. All you have to go on is the body, which isn't real. The Course's healing is all done at the level of the mind. Sometimes the physical will be affected and sometimes the healing will have some other result you can't see. If someone is doing the Course and they only have one leg, are you going to judge them as a failure if they don't grow back the missing leg? Remember, it's the mind that's being worked on. Once again, don't go by results you may or may not see on the level of form.

GARY: So there's still hope for me as a healer.

ARTEN: You *are* a healer, Gary. So is everyone who practices true forgiveness. As the Course teaches you,

It is not the function of God's teachers to evaluate the outcome of their gifts. It is merely their function to give them.[20]

Again, who's really being healed? The answer is both as one, for there *is* only one.

PURSAH: The time has come for us to take our leave. We're proud of you, buddy. Keep those forgiveness thoughts coming.

GARY: Say, that thing where you transported me over to Portland. While you're here, you wouldn't consider taking a little side trip to Maui, would you?

PURSAH: Don't worry, Gary. You'll see Hawaii again. It's in the script. In fact, it's already happened; you just don't know it right now.

A couple of years later, through a series of seemingly unrelated events, Karen and I would find ourselves vacationing in Hawaii, winding our way along the beautiful local pathways and gently debating the possibility of moving to the Islands of Aloha.

11

A *Very* Brief History of Time

...Time lasted but an instant in your mind, with no effect
upon eternity. And so is all time past, and everything exactly
as it was before the way to nothingness was made. The tiny tick
of time in which the first mistake was made, and all of them
within that one mistake, held also the Correction for that one,
and all of them that came within the first. And in that tiny
instant time was gone, for that was all it ever was.[1]

FOR as long as I could remember, I had been fascinated by the
subject of time. In April of 1997, eight months after I had last
seen them, Arten and Pursah came to me for their eleventh appearance. I had my questions ready.

ARTEN: Hey, timeless guy. How are you?

GARY: I don't know; let me check... I'm pretty good. It's great to see
you guys!

PURSAH: And us you. You have some questions in your mind, so
let's get right down to business.

GARY: All right. First, I'm really grateful to you guys for coming to
me like this. I've been looking for spiritual answers ever since I was
twenty and I read that Hermann Hesse book that was based on the
life of the Buddha.

ARTEN: *Siddhartha.*

GARY: Yeah, that was really good. But I've never come across anything with the magnitude of the Course. Talk about comprehensive!

And I really love you guys so, thanks a lot, man.

PURSAH: Then you're satisfied?

GARY: Are you kidding? I'm *stratisfied*.

ARTEN: And we thank you, buddy. Gratitude is a good thing, although from now on your gratitude should be directed toward God. It's He that made your salvation inevitable by making sure the memory of Heaven could never be obliterated from your mind.

GARY: O.K. So as for business, I would have gotten in a fight the other day if it wasn't for the Course. I was at the gas station and this guy blocked me in just as I was about to leave, and I was in a hurry. I asked him politely enough if he could let me out 'cause I was in a rush, and he just looked at me with this unbelievably condescending and disgusted look and said, "Tough!" I couldn't believe it. There was a part of me that wanted to rearrange his face.

PURSAH: What *is* it with men and cars? Anyway, you saw him as being really ignorant?

GARY: Oh, he was worse than that. People who talk at the movies are ignorant. This guy was the world champion flamer. Mother Teresa would have been tempted to slap him.

ARTEN: We saw what you did. You got angry for a few seconds, then you turned around and got in your car and said these lines from the Course:

I am as God created me. His Son can suffer nothing. And I am His Son.[2]

GARY: Yeah. Then I thought that if I'm as God created me, I can't be a body, and neither can this guy. I could let my true strength take over and not be affected by this poor man who thinks he has to be tough because he's really afraid. I started thinking about the things you said in your forgiveness examples. I realized forgiveness is better for me even on the level of form, because when I'm angry I'd forget that if I hit this guy, he probably would have killed me.

ARTEN: Very good. Every way you look at it you win. By the way, violence is a highly overrated problem-solving technique. Look at the international level. If retaliation worked, then countries that engaged in it would be very secure, right? Are they?

GARY: Nope. It just creates a vicious cycle.

ARTEN: Well, instead of creating a vicious cycle you prevented one. Forgiveness is where it's at for the rest of your life if you're smart — and you *are* smart.

GARY: Thanks. So it's time to play twenty questions about one of my favorite subjects. I think I know the answer to this first one — but from a linear view of time, I would assume that you, as enlightened Beings, would have had to achieve your salvation in the *past* in order to appear to me as enlightened Beings *now*.

ARTEN: You really answered your own question when you said from a *linear* view. We were enlightened in your future, as you will be. There is only *one* time, or in terms of the illusion, there *was* only one time. You took this one time and, just like with the illusion of space, you divided and sub-divided it into seemingly endless parts so they'd look different instead of the same — just as you made up countless people who would seem different instead of the same. Time and space were necessary because there had to be a place for these people to seem to operate *in*. This helps cover up the fact that they're operating in a dream. As the Course says,

> *There is only one time, or in terms of the illusion, there was only one time. You divided and subdivided it into seemingly endless parts so they'd look different instead of the same.*

> ...Ultimately, space is as meaningless as time. Both are merely beliefs.[3]

GARY: You said before that I'm a non-spatial being having a spatial experience; you could also say I'm a timeless being having a time experience.

ARTEN: Yes. That's why we emphasized before that the mind is outside of time and space. When you wake up you realize that all of time and space, and all of the things that appeared to happen there, were just a dream. Your mind merely seemed to go to sleep for a while.[4] As the Course puts it, referring to your mind,

...It dreams of time; an interval in which what seems to happen never has occurred, the changes wrought are substanceless, and all events are nowhere. When the mind awakes, it but continues as it always was.[5]

GARY: That experience of revelation I had; that was just a preview? It's gonna be that way all the time?

ARTEN: Yes.

GARY: I don't know if I could stand that kind of ecstasy.

ARTEN: Give it a shot; you'll love it. Nobody's left out, Gary. Everybody you ever knew is included: your parents, your friends, your relatives, your lovers — everyone, because they are all one with you. The feeling of wholeness is beyond the beyond.

GARY: I want it. So let's keep going here before I forget half of the things I wanted to ask you. For example, it seems the Course is saying that *everything* is just a symbol of separation, and as you've indicated, that would include time itself. I take it that each dream lifetime of ours is just a way of continuing this, but the truth is it really happened all at once?

ARTEN: Yes. Consider what the Course says about that.

Each day, and every minute in each day, and every instant that each minute holds, you but relive the single instant when the time of terror took the place of love. And so you die each day to live again, until you cross the gap between the past and present, which is not a gap at all. Such is each life; a seeming interval from birth to death and on to life again, a repetition of an instant gone by long ago that cannot be relived. And all of time is but the mad belief that what is over is still here and now.

Forgive the past and let it go, for it *is* gone.[6]

GARY: So each day is like a different lifetime, where you seem to fall asleep at night, or die, and then start another one. Within each full lifetime identity, you have phases of your life that are so different that they may as well be distinct lifetimes. Plus, your body changes so much it's as though you occupy several different bodies during a lifetime. It's really all in the mind, or more accurately, a projection of the mind. As that quote is saying, it's all just a reliving of that *first* instant when we thought we had separated ourselves from God. In every instant we have the ability to change our minds about our reality.

ARTEN: Yes. The American Indians used to say, "Behold the great mystery!" The Text of the Course says,

> Behold the great projection, but look on it with the decision that it must be healed, and not with fear. Nothing you made has any power over you unless you still would be apart from your Creator, and with a will opposed to His.[7]

The Course also says, shortly before that,

> …For time you made, and time you can command. You are no more a slave to time than to the world you made.[8]

As J repeatedly counsels you, you can't have both time and eternity. You've got to choose.

> There is no part of Heaven you can take and weave into illusions. Nor is there one illusion you can enter Heaven with.[9]

GARY: The great projection of time and space is just like a movie, then — a very intense movie.

ARTEN: Yes. Once you really understand that, then the question becomes who are you going to watch the movie *with?* You can watch it with the ego and listen to its interpretation, or you can watch it with the Holy Spirit and listen to Its interpretation.

GARY: You mean His interpretation.

ARTEN: Technically, "Its." Don't forget, J is speaking as an artist correcting the Bible that was allegedly based on his teachings. That's why he uses Biblical language.

GARY: Is it true they cut a lot of stuff about reincarnation out of the Bible?

ARTEN: Yes, during the fourth century of the common error.

We'll keep most, though not all of our remarks about the Bible to the century Thomas and I were involved with.

PURSAH: Now, we talk about watching the movie with J or the Holy Spirit and listening to the right-minded interpretation. That brings up an important point. Even though your experience is that you are watching the movie *here,* you're not really watching it here. You're watching it on a higher level, and your *experience* is that you are in a body watching it here. Not only that, but you're watching something that's already happened — like watching a re-run on television that you've repressed or forgotten. Consider these startling passages from the Workbook; taken together, they give an overview of the Course's teachings about the illusion of time.

> ...The revelation that the Father and the Son are one will come in time to every mind. Yet is that time determined by the mind itself, not taught.
>
> The time is set already. It appears to be quite arbitrary. Yet there is no step along the road that anyone takes but by chance. It has already been taken by him, although he has not yet embarked on it. For time but seems to go in one direction. We but undertake a journey that is over. Yet it seems to have a future still unknown to us.
>
> Time is a trick, a sleight of hand, a vast illusion in which figures come and go as if by magic. Yet there is a plan behind appearances that does not change. The script is written. When experience will come to end your doubting has been set. For we but see the journey from the point at which it ended, looking back on it, imagining we make it once again; reviewing mentally what has gone by.[10]

GARY: When he says *we* undertake the journey, he means he's watching it with us, and he'll help us if we ask.

PURSAH: Exactly. Continuing later in the Workbook, J connects the concept of oneness to the two words we have said express the absolute truth, "God is," and then connects it to the subject of time by saying,

...It returns the mind into the endless present, where the past and future cannot be conceived.[11]

And continuing,

...The world has never been at all. Eternity remains a constant state.[12]

He also says,

This is beyond experience we try to hasten. Yet forgiveness, taught and learned, brings with it the experiences which bear witness that the time the mind itself determined to abandon all but this is now at hand.[13]

Continuing along the same lines, referring to the Holy Spirit,

All learning was already in His Mind, accomplished and complete. He recognized all that time holds, and gave it to all minds that each one might determine, from a point where time was ended, when it is released to revelation and eternity. We have repeated several times before that you but make a journey that is done.

For oneness must be here. Whatever time the mind has set for revelation is entirely irrelevant to what must be a constant state, forever as it always was; forever to remain as it is now.[14]

GARY: If it's all done already and I'm just watching a dream movie that's being projected by my hidden unconscious — and my *seeming* movements are being manipulated like a robot anyway — then I don't have to worry about it, do I? I could just do whatever I feel like and salvation is still bound to come anyway, right?

PURSAH: Well, no. You still have to do your job. As J says after the quotations we just spoke,

Suffice it, then, that you have work to do to play your part. The ending must remain obscure to you until your part is done. It does not matter. For your part is still what all the rest depends on. As you take the role assigned to you, salvation comes a little nearer each uncertain heart that does not beat as yet in tune with God.[15]

GARY: I don't know if I like that. All the rest depends on *my* part?

PURSAH: The dream wasn't made up by somebody else, remember? Once again, can the world be saved without you? The answer is no. You know what your job is, just like you knew at the gas station.

GARY: Forgiveness. I'm really forgiving myself; it just doesn't look that way.

PURSAH: Absolutely. As the Course tells you in many different ways, again and again and yet again, in never uncertain terms,

Forgiveness is the central theme that runs throughout salvation, holding all its parts in meaningful relationships, the course it runs directed and its outcome sure.[16]

GARY: I hear you, J. Hell, I was just kidding. I already said I'd do it.

PURSAH: We know you will. You can either be delayed indefinitely or you can break free. The choice you make is no less than what is described in the following — where J himself asks you, in every situation, to make the same decision he did.

Choose once again if you would take your place
among the saviors of the world, or would remain
in hell, and hold your brothers there.[17]

GARY: You couldn't be any clearer, although some of those quotes about time are pretty esoteric. I need to get a second wind to handle all this.

PURSAH: Just try to remember for now that time *seems* to have a future still unknown to you, but it's really already done. You can't change the ego's script; all you can do is switch over to the Holy

Spirit's interpretation — which, as we emphasize, *is* His script. That's why J said to us two thousand years ago, "Who among you by worrying can add one minute to your life?" The truth is, the story of your life — and it's *only* a story — has already been written. Talk about a story, you're not even really watching it here! You think you are, but you're really reviewing it mentally at the level of the mind. Once again, you're the part of the mind that observes and chooses, while the dream movie was caused by the first choices you made with the ego.

As far as getting your second wind is concerned, there's certainly nothing wrong with reaffirming your commitment. Remember that no matter how

> ❦
> *Your salvation always comes down to a decision you are making right now. There's no getting away from that.*

big the job may *seem* to be, and no matter how many dimensions of time there are, or alternate universes with their own dimensions, there is still that same simplicity we have described that you can never really escape: Your salvation always comes down to a decision you are making right *now.* There's no getting away from that. No matter what appears to be going on for you, the choice is really very simple and immediate. Whenever you remember that, you'll know which interpretation of the dream you should listen to — even after your body appears to pass away.

GARY: That reminds me! I was dreaming in bed about a month ago and something fearful happened in the dream. I remembered to ask J for help in the dream, and I felt his strength take over.

PURSAH: Yes. At some point — and you've reached that point — the Course's thought system becomes so much a part of you that you'll choose the strength of Christ even when you're asleep at night, which means you'll often choose that same strength automatically after you lay your body aside. That should be a comforting thought for you, not only because it will make you less fearful of death, but because it confirms that even if you died today you'd still take your learning with you — even though you're not a master.

GARY: Don't be so linear.

ARTEN: Now that we've gotten this far in our timeless discussion of time, don't forget to ask us some of the questions you had in your mind before we came here.

GARY: Sure. I've mentioned this before, but it helps me to be patient if I remember that the Course is saying the separation was completely answered and healed immediately. The reason we seem to be waking up slowly is so we won't be terrified.

ARTEN: That's correct. Reality is very different than your present experience, as you've seen for yourself. Getting used to it slowly is highly recommended. Even most mornings you wake up gradually from your dreams — unless the alarm clock gives you a rude awakening. Well, the larger mind appears to be waking up from the dream slowly, and when a seeming individual awakens from the dream it's symbolic of the larger mind's gradual awakening — even though you can tell from the quotations we're using that the dream was really over instantaneously. The question is, how long do *you* want to wait to be completely prepared for Heaven? As the Course reminds you,

> **...Your brothers are everywhere. You do not have to seek far for salvation. Every minute and every second gives you a chance to save yourself. Do not lose these chances, not because they will not return, but because delay of joy is needless.**[18]

We've quoted the Course before about God willing that His Son be wakened gently, but you have to realize that your mind must contemplate an idea at least a dozen times or so before it really starts to sink in. While it may be your mind that thinks and sees and hears, not your body, that means it's also your mind, under the dominance of the ego, that *refuses* to really think and see and hear right-minded ideas — no matter what their form. That's why the thought system of the Course is essential when it comes to gradually peeling away the layers of your ego through the use of interconnected principles that continuously support each other and become dominant over the wrong-minded way of looking at the great projection.

GARY: I get the importance of the structured thought system and how it works. Some people resist the idea of having their mind trained because they're afraid it means being brainwashed or tricked into giving up their independent thinking.

ARTEN: If they want brainwashing they can always join a cult, but as long as they stick to the Course as a self-study method, they'll realize that it's their *own* power of decision that's being utilized, not given up. Besides, in their present condition they've actually already been brainwashed by the ego, and will remain so until they reclaim their minds. As the Course explains about the need for training,

...You are much too tolerant of mind wandering, and are passively condoning your mind's miscreations.[19]

GARY: I'd never do that. Just kidding. Also, most people assume it's what they believe in their conscious mind that matters, when the truth is it's what they believe in their unconscious mind that makes all the difference — and they can't change that on their own.

ARTEN: You've got it. That's why the Holy Spirit is the way out.

GARY: So if I keep up this forgiveness game I can get plucked out of the illusory hologram?

ARTEN: Why not? It's only because of your mistaken beliefs and wrong-minded thinking that you got plucked into it.

GARY: That reminds me, what we call the Big Bang, which was symbolic of the separation and the projection of the universe — does it mean the universe is eventually gonna start going the other way and collapse into itself at the end?

ARTEN: To borrow one of your words — nope. It's true that the Big Bang symbolized separation, but what you should remember is that on the level of form it was so tremendous it rendered an unfathomable force of energy. This in turn pre-determined *all* physical laws and the fate of every cell and molecule, how each one would evolve and which direction they would go in. When we say the movie has already been filmed, we're saying that everything that would seemingly occur was already set in motion at that instant, and in fact couldn't really occur any other way. All the different dimensions and scenarios are simply symbolic of different big bangs within the Big Bang that occurred at that same instant. Even though it was all over immediately, you still have to wake up in order to recognize reality.

GARY: So, on this level we suffer under the illusion that we forge our own destiny when the truth is that every physical law was already set in motion at that instant. Everything that happened would have had to happen exactly the way it did, no matter what we tried to do about it?

ARTEN: That's correct. The mechanism of how the body robots are manipulated by unseen forces is simply a part of the acting out of the pre-determined script. Remember this: Since it was your decision to side with the ego and make the separation real it means, once again, that this script is an example of *self* pre-determination that was agreed to by you on a different level, not a case of you being a victim. Now you have the Course to teach you how to change your mind about the whole thing.

What you are witnessing here is like an ego recording, and it's up to you when you want to listen to a different tune. The universe doesn't have to collapse onto itself in order to end. What has to happen is that everyone has to wake up, *then* the dream universe will simply disappear — because an insignificant dream was all it ever was.

To keep you sucked in, the script seems to move faster and faster as time goes on, and your attention span gets shorter and shorter. Until you destroy your civilization and start all over again with little memory — like starting a new lifetime.

GARY: I know what you mean about faster and faster; it's true with everything. Look at the movies. The editing of movies and television in the last thirty years has speeded up so much it's almost laughable. They must seriously believe everybody has attention deficit disorder. Real conversations are becoming more and more rare. Everything is dumbed down. As far as the images are concerned, the philosophy sometimes is that if you can see it, it's too slow.

ARTEN: Yes; more and more style and less and less substance — like with your politics. Do you realize that Abraham Lincoln, the first great Republican President...

GARY: And the *last* great Republican President.

ARTEN: You give yourself away, but do you realize Lincoln could not be elected today? He didn't have a good speaking voice, and he actually took the time to think about the answer to a question. If you did that in a debate today you'd be called stupid. Imagine having a thoughtful answer instead of a clever, pre-written sound byte? Politics, movies — they're going the same way. It's all style and speed, and what does that do for people except tune them more and more into the madness?

GARY: Yeah. Time flies when you're going crazy. I do like the movies, I just felt like pointing out the way the editing is going. Hey, what you said before about multiple choice scripts — that seems to contradict the idea of the whole movie already being written.

ARTEN: Actually, it doesn't — because it has to do with the fact that there are several dimensions open to you and it's possible to switch from one to the other. Yet it's still a closed system, and the very fact that it's limited and fixed supports what we've been saying. The ego's script is like a carrot and a stick. It tries to suck you into thinking you have freedom *within* the script when the only real freedom you will ever find is completely outside the whole mess.

GARY: As for the multiple choice script, are you saying that by making different decisions I could wake up one morning and without knowing it I could be in a different dimension that looks just like this one, except it had its own big bang boom within the whole she-bang of the Big Bang and thus has its own variation of the script?

ARTEN: Yes, you could.

GARY: That's wicked excellent.

ARTEN: Is it? Once again, you have to remember it's still an illusion within a fixed system. An illusion is still an illusion — and *that's* still an illusion, and there's only one way out. The ego's script is simply *all* of time, which is already over. The Holy Spirit's script is the for-giveness of all the people in your life — no matter where you may appear to be. That's how time disappears.

PURSAH: One of the best ways to get the distinction between the ego's time and the Holy Spirit's timelessness is to remember that the Holy Spirit's lessons of true forgiveness lead to the *undoing* of time by rendering it unnecessary. This undoing is accomplished at the level of the mind — outside of time — and instead of changing time, collapses it.

GARY: Like that day I was at the movies and I drove home at a different time because I no longer needed some particular forgive-ness lessons — having already been practicing forgiveness?

PURSAH: That's right, you lucky stiff. Oh wait; I was going to save that particular description of you for the discussion about sex.

GARY: Funny. You should be on TV.

PURSAH: Oprah?

GARY: She's great, but even she may not be open-minded enough for all of this.

PURSAH: We'll see. Any more questions before our time runs out? Just kidding, of course.

GARY: Yeah. Some people believe reincarnation leads to the evolvement of the soul. True?

PURSAH: Think, Gary. Your soul is *already* perfect, or otherwise it wouldn't be a soul; it would just be something you're mistaking for a soul — like your mind, which people do mistake for the soul, or a projection of your mind, which includes bodily-shaped ghostly images that people think are souls. Evolution is something that appears to happen on the level of form, but it's just a dream. Once your mind has learned all its forgiveness lessons then it awakens to spirit or soul, and everything else is gone except Heaven. Most people think of their soul as being an individual thing because they can't help but think of themselves as individuals. When that false belief is gone, then you know that there is really only *one* soul — which is our unlimited oneness as spirit.

> ❧
>
> ***Evolution appears to happen, but it's just a dream. Once your mind has learned all its forgiveness lessons it awakens to spirit, and everything else is gone except Heaven.***

GARY: Reincarnation is also just a dream?

PURSAH: Yes, but as we've been trying to explain, since it's something that appears to happen we talk about it as though it does. When your dream lifetime is over, you *see* yourself as leaving the body and having other adventures, but you're not really going anywhere. You're just watching the mind's projections, or as we've often called it for your benefit — a movie.

GARY: O.K. Now here's a question that might make you think I lack faith in you, but that's not the case. I was just wondering... You said you were in the body for eleven years after being enlightened, but the

Course seems to indicate that the body doesn't support enlightened Beings; it says that if you were in constant communication with God then the body wouldn't be long maintained and that our task is to become perfect here and then we're seen no more. Eleven years seems like a long time to hang around after your enlightenment. What do you have to say for yourself?

PURSAH: I'll answer that, but let me caution you about something. Don't nitpick the Course to death. As we've said, all the details of the Course's teachings should be put within the context of its larger teachings on forgiveness. As far as hanging around for eleven years, I remained visible in the dream in order to help Arten. I deliberately kept one foot in the door, so to speak, so I could be with him and help him to be with me forever. As for the body not being long maintained, don't forget that J had a ministry for several years during which he was clearly enlightened. While it's not possible to be completely in communion with God and maintain the body, there is an in-between place, which the Course refers to as the borderland,[20] which is a place of forgiveness where one can do some work that is helpful while appearing to be in this world, and also experience their enlightenment at the same time.

GARY: That's what the Course also calls the real world?[21]

PURSAH: That's right. Thank you for not losing faith, although we've already indicated that faith in us personally is not essential. Whether you believe in us or not, you can always trust the Holy Spirit. Do you remember what the ten characteristics of a teacher of God are in the Course?

GARY: Sure. A teacher of God is trustworthy, loyal, helpful, friendly, courteous, kind — oh, wait a minute. I used to be a Boy Scout.

PURSAH: You're certainly not one anymore. The characteristic I was chiefly referring to is trust. As the Course says about your Teacher,

...The Holy Spirit must perceive time, and reinterpret it into the timeless. He must work through opposites, because He must work with and for a mind that is in opposition. Correct and learn, and be open to learning. You have not made truth, but truth can still set you free.[22]

Because you cannot yet experience eternity completely you need miracles, or acts of true forgiveness, in which you give to your brothers and sisters in order to give to yourself and be healed by the One you trust, the Holy Spirit. As the Course says,

> ...In time the giving comes first, though they are simultaneous in eternity, where they cannot be separated. When you have learned they are the same, the need for time is over.
> Eternity is one time, its only dimension being "always."[23]

ARTEN: To start summing up our discussion, the Course teaches you,

> ...Time and eternity are both in your mind, and will conflict until you perceive time solely as a means to regain eternity.[24]

You will not be able to do this anywhere near as quickly by utilizing the ordinary methods that the world has emphasized to date. For example, the Course makes a commentary on such approaches by asking you the following rhetorical question.

> ...Can you find light by analyzing darkness, as the psychotherapist does, or like the theologian, by acknowledging darkness in yourself and looking for a distant light to remove it, while emphasizing the distance?[25]

GARY: What a smart ass! I'm gonna write a strongly worded letter to the Foundation for inner pizza, there.

ARTEN: In the meantime, look up and remember these quotes we've been saying about time. The more you consider them, the more meaningful and profound they will become. In your future, Pursah and I will tell J after reading his Course that his countenance shakes a spear.

GARY: I hope you'll tell me what that means.

ARTEN: Sure. The gentleman who wrote the Shakespeare material was an Earl whose family's crest bore the image of a lion shaking a spear. To honor his family he was sometimes toasted at Court with the phrase, "Your countenance shakes a spear." But this Earl was forbidden by Queen Elizabeth the First, who was a political genius and very controlling, from putting his name on his work. There was a social stigma attached to the stage at that time. Plays, especially comedies, were not considered to be serious literature and were beneath the dignity of royalty.

GARY: That's funny — Shakespeare not being serious literature.

ARTEN: Illusory times do change, and Shakespeare, or Edward de Vere, the seventeenth Earl of Oxford, helped change them. There is only one Shakespeare, even if he is a dead white man. Although the Queen did not completely forbid him from writing, he couldn't put his name on his accomplishments.

It turns out there was an actor by the name of William Shakespeare. When de Vere found out about this man, he thought it was almost too good to be true. Here was de Vere being toasted at Court with the phrase related to his family crest, a lion shaking a spear, and here's a man in the business named Shakespeare! Edward struck a deal with William to put his name on the work and have the plays presented to the public with the actor playing the part of author. It was a sly way for Edward to get some credit for his work without actually putting his name on it. The plan succeeded very nicely, although Shakespeare wasn't really paid that much, and many of the plays were published all at once as a catalog *after* the actor named Shakespeare passed away.

Many have noticed the writing style of the Course and its similarity in beauty to the writing of William Shakespeare, so we joke with J and tell him that his countenance shakes a spear.

GARY: That's pretty cool. You guys are a lot of fun.

ARTEN: Then have fun, my friend. J did; Shakespeare did. Don't take the tricks of time seriously. What you think of as the past is an illusory happening that is taking place right *now*. The future is happening right *now,* but your mind has divided these images up to make them look like time. Yet the whole thing happened all at once and is already over. No matter what tricks the ego throws your way, just forgive and let live. The Course asks you to relinquish your judgment.

And where is time, when dreams of judgment have been put away?[26]

GARY: In a nutshell, the Course is saying that all of time was actually contained within one instant. The vast illusion happened all at once, although it didn't *really* happen, and it's actually over. The thought of separation and all the symbolic thoughts of separation therein were immediately corrected by the Holy Spirit, but we keep replaying the tape of the script of separation in our mind over and over — kind of like ghosts — until we completely *accept* the Holy Spirit's corrections, which dissolve time and return us to God.

ARTEN: You've got it. True forgiveness is the way out.

GARY: So time heals not all wounds, but forgiveness will heal all time.

ARTEN: Not bad, fellow messenger. I think your countenance just shook a spear.

12

Watching the News

You cannot see his sins and not your own.
But you can free him and yourself as well.[1]

Two of my biggest sources of information were the nightly TV network news and the Internet, and nothing pushed my buttons more than the information I received through these "conveniences." One day when I was at my computer going internuts, I came across the website of a group in the Midwest that many Course students considered to be a cult using the Course for its own purposes. I was astonished to see that this group had actually *added* its own words in between the lines of the Course. "Jesus," I said out loud, "That's like painting a moustache on the Mona Lisa."

Several years later this same cult became the focus of a national news program that had gone to Wisconsin to do a story on them. The leader of the group, a self-styled "master teacher," was infamous for confronting many of his students in an attacking and humiliating manner. On this particular day, while the cameras were still rolling, he became visibly angry and started yelling at the interviewer of the program for repeatedly asking him a question he didn't like.

Watching the show, I felt embarrassed that my chosen spiritual path was being misrepresented to the American public in this way. Didn't the Course teach that anger was never justified? Yet here was a self-proclaimed Course teacher who didn't seem capable of living its most basic ideas — all the while presenting himself as infallible.

I cringed as I watched the program — but then I realized what I was doing. Who was making all of this real? Who was the dreamer of the dream, and who was reacting to it? Who forgot that there's not really anybody out there? It was me; there was no one else around. Wasn't I condemning this other man for what were actually my own secret sins that existed in a different form, but which I didn't want to look at? Didn't I occasionally make other people wrong who didn't agree with me? Didn't I sometimes feel angry?

I then saw more clearly than ever that what the Course was saying to *me* was true; the dream was *not* being dreamed by the people in my mirror. Within my conflicts there were not really any opponents. It didn't matter that this particular upset had something to do with a teacher of *A Course in Miracles*. Miracles were all the same. The truth did not vacillate, and no exceptions or compromises were possible if the truth were to remain itself.

I forgave my brother and myself simultaneously. Because I thought the guilt was in my brother, and since I had made him up in the first place, then the guilt must really be in me. But if the separation from God never occurred, then I must be innocent also, and the reasons for this made-up projection and defense were erroneous. I joined with the Holy Spirit, and from that time forward I would never really look at anything on television or the Internet in quite the same way.

In December of 1997, when Arten and Pursah showed up for appearance number twelve, I was going through a time when my ego was getting very tired of me forgiving so much. I sensed that my ascended visitors were ready to help.

ARTEN: Hey brother. How's your world?

GARY: It's still here, which gets a little tedious sometimes.

PURSAH: Take heart, dear brother. The Course is set up so you can live what you thought was your life and gradually attain your salvation at the same time. Go at your own pace. That way you won't feel like anything is being taken away from you, and you can realize *for yourself* that the world has no value. For example, you should remember what the Manual For Teachers says about almost all of the Course's students, including you.

...By far the majority are given a slowly-evolving training program, in which as many previous mistakes as possible are corrected. Relationships in particular must be properly perceived, and all dark cornerstones of unforgiveness removed. Otherwise the old thought system still has a basis for return.[2]

GARY: I understand; the world is just a pain in the ass sometimes.

PURSAH: That's quite honest, so let's help you out a little. You occasionally get your tummy in an uproar when you watch the news. You make it good and real for yourself or else that wouldn't happen.

GARY: I've been thinking about that. When I go to the movies — and I'm sorry to keep talking about films all the time, but that's what I do. You know: so many movies, so little time. When I go there I want to forget that it's not real. That's one of the signs of a good movie — if you can suspend your disbelief. I think that's what people have done with what they think is real life; we've suspended our disbelief and we want it to be true. We make everything out to be important. When I'm sitting here at home watching the news sometimes I forget to remember it's a bunch of bull, and I do what we've all been doing forever, which is the same thing I do at the movies — I get into it like it's really happening. If I could just make a habit of remembering a little more how the Course would interpret it, then it wouldn't have the impact on me that it does. It seems to me that it's all in the remembering. Now maybe you've said that before — that remembering is the hardest part — but how do I *do* it?

PURSAH: First of all, instead of just getting up in the morning and doing whatever you feel like, why don't you do what the Course suggests in the Manual? As soon as it's possible, spend some quiet time with God.[3] Then remembering Who you are, bring your peace with you. After that, be determined to stay alert. You *know* the ego is going to try to upset you and make you think you're a body. That's why the Course counsels you about being vigilant and not being so tolerant of mind wandering. All you've got to do is focus and use a little more discipline.

The funny thing is, you can do it. I think you *know* from experience that you can do it. In fact, you do it a lot. That's why your ego feels threatened. The ego is ingenious, and as you've seen for yourself, it will come up with remarkable ways to trick you. All you have to do is be a little more ready to respond ahead of time. Once you're in that state of mind you'll have it made. You can handle the news, and you can handle anything else that comes up.

> ❦
>
> *It's no sacrifice for a teacher of God to give up the burden of judging.*

GARY: If I'm watching the news and I'm in this state of miracle readiness, then is it the same process as with other forms of forgiveness — like with my personal relationships — or are there different thoughts that would be best for me to respond with?

ARTEN: It's all the same. But yes, there can be certain thoughts that help different people more in different situations. There's a passage in the Manual that's very helpful because it reminds you that if you let the Holy Spirit take care of judgment, then it actually puts you in a much more powerful situation. It's no sacrifice for a teacher of God to give up the burden of judging.

> …On the contrary, he puts himself in a position where judgment *through* him rather than *by* him can occur. And this judgment is neither "good" nor "bad." It is the only judgment there is, and it is only one: "God's Son is guiltless, and sin does not exist."[4]

GARY: When I see that they're guiltless, whether it's on TV or in person, then my unconscious mind understands that I'm guiltless.

ARTEN: I knew you were listening some of the time we were here. You can do it, and do it consistently. Once you're there, you're there. Just be more determined. It's time for you to go from the little willingness stage to the abundant willingness stage. It's a game you can't lose, so relax.

GARY: I know, but when shit happens like these terrorists blowing up our embassies, it's hard to see the terrorists as guiltless.

ARTEN: Yes, but that's just another chance to free yourself. It may *look* more difficult, but your forgiveness opportunities are really all the same.

GARY: All right. But isn't it true that you can be guided to appropriate action as a result of your forgiveness?

ARTEN: Yes. We'll get into that, and although we almost never give advice on the level of form, before we get back to forgiveness at the level of the mind we're going to talk for a minute about the level of the world.

The United States, being in a position of power that has never been achieved by any other nation in history, has much more of a responsibility when it comes to diffusing situations than anybody else does. Take the Middle East, for example. Yes, the terrorists are psychotic — especially when they claim to be doing something for Allah. The God of the Koran, although spelled differently, is the same God as The Old and New Testaments. While the particular God presented by these religions may not always be a happy camper, it's ludicrous to think terrorists are correct in hijacking a religion and using it as an excuse for their own violent purposes. Although every religion ends up getting used by psychotics as a justification for their own insanity, the leaders of these movements have to get somebody to listen to them in order to gain power — and especially money. The question you should ask yourself is, does the United States make it harder or easier for these fanatics to gain the support of their people?

Your Presidents will try to tell you that America is hated by these terrorists and other people in the Middle East because you stand for freedom and democracy. That's false at best and a cynical lie at worst. What did the Shah of Iran have to do with freedom and democracy? How about the Emir of Kuwait? What about the royal family in Saudi Arabia? What do they have to do with freedom and democracy? Nothing. The government of the United States has become famous around the world in the last hundred years for propping up any government that will watch out for the best interests not of the local people, but of the American-based or US-dominated multi-national corporations.

The terrorists hate you for their own psychotic reasons, but your country is hated in the Middle East by average people not because you stand for freedom and democracy, but because you *don't* stand for freedom and democracy. You stand for whatever's best for American money. You care about their oil, not about them. You care about the most efficient way that your corporations, whether at home or on foreign soil, can make money in any situation — not about democracy. Most of the people in the world know this, but not the American people, who have been brainwashed by television propaganda for the last half a century into believing America can only do right. Since the mid-1970s the big corporations, through acquisition, have completely sewn up their editorial control over the news media. In the meantime, their agenda for the Middle East has been anything but altruistic.

GARY: You're saying these terrorists and fanatics gain the support of the people because we make it easy for them to hate us. I also imagine that in the case of some terrorists, when you haven't got a pot to piss in, it makes you more likely to have martyrdom as your main vocation.

ARTEN: Of course. What if all the people of the Middle East had their own free countries and economies and good educations, careers, and nice homes? Do you think they'd be as interested in blowing themselves up? Of course the *real* problem is within them.

GARY: Though communism sucked, it doesn't mean capitalism is perfect — but it *can* do good.

ARTEN: America does good and bad; that's duality. Your country is often a positive force, but usually with a hidden agenda. Even the Marshall Plan to rebuild Europe after World War Two was done just as much to promote your capitalistic ambitions as it was for humanitarian purposes. The greed of your corporations has grown exponentially since then. There has always been the element of an empire based on money underneath the surface.

GARY: You mean like when America stole the independent country of Hawaii back in 1893?

ARTEN: A fine example. Most of the people of the Middle East see you as being perfectly willing to steal anything you can, just as you stole your own vast country from the Indians. The fact that you pay for oil doesn't change how the people of other regions *perceive* you through the lens of their own unconscious guilt. Perhaps you should help them more to see you differently.

GARY: What if we didn't need their oil?

ARTEN: Politically, that would be the most brilliant move you could make. Then you wouldn't have to do anything in the Middle East that wasn't good. You could support freedom and democracy instead of just yourselves. Of course the truth is you already have the technology to free yourself of your addiction to foreign oil, but because that's not what would be best for the bottom line of your corporations at this time, you can forget about it.

When President Eisenhower left office he warned your nation about the power of what he called a "military-industrial complex." While there is nothing in your Constitution about capitalism, America is not a democracy — it is now a moneyocracy. Your banks, their legal loan shark credit card companies, the insurance companies and your major, multi-national corporations seek to ultimately become above the law and own the world. They own America and its political process, and will continue to insure in the future that your government of the rich, by the rich and for the rich shall not perish from the earth.

This will lead to more tragedy, and I thought it best to point out here that there are alternative methods that would be more promising than the tired process of retaliation, lies and profits.

GARY: Food for thought, anyway. Forgiveness is what the individual can do about his or her world, and nobody can ever take that away once you know how to do it.

ARTEN: Yes, once you know how to do it then you realize that you're never a victim, and what you are seeing are merely symbols of your own insanity pictured outside of yourself — except now you have a way to be free of it by releasing the other. Other people in turn will live in peace only after they are willing to look at their *own* dark side as seen in others and forgive it. When you get away from the level of form, the people of the Middle East are not the victims of America, or Israel or anybody else. Even the people of a decimated country like Lebanon, or the Palestinians, who still do not even have their own country, are not victims of the world they see. Throwing rocks at the same people that their ancestors threw at will not change anything in this generation, any more than it did in previous ones.

The people of Israel are acting out the same script they agreed to with everyone else, whether it looks that way or not. Each person on all sides must be willing to forgive the so-called evil that they *perceive* as being in their enemies, who do not really exist any more than they do. The world's inhabitants must heal their relationships and undo their unconscious guilt before violence will ever end permanently.

GARY: You mean it wasn't a good idea when I got on the Internet after the Embassy bombings and called for *A Course in Miracles* Day of Rage? Just kidding. The news sucks us into seeing someone else as the guilty party — whether it's the terrorists, or the politicians and their witch hunts, or those people who are guilty of crimes, or at least whomever the prosecutors and the news media want us to believe are guilty — because getting us to project our guilt onto others is good for certain careers and ratings. On some talk shows, the game is about whoever can put other people down the best. On the news, the more problems they can get us to worry about, the better. All of this keeps our minds running wild.

ARTEN: Precisely, which is exactly what the ego wants. As the Course teaches you,

...Preoccupations with problems set up to be incapable of solution are favorite ego devices for impeding learning progress. In all these diversionary tactics, however, the one question that is never asked by those who pursue them is, "What for?" This is the question that *you* must learn to ask in connection with everything. What is the purpose? Whatever it is, it will direct your efforts automatically.[5]

GARY: The purpose should be forgiveness and the Atonement. On TV the whole diversion is just a function of multiplicity, or one *appearing* as many. The one is me — not really me, but symbols of what's in my unconscious — and the answer is always the same, no matter what form the multiplicity takes. I guess forgiveness can be pretty simple when you remember it.

PURSAH: Yes. We told you it was doable. Not necessarily always easy, but doable. Don't forget, the images you see in what you think is your real life are no more real than the images you see on TV or at the movies.

GARY: I'm trying to remember. You know what I really don't like, though: that all this stuff I've learned about the markets isn't real —

like the Fibonacci sequence and ratios and the Golden Section and Gann angles and Elliot Wave Theory and my technical indicators, and all these patterns. It makes me a little disappointed that none of it's real.

PURSAH: That's true of everyone's idols and the tools they use to try to attain their dreams. Don't forget, it doesn't mean you can't use illusions *inside* the illusion, however you see fit. We've already indicated that there's nothing wrong with magic that's used at the same time as forgiveness, and that would apply to the tools for whatever career you've chosen.

GARY: So I can be forgiven all of my illusions, no matter what they are, and I can get home even faster.

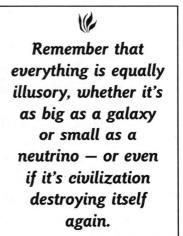

Remember that everything is equally illusory, whether it's as big as a galaxy or small as a neutrino — or even if it's civilization destroying itself again.

NOTE: At this point some gunshots went off in the woods very close to my house — a situation that wasn't uncommon near Christmas, even though deer hunting season had ended a few weeks earlier. It wasn't unheard of for citizens of Maine to be killed in their yards, or even their homes, by hunters.

GARY: Don't worry, none of them hit me. It's just some rednecks blowing away a few defenseless animals for pleasure.

ARTEN: You've never fired a gun, have you?

GARY: No. That's because a man who feels a need to fire a gun secretly feels inadequate about his penis. And a woman who feels a need to fire a gun is secretly jealous because she doesn't *have* a penis. That's just my opinion. Maybe I'm still upset about that woman near Waterville who was out in her yard with her children; a hunter mistook her for a deer and snuffed her.

ARTEN: You're slipping, Gary. Forgiveness, remember?

GARY: I'm taking the day off!

ARTEN: We'll move along anyway. Remember that everything is *equally* illusory. It doesn't matter if it's as big as a galaxy or as small as a neutrino. It doesn't even matter if it's civilization destroying itself again. It's all the same.

GARY: Does civilization always destroy itself?

ARTEN: Usually. For example, intelligent humanoid life migrated from Mars to the Earth. It didn't *evolve* on Mars, but had migrated there as well. Civilization on Mars had been mostly destroyed at that point, so it was just as much an escape to Earth as a migration. Also, there are times when most of the life on a planet is destroyed by an asteroid hitting the surface.

GARY: It's always something, isn't it?

ARTEN: It's always something until it's nothing. When J spoke to you and said, "Renounce the world and the ways of the world; make them meaningless to you," he meant that what you're seeing doesn't exist. It's nothing because it's not really there. How can nothing mean anything? If you make it mean something, good or bad, then you're trying to change nothing into something. The only thing you should make it is meaningless.

At the same time, don't try to take other people's idols and dreams away from them. Remember how important some things have been to *you*. Do you remember when you were a kid and you went to see The Beatles play in Boston?

GARY: Sure I do.

ARTEN: Is there any way that anybody could have told you that wasn't important?

GARY: I see what you mean. George Harrison was my idol. I modeled my guitar playing after his. There's no way anybody could have told me that wasn't the most important thing in the world at the time.

ARTEN: Remember that when you're tempted to criticize others for having their dreams. They'll give up being attached to their illusions when the time is right.

GARY: I won't even ask you for more information about Mars. I have enough to take in right now.

PURSAH: It's not important, Gary. But you didn't really think you were a descendant of an ape, did you? There are many different humanoid types. The ego makes bodies, which was really done all at once, but in time they appear to be separate. Bodily images are projections; guilt and fear make them seem solid, then the script is set up to make it look like bodies are the function of a natural process. Death becomes as natural as life, yet there *is* no death.

GARY: I got it. I also get the idea about the news being set up to make us react and see others as guilty, which is the same purpose as the rest of the illusion. I see it even in the regional news here.

PURSAH: Yes. For example, the local police might want to make it look like they're doing something, so they call up the town newspaper and then arrest the local call girls.

GARY: There goes my social life.

PURSAH: Seriously, the important point we want to leave you with is this. The book you are writing isn't about you, and it's not about us. We came here to give people a spiritual message, a message that not everyone is ready for yet, and this is it: When you are ready to accept that the *only* thing that really matters in your illusory lifetime is the successful completion of your lessons of true forgiveness, then you will be truly wise indeed.

Despite your wisecracks, you, my brother, are doing superbly. You *always* forgive — even if it sometimes takes you a few minutes or a few hours. You're winning. Accept that and let it make you even more determined to persevere.

ARTEN: In the months ahead, don't ever forget that the goal is the only thing worth having, and this world isn't. You think the universe is of value because you're used to it and, except for a few recent experiences, it's all you remember, at least in this lifetime. The Course asks you,

> Is it a sacrifice to give up pain? Does an adult resent the giving up of children's toys? Does one whose vision has already glimpsed the face of Christ look back with longing on a slaughter house? No one who has escaped the world and all its ills looks back on it with condemnation. Yet he must rejoice that he is free of all the sacrifice its values would demand of him.[6]

PURSAH: That's it for today, beloved brother. Happy holidays and continued success — even when it's hard. We'll leave you with these words from the Course to encourage you.

Have faith in only this one thing, and it will be sufficient: God wills you be in Heaven, and nothing can keep you from it, or it from you. Your wildest misperceptions, your weird imaginings, your blackest nightmares all mean nothing. They will not prevail against the peace God wills for you.[7]

13

True Prayer and Abundance

I once asked you to sell all you have and give to the
poor and follow me. This is what I meant: If you have no
investment in anything in this world, you can teach the
poor where their treasure is. The poor are merely those
who have invested wrongly, and they are poor indeed![1]

ARTEN and Pursah had promised me they'd talk about true prayer
and the way to receive guidance on how I should proceed in my
everyday life. I thought this might be the subject of our next discussion because I had recently felt a desire to spend time studying and
applying one of the Course's related pamphlets, titled *The Song of
Prayer,* which also dealt with those topics. My ascended friends
were scheduled to reappear in August of 1998 but before that, over
the 4TH of July weekend, I was destined to pay a visit to the man
whom Pursah had said would come to be viewed as the Course's
greatest teacher.

For the previous five years, ever since my study group facilitator
had handed me some tapes by Ken Wapnick, I had occasionally
listened to Ken's teachings. I didn't really like to read, and these
cassette tapes were especially helpful to me in my understanding
and application of the Course. Although it would be possible for me
to study the Course on my own I liked having help, and I knew I
wanted very much to do a workshop with Ken in person.

As Karen and I drove the ten hours it would take us to get from
rural Maine to Roscoe, New York, a rural town in the Catskills, I was
happy that my five years of procrastinating on this trip were over.

I was even happier when I saw the idyllic setting of the Foundation for *A Course in Miracles* on beautiful Tennanah Lake.

We would stay there for the next couple of nights and do a workshop called "Time and Eternity" along with 150 other students. A high percentage of these people were from the New York City area, but there were also students from all over America as well as a few international visitors. As I shyly talked to my fellow students I realized that most of them were on the upper end of the intelligence scale — something I'd expect of serious students of the Course.

During the three days we spent in Roscoe, I got to meet Ken and chat with him a couple of times in the lunchroom. Two of the things that surprised me the most were his easygoing manner and excellent sense of humor — things that didn't always seem as evident on his cassette tapes.

Although it's not really possible to put an experience such as this into words, it suffices to say that I found the workshop to be a transforming event. I came away with the conviction that while I couldn't always control *what* appeared to happen in my life, I could always control how I looked at it — and thus how I felt about it.

A couple of years later, in June 2000, I would go to Roscoe and do a second workshop with Ken. This time I'd be surprised to find out that the Foundation was leaving Roscoe and moving three thousand miles away to the city of Temecula in southern California. Although a little disappointed at first, I was sure Ken and his wife Gloria knew what they were doing and were being guided by Jesus — and I also knew that California was the Mecca of open minded spirituality. I hoped I'd get to go visit the Foundation out west someday, but I'd always be thankful for the workshops in Roscoe and the chance to meet Ken.

Back at home, I thought a lot that summer about the subject of scarcity and abundance, knowing I wanted to talk to Arten and Pursah about it. It was amazing to me that the American people thought they needed so many things. During the Great Depression, if you had a roof over your head and enough food to eat then you were grateful. Yes, there were rich people then, but survival was the strategy for most citizens. If you weren't cold and hungry you were doing well. After World War Two was over, and up until the early

1950s, Americans were very tight-fisted with their money. All but the very young still had the Great Depression in their minds, and saving was in fashion — much to the chagrin of America's corporations. Then the first coast to coast television broadcasts took place in 1951.

For the first time, an entire nation could watch television advertisements that showed them all the things they didn't have and all the reasons they'd be better off if they did. People had no idea how vulnerable they were to suggestion and greed. By the mid-1950s business was booming. It was now as American as apple pie to spend instead of save. People bought things they would have earlier gone without and never missed. From watching television, the idea of keeping up with the neighbors had taken root. The capitalistic steamroller took off, and Wall Street right along with it. Maybe that wasn't bad in the material world, but what was it doing to the minds of the people? It simply made them more and more focused on the physical, which was in perfect alignment with the ego's hidden script, keeping their minds away from mental discipline.

Another point of interest was that if the people *didn't* see it on television, then it didn't matter. On September 11, 1973, not much was made of the fact that the democratically elected President of Chile was killed by people hired by the CIA, and a right-wing puppet of the United States installed in his place. The torture and murder of so many of the Chilean people that followed was shameful to the world, but not to most Americans, who did not see the story accurately reported on their television networks.

In the 1990s, the American people didn't know that their country, even if it wanted to, would not be allowed to join the European Union. By European law, the fact that the death penalty was allowed here would make our nation too barbaric to qualify for membership.

Still, this was all part of a pre-conceived script, and I only had two lenses to see it through. Forgiveness didn't always come quickly to me, but it *did* always come eventually.

In August of 1998, I was at home on a rainy afternoon when Arten and Pursah popped in for visit number thirteen. A smiling Pursah opened the discussion.

PURSAH: Hey, Gary. It's great to see you, as always. We're happy you went to see Ken. Of course you could learn from him without actually going to see him, but it's fun that you went.

GARY: You bet, and it was cool meeting him, too. For a scholar, I was surprised at how funny he is.

PURSAH: One of the Holy Spirit's finest tools is laughter, my brother. If you take the world too seriously, it will take you.

GARY: Yeah. I wish I could remember to laugh a little more often. I still delay my forgiveness too much sometimes. I'm sure you're aware of what I want to talk about today. I'd like to be better at receiving guidance, and I appreciate you indulging my current interests so much.

PURSAH: It's all part of the plan. Let's discuss a Source of guidance that is *not* of this world. We won't stay here very long today, so let's get right to it. You read the pamphlet *The Song of Prayer,* right?

GARY: I sure did. It's one of my favorite things.

PURSAH: Then let's talk about what true prayer is and how you can get a secondary benefit from it by not trying to get a secondary benefit from it.

GARY: A quick question first?

ARTEN: We only show up to serve.

GARY: Well, I've been thinking about the devotion of real spiritual messengers, from Saint Francis to Mother Teresa, and it makes me wonder if I'm really worthy to be one of God's messengers. I'm not always that devoted, you know?

ARTEN: Remember something always: your forgiveness proves your devotion. You're getting used to forgiving a lot now, and you forget that it was never natural for you until the last few years. Every time you forgive, think of it as being a gift to yourself *and* to God. You'll do fine.

GARY: Thank you; I'll try it. But I also feel like I don't have the drive that I should to write our book, or go running around trying to be a spokesperson for the Course. I don't have a good speaking voice.

ARTEN: You don't have to do that if you don't want to, but if you choose to then remember something. Moses didn't have a good speaking voice; Hitler did. It's the message that matters, not the form of it. Besides, you might be surprised if you give it a shot. Just remember that you're talking to yourself. There's nobody out there, and you can remember that anytime you want.

As far as drive is concerned, whether it's a sex drive or a drive to work, people have it because they fear death. They have a deadline, so to speak. A slacker like you simply has your fear of death show up in other ways. When it does, remember how erroneous your fear of death and fear of God really are.

> **If you remember you're not a body, then you can step back and see that what you desire is valueless.**

GARY: Actually, I do have that fear about not being able to live in Hawaii. I guess I've wanted it a lot more than I realize.

ARTEN: First of all, you shouldn't feel guilty about wanting to live there. Why not live there? Everybody's got to live somewhere. It's just a preference. Why make such a big deal out of it? The whales are smart enough to go there for the winter. Why shouldn't a nice Pisces guy like you go too?

GARY: I don't see the means to stay there for any long period of time yet.

ARTEN: That's because you've been putting the cart before the horse. Lucky for you we're going to talk about how to put the horse before the cart today.

PURSAH: One thing you want to understand is that you're innocent no matter *what* appears to happen in your life. Some people feel guilty for being poor and some people feel guilty for being rich. Don't you think you've been both poor and rich in your numerous dream lives? Yet neither one is true. It's just a dream!

As we've suggested, if you have a good feel for the basics of the Course's thought system then you should be able to apply what you've learned to anything. For example, when you have a deep desire for anything then you must think you're a body, or separate from God in some way. What else could want something? If you're spirit, or joined with God, then you need nothing. If you remember you're *not* a body then you can step back and see that what you desire is valueless.

Once again, we're not talking about giving up everything physically; we're talking about the way you look at it. If you need something — and you would have to lack it to need it — then you can remember that it's just a substitute for God, and that a sense of separation from Him is the only real problem. You're having a dream of scarcity, but it's not true. Instead of making one thing on the level of form more important than another thing, you can remember that it's really all the same in its nothingness.

Christ needs nothing. If you need something then you're coming from weakness, but if you need nothing then you can come from the strength of Christ.

GARY: What if I just love Hawaii and choose it because it's beautiful?

PURSAH: One way to do that is to consider the beauty that you see, or even just think of, to be a *symbol* of your abundance as Christ. That way, if it rains on your birthday and you can't go out and look at the beauty, it's still there where it really always was in the first place — in your mind.

ARTEN: In your case, lack shows up in the form of financial problems. That's a result of your unconscious guilt. Don't feel bad about that. There are worse ways for your unconscious guilt to play itself out. For example, your problems are preferable to serious health problems and a lot of the other things people have to contend with. You know how to forgive; you have perfect blood pressure; you look many years younger than you are. Count your blessings and be grateful that most of your lessons are gentle ones, and that your forgiveness is awakening you to the awareness of what you really are.

GARY: I *have* been getting a pretty good idea of how to pray and be with God, but I'm not sure I understand this idea of a secondary benefit.

ARTEN: All right. We'll go over it briefly for you and then we'll leave so you can practice. Practice makes perfect.

Look at it this way. If the illusory universe is in perpetual change and God is changeless and eternal, which would you rather have as your source? Your problem of scarcity, which is symbolic of the thought of separation, is amplified by the fact that you are putting your faith in something that can't be counted on. If you see your source of supply as being something in this world, for example your career, a specific job or your own abilities, then when something changes — as it always does in this world — you could be out in the cold. An illusory source can be lost.

What if your Source cannot change or fail? Then you're putting your faith where faith is justified. Now you can see your transitory careers and endeavors as simply tools that can be used as symbolic expressions of your constant supply. Now your Source becomes a bottomless well where you can go for guidance that will always come in some form of inspiration. If your tool happens to break, so what? You don't have to be attached to it because it's not your Source. If your Source is constant, then one tool can be easily and quickly replaced by another one — through the very natural occurrence of inspiration. You can relax knowing that you *can't* lose your Source.

GARY: I've already experienced some of what you're talking about, but could you be a little more specific about what it looks like?

PURSAH: Yes. J's instruction in *The Song of Prayer* is quite specific, but joining with God is abstract. Later on, usually when you don't expect it, an answer to your problems will come to you out of the blue, if you will, as an after-effect of joining with God. I'll repeat for you, because you've already read it, part of what this gem of a pamphlet says.

The secret of true prayer is to forget the things you think you need. To ask for the specific is much the same as to look on sin and then forgive it. Also in the same way, in prayer you overlook your specific needs as you see them, and let them go into God's Hands. There they become your gifts to Him, for they tell Him that you would have no gods before Him; no Love but His.[2]

As one example, when you meditate you might visualize yourself taking J's or the Holy Spirit's hand and going to God. Then you might think of yourself as laying your problems and goals and idols on the altar before Him as gifts. Maybe you'll tell God how much you love Him and how grateful you are to be completely taken care of by Him — forever safe and totally provided for. Then you become *silent*. You have the attitude that God created you to be just like Him and to be with Him forever. Now you can let go of everything, join with God's

Love and lose yourself in joyful Communion with Him.

A couple of days later, you might be eating a sandwich or working on the computer and all of a sudden it hits you; an inspired idea just comes to you. The word *inspired*, as you know, means "in spirit." By joining with spirit you've been given the answer. People are always looking for God to answer their prayers. If they knew more about how to pray then they'd know *how* the answer is given. His answers don't come in the form of physical answers, they come to your mind in the form of guidance — an inspired idea, which the pamphlet describes as an echo of God's Love:

> **...The form of the answer, if given by God, will suit your need as you see it. This is merely an echo of the reply of His Voice. The real sound is always a song of thanksgiving and of love.**[3]

That's the key: joining with God in love and gratitude. You forget everything else and get lost in His Love. *That's* what it is to be filled with the spirit. That's the Song of Prayer. The echo is a fringe benefit, but that's not the purpose of the prayer. It just happens naturally when you join with God and love Him.

> **You cannot, then, ask for the echo. It is the song that is the gift. Along with it come the overtones, the harmonics, the echos, but these are secondary.**[4]

GARY: Wouldn't it be possible for something to happen in the world that would suit my need as I see it?

PURSAH: God's answers are internal, not external. If something shows up in the world it's a symbol. Don't think that God acts in the world; He doesn't. The *results* of following your guidance can show up in the world as symbols of safety or abundance.

ARTEN: Now you can come from a position of strength rather than weakness. You may find yourself being more patient and relaxed in your work, and thus more effective. By emptying your mind of your perceived desires when you go to God, you can experience His Love. Upon returning to the world where you *think* you are, you can remember more regularly where you *really* are — with God. At times you will see, very naturally and very clearly, what you should do in this world to solve your problems — or if you are faced with an important decision, exactly what that decision should be. The most striking evidence of this approach's validity will be that it works. As you accept the gifts of your Father, remember that you are eternally with Him.

> **...God answers only for eternity. But still all little answers are contained in this.**[5]

PURSAH: We're going to leave now, but only in form. When we disappear, we want you to join with God — and we will be there. When you go to God you are not trying to get anything — you simply love Him. In doing so you find that you *are* loved by Him, for now and for eternity.

> **...In true prayer you hear only the song. All the rest is merely added. You have sought first the Kingdom of Heaven, and all else has indeed been given you.**[6]

14

Better Than Sex

Revelation induces complete but temporary suspension of
doubt and fear. It reflects the original form of communication
between God and His creations, involving the extremely
personal sense of creation sometimes sought in physical
relationships. Physical closeness cannot achieve it.[1]

I HAD noticed many things in my life about sex. Three of the most
interesting were:

- Although sex was as "natural" as anything in nature could
  be, people were always trying to make other people feel guilty
  about having it.
- People kept doing it anyway, even if they did feel guilty.
- Although one wasn't supposed to point it out in a sexually
  obsessed society, sex didn't really make anybody happy.

As a musician, I had known quite a few people who engaged in
an unusually large amount of sexual behavior and were still miserable. Sex was a very transitory experience. People *assumed* that other
people who got a lot of sex were happier as a result, but that wasn't
really true. If someone seemed content, it was because they had
some kind of internal happiness that was not ultimately dependent
on temporary gratification.

One of the things I liked about the Course was the fact that sex
wasn't even an issue. There was no judgment made about behavior.
The only question was: Does the student want to have the body or

spirit for an identity? If one chose the spirit, that didn't mean one couldn't have sex. To *insist* on celibacy for yourself or anyone else would be a judgment rather than forgiveness, yet it would be perfectly appropriate for someone to *choose* celibacy if they wanted to. Not having the body as their identity simply meant that at some point students should remember who they and their partners really were. For those in love, sex could be used as a symbol of joining and an expression of their love. The key was an awareness — even if that awareness was temporarily forgotten in the heat of the moment — that their partner was not really a body but Christ. In turn, how they thought of the other person is what established their *own* identity in their mind.[2]

A powerful advantage of *A Course in Miracles* is that instead of merely telling you to believe you are not a body, it actually gives you the means to experience something beyond — and better. Most people have no idea of how good they could really feel. A chief goal of the Course is to lead the student to an Identity, and associated experiences, that are not of this world. These non-intellectual experiences, which are paradoxically the result of intellectual processes, are in fact the forerunner to the Holy Spirit's permanent answer to this world. Most people would hesitate to give up the world, but would they be so hesitant if they were given a clear taste of the alternative? Given an authentic spiritual experience, they would find the material world a cruel joke compared to what's available.

All experiences, including sex, are mental states — even if the illusion is that they take place in the body. I remember visiting a church in Boston to hear a lecture by two Buddhist monks who grew up near the border of India and Tibet. After the lecture, people in the audience were given the opportunity to ask questions. Most of them were the nice "spiritual" questions people usually ask. Then one woman had the courage to get up and ask the monks how they could go so long — in one case, thirty years — without having sex. The monk who had been celibate the longest, and who spoke English as well as the Dalai Lama, thought for a minute and then surprised the audience with his reply: "When you're coming all the time, it doesn't make any difference."

From the vantage point of my new experiences, I could now see that happy monk's answer in sync with the Course's answer to the dilemma of giving up the changing, illusory universe. What the Holy Spirit offered was *constant,* compared to the precarious and unreliable experience of each seemingly separated mind. The eternal Word of God could *not* really become temporary flesh, except in unreal dreams, but the flesh *could* be brought to the truth.

Given my desire to talk about the subject of sex during our next meeting, it was with happy anticipation that I would go into my living room in April of 1999, each time hoping for Arten and Pursah's next expected appearance. Then, late in the evening of what New Englanders call Patriots Day, I received the visit I was waiting for.

> *A dream is nothing, and sex is nothing. But I wouldn't recommend that you turn to your partner after making love and say, "That was nothing."*

ARTEN: Hey Gary.

PURSAH: Hey Gary.

GARY: Hey guys. I'm psyched! Thanks for coming. It seems like so long since I've seen you.

PURSAH: We're always here; you just don't always see us. Speaking of a long time, after this visit our last three appearances will all be in December — the next three Holiday seasons — '99, 2000, and 2001. You already know enough to forgive, and we know you'll continue with your chosen path. At this point we're just coming to support you and add a few observations for your benefit. Since sex is part of what you call life, and since we already know you want to talk about it, where would you like to begin?

GARY: Good old Pursah; always right to the point. You already talked about how the Course teaches that temptation wants to convince me I'm a body, so I guess the question is: How do I live the normal life you said I could live, practice the Course, and still not feel bad about that body identification part of my dream life?

ARTEN: By remembering what it is and forgiving it at an appropriate time. A dream is nothing, and sex is nothing. But I wouldn't recommend that you turn to your partner after making love and say,

"That was nothing."

GARY: I *knew* I was doing something wrong.

ARTEN: However, you can realize what the truth is whenever you want to. For example, the Course says very early on,

> ...Fantasies are a means of making false associations and attempting to obtain pleasure from them. But although you can perceive false associations, you can never make them real except to yourself. You believe in what you make. If you offer miracles, you will be equally strong in your belief in them.[3]

GARY: So it's all a fantasy, and the sexual part of it is an attempt to derive pleasure from a false association. I take it part of that would be the fact that we've made a false idol out of the sexual feeling — like a substitute for God.

PURSAH: Yes. Listen to this quote from the section of the Text called "The Anti-Christ." J is talking here about different kinds of idols, and sex would certainly be considered one of them.

> Let not their form deceive you. Idols are but substitutes for your reality. In some way, you believe they will complete your little self, for safety in a world perceived as dangerous, with forces massed against your confidence and peace of mind. They have the power to supply your lacks, and add the value that you do not have. No one believes in idols who has not enslaved himself to littleness and loss. And thus must seek beyond his little self for strength to raise his head, and stand apart from all the misery the world reflects. This is the penalty for looking not within for certainty and quiet calm that liberates you from the world, and lets you stand apart, in quiet and in peace.[4]

GARY: Now you're really getting me in the mood.

PURSAH: Fear not, dear brother. As J tells you,

> This course does not attempt to take from you the little that you have.[5]

It merely puts you in a position where you can claim your natural inheritance, which is far greater than any bodily feeling you can conjure up.

GARY: You know, before the Course I wouldn't have thought so — but the Holy Spirit is actually offering me something better than sex. In fact, it's not even close.

PURSAH: That's correct. At the same time, He doesn't seek to deprive you of what you temporarily perceive to be your desires. Speaking of your desires, Karen isn't here tonight?

GARY: Nope. She went to New Hampshire to do some shopping with her mother. She's spending the night there with her.

PURSAH: A likely story.

GARY: Funny. You know I was telling her a few weeks ago about when I was a teenager and I went to a dance at a Catholic church hall. I was dancing a slow dance, really close to this girl. All of a sudden, a nun came running over and stuck a ruler between us and said, "Now kids, let's leave enough room in there for the Holy Spirit." I always got a kick out of that.

ARTEN: Yes, most religions have always sought to repress sexual expression — until it's time to get married and make more bodies for the church, of course. Telling people to repress their unconscious, pre-programmed desires is like telling a bird not to fly. Do you remember that self-righteous minister at the Baptist church when you were in high school, who used to speak out against the evils of sex — all the while he was going after half the women in the congregation?

GARY: Oh, yeah! We called him "Old bless 'em and undress 'em."

ARTEN: So when you're in high school and you're helplessly horny, how likely are you to listen to a hypocrite like him?

GARY: Not very.

ARTEN: No, which leads us to a subject that isn't funny, but which we should cover briefly.

For the first 750 and some odd years of the church's official existence, from 325 to around 1088, there was no such thing as a requirement for priests' celibacy. Then Pope Gregory, who had no sense of humor, insisted on all priests being celibate — even the ones who at that time were married! Of course that begs the question, what could Gregory's decision possibly have had to do with J?

GARY: Ah, nothing?

ARTEN: Precisely. So for the last 900-plus years, priests have had to be celibate. In some cases that's fine, but in other cases it has led to instances of sexual abuse that would not otherwise have occurred if only the priest had a legitimate outlet for his sexual desires. The illusory universe is a place of tension and release. That's duality. You see it all through what you call nature. You even find it in music. It is not natural to make someone give up certain kinds of behavior until they themselves are completely ready to, nor in the case of most priests is it necessary anyway. And yes, there are child abusers who shouldn't be priests no matter what the rules are.

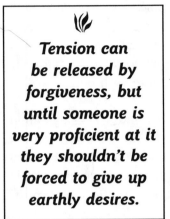

Tension can be released by forgiveness, but until someone is very proficient at it they shouldn't be forced to give up earthly desires.

Now with the Course the tension is released by forgiveness, but until someone is very proficient at it they shouldn't be expected to give up most earthly desires. That's something that comes naturally with the maturity of a mind that is advanced in the ways of true forgiveness.

Even J was not always celibate, and though he didn't need sex the last few years of his life, he *was* married for the final fifteen years.

GARY: Excuse me?

ARTEN: Today, you find that idea to be unusual. Yet if you were there two thousand years ago, what would have been very unusual was a Jewish man of J's age to *not* be married. It wasn't until over a thousand years later that the Pope decided you had to be celibate to be a priest. Only because of your warped view of history, along with centuries of projection of unconscious sin and guilt onto sex, do you now see the idea of J being celibate as a necessity.

GARY: Hey, I don't give a rat's ass! Somebody else might.

ARTEN: Then let them know the way it really was. The whole idea about sex being a bad thing never came from God and it never came from J. If you think there's something wrong with sex then you may as well think there's something wrong with eating food. They are both normal activities for a body, and any idea to the contrary is completely made up by people, not spiritually inspired. Yet it's perfectly appropriate for someone to give up sex if they *themselves* feel inspired to do so as an expression of what they really are.

GARY: Yeah, I was thinking about that recently. Say, who was J married to, that Mary Mag'dalene chick?

ARTEN: As a matter of fact he was. Many nowadays think of her as being a prostitute, not that the Bible says she was one. It doesn't. The Bible had so many prostitutes in it that people assume Mary Mag'dalene was one too. She wasn't; she was J's beloved wife. Incidentally, by Jewish law at that time a person's dead body could only be anointed by their family members, and if you look in your New Testament you'll find that even though J's body was no longer there, Mary Mag'dalene was allowed to go to the tomb in order to anoint it. What should that tell you?

GARY: Pretty interesting.

ARTEN: The whole point is simply that people have a lot of assumptions, but J didn't come to the world in order to start some religion so people could make other people wrong for having bodies and wanting to use them. He taught forgiveness, and still does, in order to teach people the total insignificance of the body — and lead them to their true Identity as Christ.

GARY: So I can live and forgive simultaneously — and it's possible to have both an erection *and* a resurrection.

ARTEN: That's true — just not at the same time! At some point you'll have to choose the body or spirit, once and for all.

PURSAH: Speaking of bodies, it doesn't really matter what a person's sexual preferences are or what they're into. Right now certain body parts are more important to you, but no body part is really any more important than any other, just as no body is really any more important than any other. They're really all the same in their unreality. Incidentally, that would apply to that fetish of yours.

GARY: You mean my attraction to a woman's tummy and her bellybutton?

PURSAH: Yes. That fixation is more common in the Middle East, by the way. You should understand that people make associations in the mind, but they are played out on the level of form in order to make people feel a certain way. Sometimes they are designed to make you feel different and thus guilty.

It's not generally known that there are two stages of sexual development for the human body. Everybody knows about the second stage, which is puberty, but most people don't realize that sexual preferences are usually determined during the first stage of sexual development — and *that* takes place when you're just a child. For example — and keeping in mind that your parents are a made-up substitute for your relationship with God — a child may be playing near his mother's feet, and he makes an unconscious association between the feet and her. Then when he reaches puberty he finds that he's sexually aroused by a woman's feet. His mother symbolized God, and the feet symbolize his mother.

It's just one false association and substitution after another, and it's often pretty simple — but then it's denied and projected. The whole thing was decided ahead of time, but that's how it appears to play itself out in the world. In your case you have a thing for a woman's bellybutton. Whatever turns somebody on, it always goes back to a very early age and something that was an association that then became an unconscious memory. That association then resurfaces later on in the *form* of a particular sexual desire.

GARY: That makes sense. I have felt different at times because of it, and I guess that's the equivalent of guilt. Obviously forgiveness is the correct response.

PURSAH: Yes. Remember, no matter what your preferences are, the Course isn't about changing your behavior. If your behavior changes then so be it. If it doesn't, don't worry about it. You might not even want it to. The important thing is to understand your total innocence.

GARY: Thank you.

ARTEN: Speaking of associations, a man has a connection between Heaven and his mother's womb. That connection is also there for a woman, but it shows up more in the form of a man wanting to get inside of a woman, and sometimes a woman wanting to.

GARY: That would explain why a man is born through a woman's vagina, and then he spends the rest of his life trying to get back in there.

ARTEN: I'm glad *you* said it.

GARY: Speaking of preferences, how come a Muslim in the

Middle East gets to have four wives and us American guys can only have one?

ARTEN: Actually you *are* allowed to have four wives in this country — just not all at once.

GARY: Oh, yeah. Maybe it's more fun that way. We better move on; I think I'm getting myself into trouble here.

ARTEN: You, Gary? Never.

GARY: Hey, Pursah, do you have any advice for women about sex?

PURSAH: Yes. Beware the one-eyed serpent.

GARY: Cute. Anything else?

PURSAH: You don't have to worry about women and sex. They talk to each other about it; it's practically a cult. Not having the macho virus, they're often helpful to one another. Once again, at some point it always comes back to forgiveness.

GARY: You know I always thought when I got a little older I'd settle down and have three children; you know, one of each, and do the family thing. Now I'm not so sure. It seems to me all special relationships depend on a past and a future, just like all judgment does. I'm not saying I think there's anything wrong with kids, it's just that I'm not so sure about the need to have them anymore.

ARTEN: Continue to join with God and you'll be guided in that matter. Ultimately, a savior of the world joins with God in the same manner that a nun marries Jesus, but it's not necessary for you to do that completely right now if you're not ready. If it helps any, Gary, you're already a father.

GARY: Who said so? I deny everything!

ARTEN: I don't mean that kind of a father, buddy. I remind you about this interesting statement from the Workbook.

> Release the world! Your real creations wait for this release to give you fatherhood, not of illusions, but as God in truth. God shares His Fatherhood with you who are His Son, for He makes no distinctions in what is Himself and what is still Himself. What He creates is not apart from Him, and nowhere does the Father end, the Son begin as something separate from Him.[6]

GARY: Cool. You're saying I really get to be *exactly* like God when I'm in Heaven?

ARTEN: Yes — exactly like Him.

GARY: It's gonna be pretty awesome, isn't it?

ARTEN: You got it. Keep preparing yourself with your forgiveness, and when you're ready to return to your natural state you'll be there with God. That is His promise, not just ours. As J goes on to instruct you in that same Workbook Lesson,

> ...Deny illusions, but accept the truth. Deny you are a shadow briefly laid upon a dying world. Release your mind, and you will look upon a world released.[7]

PURSAH: So brother, do you have any questions before we return to whence we came?

GARY: Not that I can think of right now. It's funny how things get put into perspective. When I was a kid I used to think my generation was so much cooler than my parent's generation. And both my parents were musicians! Now I can see that every generation thinks they invented music and sex and that their parents aren't cool. Before you know it they have a bunch of kids who grow up and think *they* invented music and sex and *their* parents aren't cool.

PURSAH: Very observant. It's all style and hormones. The real idea behind it, which is the ego's idea of separation, remains the same. Your job is to replace that idea with the love of the Holy Spirit.

GARY: Yes, and I think I appreciate how powerful the mind is now, even on the level of form. I was reading in the newspaper that girls are showing signs of puberty at an earlier age. Scientists are looking for physical reasons, like genetics and the social environment. What their methods can't even allow them to consider is that the mind is responsible for this — and that constantly bombarding everyone with sexual images just because it's the best way to sell stuff is actually triggering changes in children's bodies. I'm *not* saying this to pass judgment on sex, but I think it points out that the mind runs the body — not genetics or the environment or evolution.

ARTEN: What you say is true. Bodily identification reinforces itself, and spirit identification releases the body. Each one must make that personal choice. Forgive the dream figures, my brother, and your reward will be your Self.

PURSAH: Perhaps it will be best to leave you with a statement from the Text that will remind you of the way home. We'll see you around Christmas. Until then remember your purpose, which is the Holy Spirit's, and remember these words:

> From the forgiven world the Son of God is lifted easily into his home. And there he knows that he has always rested there in peace. Even salvation will become a dream, and vanish from his mind. For salvation is the end of dreams, and with the closing of the dream will have no meaning. Who, awake in Heaven, could dream that there could ever be need of salvation?[8]

15

Looking Into the Future

The presence of fear is a sure sign that
you are trusting in your own strength.[1]

THE end of the millennium was a time of changes for Karen and
I. We moved out of the house we had lived in for ten years and
moved to an apartment in town that offered a new world of conveniences in place of the challenges of country living we had grown
accustomed to. We had often thought of moving but stayed where we
were for the benefit of one of our best friends, our dog Nupey. But
after fifteen years of giving us unconditional love, Nupey had made
her transition that year to a doggie-dream afterlife.

Zoroastrianism considers dogs to be spiritually equal to humans,
and there was nothing in my observations that would cause me to
disagree with that. Buddhists believe that mind is mind, and it
doesn't really matter what the container appears to be. Once again, I
saw no reason to argue. We knew we'd miss our Nupey, but that
someday she'd be with us in Heaven, which was our reality.

We had also made a long desired visit to Hawaii that autumn, and
we saw our move to an apartment as part of a longer range plan to
live in a condo on either Oahu or Maui. In the meantime, I had much
to think about as the world prepared for an important rite of passage.

For the previous decade I had heard constant predictions about
terrible things happening around the turn of the century. New Age
writers and speakers had been falling all over each other to predict
great changes in the climate caused by, among other things, a shifting of the earth's magnetic poles — leading to great flooding, earth

quakes, icy conditions where warmth presently existed and summer heat where winter conditions now ruled. Terrible earthquakes would reshape the world, and only the spiritually advanced would be guided to safety. These prognostications didn't sound very different than the warnings of the end times I had heard from enthusiasts of the Book of Revelation. Yet that book could be interpreted, and has been, in almost any way a reader wants to see it.

It was entirely possible that most of these interpretations had little to do with what the zealous writer of the book had in mind. For example, rather than predicting the coming of an anti-Christ who would somehow be connected to the number 666, it was entirely possible that the number was a Hebrew reference to the Emperor Nero, and was never meant to describe anyone else except that particular, well-hated enemy of Christianity. It was also very possible that the writer of Revelation, like many other Christians of the time, saw the return of J in physical form as occurring within just a few years of their writing, making them wrong by almost two thousand years.

However, human nature dictates that if a modern-day minister desires success, one of the best techniques is to pull out all the stops and vigorously warn followers of the terrible wrath of God about to manifest as "the end of the world." It had worked on those with unconscious guilt for two thousand years and it was still working today, not just for Christians but also for New Age speakers and their listeners — the very people viewed by conservative Christians as being tools of the devil.

In the history of the world there had *always* been earth changes and always would be, but not at a time artificially set by people. The time for all events was set in the unconscious mind that people were oblivious to. Arten and Pursah were right; the ego loved rude awakenings, and terrible tragedies usually happened when people *didn't* expect them, not when they were looking for them. The first few decades of the new millennium would probably bring their share of terrific good times and sickening bad times — but no end times. The ego had a good game going. Why not keep it going a little longer?

Arten and Pursah had told me early on that they wouldn't reveal much about the future. Still, I was a speculator, and I thought it might be fun to see if I could pry some information out of them about what was to come in the new millennium. I knew they'd been watching me, and I knew I wasn't disappointing them with the way I was doing my forgiveness homework. Even though I initially disapproved of much of what I saw in the world, I would still remember to forgive my brothers and sisters. After all, when I forgave instead of holding people prisoner to guilt, who was it who was really being forgiven? In our conversations, I myself had earlier quoted the Course as asking,

> ...Can you to whom God says, "Release my Son!" be tempted not to listen, when you learn that it is you for whom He asks release?[2]

> ## 🌿
> *Always remember to let other people have their beliefs. It's not necessary to get other people to agree with you.*

I had just finished unpacking some boxes in our new apartment when Arten and Pursah suddenly appeared on the same couch they had projected their image onto so many times before.

ARTEN: Hey bro, as they say in your favorite islands. How did you like your vacation in Hawaii?

GARY: It was great, man. Thanks. I love that place. The people are so laid back, saying things like "Ain't no big thing, brother" — and they mean it. How can you beat that? What a great trip!

PURSAH: As long as it wasn't a guilt trip. Really, we're glad you had a good time. This is a nice little place you have here. You might get used to condo living.

GARY: You bet. I won't have to cut the grass anymore.

PURSAH: You went to two study group meetings when you were in Hawaii?

GARY: Yeah, we did. It's fun seeing how different people look at the whole thing. The first group on Oahu understood the non-dualistic nature of the Course, and the one on Maui didn't. I could really tell the difference when they talked about it. I didn't say anything, though.

PURSAH: Good for you. Always remember to let other people have their beliefs. It's not necessary for you to get others to agree with what you think, and it's not necessary for people, whether they study the Course or not, to agree with the things you'll be reporting in your book. Just put the truth out there and leave the rest of it up to the Holy Spirit. Everybody learns and accepts exactly what they're supposed to learn exactly when they should. You couldn't change that if you wanted to — and you shouldn't want to. It's just a dream! Yes, say what you think, but don't make others wrong. Don't disagree with them; just say what you know is true in a nice way. Then back off; never confront. You hear me, bro?

GARY: Loud and clear. So tell me, is peace gonna break out in the new millennium?

ARTEN: Well, no. For one thing, you can't have peace until people stop identifying with their particular nations and start seeing all of their brothers and sisters — and thus themselves — as spirit. When you're limitless you don't have any borders to defend, and thus nothing to kill for. That doesn't mean you can't go sing *The Star Spangled Banner* at Fenway Park; it means that while you appear to live your normal life you know in your heart where you *really* belong, and that the way home is not through defending illusions with illusions but by forgiving them.

GARY: Excellent. So, give it to me straight. Is the Apocalypse at hand with the turn of the century? I don't think so, but tell me anyway.

ARTEN: The idea of the Apocalypse is older than the hills. It's actually pre-Jewish. It goes back to Persia and Zoroaster. Of course we had our own version with Daniel, and the Christians have Revelation. The New Age dudes and dudettes have their "earth changes." It's all the same fear. Do you know what the best thing is about the Book of Revelation? Ultimately, evil is overcome not by force but by love. That's what the lamb is all about. Love is stronger than fear, and that's what the Bible means when it says good will always overcome evil.

Let me give you a quick example of love overcoming fear and the Holy Spirit working in a situation you probably didn't even know about, but which came *extremely* close to killing you and everybody you know.

In 1983 the Soviets believed that Ronald Reagan was preparing to attack them. America was undergoing its biggest peacetime military buildup ever, and then something happened that no one anticipated. On September 25, a software glitch in Russia caused their computers to interpret sunlight bouncing off of the tops of clouds as incoming American missiles. The Soviets were within five minutes of ordering an all-out attack. If they had, 100 million people would have been killed on *each* side immediately. Every major city in both the United States and the Soviet Union would have been completely destroyed, and the world would have been nothing but a living hell for the survivors, who would have envied the dead.

GARY: Shit, man. What stopped it?

ARTEN: Just one man. This is an example of someone listening to the Holy Spirit without even thinking about it that way. His name was Colonel Petrov, and he courageously went against procedure, insisted the computers were wrong and aborted the attack. For his noble efforts, he was eventually forced out of the military by his superiors who, with their mental blinders on, *would* have let the attack go forward rather than risk being wrong. Colonel Petrov listened to love instead of fear. You and your loved ones have been able to live the last two decades because of it.

GARY: Wow. Militarism and nationalism are really making the world a safer place, huh?

ARTEN: Obviously. That colonel did one of the most loving things in history. He saved most of the human race, and nobody knows who he is.

GARY: I'll give you a call when life is fair.

ARTEN: Only life in Heaven is fair, because it's perfect. That's what God's Son is worthy of. Here on earth, we'll tell you what you can expect in general this coming century. You can expect everything to be bigger, faster and scarier. The twentieth century was ridiculous in its violence, its seeming speed-up of industrial and technological progress and its frightening headlines. This century you can expect more of the same — only bigger, a lot faster and even scarier. That's what the ego likes.

You won't have earth changes but you *will* have more violent weather and greater extremes in temperatures, both hot *and* cold. People think you're getting global warming because of all the pollution you put into the atmosphere and that's true, but you'll also get colder extremes as well. Fooling with the atmosphere causes both. This will lead to conflicting scientific studies that will confuse people and give the corporations enough of an excuse to go right on doing what they're doing. After all, if the science isn't conclusive, then why should they do anything they aren't forced to? So what if more and more of your children get asthma and acid rain kills all the lakes?

These same corporations, through the small print in your trade agreements, will seek to replace the laws of nations with the decisions of international councils. That will put them in a position where they don't have to follow the laws of many countries and will not have to pay the money from lawsuits that they lose to individuals, effectively placing them *above* the law. In the 20TH century money became more important than people in your country. In the 21ST century, money will become more important than the laws that are passed by your elected officials, who owe the money for their campaigns and thus their elections to these same corporations anyway. Thus the big money will put itself in a position of total authority. The process of legislative democracy, which is already a sham, will become more and more like a professional wrestling match where it's all for show and the result has already been determined.

GARY: But no earth changes?

PURSAH: Sure, there will be earthquakes, tsunamis and hurricanes that kill thousands of people and scare the hell out of everybody. If you really think about it, haven't there *always* been earthquakes, tsunamis and hurricanes that killed thousands of people and scared the hell out of everybody?

There was an earthquake in China in the 1960s that killed a *half-million* people. If that happened today in California, everybody would think it was the end of the world. But it wouldn't be the end of the world. Unfortunately, it would simply be a continuation of the same kind of thing that has always happened in earthquake-prone areas — only bigger and scarier. In order to have a good economy you need cities on the ocean with good ports, and of course a lot of these cities just happen to be on the Pacific rim. Even a city like St. Louis, which is on the Mississippi River, is sitting right on an earthquake fault. Most people don't even realize that New York City is on an earthquake fault. How convenient a set-up for the ego's lurid script.

ARTEN: As far as your climate is concerned, one of the biggest problems in this coming century will be the alternation of floods and drought. Within thirty years, hydrogen-powered cars and various hybrids will start to dominate, first in Europe and later in America — but only after your corporations have sucked every dollar they can out of the use of gasoline-powered vehicles. Many oil-related companies will remain in existence because of other products, but hydrogen powered cells are the energy of the future.

As for other forms of travel, right now it takes five hours to fly from New York to Los Angeles; later in this century you'll have commercial airliners that will make the trip in 30 minutes.

There will be good and bad, as there must always be with duality. The world will still be made up of the haves and the have-nots. For good news, I should point out that with the fall of communism the world is set up to gradually undergo the biggest economic expansion in human history — and your Dow Jones Industrial Average will trade at the 100,000 level within fifty years.

NOTE: The week Arten spoke these words the Dow Jones Industrial Average hit a record high for that time of 11,750 — and then a bear market began. The Dow and most stock markets will have to forge a stunning increase in the next fifty years for Arten's prediction to pan out.

GARY: So much for the end of the world.

ARTEN: Yes. Now, let me ask you something. On one of your trips to New York City you went up to the top of the Empire State Building, right?

GARY: Yeah! That was really cool.

ARTEN: Why did you go up there?

GARY: Well, I guess it meant a lot to me. You know; all the movie history and the fact that it was the tallest building in the world for a long time.

ARTEN: Yes. And why was the World Trade Center built a few stories higher?

GARY: So it would be a little bigger.

ARTEN: Precisely, but you went to the top of the Empire State Building because it meant more to you.

GARY: Yeah; so?

ARTEN: One building meant more to you, but the other place means more to others. Not everyone's idols are the same, but they all have one thing in common. What do idols seem to give people, no matter what form they may take? As the Course explains,

> ...It must be more. It does not really matter more of what; more beauty, more intelligence, more wealth, or even more affliction and more pain. But more of something is an idol for. And when one fails another takes its place, with hope of finding more of something else. Be not deceived by forms the "something" takes. An idol is a means for getting more. And it is this that is against God's Will.
>
> God has not many sons, but only one. Who can have more, and who be given less?[3]

GARY: I know it's true, but it doesn't usually stop me from wanting more. Until I forgive, that is. You know I did that when I hiked to the top of Diamond Head. It was the greatest view, and I gave it to God. I realized I was just trying to take His place by being on top, so I joined with Him instead. I guess there are variations on forgiveness, depending on the situation. The important thing is to forgive no matter what the appropriate form. I'm not saying people shouldn't go to the top of things and have a good time; I'm just saying sooner or later it's time to forgive.

ARTEN: That's all you need do, my brother. I assure you that the 21ST century will not deprive anyone of opportunities to do so. For example, these terrorists we've talked about. What would give them more?

GARY: Well, I imagine they'd have to do something bigger; something to freak people out that's never been done before. I suppose they'd have to keep outdoing themselves and each other.

ARTEN: Exactly. After that it would have to be something bigger again, no matter how long it took. In the 21ST century, the biggest threat to safety in the West will be the threat of nuclear and biological terrorism. Conventional bombings will continue, but the need to make them bigger will make itself tragically apparent.

GARY: Will terrorists manage to explode a nuclear device in a major city in the next century?

ARTEN: Not to scare you, but the answer to that question is unfortunately yes. After that, life in your world will never be quite the same, but it will go on. The question is, what will people use the situation for? That answer will be different for various people, but for a student of the Course there *is* only one answer. It must be used for forgiveness.

GARY: Can you tell me which city?

ARTEN: I think you know I can't do that. If I told you where it was it could change what some people do. Yet everyone who comes to this world did so with an unconscious knowledge of what was going to happen. They chose their fate, and they have the opportunities to learn their lessons from whatever occurs. You might think we'd be doing people a favor by helping them avoid their problems, but the truth is they'd just have to go through the same kinds of things all over again anyway, because the unconscious guilt would continue to play itself out until it's forgiven. Even if it doesn't always look that way to you, the best thing to do is learn how to forgive no matter *what* appears to happen. That's the only real way out of this whole nightmare — and even if it doesn't seem like a nightmare to some people, it always turns into one eventually.

> *The best thing to do is learn how to forgive no matter what appears to happen. That's the only way out of this nightmare.*

As for the attitude of the masses, with communication being what it is and everyone wanting to have what they see on television, people will become even more materialistic throughout the world. That doesn't mean that capitalism isn't better than fascism; of course it is. People have the freedom to seek the truth under capitalism, and those who sincerely seek the truth cannot help but find it. In general however, more people will make money their new god, including those who seek abundance through what they think of as spiritual means. As we've said, there's nothing wrong with money, but there's nothing spiritual about it either — and those who seek God first will find Him first.

It will take time for the principles of *A Course in Miracles* to be understood by society, and the overwhelming majority of people will continue to believe as they always have. They'll continue to live in denial. They will try to bring God into the world and spiritualize the universe, thinking there is some kind of compassionate intelligence behind what is really a murderous thought. They will see death as part of a "circle of life," when it is really just a symbol of the great mistake. So they'll gloss everything over. Nobody will talk about the fact that half of your homeless and your prisoners *should* be getting treatment in mental institutions, or that more police die by suicide than in the line of duty.

In your often backwards and uncivilized nation, where national healthcare is enjoyed by those in your Congress but not by the people, about 8000 of your citizens will be killed this coming year with guns — while in your neighboring country of Canada, only about 100 people will be killed with guns. Your country has a tradition of violence, and extreme problems require radical solutions. Yet the fanatics in your country who treasure weapons more than people will continue to have their way against the will of the majority, and deny that their clearly insane policies cause thousands of people their lives each year — all while the ego smiles with delight.

In the coming century, humans will walk on the planet Mars and eventually discover shocking anthropological evidence that intelligent life has existed there. There will also be the first contact made between human beings and life from a planet other than Earth, but this humanoid life form will not be from Mars.

Throughout all this, the more things change the more they will stay the same.

Now here's something you probably didn't notice about all of these things; they are *all* forgiveness lessons! All of them are somehow connected to bodies, because relationships play into every situation in some way eventually. Not only is it your task to forgive what you see on television or read on the Internet, but it is *especially* vital for you to forgive the bodies your eyes see as the relationships in your every day life. These people are there for a reason. As J says,

Salvation does not ask that you behold the spirit and perceive the body not. It merely asks that this should be your choice. For you can see the body without help, but do not understand how to behold a world apart from it. It is your world salvation will undo, and let you see another world your eyes could never find.[4]

Or you can continue to worship your idols. But how wise would that be? As the Course also counsels you,

Seek not outside yourself. For it will fail, and you will weep each time an idol falls. Heaven cannot be found where it is not, and there can be no peace excepting there.[5]

GARY: Yet I can still live my life, pursue my goals and forgive at the same time. It's all about giving up psychological attachment. That's pretty good.

ARTEN: Yes, and you may find that your goals will change as a result of the inspiration and guidance you receive from practicing true prayer and forgiveness. Obviously, you have been undergoing a process of becoming one of God's messengers. This isn't your first lifetime where you've been a messenger for God, so it shouldn't feel unusual to you. You should always remember what the Course says about it.

There is one major difference in the role of Heaven's messengers, which sets them off from those the world appoints. The messages that they deliver are intended first for them. And it is only as they can accept them for themselves that they become able to bring them further, and to give them everywhere that they were meant to be. Like earthly messengers, they did not write the messages they bear, but they become their first receivers in the truest sense, receiving to prepare themselves to give.[6]

GARY: I get it. And I'm doing it — some of the time.
ARTEN: Actually, a lot of the time. It just takes you a while in

certain circumstances, but your consistency in forgiving everything eventually is impressive. Any lag time you can eliminate would simply contribute to your own peace — and isn't that the immediate goal?

Everyone will have their own particular forgiveness lessons, and as they go along and forgive with the Holy Spirit, and put everything they do more and more under His control, they — like you — will reach the immediate *and* eventually the long term goal of the Course. As J tells everyone in the Manual,

> ...To follow the Holy Spirit's guidance is to let yourself be absolved of guilt.[7]

He also says in that same section,

> ...Do not, then, think that following the Holy Spirit's guidance is necessary merely because of your own inadequacies. It is the way out of hell for you.[8]

GARY: I believe it. You're preaching to the choir now, man. I know what you're doing. I always have to be reminded — and you're not just talking to me anyway, are you?

ARTEN: You got it, buddy.

PURSAH: *A Course in Miracles* is a presentation of the absolute truth, which we have said can be summed up in just two words, but only accepted by a mind that has been prepared for it. Two thousand years from now, "God Is" will still be the absolute truth, and God will still be perfect Love. The *real* truth *doesn't* change. To accept it however, requires the kind of mind training the Course gives you. Some people may not choose to be prepared in this lifetime. They want the meaning of God and the world to be open to their own ideas. That's fine if that's what they want for now. But as J asks you in his Course,

> Would God have left the meaning of the world to your interpretation?[9]

GARY: Him and his smart-ass rhetorical questions.

PURSAH: Yes. It's not easy being humble when you know everything. In general, I think J's done a pretty good job.

ARTEN: For those who care to join him, as we have, we are honored to join with you. For as the Course declares near the end of the Manual,

Through you is ushered in a world unseen, unheard, yet truly there.[10]

PURSAH: We love you, Gary. And now we'll forgive you if you party like it's 1999.

16

Notes on Raising the Dead

*Embodiment of fear, the host of sin, god of the guilty
and the lord of all illusions and deceptions, does
the thought of death seem mighty.*[1]

ONE night I was at a shopping mall about thirteen miles from
home when a young man was stabbed, which was an unusual
occurrence for the area. I watched as the man came running in from
the parking lot, stumbled through a drugstore holding his cut throat
and then fell into the mall that was crowded with shoppers passing
through it. The terrified man then rolled over face down and bled
to death.

There wasn't much that I or anyone else could do for the poor
guy, who was hurt beyond repair. I helped hold the crowd back and
kept people moving so the emergency medical technicians, who
arrived quickly, could do their jobs. I would occasionally glance back
at the stabbed man and be surprised by the amount of blood a
human body can hold. As the man lay dying on the floor, the pool of
blood that was spilling from his throat completely encircled his body
and was making an ever-widening oval around him. The crowd of
people passed by silently as if viewing an open casket at a funeral
reception, rendered mute by the thought of death that surrounded
us all.

As I participated in the ghastly scene, it didn't feel to me like I was
really there. As I looked at the body I said in my mind to the man,
"That's not you. It can't be you. This isn't us. We are Christ." The
body, the blood, the thought of death; none of it seemed any more

real than a movie. It wasn't that I had become incapable of being shocked. On a bad day I could still have my reactions. But this particular collection of images brought home to me the unreality of the body, and how counterfeit the idea was that anyone could be contained within such a temporary and fragile vessel. This young man's life was over less than a third of the way through the average journey; all his hopes, dreams, fears and joys carried back to the illusory mind they had come from. Was that really something that could be referred to as life?

Later, I asked the Holy Spirit if my thinking this way was a form of denial. The answer that came to me was yes, absolutely — it was a denial of the ego. My thinking at the scene hadn't stopped me from doing everything I could to help, or as my teachers would put it, the things I would have done anyway — except that as I did them, my mind was being led away from error instead of toward it.

In December of 2000, while I had been contemplating the subject of death and also marveling at the spectacle of an American presidential election being decided by an appointed Supreme Court rather than the will of the voters, Arten and Pursah appeared to me for the sixteenth time.

ARTEN: There's not much to say about the experience at the mall. It kind of puts things into perspective.

GARY: That's right; this really isn't us. I know it. I've had a lot of experiences that told me so, but that's the first time an ego trick that was *supposed* to convince me of the reality of someone else's body was used by the Holy Spirit to teach me the opposite.

ARTEN: Very good. We'll come back to the subject at hand in just a minute. But briefly, you weren't happy with the way the election came out?

GARY: What election? We may as well have not even had it. The corporate-bought and paid-for candidate loses by half a million official votes, not to mention another million disqualified votes — mostly in minority areas — and then the Supreme Court makes him President, with the deciding vote being cast by someone who was appointed by his father! Another Supreme Court justice, who said in public that he believes he's in a "cultural war" with his opponents, actually wrote in his decision that it would be wrong to continue to count votes in Florida because it could call into question the legitimacy of the Bush election! I've got news for you, man, democracy is dead.

ARTEN: Wounded, but not dead. It's true that in your country the will of the people can often be manipulated by the hidden powers-that-be, including the modern, all-corporate news media. In cases where it can't be manipulated, it can be gotten around. Eventually, a *New York Times* investigation, which will be ignored on television, will conclude that if *all* the votes in Florida had simply been recounted, then Gore would have won the election. But most Americans are too preoccupied with their own ambitions to care about the common good. This results in a politically illiterate public that can usually be conned into accepting long-term negative consequences — many of which they don't even know about.

It doesn't always involve the President. We could tell you stories, like when your banks and the Federal Reserve Board deliberately created the inflation of the late 70s and early 80s so average Americans would have to become slaves to the banks for life just to own their own homes. Now instead of borrowing $30,000, people had to borrow $130,000 or $230,000 — and pay the banks back four times as much. Notice that when inflation came down, the prices didn't. Pay never went up anywhere near as much as prices did. President Carter, who was a nice spiritual man, was the perfect patsy to take the fall for it politically.

GARY: You know, I remember something about that. President Ford knew inflation was a problem; everybody did. He even had these "WIN" buttons that stood for "Whip Inflation Now." But when Carter was elected President, the Federal Reserve Board spiked interest rates *down*. They said publicly they were trying to avoid a recession, but it was really like throwing gasoline on a fire. Wow, what a scam. Most of us don't pay much attention to stuff like that. People had to pay attention to these election results, but I doubt if it will change anything.

ARTEN: Look on the bright side. You won't be as interested in politics after this.

GARY: That's good? Isn't that just what the corporate owners of the country want?

ARTEN: It's good in a way, because one thing I can guarantee you about politics is that it will always be consistent. No matter what side you're on, the other side will always be there right in your face. That doesn't mean you shouldn't continue to vote as a way of registering your opinion. You've always voted. Most Americans, while claiming to be patriotic, don't even bother to do that. But you should vote, forgive, and have *that* be your real contribution to politics.

GARY: Even if the results are a fraud?

ARTEN: It's all perception, brother. Republicans would say Kennedy stole Illinois in 1960.

GARY: Yeah, but even if Mayor Daley of Chicago miraculously produced some votes for Kennedy among the deceased, Kennedy still had enough electoral votes to win that election *without* Illinois. You can't say that for Bush and Florida. Besides, Kennedy won the national popular vote too. As you've pointed out, there's been a lot of weird stuff that's gone on since 1960 to change the country, and not for the better. As far as I can see Eisenhower was right about the military-industrial complex, and one of the earliest major parts of their absolute power grab was the murder of Kennedy.

ARTEN: We're not going to go any further into the details of that, but we *were* talking about politics and elections. The point is that even if some of them have been fraudulent, you win a few and you lose a few. That's duality. It's only with God that you can't lose — which is why your real job always comes back to forgiveness. So, can you forgive this election?

GARY: All right, my brother. I'd hate to have my body die and still have something stupid like that be unforgiven.

ARTEN: Excellent. Because you sometimes think of yourself as a speculator and a capitalist, we've occasionally taken the time to talk with you about money and politics. But you're not really those things, and it doesn't matter if you're accurate about the details of your grievances on the level of form. What you're seeing isn't really there. You made it up. Given what you know, you don't have any logical reason to be projecting your unconscious guilt onto the rich, especially since you wouldn't mind being one of them. That means you have a perfect opportunity to forgive yourself by forgiving the other. The truth is all these things are forgiveness lessons and all forgiveness lessons are equal — up to and including death.

Until tonight you've sometimes delayed applying the forgiveness you've learned if the circumstances were especially difficult for you. When you've forgiven, as you always do eventually, and as you did even at times during the election debacle, you felt fine. Then you have a tendency to slip and allow yourself to compromise in the way you look at things. That leads to a temporary lack of peace. Misery loves company, but that doesn't mean you have to accept the invitation. It's time for you to go all the way with the truth. No more compromising. That brings us back to the subject of tonight's discussion.

> *Misery loves company, but that doesn't mean you have to accept the invitation.*

You now know beyond a doubt that you're not a body and that you can't really die, right?

GARY: Right. I also believe what both the Bible and the Course say, "And the last to be overcome will be death."[2]

ARTEN: Yes. Now if you can't die, neither can anyone else. If they can't die, neither can you. The two ideas are one.

PURSAH: Death is symbolic of your illusory separation from God. What happens when someone you love appears to die? All of a sudden you're separate. You appear to lose them just like you appeared to lose God. But it's not true. You can't really lose them any more than you can lose God. You are inseparable. You cry when a body you love appears to die, but as the Course teaches you, it's really your experience of God and Heaven that you miss.

And who could weep but for his innocence?[3]

GARY: I cried for my parents, but no matter who it is that we mourn for it's really our natural home we miss, and our true state of Being with God. We just don't make the connection because it's unconscious.

PURSAH: That's correct. You've had many different parents in your many lifetimes, and many spouses and children. A lot of them have appeared to die on you while you were still in a body. That's the way of the dream world. But it's *only* a dream world and you're really with God. The Holy Spirit's thought system is waking you up; it's up to you to do your part and *remember* Him and His thought system on this level once you've learned it.

GARY: That's why when I remember that I shouldn't hold any grievances, then I don't. There's not really any injustice if I made it all up, and made it all up for a reason. I feel at peace when I remember that, but then I forget to do it and I get sucked back into the ego's crap.

PURSAH: Yes. And *there* you've identified one of the biggest problems for all serious students of the Course.

GARY: Once you know and understand the truth, it can still be very hard to remember it when shit happens, especially when it has to do with something that's important to you.

PURSAH: Precisely. Vigilance can be difficult, yet it's mandatory. You need to recommit yourself once in a while to being even more vigilant. It's your own happiness that's delayed when you fail to remember the truth the Holy Spirit holds out to you. As the Course asks,

What is a miracle but this remembering? And who is there in whom this memory lies not?[4]

GARY: I know from experience that I can do this Course when I remember to.

PURSAH: Yes, you can. You can do it regardless of the problem you face, including the death of those you love and the death of your own body, which, as we've told you, will occur at a point in the script that's already been determined — by you. Why worry about it? It's just another one of your forgiveness opportunities. Whatever happens, the smartest thing you can possibly do is take advantage of it by forgiving it — preferably sooner rather than later.

ARTEN: You fear death consciously and are attracted to it unconsciously. You once said it was like a moth to the flame. The attraction of death is the third of what the Course describes as the four major obstacles to peace,[5] and your fear of death is subordinate only to your erroneous fear of God. You could say the fear of death is symbolic of the fear of God, and without guilt in your unconscious mind it will be impossible for you to fear either. J wasn't afraid of death, and he certainly wasn't afraid of God. There's no more need for you to fear your Father than there was for him to.

You should look at the illusory death of your physical body as graduation day. It means you've gotten all you're supposed to get out of this particular, temporary classroom. The lessons have been learned! It should be a celebration. I assure you it will be a lot of fun. In most cases, if people knew what freedom from the body is like they wouldn't mourn the dead — they'd be jealous. The problem is that the fun doesn't last. As we've stressed, the guilt catches up with you and causes you to hide in a security-blanket body again. It's just a continuation of the dream of birth and death.

GARY: That's why I want to make sure I take advantage of my forgiveness chances *now*. That way death will be more fun, and I can be more advanced in my progress whether I appear to be in a body or not. If I happen to become enlightened this time around, so much the cooler. If not, I'm still a lot better off. You've talked about reincarnation, but I understand now that it's only something that appears to happen; I'm just dreaming that I'm going from one body to the next.

ARTEN: That's right. Concerning reincarnation, it doesn't really matter what one's personal belief is about it, as long as you forgive. The Course says,

All that must be recognized, however, is that birth was not the beginning, and death is not the end.[6]

GARY: So consciousness, even though it's an unreal state, does continue after the seeming death of the body. When you completely awaken from the dream, consciousness disappears and you experience your oneness with God and All Creation.

PURSAH: Right as can be, brother. Everyone will re-enter the Kingdom together because, as we've talked about, time is just an illusion. There's no long waiting period in between being enlightened and waiting for someone else to be enlightened, because enlightenment is a state of Being that is beyond the confines of time and space.

The mind made time and space and therefore must, by definition, actually be outside of it. One more thing: it's all right to mourn the death of a loved one at first. It's later on that most people will forgive something like that. Be appropriate in the way you deal with people.

GARY: You mentioned something a long time ago about J healing some people who were already dead. I assume Lazarus was one of them, but how did J do it?

ARTEN: The act of raising the dead is no different than healing the sick. The real healer is still the mind of the patient. You are joining with that mind in order to *remind* it of its true Identity. J was so advanced he wasn't willing to compromise on a very important idea. As he says in the Course, commenting on your relationship with him,

...Your mind will elect to join with mine, and together we are invincible. You and your brother will yet come together in my name, and your sanity will be restored. I raised the dead by knowing that life is an eternal attribute of everything that the living God created. Why do you believe it is harder for me to inspire the dis-spirited or to stabilize the unstable? I do not believe that there is an order of difficulty in miracles; you do.[7]

GARY: So raising the dead was no more of a big deal to him than healing the sick, or forgiving someone for saying something unkind to him or any other miracle. They're all equal. With life being an eternal attribute of everything God created, J knew death didn't really exist. Only what God created is real, and what He created will never die.

ARTEN: Yes. Don't forget the body is just a symbol. J wasn't making Lazarus' body out to be anything special, any more than he would make his own body special. Having the mind temporarily re-animate the body projection was symbolic. The body itself is insignificant. The whole point was simply to teach that there *is* no death. Despite what the Bible says, Lazarus didn't stay in his body long after J raised him. He laid his body aside and went on to his transition gladly and peacefully, because he'd been shown there was absolutely nothing to fear.

GARY: O.K. So when J joined with Lazarus' mind while everyone thought he was dead meat in the tomb, it was like J was joining with his own reality as Christ or the Holy Spirit and joining with Lazarus as one at the same time. Minds are joined, so J could shine his love into Lazarus' mind and they'd both be one with the Holy Spirit, which J knew was their real Identity anyway. That in turn *reminded* Lazarus of what he really was, causing his mind to re-animate his body projection as a symbol of the denial of death.

ARTEN: We chose you wisely, brother. Don't forget, J was as advanced as anyone can possibly be in his ability to join with others at the level of the mind and remind them of their innocence, which is why he was such a great healer. Don't be disappointed if you don't raise the dead on your first try.

GARY: I understand. If the day comes when I'm blessing someone whose body is very dead and they happen to get up and start walking around, then I'll take that as a pretty good indication that I'm on to something.

ARTEN: Very good. We told you years ago that you wouldn't be able to grasp how we project our bodies, but you understand so much more now that you are well on your way toward the goal. To summarize, you project your bodily image in the same way you project images when you're dreaming at night. Your mind is projecting a movie, then in your experience it appears that your body's eyes are seeing your own body as well as those other bodies — but it's actually your seemingly separated mind that's viewing its own thoughts, projected from a different, hidden level.

When the mind returns to wholeness there *is* no separation of levels, and thus no movie being projected and no bodies to view. Your body then disappears from the movie. Like all else, the body is a mental experience and not a physical one. It never existed! But it's possible for an enlightened Being's love to be given form in the dream, like J after the crucifixion. This love is now the Holy Spirit's love. After all, you'd have to be one with Him in order to be enlightened in the first place.

PURSAH: You, dear brother, will continue to learn and grow as the years go on, and as your awareness increases you'll understand more and more about such things. Once again, it would be helpful if you'd be even more willing to forgive from this point forward. You've forgiven a lot in the last few years; why not be even more determined?

GARY: I hear you. The Course says a lot about not compromising, and I think I'm ready to be more serious about that.

PURSAH: Excellent. Let others compromise the Course. It's not your job to stop them, only to forgive them. You have no need for compromise — and there isn't really anyone else out there. There is only *one* ego appearing as many. Among the seemingly separated ones there is no belief where compromise is more willingly accepted than the belief in the dream of death. As the Course puts it,

> ❦
>
> **There isn't really anyone else out there. There is only one ego appearing as many.**

...If death is real for anything, there is no life. Death denies life. But if there is reality in life, death is denied. No compromise in this is possible. There is either a god of fear or One of Love. The world attempts a thousand compromises, and will attempt a thousand more. Not one can be acceptable to God's teachers, because not one could be acceptable to God. He did not make death because He did not make fear. Both are equally meaningless to Him.

The "reality" of death is firmly rooted in the belief that God's Son is a body. And if God created bodies, death would indeed be real. But God would not be loving. There is no point at which the contrast between the perception of the real world and that of the world of illusions becomes more sharply evident.[8]

GARY: Once again, the real world is what I'll see — not with my body's eyes but with my attitude — when I've completely forgiven the world so I'm not projecting any unconscious guilt onto it. That would also have to mean that *I'm* completely forgiven, and that perception and time are coming to an end for me.[9]

PURSAH: That's correct, my brother. It's nice to see you do your Course reading homework, as well as your forgiveness homework.

GARY: Thank you. Speaking of the belief that God's Son is a body, I noticed this year that scientists called the map of the human genome, which is the complete schematic of the human genetic code, the "book of life." They said it determines who you are!

PURSAH: Yes. They worship the complexity and so-called beauty of the body and ignore the mind that runs it. That's like thinking that a computer, which can do nothing, is important and the programmer who tells it what to do should be ignored. The ego has temporarily succeeded.

Remember, if something will help researchers discover treatments for illnesses that can help people, we would not be opposed to it. We've already indicated that most minds can heal the body easier if there is a treatment involved that the person can accept without fear. But remember something *else*. There are people who have all the physical reasons to have heart disease and Alzheimer's disease, whose arteries are all clogged up or have an unlucky family history, yet they show no symptoms of the diseases whatsoever. It's always the mind that decides whether or not to get sick — and whether or not to get well.

GARY: Cool. Hey, I know something I've meant to ask you for years and I always forgot. Is the Shroud of Turin really the burial cloth of J, and did he intentionally leave his image on it as a sign of the resurrection?

ARTEN: We don't want to throw a wet dishrag on something people are excited about, but the Shroud is a brilliant forgery, so great as to be the work of a genius. There have been conflicting scientific tests, some of which seem to indicate that the Shroud is authentic. There are other explanations for the results. You have to realize that the Shroud was made at a time when it was *very* important for churches to have religious relics of famous figures. They were considered to have great power back then.

Let me ask you this: Do you really think that J would leave something behind to glorify the reality of his bodily image? No. With resurrection, the body just disappears. By the way, the image on the Shroud is not what J actually looked like, any more than the paintings of him are. Physical evidence isn't necessary, Gary. Faith is all you need. J's body was nothing to him. Don't try to make an image of it important now.

The body, the universe and everything in it are just pictures in your mind, parts of a virtual reality game. Perhaps at times it's a rather convincing forgery of life, but like the Shroud, it's a fake. Don't look there for your salvation. Always look where the Answer really is — in the mind where the Holy Spirit abides — and you'll find it. Remember, we say God is, and then we cease to speak because there *is* nothing else.

PURSAH: As we close our discussion on the topic of death, remember what the Course says about your seeming life and death in this world.

> …In any state apart from Heaven life is illusion. At best it seems like life; at worst, like death. Yet both are judgments on what is not life, equal in their inaccuracy and lack of meaning. Life not in Heaven is impossible, and what is not in Heaven is not anywhere.[10]

J calls you to be with him, and join him where life really is!

> The First Coming of Christ is merely another name for the creation, for Christ is the Son of God. The Second Coming of Christ means nothing more than the end of the ego's rule and the healing of the mind. I was created like you in the first, and I have called you to join with me in the second.[11]

If you are ready to answer the call, then knowing how deep unconscious guilt can be, you will become more and more determined to forgive your brother every chance you get.

> …And you will be with him when time is over and no trace remains of dreams of spite in which you dance to death's thin melody.[12]

17

The Disappearance of the Universe

The images you make cannot prevail against
what God Himself would have you be.[1]

SEPTEMBER 11, 2001: When Arten and Pursah had first appeared to me nine years earlier I was at war. Now I was at peace most of the time and the United States was at war.

On this day the World Trade Center, the Pentagon and four commercial passenger airliners became the targets of terrorists, destroying all the targets except for the Pentagon, which was heavily damaged. Thousands of unarmed civilians were murdered and the American people, except for a very small minority, were in no frame of mind for *any* kind of forgiveness.

This was a new kind of war for a more complex world. The ego's script no longer called for wars with a clearly defined and visible enemy. It would be much more fearful to have ongoing enemies who could seldom be seen or predicted, didn't abide by any of the "rules" of war, and fanatically believed it was God's desire that they kill Americans. How could a war like this ever *really* be "over"?

That Tuesday morning, along with millions of others, I stared in numbed silence as the live pictures on my television screen showed the second tower of the World Trade Center collapsing. The combined pictures of the attack produced some of the most awful images ever; images that, although the public didn't realize it, symbolized the separation from God, the loss of Heaven and the fall of man. On the level of form, this was the insane thought system of the ego being carried out to an illogical extreme. The victimizers in this lifetime's script would surely be among the victims in another.

While watching the hellish catastrophe and its results, I almost cried as I visualized the horrific nightmare that was undoubtedly being experienced by those in and around the buildings. Then, in a miracle born of habit, I asked J for help. Almost instantaneously a couple of thoughts came into my mind — thoughts I had read at the very beginning of the Course many times, but which had never seemed any more appropriate for me to apply than at this terrible moment.

There is no order of difficulty in miracles. One is not "harder" or "bigger" than another.[2]

As I joined with J, I felt almost embarrassed for a minute about feeling better in the face of what appeared to be happening. Could it really be that simple? Could I actually deny the ability of anything not of God to affect me? Was there really *no* hierarchy of illusions, including any manner of death? Could I sincerely be vigilant only for God and His Kingdom? Were all the images of the world just temptations designed to persuade me that I was a body so I'd judge others and keep my unconscious guilt, my reincarnation dream-life cycle and the ego intact? Was the Holy Spirit's forgiveness really the way out, leading to the peace of God, my return to Heaven and the disappearance of the universe?

I finally knew for sure that the answer to all of these questions was yes. Although I'd still feel bad at times over the next several days, I also knew that whatever feelings I had were nothing compared to what they would have been if I didn't have J and his Course. That did *not* mean that action wouldn't be appropriate in a crisis like this. Yet as far as I could determine, the ego had set up a no-win situation.

If the United States took *no* military action it would not deter psychopaths and would probably encourage them, as was the case with Hitler. If America took military action, which seemed inevitable, it would probably result in other terrorist attacks, including assassinations, even if the U.S. military action was successful. Who knew when these attacks might come? There had been eight years in between the two separate attacks on the World Trade Center. How many more years would the terrorists be willing to wait to strike inside the U.S. again? America could retaliate and be attacked, or not retaliate and still be attacked, and it could happen at any time in the distant or not too distant future. This was a dilemma for which I saw no easy answer. As was often the case with the ego's script, the plot added up to "damned if you do and damned if you don't."

In any case, my job was forgiveness, and I decided to leave the decisions as to what the country should do up to the politicians. That was *their* job, because that's what they wanted — not that they couldn't practice true forgiveness in any situation if they learned how. I'd give money, give blood, and give my forgiveness. It was possible to do these things without revenge in my heart, without anger, judgment or guilt. No matter what appeared to happen, I'd always remember that the attacks on America only proved that this world wasn't God's world, and no one in their right mind would come here — except to teach others how to leave. But I *could* have a happy dream of forgiveness here; the dream that led to the real world.

I was also very thankful that Arten and Pursah had promised me one more visit at the end of the year; I wanted to discuss this uncharted situation with them. Yet didn't I already know what they'd say? I could almost hear Pursah now. "Miracles are all the same, Gary, whether you want to believe it or not. And if the students of the Course don't forgive, who *will*?"

In late October, I attended the tenth annual *A Course in Miracles* Conference held in Bethel, Maine. While there I got to meet many wonderful Course students and teachers, including Jon Mundy, one of the earliest of all Course teachers, who had been introduced to *A Course in Miracles* in 1975 by Helen Schucman, Bill Thetford, and Ken Wapnick at Ken's New York City apartment. I loved the Bethel Conference and realized for the first time that some of my long dreaded shyness had disappeared. This made me think that maybe if the Holy Spirit guided me to do so in the future, I'd start traveling more in order to meet with others who study the Course.

On December 21, Arten and Pursah appeared to me for the last of our scheduled meetings.

PURSAH: Hello, my dear brother. That's what I called you the first time I saw you, remember? We're happy to see you, but we know it's been a rough time in America. How are you doing?

GARY: All things considered, I'm doing very well. Being a stock and options trader, I identified with some of the people in the brokerage firms at the World Trade Center. A lot of them didn't make it out. I know we all chose the script, but we didn't choose it at this level and it's been a terrible experience for a lot of people and their families, and it's made Americans feel less safe — at least temporarily.

As I'm sure you know, about a week after the attacks I went with my brother, who was up from Florida, to see the Red Sox at Fenway as our way of saying the terrorists weren't gonna affect our lives. One thing that really made me feel great was during the seventh inning stretch when all us fans who usually boo those Yankees got up and sang, "New York, New York," as a way of showing our support for the people of the Big Apple. For all of us who were there it was pretty moving.

PURSAH: Yes. A way of joining. A lot of people in New York heard about that and appreciated it. I must say, you did a good job with your forgiveness on the day of the attacks.

GARY: I was trying to get different parts of our book together and I didn't have the TV on before the attacks. When I did start watching, it took a while for them to say what was happening. When they said one of the Towers was down, I couldn't believe it. I thought it must be a mistake. The whole thing couldn't be *down*. When the second one went down, I almost lost it.

ARTEN: But you remembered J.

GARY: Yeah; that never fails. As soon as I remember him the separation's over — it never happened. Yet in a situation like that it can feel a little inappropriate to stop sympathizing with the victims.

ARTEN: Of course. As you know, we have nothing against being appropriate. You can still identify with them as Christ, and there's no difference between feeling bad and feeling guilty. A mild upset is no different than tremendous rage or grief. The idea of levels was made up by you. Remembering the truth can bring you peace no matter what the seeming event or person is who is being forgiven. As long as you remember the truth, you're doing your job.

Sometimes your dream seems like a nice one, but then without warning it becomes a nightmare. That's the re-enactment of the separation from God. Yet neither the bad or the good that seemed to precede it are true. As the Course reminds you,

> ...Fairy tales can be pleasant or fearful, but no one calls them true. Children may believe them, and so, for a while, the tales are true for them. Yet when reality dawns, the fantasies are gone. Reality has not gone in the meanwhile.[3]

PURSAH: You want to make sure you continue to forgive no matter what appears to happen. This *is* temptation to regard yourself as a body; first by reacting as a person to the tragedies that occurred on 9/11, and then by identifying yourself as an American and responding like one. No fine, upstanding American is going to take something like *this* lying down, right? Then there you are, right in the same old vicious cycle — unless you forgive. If some people think it would be wrong to forgive such a thing and teach only love instead of fear, then perhaps they should remember that the crazy people who committed these acts would never have done so if only someone had taken the time to teach *them* how to forgive.

In a case like this, most Christians won't even bother to ask what Jesus would do. That's because the answer wouldn't match their feelings. As we've indicated before, the answer would always be the same — he'd forgive. There's no debating that. If he forgave people for killing *his* body, do you really think he'd retaliate now? Of course I'm talking about the historical, uncompromising J and not the go-either-way, mumbo-jumbo religious icon. I say that for Christians who have ears to hear. As far as the attacks on America are concerned, we'll talk shortly about the best way to proceed in matters like this.

Always remember that your state of mind and the resulting goal you will achieve are in your own hands, because there are really only two things you can do — judge as an expression of fear, or forgive as an expression of love. One perception leads to the peace of God and the other perception leads to war. As the Course teaches,

> You see the flesh or recognize the spirit. There is no com-
> promise between the two. If one is real the other must be
> false, for what is real denies its opposite. There is no choice
> in vision but this one.[4]

And,

> The lessons to be learned are only two. Each has its out-
> come in a different world. And each world follows surely
> from its source. The certain outcome of the lesson that
> God's Son is guilty is the world you see. It is a world of
> terror and despair.[5]

ARTEN: It's totally up to you where you want to build your treasure. It's also up to you which spiritual path you want to use to help
you if you choose to build your treasure in Heaven. If you choose
this path, as we did during our final lifetimes, then we ask that you
simply pay attention to what this self-study Course is really saying
— then use it and not try to change it. For as J explains,

> ...The Holy Spirit is the translator of the laws of God to
> those who do not understand them. You could not do this
> yourself because a conflicted mind cannot be faithful to one
> meaning, and will therefore change the meaning to preserve
> the form.[6]

GARY: All right. I don't want to wait, so please tell me about the
best way to proceed in matters like the 9/11 tragedy.

PURSAH: Think back to our discussion about true prayer and how
to receive guidance. That's how you can be inspired and receive creative solutions to your problems — and it applies to any problem,
without exception. Join with God and experience His Love, and the
answers on the level of form will come to you as a natural extension.

There could be no finer example of inspired problem solving than
the way Gandhi drove the British Empire out of India without ever
firing a shot. His well-organized and very public non-violence eventually turned the opinion of the British people against their own

army and in favor of Indian independence.

GARY: That's true, but it worked because the British themselves *are* very civilized. Nonviolence isn't gonna work against someone who doesn't give a damn if people get killed, or enthusiastically *wants* them to get killed.

PURSAH: You're right, but it brings up an important point. The inspired answers are different for different situations and different people. There is no one answer to every problem. True inspiration will apply to whatever is happening with *you, now*. For Gandhi, what he did worked at that place and time. In your case, you may have a different kind of problem that calls for an even more creative solution. How are people going to be inspired if they don't learn what it is that produces true inspiration and then practice it?

> *The Holy Spirit works with every seeming individual on a case by case basis, and each one's focus should always be on working with Him.*

We've mentioned that as the most powerful force in the history of this world, the United States has much more responsibility than any other country when it comes to finding creative solutions to problems. Government is not your chosen profession, but you should use what you've learned in your own life and share your experience with others. The day will come when a President will emerge who knows how to join with God in true prayer and find genuine inspiration. The Holy Spirit works with every seeming individual on a case by case basis, and each one's focus should always be on working with Him.

GARY: We already touched on the idea of having the United States become totally free of its addiction to oil and not having to be involved in the Middle East, except to do good. It seems that would be a logical starting point.

PURSAH: Yes it would, but that's not going to happen any time soon, and you as an individual can't make it happen. You *can,* however, be inspired as to what to do in your own life. As each one learns to do the same, the illusory world can't help but seem to benefit at the same time.

ARTEN: Choose between the strength of Christ and the ego's weakness. The world is asleep. Save time in your awakening and you can't help but assist others on the level of the mind. You don't usually see what your forgiveness is accomplishing, but I assure you it's vital, and the Holy Spirit's plan cannot be complete without you.

The Course says,

Perception's laws must be reversed, because they *are* reversals of the laws of truth.[7]

Be a part of this thought reversal by concentrating on your *own* forgiveness lessons instead of somebody else's. We are honored to have participated with you in this project to make more people aware of the truth. That doesn't mean you should try to lead others. That's the Holy Spirit's job. *Your* job is to follow Him and allow your seemingly personal perception to be reversed. If you focus on your own learning opportunities, you'll save immeasurable time.

You've grown so accustomed to the ego's notional world of ephemeral bodies that it will take additional determination and discipline for you to continue to break free. We have complete confidence that you will succeed.

PURSAH: Instead of imprisoning the body robot dream figures, release them as they act out for you. Sometimes you may want to use thoughts like this from the Workbook to get your day off on the right foot.

**Today I let Christ's vision look upon
All things for me and judge them not, but give
Each one a miracle of love instead.**[8]

ARTEN: Don't ever forget the forgiveness thought process Pursah gave you. That is the way the Holy Spirit wants you to think on this level in order to help Him bring you to where levels do not exist. In fact, you will not even recall the concept of levels when the universe disappears and you return home. As the Course says,

You will not remember change and shift in Heaven. You have need of contrast only here. Contrast and differences are necessary teaching aids, for by them you learn what to avoid and what to seek. When you have learned this, you will find the answer that makes the need for any differences disappear.[9]

PURSAH: As you read the Course, you will see for yourself that the things we have said about it are true. The following quotation is very representative of the statements J makes about the thought system of the ego, which is the thought system of the world.

Guilt asks for punishment, and its request is granted. Not in truth, but in the world of shadows and illusions built on sin.[10]

Yet the Course also teaches a distinct thought system that cannot be blended with the ego, but has come forth to replace it. You are learning it well. You will forgive the world in the manner that J teaches you, just as he did.

...And we are saved from all the wrath we thought belonged to God, and found it was a dream.[11]

GARY: I believe you. I knew there had to be more to J than what the churches told me when I was growing up. A lot of this somehow has a familiar ring to it. I take it the thought system of love was exactly what J's attitude reflected when you were there with him two thousand years ago?

PURSAH: Absolutely! There was nothing left in him but love. His forgiveness was perfect.

GARY: And your sometimes, shall we call it, *direct* teaching style was strictly for my benefit?

PURSAH: You and others. Sometimes you have to go a little overboard to get someone to pay attention. In this day and age that would apply to many other members of the raucous society you appear to live in. You, dear brother, have been set firmly in the right direction now.

You *are* learning perfect forgiveness here as all ascended masters did, and perfect Love will be all you know in Heaven. Remember, when you wake up from a dream, the dream disappears. It will be gone completely. You will not miss anyone, because everyone you ever knew and loved will be there — because they will be one with you. It's awesome.

GARY: All right! So, do you have any last-minute instructions for our book?

ARTEN: Because you're going to be noting the quotations we used from the Course, we decided to arrange it so that by the time you're finished writing our book you will have used exactly 365 of them — one for each day of the year. These quotations, if read by themselves, constitute a refresher on what *A Course in Miracles* is saying. Although some of them are paraphrased, they can be read in exact order by going from note to note — and they give a presentation of J in his own words. Only a couple of them were used more than once, and they can be employed over the span of one year as a thought for the day to help keep readers on their toes. In any case, people can choose however they want to use our book in the future.

Also, as you suggested a long time ago, you might want to get rid of your notes and especially those voice-activated cassette tapes as soon as you're finished with them. You wouldn't want to see them showing up for auction on the Internet someday. Aside from that, just finish the book and do the things with it that we talked about in private. Don't feel any pressure. Our message is timeless.

GARY: Cool. You know some of those tapes didn't come out so hot anyway. I had to fill in a lot of blanks. It's a good thing I took notes. You said the book doesn't have to be a literal transcript anyway, right?

PURSAH: That's right. You know J also told Thaddaeus and I, back about twenty centuries ago, that we shouldn't feel any pressure. He said salvation would come to each mind when it was supposed to. As he stood there, in a body that was supposed to be already dead, he advised us to just give people our love, our forgiveness and our experience — and let the Holy Spirit take care of the rest.

GARY: Wow. That must have been incredible. You know, I wish I knew *you* back when you were Saint Thomas; I'll bet you were one interesting dude.

PURSAH: I wasn't a Saint yet; that was a later church action, remember? Actually, you *did* know me when I was Thomas. In fact, you knew me better than anyone.

GARY: What do you mean?

PURSAH: You and I are even closer than you think.

GARY: What are you getting at?

PURSAH: You see, Gary, *you* were Thomas.

GARY: What do you mean, I was Thomas?

PURSAH: You were Thomas two thousand years ago, and you'll be *me* in your next lifetime.

GARY: What?!

PURSAH: It's all part of the script, dear brother, and you must play your roles. You've had many lifetimes that were very interesting, and some that weren't so great. That's true for everyone.

GARY: Are you telling me that you're appearing to *yourself* in your previous lifetime, and that I'm you? I was there with Thaddaeus and J two thousand years ago as Thomas? I wrote *The Gospel of Thomas?* I'm gonna be you, a woman, the next time around? And that'll be my final lifetime — the one where I actually achieve enlightenment?

PURSAH: You've got it. Very good, Gary. You know it would take someone with a spiritual background to get that. Try to understand that I came to help you, and to help others through you — and so did Arten. It's all part of the Holy Spirit's holographic plan of forgiveness.

You and Arten have known each other in many lifetimes, including the one where you were Thomas and Thaddaeus. You know him in this lifetime too, but we'll let you figure out who that is. Having me — your future bodily image as Pursah — appear to you and assist you in this lifetime is a part of the plan, and it reflects the law of Heaven that I ended up helping myself. It's *always* yourself who you are really helping. By the way, you're seeing a 32-year-old version of Pursah's body to help you pay attention. I think it worked very nicely.

A part of your mind completely knows the past, present *and* the future. The Holy Spirit, looking back from the end of time, decided that in some cases He'd use the future to help heal the past — just as He uses the present to heal the future. The world really does have to get used to thinking more holographically instead of the old-fashioned, linear way.

GARY: So I'm your pre-incarnation?

PURSAH: Yes, but we really happened all at once. We visit you now from *outside* of time.

GARY: I don't know what to say.

ARTEN: Excellent. A fine qualification for a student, remember? I know it's a mind blower. Get used to it. You have a lot of fascinating things in store. Just keep doing your forgiveness homework. Remember, you need to forgive all of it, no matter what may appear to happen in the future. Only God is real.

We apologize for not revealing this sooner, but you wouldn't have been quite ready to accept yourself as the reincarnation of a famous saint without thinking it makes you special. Now you'll be ready to see it as just another lesson in the classroom. Most people assume that just because we were called saints by the church then it must mean that those lifetimes as two of the original disciples were our final ones — the ones where we achieved mastery. It doesn't work that way. Nobody can really judge someone else's level of spiritual achievement. Only the Holy Spirit has all the information necessary to do that.

You weren't supposed to start remembering you were Thomas until this point in time. The reason you always had that yearning to know what it was like to be there with J as a student of his two thousand years ago was because you *were* there, and you *were* a student of his two thousand years ago. You were just trying to remember.

GARY: I can see that. It's kind of like trying to remember a dream you had in bed the other night, but you can't quite put your finger on it. I guess that's what it's like trying to remember Heaven on a more consistent basis, too. This is all gonna take a little getting used to; I can't believe I wrote *The Gospel of Thomas.*

PURSAH: Yes, but your life as Thomas wasn't your final one, and you eventually wrote another spiritual book. As time went on, it was read a lot more widely and pointed a lot more people in the right direction. It was called *The Disappearance of the Universe,* and you're going to finish it a few months after we leave here tonight. In a way, you could even call it the second *Gospel of Thomas.* Get busy, you slacker.

GARY: This is a lot for me to take in all at once. I don't know if I like the idea of having to study the Course in more than one lifetime in order to be enlightened.

PURSAH: Some people will study the Course in more than one life-time, and some will be enlightened during the first lifetime where they study it. In *either* case, it's a process. You've made tremendous progress and you'll continue to. Like almost all people, you have some very deeply buried guilt you don't know about, which is why you still have some fear. It will take even more forgiveness, chipping away at unconscious guilt, for you to wake up completely. *That's* why we keep emphasizing forgiveness; it's what wakes you up. You're already in the process of awakening! Your eyes are opening, and fin-ishing the job after just two final lifetimes of work is a lot better than taking another hundred lifetimes to do it. I assure you that without the Course, it *would* have taken another hundred.

Also, I know from experience that your study of the Course as Pursah will come even easier to you, because you'll already have a familiarity with it from this time around.

GARY: Will I remember all this during that next lifetime?

PURSAH: You still ask good questions, dear brother. Interestingly, you'll remember just enough and forget just enough of this to make your last remaining learning experiences possible. You'll procrastinate in reading the book you wrote in this lifetime until long after the for-giveness lesson at the university I described to you. You'll study other things before that, including the classic Wapnick materials. Once you get to the point in your life where you read *The Disappearance of the Universe,* you'll put the pieces of the puzzle together and remember everything. Your awareness would have expanded to that of an ascended master, plus Arten would have been in your life for a while helping you. You'll remember a lot of things together.

Of course I'm speaking in the past tense because it's already hap-pened for us, and in a larger sense, everything has already happened. The two of you were able to forgive everything, and you held no grievances. You weren't afraid because you didn't value wrongly, and you chose the strength of Christ at every opportunity.

Incidentally, we're not using our real names from that lifetime or else some people in the future would be watching to see if they can figure out who we are, and that might complicate things. I really did have a Southern Asian name, but it's been changed for the benefit of these discussions.

GARY: Boy, it's funny how it all fits together.

PURSAH: That's the nature of a hologram, but it still has to be forgiven along with the Holy Spirit if you want to find your way out. *Wanting* to find your way out of it only comes when you recognize the true nature of the illusory universe. Don't get sucked in by your success; don't always expect agreement either. You don't have to wait for everyone in the universe to wake up and smell reality.

You're very fortunate that during your thousands of lifetimes you got to be friends with both J and the Great Sun. If you're ever tempted to think that makes you special, then remember this: *Everyone,* during at least one of their many incarnations, or incarcerations — either would be accurate — will happily get to be a friend and or follower of an enlightened one who still appears to be in a body. Sometimes that enlightened Being is famous or at least well known, but usually he or she is not. We told you that most enlightened ones don't seek out a leadership role, but they do tend to attract some friends and followers, and it's often a very important learning experience for those people. We also pointed out to you that J was not as famous as John the Baptist was during their lifetimes. J became much more famous *after* the crucifixion and the resurrection, but even before that he had his loyal friends and followers, who included us.

Today, there are more lucky people than ever who either are or will be enlightened this time around by having the unconscious guilt in their minds completely healed by the Holy Spirit. The number of them has gone up in the last couple of decades, mainly because there are a lot of people studying and practicing the Course. You thought I was going to say it's because the world is more enlightened. I'm sorry, but salvation is not a critical mass thing. People cannot be enlightened by the thinking of others, or simply by being in their presence. But they *can* be pointed in the right direction.

Most of the people who are enlightened today, or soon will be, are not going to be written about in the annals of spiritual history. That doesn't matter. How could it really matter in a dream? If they truly know it's only a dream, then why would *they* think it's relevant if others know about them? Do the details of their lives really mean anything? No. But there are still friends who will greatly benefit through the sharing of their experience.

ARTEN: You know what *you* are destined to continue to learn from. There is no substitute for reading the Text of the Course and the Workbook, even after you've already done the lessons. Use your mind to choose between the body and true spirit, and by doing so forgive the world. It is through your forgiveness that your ego will be undone. As the Course so movingly puts it,

> Salvation is undoing. If you choose to see the body, you behold a world of separation, unrelated things, and happenings that make no sense at all. This one appears and disappears in death; that one is doomed to suffering and loss. And no one is exactly as he was an instant previous, nor will he be the same as he is now an instant hence. Who could have trust where so much change is seen, for who is worthy if he be but dust? Salvation is undoing of all this. For constancy arises in the sight of those whose eyes salvation has released from looking at the cost of keeping guilt, because they chose to let it go instead.[12]

PURSAH: J has made it very clear how important your salvation is to him. As your ego is gradually undone, you get closer and closer to the beginning; that moment where you made the one mistake that resulted in all the others. Then you will get to choose once again for the final time, resulting in your return to Heaven and eternal Oneness with God. J will be with you every step of the way. For as he says to you in the Workbook,

> ...I have forgotten no one. Help me now to lead you back to where the journey was begun, to make another choice with me.[13]

There could be no better way to close our quotations from our leader. We love you J, and we thank you for your eternal light and certain guidance. We are your disciples until time has ended for everyone.

And we love you, Gary. We have one more message for you to

deliver, but you will hear our voices combined into one, for they are really the Voice of the Holy Spirit, Who will still be here with you when we appear to leave.

GARY: Will I ever see you again?

ARTEN: That's up to you and the Holy Spirit, dear brother. You should talk to Him about it, as you should everything else.

GARY: Don't go yet.

ARTEN: It's all right. You'll see. Everything's going to be all right.

NOTE: With that, Arten and Pursah's bodies began to merge into a beautiful spectacle of glorious and pristine white light, slowly filling the room until all I could see and feel was the wonderful, warm glow of the light that was encompassing me. Then I heard the following statement from the Voice, after which the light expanded into a brilliant flash and then was gone — leaving me in the room to think about everything that had happened, and all the help I would need on the path that stretched before me.

ARTEN AND PURSAH AS ONE: I love you my brothers and sisters, who are really Me but do not yet fully know it. Be grateful for the opportunities to forgive each other and thus yourselves. Replace your grievances with love. Let your minds be led to the peace of God, and the truth that is within you shall come to your awareness.

You may recall that near the beginning of these discussions, Arten was describing J as a light leading the children back to their true home in Heaven. It turned out that all of the children finally found their way home. Then, just as they all recognized that they are one and found themselves to be innocent, the no longer seemingly lost, split-off part of the Christ Mind was welcomed back by God into the Kingdom of Life, never to be seen again. The false universe disappeared, back into the void that was never there. The illusory mind was freed into spirit, to love as was intended.

Now Christ is so happy that It can't contain Itself, so It extends beyond infinity. And all the foolish ideas of a child's dream do not exist to be remembered. There are no borders or limits, only fullness and wholeness. There is no past or future, only safety and joy. For

Christ is anywhere, because God is everywhere. Unlimited forever, there is no distinction made between Them. All that remains is One, and God Is.

About the Author

GARY R. RENARD was born on the historic North Shore of Massachusetts, where he eventually became a successful professional guitar player. During the Harmonic Convergence of 1987 he heard a Calling and began to take his life in a different direction. At the beginning of the 1990s he moved to Maine, where he underwent a powerful spiritual awakening.

As instructed, he slowly and carefully wrote *The Disappearance of the Universe* over a period of nine years. Today, he is a private investor who writes, travels and discusses metaphysical principles with other spiritual seekers.

About *A Course in Miracles*

The authorized three-in-one volume of *A Course in Miracles,* comprising the Text, Workbook, and Manual for Teachers, is available in both hardcover and softcover English editions, as well as a variety of translations, from the Foundation for Inner Peace (FIP), the original publisher. Related publications from FIP that are mentioned in this book include two pamphlets authored by Helen Schucman — *Psychotherapy: Purpose, Process, and Practice* and *The Song of Prayer* — and *Journey Without Distance*, a brief history of the origins of the Course authored by Robert Skutch.

These publications are available through many bookstores or direct from the publisher by writing or calling

> **Foundation for Inner Peace**
> PO Box 598
> Mill Valley CA 94942-0598
> (415) 388-2060

or online at **www.acim.org**.

A comprehensive history of the Course, including an overview of the criticism and controversies it has engendered since its publication, is available in the Fearless Books title *The Complete Story of the Course* (see last page of this book).

Index of References

In the following Index the first numeral listed is the footnote number, followed by the standard designation of the page number of a quoted reference or direct paraphrase from *A Course in Miracles* or its two related pamphlets. Course references are signified as follows:

T Text
W Workbook For Students
M Manual For Teachers
PR Preface
CL Clarification of Terms
P *Psychotherapy: Purpose, Process, and Practice* pamphlet
S *The Song of Prayer* pamphlet

All page numbers are for the second edition of the Course, printed 1992 and after.

Frontispiece / **Arten and Pursah Appear**

1.M64. 2.M62.

The J Underground

1.T109. 2.W159. 3.T411. 4.T153. 5.CL79. 6.T89. 7.W323. 8.T237. 9.W268. 10.T664.

The Miracle

1.W473. 2.M1. 3.T489. 4.T16. 5.W1. 6.PRvii. 7.M7. 8.CL89.

9.M10. 10.T14. 11.T7. 12.W25. 13.T14. 14.T325. 15.T6. 16.T8.
17.CL85. 18.T13. 19.W1. 20.W2. 21.T499. 22.T1. 23.T85.
24.T337. 25.T202. 26.T96. 27.T138. 28.W304. 29.CL89. 30.T84.
31.T38. 32.PRxi. 33.T623. 34.W2. 35.CL81. 36.T19. 37.CL83.
38.T94. 39.CL89. 40.T463. 41.T445. 42.T617. 43.T207. 44.M12.
45.T6. 46.CL77. 47.PRix. 48.T403.

The Secrets of Existence

1.T493. 2.W1. 3.Ibid. 4.M31. 5.T660. 6.T257. 7.T586. 8.T75.
9.T236. 10.T4. 11.T182. 12.T42. 13.Ibid. 14.Ibid. 15.T312.
16.T67. 17.T74. 18.T98. 19.T60. 20.T373. 21.W48. 22.T138.
23.T60-61. 24.T1. 25.T154. 26.T1. 27.T420. 28.T84. 29.T202.
30.T183. 31.T146. 32.T641-642. 33.W324. 34.T179. 35.CL77.
36.T620-621. 37.T177. 38.T145.

The Ego's Plan

1.T138. 2.T354. 3.T215. 4.T652. 5.T3. 6.W115. 7.T668. 8.T617.
9.T666. 10.W125. 11.T438. 12.T412. 13.T410-414-415. 14.T415.
15.T8. 16.T376. 17.T223. 18.T202. 19.T217. 20.W305. 21.T454.
22.Ibid. 23.T51. 24.T638. 25.T587-588. 26.T239. 27.Ibid. 28.W73.
29.T239. 30.T438. 31.T376. 32.T142. 33.PRxii. 34.T27. 35.T8.
36.T346. 37.W141-142. 38.T169. 39.T651.

The Holy Spirit's Alternative

1.T80. 2.CL89. 3.W294. 4.T97. 5.T98-99. 6.W178. 7.W181.
8.T651. 9.T88. 10.W243. 11.T217. 12.T443. 13.T59. 14.T257.
15.Ibid. 16.T82. 17.T583. 18.CL87. 19.PRxi. 20.W437. 21.CL87.
22.CL89. 23.Ibid. 24.T108. 25.W384-385. 26.T9. 27.T349.
28.T261. 29.T51. 30.T327.

The Law of Forgiveness

1.W468. 2.CL77. 3.W159. 4.W487. 5.CL77. 6.T25-26. 7.W386.
8.W382. 9.T82. 10.W401. 11.T95. 12.M51. 13.T594. 14.T595.

15.T600. 16.T601. 17.T431. 18.W249. 19.T183. 20.T599.
21.W34. 22.Ibid. 23.T3. 24.W357. 25.W348. 26.Ibid. 27.W468.
28.T92. 29.T94. 30.T618-619. 31.T564. 32.T668. 33.T6. 34.M11.
35.Ibid. 36.T109. 37.T6. 38.T668.

Enlightenment

1.W357. 2.W401. 3.T385. 4.T67. 5.T221. 6.W407. 7.T93. 8.T88.
9.T7. 10.W323. 11.W443. 12.CL77. 13.T147. 14.T635. 15.T584.
16.T666. 17.M68. 18.Ibid. 19.Ibid. 20.Ibid. 21.W449. 22.W455.
23.T214. 24.T384. 25.T194. 26.T195. 27.Ibid. 28.M67. 29.W323.

Near Life Experiences

1.S22. 2.W346. 3.Ibid. 4.T81. 5.W119. 6.W298. 7.W291. 8.Ibid.
9.W316. 10.T322. 11.T7. 12.T8. 13.T7. 14.Ibid. 15.T60-61.
16.T16. 17.T7. 18.M62. 19.Ibid. 20.Ibid. 21.Ibid. 22.Ibid. 23.Ibid.
24.T95. 25.T325. 26.W339. 27.W321. 28.T329. 29.W479.

Healing the Sick

1.M18. 2.T257. 3.T667. 4.P17. 5.M46. 6.M18. 7.Ibid. 8.Ibid.
9.T667. 10.Ibid. 11.Ibid. 12.M19. 13.Ibid. 14.M42. 15.W270.
16.Ibid. 17.T84. 18.T84-85. 19.T184. 20.M20.

A *Very* Brief History of Time

1.T550. 2.T667. 3.T14. 4.W319. 5.Ibid. 6.T552. 7.T473. 8.Ibid.
9.Ibid. 10.W298. 11.W323-324. 12.W324. 13.Ibid. 14.Ibid. 15.Ibid.
16.Ibid. 17.T666. 18.T175. 19.T29. 20.T546. 21.T547. 22.T80.
23.T174-175. 24.T181. 25.T172. 26.T624.

Watching the News

1.S10. 2.M26. 3.M40-41. 4.M27. 5.T67. 6.M33. 7.T268.

True Prayer and Abundance

1.T220. 2.S2. 3.Ibid. 4.Ibid. 5.Ibid. 6.Ibid.

Better Than Sex

1.T7. 2.T667. 3.T15. 4.T619. 5.W245. 6.W244. 7.Ibid. 8.T354.

Looking Into the Future

1.W77. 2.T666. 3.T621. 4.T661. 5.T617. 6.W289. 7.M70. 8.Ibid.
9.T640. 10.M72.

Notes on Raising the Dead

1.W309. 2.M67. 3.P9. 4.T447. 5.T416. 6.M61. 7.T65. 8.M66-67.
9.W443. 10.T493-494. 11.T64. 12.C90.

The Disappearance of the Universe

1.T667. 2.T3. 3.T170. 4.T660. 5.T646. 6.T115. 7.T554. 8.W478.
9.T267. 10.T554. 11.W485. 12.T660-661. 13.W330.